KATHLEEN DAY

Broken Bargain

BANKERS, BAILOUTS, AND

THE STRUGGLE TO TAME WALL STREET

Yale

UNIVERSITY PRESS

NEW HAVEN & LONDON

Published with assistance from the foundation established in memory of Philip
Hamilton McMillan of the Class of 1894, Yale College.

Yale University Press books may be purchased in quantity for educational,
business, or promotional use. For information, please e-mail sales.press@yale.edu
(U.S. office) or sales@yaleup.co.uk (U.K. office).

Chapters 11–14 adapted in part from Kathleen Day, *S & L Hell: The People and
the Politics behind the $1 Trillion Savings and Loan Scandal.* Copyright ©
1993 by Kathleen Day. Used by permission of W.W. Norton & Company, Inc.

Set in Times Roman type by IDS Infotech, Ltd.
Printed in the United States of America.

Library of Congress Control Number: 2018943787
ISBN 978-0-300-22332-3 (hardcover : alk. paper)

A catalogue record for this book is available from the British Library.

This paper meets the requirements of ANSI/NISO Z39.48-1992
(Permanence of Paper).

10 9 8 7 6 5 4 3 2 1

This book is for my family,
especially my son, Ian, who wasn't here for the first one,
and my brothers and our parents, who were

"It is difficult to get a man to understand something,
when his salary depends upon his not understanding it!"

Upton Sinclair, I, Candidate for Governor: And How I Got Licked

CONTENTS

PREFACE

THIS BOOK BEGAN AS A STORY IN THE *Washington Post* in 2008 in which I compared the thrift crisis of the 1980s to the mortgage crisis of 2007. That story led Georgetown University to ask me to teach an ethics course for a new graduate program in real estate, based on my first book, *S&L Hell.* The thinking was that one similarity between the thrift crisis and the mortgage crisis was that both involved real estate.

The course became a walk through the recent, major U.S. domestic financial crises and their international ties, from the 1920s through the mortgage meltdown. From the beginning, it was rooted in finance: without an understanding of the basic principles of finance, one can't understand what went wrong in any of these situations. This is not to condemn finance or the people in the industry. To the contrary, it is to recognize the essential role that finance plays in society by studying the damage it inflicts when it goes awry. As Robert J. Shiller, a Nobel Prize–winning economist and frequent critic of Wall Street, puts it: "Among the general public, there is clearly a tendency to think of the financial professions as focused on conspiring against them instead of contributing as constructive organs of civil society. Of course, conspiracies here and there are part of history, and part of finance too, but we should not assume the universality of those instances of calculated manipulation and deception," nor forget that the "powerful tools . . . [of finance] help all individuals in our society achieve their varied goals."[1]

Finance is not institutions but people, the decisions they make and the ethics issues their actions raise. In 2013, I was asked to bring an expanded version of the course to Johns Hopkins Carey Business School, where it has evolved into a history of banking and of major U.S. financial crises and, eventually, this book.

U.S. financial history can usefully be broken into two parts: the era before the 1929 crash, which, financially speaking, seems very different and distant to modern eyes, and the era that came after the crash, when much of the financial system we know emerged. While this book focuses on events from the 1920s onward, it also traces the country's earlier financial history, including back to the American Revolution, albeit much more quickly.

I have covered financial services for several decades, starting at *USA Today* at its founding nearly forty years ago, then at the *Los Angeles Times,* and most recently, for more than two decades at the *Washington Post.* After a time, patterns appeared. Not only were those people in industry and government who were involved in one crisis often involved in the next, but key concepts, from moral hazard to easy credit, played out over and over.

Many, many people in government and the private sector served as sources for this book and for the decades of reporting on which it rests. Many wish to remain anonymous. I thank them for countless instances of help, direction, and enlightenment over the years. They know who they are.

Some people and institutions that have helped me I can thank by name. I do so with the caveat that any mistakes in the book are mine alone.

Alice Martell has been an agent extraordinaire, embracing the idea of this book even as she pushed me to shape it more deeply and clearly. Likewise, William Frucht has been an editor extraordinaire, providing invaluable enthusiasm, thoughtfulness, insight, and editing throughout. In addition, I thank all the other people at Yale University Press who helped bring this book to life, especially Karen Olson, whose wisdom, good humor, and steady hand kept the process on track, and to Julie Carlson, whose good eye and ear and painstaking focus and patience brought the book to the finish.

Colleagues at Johns Hopkins Carey Business School provided support and encouragement, and several deserve special thanks: Librarian Feraz Ashraf helped me track down countless books and navigate the university's incredible research tools; and librarians Alan Zuckerman and Heather Tapager ferreted out several essential details that had eluded me despite hours of trying.

I thank W.W. Norton & Company, Inc., publisher of my 1993 book *S&L Hell: The People and the Politics behind the $1 Trillion Savings and Loan Scandal,* for permission to use portions of it in Chapters 11–14. I also thank the Will Rogers Memorial Museum for permission to quote the humorist.

Several archives deserve tribute for preserving books and other materials about the country's financial history and for making them electronically accessible to the public: FRASER, the "digital library of U.S. economic, financial, and banking history" maintained by the Federal Reserve Bank of Saint Louis; The Gilder Lehrman Institute of American History; Google Books; the HathiTrust community of U.S. and international research libraries; The U.S. National Archives and Records Administration; and the Library of Congress.

Special thanks to Craig G. Wright, archivist at the Herbert Hoover Presidential Library in Iowa, who found several documents that I had not seen before in published accounts of how deposit insurance came to be.

Thank you to David Barr, Christine Blair, Lee Davison, Amy Friend, Robert M. Garsson, Thomas Herzog, Kathleen Keest, Nell Minow, Mary Moore, Raymond Natter, Lew Ranieri, Ellen Schloemer, David Skidmore, Jesse Stiller, and Ed Yingling. Special thanks to Michael Bradfield, former general counsel of the Federal Reserve under Paul Volcker and then of the Federal Deposit Insurance Corp. Bradfield passed away in August 2017, taking with him a vast repository of banking history and wisdom. Our conversations informed my research, and his knowledge and guidance over the years have been invaluable. I am humbled that he took time to help me in the last months of his life.

Many scholars provided essential help. I'm grateful to Martha Olney at the University of California at Berkeley, Stephen Ryan and Richard Sylla at New York University Stern School of Business, Arthur E. Wilmarth Jr. at George Washington University, and Elicia P. Cowins at Washington and Lee. I give special thanks for the work of two banking historians, Susan Estabrook Kennedy and Helen M. Burns, whose scholarly, exhaustive books chronicle so well the banking crises of the early 1930s. No one can understand that period without relying on their meticulous research.

Writing a book is lonely, but no author works alone. I thank my family and friends for their support and for their forgiveness for all the dinners and events missed and for the eccentric hours of research and writing. My husband, Charles, most especially deserves credit for supporting this project. I appreciate daily his intelligence, good judgment, and patience, not to mention his willingness to live among stacks and stacks of books (and shoes). I have special gratitude for Mireya Malespin and to former colleagues at the *Washington Post* and *Los Angeles Times,* whose work, encouragement, and friendship continue to inspire.

Finally, an unexpected pleasure in writing this book was the research it required on the founding fathers. Reading and rereading their work reminded me that, although each was imperfect—often profoundly so—their collective brilliance endures and, while always remarkable, is particularly reassuring during the current, troubled period in U.S. history.

BROKEN BARGAIN

Introduction

IN JUNE 2007 AT A PRIVATE NEW YORK dinner between U.S. regulators and the nation's top bankers, Citigroup CEO Charles Prince turned to plead with Treasury Secretary Hank Paulson: "Isn't there something you can do to order us not to take all of these risks?" Prince made a similar point two weeks later while talking to the *Financial Times* about the growing subprime mortgage crisis: "When the music stops . . . things will be complicated. But as long as the music is playing, you've got to get up and dance." A few months after that, he resigned. Citi had just announced it would have to write down the value of its subprime holdings by as much as $11 billion.[1]

At the time of the dinner, the subprime mortgage meltdown had been unfolding for six months, yet neither the Wall Street bankers nor the Washington policymakers in attendance that night recognized its magnitude. Eventually it would stand out as the biggest financial crisis since the Great Depression. Yet it was only the latest in a series of crises that have forced policymakers and industry executives to wrestle over the government's proper role in financial markets. Prince's question raised what has become a key issue for Americans and their economy: Can and should government save bankers from themselves before calamity strikes?

This wasn't always a serious question. Before the 1929 crash, Americans didn't view the president of the United States or the chairman of the Federal Reserve Board as the stewards of the financial markets. Bankers didn't expect taxpayers to bail them out, and depositors, by and large, didn't expect Uncle Sam to guarantee their money.[2]

That has changed. Nearly a century after the 1929 crash, Prince's plea shows that even those who usually oppose government regulation nonetheless expect and even want stewardship. Some have called the crash and subsequent Great Depression "the defining moment" that caused this shift in worldview and persuaded both bankers and the public to accept, indeed embrace, a government role in regulating financial services.[3] Defining that role has been a work in progress ever since. How can government create and police a level playing field that fosters efficiency and competition but also prevents reckless behavior that seems profitable at first but then causes massive losses, puts taxpayers at risk, and imperils the nation's financial and political well-being?

The need that Prince captured in his plea started with a social contract forged in the early 1930s, when Congress and the White House demanded stricter regulation of banks in exchange for giving them federal deposit insurance—a taxpayer-backed safety net in times of crisis. President Herbert Hoover pushed for deposit insurance as the only way to restore confidence during that dark time. His successor, Franklin Delano Roosevelt, opposed it on the ground that it would encourage sloppiness among bank managers and "moral hazard" among depositors, who would become indifferent to whether the banks holding their money were well run. Big banks sided with FDR. But as the Depression worsened amid a wave of bank failures, he eventually agreed to accept deposit insurance, albeit only if strong oversight to protect taxpayers was part of the package. Deposit insurance would protect individuals, but that was never an end in itself. It was a steppingstone to the larger goal of preserving the stability of the financial and political system.

In one important sense, federal deposit insurance worked. Bank panics and failures essentially stopped as soon as Congress put the insurance system in place, and that relative financial calm lasted nearly fifty years. Deposit insurance, coupled with the creation of the Securities and Exchange Commission and other oversight agencies during the 1930s, produced a new era in commercial and investment banking.

Since the 1970s, however, industry executives and policymakers have more and more insistently opposed the regulation of financial services, maintaining that government rules and oversight impede innovation and hobble consumer choice. Financiers are happy to benefit from deposit insurance, but they and many of their regulators have argued that markets "always self-correct" and that bankers can largely self-regulate because practices that put their institutions at risk of insolvency would be against their own interests.[4] Events have proved them wrong.

Financial crises and the responses to them, especially over the past century, can't be fully understood as discrete occurrences. They are best considered together as part of a centuries-long experiment in enhancing free markets by, paradoxically, regulating them to promote fairness and efficiency while taming excess. We're still trying to get the formula right.

This book provides a concise history of U.S. finance and the corporate form—the two go hand in hand—with a focus on increasingly serious crises since 1929, when the regulatory landscape we know largely took shape: the thrift crisis of the 1980s; the implosion of the hedge fund Long-Term Capital Management; the failure of energy behemoth Enron amid a series of accounting scandals; and the housing meltdown known as the Great Recession. Each of these catastrophes evolved from the one before. Telling their stories in sequence helps illustrate their connectedness and provides the history needed to better anticipate and prepare for the next financial crisis.

Since the beginning of the Republic, Americans have been preoccupied with questions about banks, money, and credit, with the power they wield and with the surprisingly inseparable issue of how to create corporations for practical purposes while limiting their destructive influence. From the value of the currency in people's pockets to what, exactly, currency is and how it relates to paper, metal, and, in modern times, computer bytes, time and again the economist, the farmer, and the factory worker alike have put banking at the center of American politics. Few topics have engendered as much controversy or been as entwined in the country's wars, its politics, and its daily life. The history of the United States can be told through any number of lenses—the growth of the military; changes in transportation and migrations; trends in education, law, or architecture; the growth of rights and the struggles of various ethnic groups— but none illuminates the American story more than the evolution of money and credit, including their role in molding the modern corporation. For over two centuries, American finance has been a crowded, contentious, and raucous affair, a series of Byzantine events fraught with boom-and-bust cycles of panics, failures, and the loss of individuals' life savings. The history of banking mirrors the history of America.

While history does not stop and start in neatly designated eras, it does have turning points. In finance, the 1929 stock market crash was a major one. The cornerstone of the modern financial landscape, that is, the landscape since the 1929 crash, is a social contract—a bargain—forged in the 1930s in which banks agreed to stricter oversight and tighter rules in exchange for a government safety net in times of crisis.

To understand the near century of follies since then, however, we must know what preceded it. Before turning to my primary focus of chronicling the major financial crises since the 1920s, I begin this book with an overview of the first 150 years of banking in the United States, from the Revolution through the 1920s. Central to that history is the fight between Alexander Hamilton and Thomas Jefferson over how to control and harness banking to bolster democracy. Their debate has been relevant to every financial crisis since.

PART ONE

E PLURIBUS INC.

The Danger and Necessity of Banks

IN FEBRUARY 1791, AMID A "VARIABLE" Philadelphia winter that blew "sometimes very cold, and then very mild," Secretary of State Thomas Jefferson and Treasury Secretary Alexander Hamilton took up a debate whose outcome would shape American law ever after: Did the U.S. Constitution, ratified two and a half years earlier, allow the federal government to charter a bank?[1]

Hamilton wanted a federally chartered bank to help consolidate and pay off the debt the federal and state governments had incurred during the Revolutionary War—about $100 million, or roughly $2.4 billion today.[2] That the federal government would assume the states' debts had been decided a year earlier, in 1790, in a bargain that Hamilton, Jefferson, and James Madison struck over dinner. Hamilton agreed to support putting the nation's capital by the Potomac River in exchange for Jefferson's and Madison's support for his debt plan.[3] Twelve months later, Congress passed legislation to create the federally chartered bank that Hamilton deemed essential to that plan. Serving as the nation's central bank, it would create a viable national currency that could be used by citizens of all states, including to pay taxes to retire war debt, and that would allow the government to more easily borrow money and pay its bills. President George Washington now had to decide whether to sign or veto the law.

Jefferson, Madison, and Attorney General Edmund Randolph objected to the legislation, arguing that the Constitution did not authorize the federal government to charter—incorporate—any institution, let alone a bank; only states could do that. When the Constitution was being drafted, Madison had supported giving the federal government some power to grant incorporations. The notions of corporations and banks proved so divisive, however, that those supporting such institutions had decided to leave out mention of either in the document for fear of undermining popular support for it.[4]

Jefferson, Randolf, and now Madison too, argued that Hamilton's bank would violate the relationship of state power to federal power set out in the Constitution. The three Virginians made a powerful trio whose opposition to Hamilton forced Washington, also a Virginian, to settle one of the new country's first major fights over how to interpret its overarching legal document. So now, in February 1791, he asked Hamilton, why were they wrong?

Hamilton worked all night on his response, defending the idea for his bank in some fifteen thousand words that represented a landmark interpretation of the Constitution. He argued that the Constitution's "necessary and proper" clause, which authorized Congress "to make all Laws which shall be necessary and proper for carrying into Execution" its duties under Article I, gave the federal government "implied" powers. Chartering a bank, he said, was "necessary" for managing the nation's currency, debt, and credit, which the Constitution had made the purview of the federal government with the words "to coin money and regulate the value thereof."[5]

Jefferson mistrusted paper money, the creation of which would be one of the bank's main purposes. He also mistrusted the closely related concept of incorporation, and a federal bank charter was just that, federal incorporation of a bank. The power to create corporations called to his mind the monopolies granted by kings and queens for projects such as the Bank of England. Jefferson argued, with Randolph and Madison, that any power the Constitution did not forbid and did not expressly give to the federal government fell to the states— an idea already enshrined in the Tenth Amendment, written by Madison. Hamilton was making his case before Washington for implied powers eighteen months after Congress approved the Tenth Amendment, which would be ratified by the states along with the rest of the Bill of Rights at the end of the year. The amendment is straightforward: "The powers not delegated to the United States by the Constitution, nor prohibited by it to the States, are reserved to the States respectively, or to the people." Hamilton, however, maintained that these words did not preclude the Constitution from providing implied powers as a means of fulfilling powers specifically "delegated."[6]

Hamilton won the argument. Washington signed the legislation and ten months later, on December 12, 1791, the Bank of the United States—now known as "the first" Bank of the United States—opened in Philadelphia as the first central bank of the new nation under its new Constitution. Congress restricted it to a twenty-year charter.

More broadly, the arguments Hamilton used to persuade Washington to sign the bank into creation also established an interpretation of the Constitution that Jefferson and Madison feared would enable the federal government to seize too much authority under the guise of "implied" powers. While many agreed with them, and still do, generations since have found Hamilton's interpretation indispensable to the federal government's ability to adjust to the needs of a growing nation and changing times. Jefferson and Madison eventually would bend their positions, at least temporarily, during their own presidencies. Still, Jefferson told Madison ten months after Washington signed the bill that he thought any Virginian who officially recognized a federally chartered bank was guilty of "high treason" and should "suffer death accordingly."[7]

Most people don't dwell on exactly how money gets its value, but they care intensely about how much the money in their pocket can buy. Banks didn't exist in colonial America. People instead relied on private credit or state-issued currency to conduct business. When banks began to appear during the Revolution, they intertwined with notions of incorporation, a designation a government gives to protect an organization's shareholders from personal liability. An incorporated organization, including a bank, can raise funding more easily when investors' vulnerability to loss is thus limited. Although many colonists mistrusted both banks and corporations as well as the government's role in creating them, they nonetheless looked to government to provide "sound money and cheap credit."[8] A bank's main purpose in early America was to provide paper currency backed by gold, silver, or some other asset. Each bank issued its own notes. Trust in the bank meant trust in its currency.

For Jefferson—the red-haired gentleman farmer who wrote the Declaration of Independence—his often-quoted statement that "banking establishments are more dangerous than standing armies" was the beginning and end of the subject.[9] Whatever the Constitution did or did not allow, banking was dangerous because it concentrated power and encouraged speculation, which he saw as a form of gambling. Though he considered state-chartered banks legal under the Constitution, he found them suspect, too, and for what he considered the worthiest enterprise—agriculture—avoidable and unnecessary.

Hamilton acknowledged that banks could fuel excessive speculation by over-extending credit or debase paper currency by issuing too much of it. But he also understood that sound credit and currency—emphasis on the word "sound"—were indispensable to manufacturing and industry, which he, unlike Jefferson, saw as America's future. Only a central bank could create a national currency. Hamilton—the orphaned genius who rose from a hard-luck childhood of poverty in the Caribbean to become a force in the Revolution and then in shaping the political and financial systems of the United States—understood that to manage such a currency, the bank would have to earn the public's "full confidence."[10]

In short, he understood the paradox of banking: When people trust a bank and know they can access their money, they don't want that money all at once, but when they think a bank is in trouble and they can't get their money right away, they want it and start runs. In Hamilton's day, a run consisted of customers demanding that paper currency be converted to gold or silver. Banks, of course, do not simply keep depositors' money in their vaults: they lend it out at interest so that others can put it to profitable use. If too many depositors demand their money all at once, as happens during a run, a bank has to require early repayment of its loans to keep up with withdrawals. Many borrowers can't pay in full on such short notice, leaving a shortfall that could make the bank unable to honor its obligations, even though it might have done so given sufficient time. A run can thus push an otherwise healthy, well-run bank into insolvency. Its collapse would cost individuals their savings and the community a source of credit. The only tonic was confidence. Confident depositors let their money sit at a bank, allowing it to be put to work as loans. "It is a well-established fact, that banks in good credit can circulate a far greater sum than the actual quantum of their capital in gold and silver," Hamilton told Congress in arguing for a nationally chartered bank. "A great proportion of the notes which are issued, and pass current as cash, are indefinitely suspended in circulation, for the confidence which each holder has, that he can, at any moment turn them into gold and silver."[11]

Precisely because he thought banking both necessary and potentially harmful, and because it rested on public confidence, Hamilton saw it from the start as an enterprise in need of oversight. In addition to issuing currency and making loans, the central bank would have the duty of policing state-chartered banks to ensure they kept up standards for the currency they printed. Contrary to what some argue today, oversight of other banks has never been an add-on to a central banker's duties by members of Congress who couldn't think how else to police the banking system. Its seeds were there from the start and always central to its mission.

The first Bank of the United States was owned partly by government and partly by shareholders. Maintaining confidence in the bank—and its currency—would require the government to keep watch over the private investors and vice versa, to make sure neither gave in to the temptation to print too much money. Issuing some notes in excess of available gold and silver was proper, but too much of this would create an inflationary spiral that would devalue the paper, spark runs, and undermine the economy. Public shareholders were needed as watchdogs, Hamilton told Congress, because "it would, indeed, be little less than a miracle" if a government weren't tempted to print money in time of need. "What nation was ever blessed with a constant succession of upright and wise administrators?"[12]

Likewise, Hamilton required that shareholders allow federal officials to inspect the bank to ensure that its executives behaved prudently. He saw a federal bank charter—like any corporate charter—as a privilege granted by government on behalf of the public. It came with obligations, whose fulfillment the government had a duty to ensure. "If the paper of a bank is to be permitted to insinuate itself into all the revenue and receipts of a country," Hamilton told Congress, "if it is even to be tolerated as the substitute for gold and silver in all the transactions of business, it becomes, in either view, a national concern of the first magnitude. As such, the ordinary rules of prudence require that the government should possess the means of ascertaining, whenever it thinks fit, that so delicate a trust is executed with fidelity and care." Congress agreed: it authorized the secretary of the Treasury, in this case Hamilton, to inspect the first Bank of the United States once a week.[13]

"Public utility is more truly the object of public banks than private profit," Hamilton wrote. "And it is the business of government to constitute them on such principles that, while the latter will result in a sufficient degree to afford competent motives to engage in them, the former be not made subservient to it."[14] Hamilton's idea of a public-private institution has infused the concept of central banking in the United States ever since. He thought of it as a system to insure soundness, but, by distributing power, his scheme's legacy also has been to avert many a political stalemate over the contentious issue of banking.

A Cheat upon Somebody

TO CONGRESS, HAMILTON DEFINED A BANK AS "a deposit of a coin or other property as a fund for circulating a credit upon it which is to answer the purpose of money."[1] He wrote that "every loan which a bank makes is, in its first shape, a credit given to the borrower on its books, the amount of which it stands ready to pay, either in its own notes [paper currency], or in gold or silver, at his option."[2] This definition still holds, though today we might say that a bank is an institution that takes deposits and makes loans, in the process creating money each time it acknowledges it owes someone money. Compare Hamilton's description to this modern textbook definition:

> A bank account is nothing more than a debt from the bank to the depositor; the bank owes the depositor money in the account. When one makes a deposit in a bank, ownership of the money deposited flows to the bank; the depositor no longer owns the money, but she *does* have a debt owing to herself from the bank. And this debt can be spent with checks or through the more modern electronic orders upon banks to move money in the deposit elsewhere. . . . When someone borrows money from a bank and a bank establishes a bank account for that amount, the bank has simply acknowledged a new debt from the bank to a depositor. . . . Lest this get too intricate, the underlying message is that banks perform a function that is normally thought of as one belonging to government: they create money. While the United States government does of course create money—it prints bills and mints coins—that money is but a trickle compared to the amount of money that banks create through the lending of money and supporting establishment of debts to its depositors.[3]

Most of Hamilton's contemporaries kept it simple: "I use the term, banking, in that sense in which it is universally understood in the United States, that is to say, as implying the permission to issue a paper currency," said Albert Gallatin, Treasury secretary from 1801 to 1814 under Presidents Jefferson and Madison.[4]

Gallatin focused on the day-to-day aspect of banking that most people care about: having enough money to get about town, buy food, and pay bills. Today, though most people wish they had more cash in the sense that they wish they were wealthier, they rarely fear having no physical currency. Occasionally a grocery cashier might be too short on dollars to break a twenty-dollar bill, or one might lack change for a parking meter, but such shortages are quickly remedied and, with electronics, quickly fading. In Gallatin's time, people often found coined money scarce. There was little precious metal in North America at the time. Many considered paper money an essential convenience for commerce, and before the birth of the nation many local governments issued it, often not backed by gold or silver but by land, of which there was plenty, or simply as "fiat money," backed only by the government's word. These shortages, combined with the workarounds, explain why the public simultaneously mistrusted banks and yet called for more of them.

Commercial banks didn't appear until the early 1780s, during the Revolutionary War. Many early Americans were unfamiliar with and therefore wary of them, and more comfortable with the idea of a government issuing paper money directly. Some—including Hamilton, Benjamin Franklin, and Thomas Paine— viewed government-issued paper fiat money as an evil (albeit a sometimes necessary one, such as during the Revolution), but saw paper money issued by a well-run bank and backed by gold or silver as indispensably useful. Still others— Jefferson and John Adams—suspected paper currency in any form, even when backed by coin, given its potential to be issued in quantities that exceeded a one-to-one ratio with gold or silver. This view grew more intense in the decades after the Revolution and helped propel Andrew Jackson to the White House in 1829 on a "hard money" platform that held that only gold and silver should be trusted as currency, a policy that caused its own economic woes.

Modern consumers might have trouble imagining America without paper currency or its electronic equivalent. Perhaps the twenty-first-century debate over whether Bitcoin is a hoax or the future of money comes close to conveying how early Americans puzzled over paper currency. In the end many simply shrugged: they valued its practicality too much and so were happy to have a bank issue "two, three, four or five" dollars for each dollar of metal that share-holders paid in, even if that seemed a bit like magic.[5]

Jefferson understood as well as Hamilton how a bank could print more currency than it had metal in its vault, but he didn't like it. He thought it encouraged debt and speculation, enabling people to borrow to bet that an investment would rise in value.[6] Adams equally mistrusted the process of creating credit. Any paper beyond a one-to-one backing in metal, he wrote, "represents nothing and is therefore a cheat upon Somebody."[7]

Likewise, Hamilton understood as well as Jefferson the danger of too much speculation. "There is at the present juncture a certain fermentation of mind," he told Congress on December 5, 1791, just a week before the first Bank of the United States opened its doors, "a certain activity of speculation and enterprise which if properly directed may be made subservient to useful purposes; but which if left entirely to itself, may be attended with pernicious effects."[8] He was referring to a frenzy that started in July, when, ironically, the first subscriptions to the Bank of the United States itself set off a speculative bubble. Investors had to buy subscriptions, called scrips, at twenty-five dollars each, payable with gold or silver only. Each scrip was a down payment on stock in the bank, which would be issued at four hundred dollars a share. Subscribers would pay the remaining cost of the shares over two years, with 25 percent of the total price paid in metal coin and the rest in U.S. bonds. In issuing these scrips, Hamilton had a twofold aim: to create a national bank through a process that boosted demand for U.S. bonds, and to ensure that the new bank had sufficient gold and silver to issue enough paper currency to serve as a national currency. The unexpectedly quick sellout pushed up the price of a scrip to over three hundred dollars and caused a similarly dizzying rise in the price of U.S. bonds.[9]

By August, prices had collapsed as demand fell and with it public confidence. Hamilton, with express agreement from Jefferson, Randolph, Adams, and John Jay, orchestrated the nation's first "open market" intervention: he used Treasury funds intended to retire U.S. debt early to buy U.S. bonds to prop up prices and calm investors. It worked, but too well. By winter the speculative optimism had revived, sending scrip and bond prices soaring until they collapsed again in the spring, setting off a domino effect—a financial contagion—of a reverse bubble, where declining prices led to more declines and panic, just as rising prices had led to a self-fulfilling mania. Hamilton again had to step in to calm the public by buying U.S. bonds.

The collapse, now known as the Panic of 1792, was ignited by the financial failure of one William Duer, a friend of Hamilton's and his first assistant Treasury secretary. Duer was also one of the era's most indebted speculators, exhibit A for skeptics like Jefferson. Early on and continuing throughout the winter, he had borrowed widely from the private (unincorporated) and state-chartered banks that had sprung up since independence, as well as from "merchants, tradesmen, draymen, widows, orphans, oystermen, market women, churches and even common prostitutes," to buy government bonds in the expectation that they would rise in value as demand rose for national bank shares. His plan backfired when the mania broke, at least long enough to bankrupt him.[10]

Duer's financial obligations were so big and widespread that his announcement he could not repay his debts rippled through the nation's fledgling bond and stock markets. On top of that, the government sued him for improprieties while at the U.S. Treasury. An Eton-educated British aristocrat who had adopted America as his home and fought for its independence, Duer led an outsized lifestyle, indulging in lavish dinner parties and other expensive habits. His downfall landed him in jail, where he largely remained until his death in 1799. His bankruptcy sparked the nation's small banks and securities dealers to embark on a self-imposed cleanup. In May 1792, they signed the Buttonwood Agreement—for the buttonwood tree they purportedly sat under—promising to create a more transparent market that would be less prone to manipulation. The agreement simultaneously launched the New York Stock Exchange and led to stock exchange reforms.

The speculation and panic had clearly been stoked by heavy borrowing from the nation's new state-chartered and unchartered (private) banks, which bolstered Jefferson's disgust with finance—a disgust only amplified by the thought that the speculators had borrowed from those banks to buy shares of the first federally chartered bank.[11] "You will have seen the rapidity with which the subscriptions to the bank were filled," Jefferson wrote to fellow farmer, lawyer, and Virginian Edmund Pendleton in July 1791, a few weeks before the bubble burst. "As yet the delirium of speculation is too strong to admit sober reflection. It remains to be seen whether in a country whose capital is too small to carry on its own commerce, to establish manufactures, erect buildings etc., such sums should have been withdrawn from these useful pursuits to be employed in gambling."[12]

Hamilton conceded as much to Washington eight months later. Trading in stocks and bonds, he wrote, "has some bad effects among those engaged in it. It fosters a spirit of gambling and diverts a certain number of individuals from other pursuits."[13]

So Jefferson and Hamilton agreed on the hazards of banking. Jefferson thought they outweighed the benefits. Hamilton didn't. Hamilton even understood that some speculation, within boundaries, was necessary and beneficial. Jefferson didn't.

Speculators created demand that otherwise might not exist for securities. For example, they had helped finance the Revolution: they had borrowed money to buy, for cents on the dollar, millions of dollars in debt issued by the Continental Congress in the form of notes to pay soldiers and buy provisions.[14] Holders of the notes often sold them immediately, at a steep discount, willing to accept some of what they were owed right away rather than risk getting nothing if the Revolution failed. By paying the notes at full value after the war, as Hamilton's plan called for, Congress would give these speculators a sizable windfall. That rankled Jefferson and Madison, who wanted to make the original note holders whole at the expense of the speculators, whose patriotism they questioned and whose support for Hamilton's debt plan they scorned. Hamilton, in January 1790 in his *First Report on the Public Credit* to Congress, addressed this issue head on, arguing a contract is a contract. The notes were sold legally, Hamilton noted, with each side a willing participant. That the seller was desperate for the money or the buyer used borrowed funds was irrelevant. Speculators created demand for securities others deemed of little value. If the United States honored the debts at face value, it was not to favor one group over another but to preserve America's future borrowing power. That, he argued, would strengthen the economy and benefit everyone.[15]

As Washington's top aide during the Revolution, Hamilton had continually faced supply and currency shortages, a situation made worse by the inability of the Continental Congress to tax or issue paper money backed by gold or silver. Several mutinies broke out over the government's inability to adequately pay soldiers. Among the most famous occurred in 1783 in Newburgh, New York, where Washington faced down rebellious soldiers to denounce those who had incited them. He broke the spirit of the rebels as he was preparing to read a letter from a member of Congress describing the country's difficult financial position. Pausing to put on glasses, he said, "Gentlemen, you must pardon me. I have grown gray in your service and now find myself growing blind." This display of "vulnerability from their otherwise stoic leader so deeply affected the officers that some wept openly." The mutiny was over.[16] Amid the debate over a federally chartered bank, Washington and Hamilton surely had in mind such incidents and the wretched circumstances soldiers had suffered throughout the war.

Hamilton won the battle for a central bank and national currency, but decades of bickering and financial loss would pass before America accepted them permanently. Even then the debate never entirely died away.

The creation of money and credit can seem like sorcery. Many rural Americans in the early days of the United States mistrusted the process. Merchants in the city may not have fully understood it either, but they relied on it regularly and took it for granted. Jefferson preferred a homespun credit system, with no charters, no paper changing hands, and no use of the word "bank." He wrote to Adams, "It is a fact that a farmer with a revenue of ten thousand dollars a year may obtain all his supplies from his merchant and liquidate them at the end of the year by the sale of produce to him without the intervention of a single dollar of cash."[17] This was a revolving credit account and barter system rolled into one. But America was growing and needed a more formal system.

Jefferson wanted to "put down all banks" and "admit none but a metallic circulation" coined and regulated by government, which, strictly speaking, is all the U.S. Constitution allows.[18] Hamilton's answer to Jefferson's strict interpretation was the implied-powers argument. He rebutted claims that bank credit fostered harmful speculation by pointing out that people abused hard money, too. "What is there not liable to abuse or misuse?" he wrote. "The precious metals, those great springs of labor and industry, are also the ministers of extravagance, luxury, and corruption. . . . Even liberty itself, degenerating into licentiousness . . . works in its own destruction. . . . It is wisdom, in every case, to cherish whatever is useful, and guard against its abuse."[19]

The process of creating money and credit plays a complex role in how a paper currency obtains value, but in the end, as Aristotle concluded, money is simply what everyone agrees to use as money. Before the Revolution, when America had no banks, colonists bartered and extended credit to one another in the manner Jefferson describes. But they also had a reasonably good experience with paper money issued by governments or individuals, often collateralized with land. Benjamin Franklin and Thomas Paine were among many colonists who understood that paper currency fostered commerce by making transactions easier. But proponents of paper thought that to be legitimate, it had to be a proxy for something more tangible than someone's promise.[20]

Thus did the founding fathers unanimously abhor fiat money, that is, paper money with no metal or land to back it up, only a promise. Though forced to use it during the Revolution, Americans for a long time remembered the inflation it created. Some had had a positive experience with paper money before the war, but the disastrous experience of nearly worthless currency during and after it amplified the mistrust of those already wary of banks, especially as Americans engaged in a "second revolution" that, in a bid to more tightly bind the states, led them to adopt the U.S. Constitution to replace the Articles of Confederation.[21]

The upshot was that paper money, with the practicality that Americans needed but a potential for misuse that they disliked, remained a contentious issue for decades. Some disagreements centered over whether states or banks should issue it, others over whether it could safely or morally exist at all. These arguments pitted creditor against debtor and lender against farmer; at their center sat questions about inflation and deflation, and who benefited from which. If paper was backed by gold and silver, and that specie was being taken out of the country or hoarded domestically or simply wasn't produced in sufficient quantities, a shortage in the money supply would push prices down. With deflation, money in effect became more expensive. Farmers earned less on what they sold, making it harder to repay debt. Someone needing to pay taxes or repay a loan might end up selling land or other property at unfavorable prices to meet the obligation. By contrast, too much printed paper meant it bought less; lack of confidence devalued it. Prices inflated as merchants required more money to make up for paper's falling worth. As the value of paper currency fell, lenders suffered because borrowers repaid debt in notes worth less than when the loan was made.[22]

3

Inc.

THE CONCEPT OF A CHARTER PLAYED A KEY role in how early Americans viewed finance. Chartering a bank, then as now, meant incorporating it. Governments grant incorporations, and in early America that meant giving license—essentially a monopoly status for a privileged few—to build or run something, like a canal or water system, for a specified and thus limited time. Those suspicious of paper money and the banks issuing it were even more troubled that the government facilitated these activities through incorporations. It seemed undemocratic.

After the Revolution, Americans mistrusted big government. Their experience with monopoly power had been with incorporations granted by royalty to form, for example, the East India Company for exploration or the Massachusetts Bay Company to settle New England as a trading post. A charter had a characteristic that today we think of as a corporation's primary benefit: it created an artificial entity, a corporation, that limited a shareholder's potential loss to the amount of money he or she invested in the company. The corporation shouldered all other liability. Absent fraud, an investor's home, savings, or other assets, down to one's "cufflinks," would be protected from creditors should the company fail.[1] This protection encouraged people to invest more than they otherwise would.

In early America, worries about the power of a government-sanctioned monopoly abounded but were nonetheless often overpowered in the end by the practical benefits that incorporation gave a bank or the benefits that a bank's money and credit gave a community. That's what happened with Hamilton's first Bank of the United States: over Jefferson's objections, Congress and Washington awarded it an exclusive charter, allowing it to issue bank notes that could function as a national paper currency. In making his case to Washington, Hamilton described the benefits of a corporation in strikingly modern language. He wrote that it functioned as "a legal person, or a person created by act of law, consisting of one or more natural persons authorized to hold property or a franchise in succession in a legal as contra distinguished from a natural capacity." This government-given power "to erect a corporation; that is to say, to give a real or artificial capacity to one or more persons" was, he wrote, a way to entice investors to a project.[2]

Being incorporated limited not only liability but often also competition. Hamilton's bank was the only federally chartered bank and thus the only one authorized to issue a national currency. The benefits of a national currency clashed with suspicion of this power. Hamilton got his bank, but the public watched carefully as the twenty-year charter of the Bank of the United States ran its course and expired, and just as closely when the twenty-year charter of its successor, the second Bank of the United States, was granted and then eventually ended.

When the Bank of the United States was created in 1791, fewer than a handful of other banks existed in the country, and all were less than ten years old.[3] With the advent of the Bank of the United States, however, states began in earnest to issue their own bank charters, leading to what contemporaries dubbed "bancomania."[4] Thus the United States gave birth to a permanent and permanently odd system of finance, with dueling federal and state bank charters that in effect enshrine Hamilton and Jefferson's debate.

Over the next two hundred years, dual banking would become a source of competition and innovation, but also of mischief and contention. In 1792 eight new banks were established, tripling the number that had existed a year earlier, and by 1800 the number had grown to 30, by 1810 to 100, by 1816 to nearly 250, and by the 1830s to as many as 600. Between then and the start of the Civil War in 1861, the ranks of state-chartered banks swelled to 1,600.[5]

Alongside incorporated banks stood private banks, which were simply unincorporated partnerships. They sprang up as incorporated banks began to populate the landscape during the last two decades of the 1700s, though eventually many states banned them or tried to severely restrict them by barring them from issuing paper currency. A state could make more money from incorporated companies on which it could assess fees or taxes.[6] Today, state and federal laws require any bank taking retail deposits and making loans to be chartered, that is, to have permission from either the federal government or a state to operate as a corporation. By contrast, banks in early America were not required to incorporate, but many sought the designation to attract investors.[7] In exchange for the benefit of a charter, states in theory imposed some oversight by insisting that an incorporated bank meet certain criteria, like keeping sufficient reserves on hand to meet anticipated redemptions of bank notes. In practice, many states had weak standards. But however slight, the regulatory relationship between banks and government, the idea of privileges extended in exchange for oversight, began with chartering. And it began early in our history.

Hamilton's first Bank of the United States was, as its name says, the first federally chartered bank under the U.S. Constitution. But it wasn't America's first bank. That title goes to the Bank of North America, founded in Philadelphia by Robert Morris in 1781, "the blackest year of the Revolution," to provide a currency to fund the war. The bank, privately owned and controversial for the power it wielded as the de facto central bank of the Continental Congress, began a pattern that would be repeated many times until the first decade of the twentieth century, that of private bankers rescuing the federal government's finances during war or economic upheaval.[8]

In a preview of the fight between Hamilton and Jefferson ten years later, the bank, uncertain that the Continental Congress had the authority to issue a charter, hedged its bets by also obtaining one from the state of Pennsylvania.[9] Its purpose was to help the federal government sort out its finances. Because the fledgling country's currency wasn't accepted abroad, it had to pay for imports with foreign currency or gold or silver from "loans or gifts from other enemies of Great Britain."[10] But at home, with no money, the Continental Congress did what financially distraught governments often do. It printed money—Continentals. This was the first of three times that Americans would use fiat money. The other two were during the Civil War, with Greenbacks, and today, with Federal Reserve notes, which President Franklin Delano Roosevelt effectively took off the gold standard in the 1930s. (In 1971 President Richard Nixon made it official.) What gives Federal Reserve notes their value now is simply belief in the United States. In the late 1700s that belief was scarce. Worries that

America would lose to Britain set the value of Continentals at next to nothing, hence the saying "not worth a Continental."

In the spring of 1787, delegates arrived in Philadelphia for the Constitutional Convention to forge more unity among the states than existed under the Articles of Confederation. They met down the street from the Bank of North America, where a years-long political tug-of-war had only recently ended. It had pitted poor farmers in the western part of Pennsylvania against wealthier, politically powerful Philadelphia merchants, including the prominent families that controlled the bank.[11]

The bank had become a battleground when currency shortages grew following independence. Farmers in the west had to pay their creditors in ever more hard-to-find, expensive dollars, while merchants bought the farmers' goods ever more cheaply. Pennsylvania's state legislature prepared to issue paper money to ease the deflation, but the bank opposed the move, arguing that the additional currency would devalue its notes. Opponents of the bank called for the state to revoke its charter. Thomas Paine, famed author of the pamphlet *Common Sense* advocating independence from Britain, had been the western residents' ally on many issues, but now he chose to defend the Bank of North America and its state charter, prompting opponents to deride him as someone who "lets his pen for hire." The uproar largely had subsided when Pennsylvania finally renewed the bank's charter in March 1787, just two months before the Constitutional Convention began. As delegates arrived, they did so against a troubled backdrop of lingering hard feelings over the bank, staggering war debt, and a shortage of currency.[12]

The currency shortage in particular was on their minds. Protests by farmers and other debtors were erupting from New Hampshire to South Carolina.[13] The war's end had brought economic depression and crushing debt, which had forced some states to impose high taxes, yet chronic currency shortages left many citizens, particularly farmers, unable to pay those taxes or any other bills. In Massachusetts, former Revolutionary War captain Daniel Shays led one of the bigger protests, known as Shays' Rebellion, in which "thousands of indebted farmers . . . grabbed staves and pitchforks, shut down courthouses and thwarted land seizures by force." The uprising played on the fears of many founding fathers that the war had made "protest against authority habitual," blurring the thin line between a fight for liberty and a mob rebellion. George Washington was shocked that some protestors considered land "to be the common property of all," and Madison suspected they wanted to abolish debt and redistribute property. Yet the protestors' plight raised legitimate issues: debtors could not procure gold or silver coins or even paper currency. If the government wanted to collect taxes, it had to provide the legal tender with which people could pay it.[14]

Protestors like Shay wanted paper currency that they could borrow to pay debt, and, having little use for bankers, they wanted it to be state-issued.[15] The founding fathers unanimously opposed that option, given their experience with Continentals during the war. Instead they wrote into the Constitution that states could not issue coin or paper money. Beyond that they could not agree. The issue of whether federal power could be used to issue paper money or to incorporate banks proved too divisive. Consequently, the Constitution declares that the federal government can coin money and regulate its value, and that it can tax and borrow, but it is silent on whether the federal government can issue paper currency. The Articles of Confederation allowed the Continental Congress to issue paper money, and that power was in the draft of the Constitution, but framers voted it out. Their aim was "to shut and bar the door against paper money."[16] In a letter to Jefferson in October 1788, after the Constitution had been ratified, Madison commented that the subject of paper money was among a handful of issues that "created more enemies than any other" question.[17]

The Constitution also makes no mention of banks or corporations. As with the related topic of paper money, the subjects were "too touchy." Even those who favored giving the federal government powers to grant incorporation for other purposes, such as building roads, deferred to those who worried that the incorporation of banks inevitably would raise insurmountable difficulties. The delegates from New York and Philadelphia, the nation's two financial centers, also vigorously opposed the idea of giving the federal government the power to grant incorporations. Those who favored it didn't want to risk losing a vote on the issue at the convention; if the framers didn't touch the issue at all, supporters could argue afterward, as Hamilton did, "that the power existed." In his writings, Jefferson says he was told that a plan to specifically allow a federally chartered bank—probably with monopoly powers akin to those of the Bank of North America—was never presented after its would-be sponsor, Robert Morris, a friend of Hamilton's and the bank's mastermind, was persuaded that its inclusion would kill any chance of getting the Constitution ratified.[18]

The result is constitutional silence on whether the federal government can issue paper money or grant incorporations, including for a central bank or any other financial institution. By thus mentioning "money" in the Constitution without spelling out state and federal powers over corporations or banks (and their issuance of paper money), the founders created a conundrum people still argue over, even if as a practical matter Hamilton's argument has won the day. Jefferson argued that because the framers of the Constitution discussed giving the federal government the power to grant incorporation but then left it out, they clearly intended to reserve that power to the states. But Hamilton responded that accounts of the discussions varied and that, in any case, "whatever may have been the intention of the framers . . . that intention is to be sought for in the instrument itself," that is, in the Constitution, which does not specifically deny that power to the federal government. Many people argue that the founding fathers meant to limit federally issued legal tender to precious metals. True or not, the bottom line is that the courts, through a series of decisions, have used Hamilton's "implied powers" to rule that the Constitution allows federal charters, including federally chartered banks and federally issued paper currency.[19]

A flurry of state-chartered institutions began popping up at the end of the 1700s and in the early 1800s, each issuing its own bank notes. This was hardly different from a state issuing currency, which the Constitution forbids, but the public maintained the fiction that no law was being broken. Paper money from state-chartered banks, in the absence of a true national currency, was simply too convenient.[20] By the time the charter of Hamilton's Bank of the United States expired in 1811, scores of bank notes of varying legitimacy and strength were circulating throughout the states. The Bank of the United States imposed some discipline on state banks by buying up their notes and periodically redeeming them for gold and silver. The threat that it might do this warned the state banks away from the temptation to issue too much paper currency relative to the metal backing it up. The Bank of the United States also made loans, including to the federal government. State banks didn't like the oversight or the competition.

Despite its success, or more likely because of it, the first Bank of the United States could not persuade Congress to renew its charter when it expired in 1811. It lost by one vote.

Throughout his presidency, from 1801 to 1809, Jefferson maintained that the bank was unconstitutional and Hamilton's implied powers argument was nonsense. Yet he suspended his stance against implied powers long enough to facilitate the $15 million purchase, in 1803, of 827,000 square miles of land between the Mississippi River and the Rocky Mountains, doubling the nation's size. Jefferson worried he had acted illegally because, under his strict interpretation, the Constitution did not expressly allow the federal government to acquire more territory and so would need to be amended. Arguments from no less than James Madison, chief architect of the Constitution and secretary of state at the time, didn't sway him. Practicality finally did. When it was clear that an amendment to the Constitution was not possible within the time needed to close the deal, known as the Louisiana Purchase, Jefferson agreed that an after-the-fact review by Congress would have to suffice.

Jefferson's successor, Madison, was in the White House when the bank's charter expired in 1811. A year later came the War of 1812. The nation's shortage of money for the unpopular war with Britain was made worse by the absence of a central bank and the lack of a unified currency. Madison, who had been more open to the idea of federal incorporation during the Constitutional Convention than he was afterward, suddenly discovered the utility of a national bank: it could act as the government's fiscal agent—making it easier to borrow—and create a stable currency, making it easier to collect taxes.[21] Once an ardent foe of Hamilton's idea, Madison signed legislation in 1816 creating a new national bank that was much bigger than the first, though to appease critics, its charter was also limited to twenty years. This new bank, the second Bank of the United States, opened in 1817, too late to help with the war. But like its predecessor it created a stable national currency backed by gold and brought some discipline to state-chartered banks and their hodgepodge of paper money.[22]

Not everything went smoothly. The second national bank played an unintended but major role in the recession and panic of 1819 by extending too much credit when it first opened. The state banks had also made too many loans, including to western land speculators, and when economic uncertainty and a trade imbalance caused increased demand for gold and silver abroad, it created a shortage in the United States. The second national bank's reserves dwindled, forcing it to withdraw credit abruptly, causing bankruptcies and foreclosures across the country, as well as "bank failures, a drop in real estate prices and a slump in agriculture and manufacturing."[23] Public resentment of the bank grew, even as that same year the U.S. Supreme Court affirmed the bank's constitutional legitimacy in a ruling, *McCulloch v. Maryland,* that would affirm Hamilton's "implied powers" interpretation of the Constitution and thus reverberate far beyond finance. The ruling broadly defined the national government's supremacy over the states and remains a cornerstone of U.S. law.

The case arose when Maryland's state bankers—suffering, like the rest of the country, from the economic slump the national bank had helped cause—objected to its opening a Baltimore branch. The state's legislators obliged local bankers by taxing the national bank's notes, which threatened to put it out of business in Maryland. After the bank refused to pay, the state sued, arguing that the bank was unconstitutional. The case ended up in the U.S. Supreme Court, which, in an opinion written by Chief Justice John Marshall, ruled that the second Bank of the United States was indeed constitutional and Maryland's tax was not. In arguing for the legitimacy of the national bank, famed statesman and lawyer Daniel Webster quoted directly from the "implied powers" argument that Hamilton had given to Washington in 1791. By agreeing with Hamilton, Marshall broadly enshrined the first U.S. Treasury secretary's interpretation of the Constitution and established that states could not tax the federal government or otherwise interfere in legitimate federal activities.[24]

Winning the dispute was not enough to ensure survival. President Andrew Jackson, who passionately opposed the bank, killed it by vetoing legislation to renew it when its charter expired in 1836. As the nation's seventh president, Jackson brought to the White House a hard-money fanaticism and hatred of all banks, which he and his supporters blamed not only for the economic panic of 1819 but also for a series of ensuing crises. Historians debate the reasons, but the country saw a "spike in riotous behavior in the years 1834–1836," to which anti-bank sentiment clearly contributed.[25]

Among the most spectacular bank failures was the collapse of the state-chartered Bank of Maryland, one of the country's four original banks when the institution was chartered in 1790. In 1834, bad management and fraud drove it under. Its closing, coupled with other bank failures that year, cost depositors in the state an estimated two to three million dollars, "an incredible sum for the time." A *Baltimore Sun* story paints the picture: "A wealthy depositor could afford to wait for the courts to settle the bank's fate. A poor one could not. There were thousands of these small depositors with accounts that totaled $100 or $200. They couldn't touch their savings. Their frustration was multiplied because failure to pay a debt, even a $10 one, made a person eligible for debt-or's prison. The only alternative was to sell the deposit or credit at a discount. Speculators were available to snap up credits for a [cheap] price."[26]

On August 6, 1835, amid reports that Bank of Maryland's "directors had manipulated stock to their own advantage," public anger spilled onto the street. To the "cheers of thousands of bystanders," rioters broke into and trashed wealthy homes, burning personal possessions in bonfires. The violent riot left at least five dead and many more wounded.[27]

Though the Baltimore riot was unusually violent even for that violent decade, the sentiments it reflected were commonplace. A history of the city published in 1881, which includes a whole chapter on the city's "Mobs and Riots," expresses sympathy for the 1835 rioters, explaining, "There was certainly great reason for their indignation, for an outrageous wrong was done, which fell heaviest on those who were least able to bear it."[28]

But the public especially resented the national bank, a sentiment that Alexis de Tocqueville, traveling in America in 1831, found remarkable. "It is sufficient to travel across the United States," he wrote, "to appreciate the advantages that the country derives from the [national] bank. There is one above all that strikes the foreigner; the notes of the Bank of the United States are accepted at the same value on the wilderness frontier as in Philadelphia, the seat of its opera-tions. The Bank of the United States, however, is the object of great hatred."[29] He mentioned in particular the state banks' resentment over the federal bank's efforts to make them issue currency prudently.

State-chartered banks, numbering some six hundred at the time, issued notes in a variety of denominations, creating a blizzard of paper whose value varied depending on the issuer's reputation and how far one had to travel to get to redeem it. As a traveler, de Tocqueville couldn't understand why the very mobile citizenry of the United States didn't appreciate the practicality of a currency that held its value over great distances. Nevertheless, under a banner of states' rights, state banks helped fan a very personal fight between President Jackson and the directors of the second Bank of the United States. "Its direc-tors," de Tocqueville wrote, "have declared themselves against the president, and they are accused not improbably of having used their influence in order to hinder his election," which caused Jackson to attack the national bank "with all the fervor of a personal enmity" to "stir up local passions and the blind demo-cratic instinct of the country."[30]

When President Jackson vetoed renewal of the bank's charter, Congress lacked the votes to override. Senator Thomas Hart Benton of Missouri captured the anti-bank sentiment: "I object to the renewal of the charter of the Bank of the United States because I look upon the bank as an institution too great and powerful to be tolerated in a government of free and equal laws. Its power is that of the purse; a power more potent than that of the sword; and this power it possesses to a degree and extent that will enable this bank to draw to itself too much of the political power of this Union; and too much of the individual property of the citizens of these States." He called for the nation to return to "the hard money mentioned and intended in the Constitution."[31]

Jacksonians, like members of any political movement, came in many stripes. Some were state bankers or speculators who opposed the national bank for its competition and stricter rules.[32] Others, notably the "Loco-Focos," opposed state banks too, largely because those banks were incorporated and they opposed all incorporation. (This laissez-faire political party got its name from the matches they used to light a meeting after Tammany Hall politicians turned off gas lights to try to thwart their gathering.)[33] Ironically, by helping to kill the second Bank of the United States, Loco-Focos helped usher in a wave of state-chartered banks amid a laxity in oversight that led to the very state of affairs they opposed: an increase in incorporated banks.

During this period, the nation split between anti-bank extremists on the one hand and, on the other, the many state legislators around the nation who, with the closing of the national bank, wanted to create—and get money from—as many state-chartered institutions as possible. The bad habits of an over-banked country led to repeated panics over the next three decades.

Recessions and panics had occurred while the second Bank of the United States existed—in 1819, 1825, and 1833–1834, for example—but they became even more frequent after it closed in 1836.[34] There were panics in 1836, 1837, 1839, 1841, 1847, 1851, 1854, 1857, 1861, 1864, 1873, 1884, 1890, 1893, 1895, 1896, 1898, 1899, 1901, 1902, 1903, 1904, 1905, 1906, 1907, 1908, 1920, 1926, 1927, and 1929.[35] Not all were major, depending on the definition of "major," and some are better thought of as one continuous panic over several years. However one counts them, they signified that life in America was a far cry from Jefferson's vision of an idyllic land of farmers. The agricultural society was plagued with bank failures and economic downturns for over a century.

The panics always featured runs in which depositors, having lost confidence and unable to distinguish sound from unsound banks, insisted their paper be converted to coin in amounts exceeding banks' ability to comply, either because they had issued too many notes or because they could not convert assets to specie quickly enough to meet the sudden demand. The era from shortly before the second Bank of the United States closed its doors in 1836 until 1863, two years into the Civil War, is known as the "free banking" period in the United States, with "free" referring to how easily anyone could open a bank.

Despite the havoc, financial loss, and unrest that bank failures caused, elected officials, often with an eye to the bribes they could extract, increasingly made owning a bank easier. This also satisfied legislators' need to make more currency and credit available in their states once Hamilton's bank closed. Before the era of free banking, bank charters were given for a specific purpose for a specific time by specific legislative action. Now states passed laws that made chartering automatic if certain criteria were met, thus melding the corporate form to the wants of bankers.[36] The proliferation of banks comported with the Jacksonian-Jeffersonian view that even if banks were evil, putting bank ownership in the hands of a few was more evil still. When Jefferson opposed the first Bank of the United States, he specifically lauded the greater competition that state banks would bring because there would be more of them.[37]

Thus did free banking emerge from of a marriage of expediency and anti-elitist sentiment. Jacksonian populism was also accompanied by a rise in the use of word "democracy" to mean a social order of equals (at least among white men) as distinct from how the founders used it, to refer to "mob rule." "The term *democracy*. . . . until the third decade of the nineteenth century [meant] the manipulation of majority opinion by demagogues, and shortsighted political initiatives on behalf of the putative 'people' that ran counter to the long-term interests of the 'public,'" notes historian Joseph J. Ellis.[38] "In the 1780s *democracy* meant the refusal to pay taxes to reduce the federal debt incurred in the war, the preference for an inflated currency that privileged debtors over creditors, the illegal confiscation of loyalist estates, and the repudiation of any political authority that subordinated local interests to some larger, national agenda." Ellis notes that "the operative word" for the founders during the Revolution was "*republic* rather than *democracy*," and that, when they came to write and adopt the U.S. Constitution to fix the shortcomings of the Articles of Confederation, they sought a political "architecture that filtered the swoonish swings 'of the people' through layers of deliberation controlled by what Jefferson called 'the natural aristocracy.' That filtration process was what the Constitution was all about."[39]

Americans' mistrust of banks made finance a central part of the era's political debates, helped cement the views of both federalists and anti-federalists, and shaped businesses far beyond finance. Financial historian Richard Sylla argues that the corporate form we know today in the United States for all types of companies was in large measure sculpted by state banking laws in the early nineteenth century, as state officials sought to make banks and credit not only more plentiful for the citizenry but also more open to control by a broader, more "democratic" slice of society.[40]

New York and Michigan were among states that led the trend by allowing groups of people to apply for a bank charter through administrative channels rather than via the approval of the state legislature. "New concepts of the corporation were fought primarily in the one area, the business of banking," Sylla writes.[41] "When the modern concept of the corporation triumphed in American banking, it spread easily and quickly to other sectors of the American economy" and then to Europe. Eventually it came to dominate the world. Along with making a grant of incorporation an administrative function, akin to getting a drivers' license today, legislators gradually did away with time limits on corporate charters. As incorporations and their renewals became easier and more common, the notion that corporations could exist in perpetuity, which is how we know them today, did too.

In 1838, New York adopted a law often described as ushering in the free-banking era, even though some states had acted sooner.[42] New York's elected officials performed a legislative sleight of hand to get around the state's constitution, which, harkening back to the general population's long-held suspicions, required a "two-thirds majority of both houses for a corporate charter" and made granting charters en masse difficult by requiring each corporation to have "its own chartering act." The solution to bypassing these constraints was to call banks "associations" rather than corporations, thus evading the state's constitution. These entities, new name or not, clearly were "de facto, if not de jure, corporations." When a suit arose soon after, state judges determined that "the banks were corporations" but not necessarily in violation of the state constitution, rendering one of many examples in American history of an inconsistent but expedient court ruling on banking.[43] In New York, those applying for bank "association" charters didn't just chip away the time-honored notion that incorporations should be time-limited; they took an ax to it. Many sought "associations" that would operate for a hundred or even a thousand years. One applicant asked for more than four thousand years. New York did require banks to adhere to some standards, such as buying a minimum value of state bonds as a reserve against losses if a bank failed, and meeting certain capital requirements. But overall during this period, "it might be found somewhat harder to become a banker than a brick-layer, but not much."[44]

Ten years before its free-banking law of 1838, New York had pioneered several commonsense rules for banks, such as requiring that they pay dividends to shareholders from profits, not capital, and imposing limits on loans to directors. It also made shareholders liable for double the amount of their investment, a rule meant to align shareholders' interests with depositors' in making sure that executives ran banks soundly. Double liability became widespread from the Civil War to the 1930s, when it was eliminated amid other bank reforms. New York also adopted, in 1829, a novel deposit insurance system, which—though it failed after nine years because of "adverse selection, fraud and inadequate supervisory oversight"—paved the way, along with similarly failed experiments in other states, for federal deposit insurance a hundred years later.[45]

Other states' standards were much looser, if they existed at all. Michigan, for example, which adopted its "free banking" law a year before New York, led the pack in eliminating oversight. Its governor lauded the new law as "destroying . . . the odious features of a bank monopoly and giving equal rights to all classes of the community." Within a year, forty new banks had set up shop in the state. Within two years, all forty had collapsed.[46] Devolving standards and the resulting overpopulation of banks produced another phrase, "wildcat banking," to describe institutions with the most questionable practices. The derivation of "wildcat" is uncertain, but a plausible account says it came from Michigan, whose bankers bought state bonds with notes they printed but that holders found impossible to redeem because the bankers "disappeared" and "had to be hunted for in the woods, among the retreats of wild cats."[47]

In 1853, the governor of Indiana said of the situation of banking in his state: "The speculator comes to Indianapolis with a bundle of bank-notes in one hand and the stock in the other; in twenty-four hours he is on his way to some distant point of the union to circulate what he denominates a legal currency, authorized by the legislature of Indiana. He has nominally located his bank in some remote part of the state, difficult of access, where he knows no banking facilities are required, and intends that his notes shall go into the hands of persons who will have no means of demanding redemption."[48]

By then sentiment in Michigan had changed, with the governor lamenting that "At present we are giving charters to the issues of banks about which we actually know nothing, in whose management we have no participation, and are thus literally paying a large tribute for what generally in the end proves to be a great curse."[49]

By 1860, eighteen states had free-banking laws, and by all accounts the system was a free-for-all.[50] In February 1863, a reporter described the situation: "Although one nation, bound together by the ties of consanguinity, of a common language, and interstate and international commerce, we have been separated by diverse systems of currency, bounded by the state lines, and as widely variant as those which marked the alien and often hostile principalities and powers of Europe. London and Munich, Paris and St. Petersburgh are not more inaccessible to each other, except by the financial bridge of exchange, than are New York, St. Louis, Boston, and Chicago."[51]

The National Monetary Commission, which was created to study the banking system three years after a significant panic in 1907, and which helped pave the way for the creation of the Federal Reserve System, noted that during the free-banking era, "it was impracticable for a traveler to carry with him the coin necessary to meet his expenses for a protracted journey, and except coin there was nothing that was universally acceptable." The public registered its low regard for most state banks' currency with nicknames like "shin plasters of Michigan, [and] the wild cats of Georgia."[52]

Amid the chaos of state banks, people began to ask the obvious: if the U.S. Constitution barred states from issuing currency, either coin or paper, could states legally accomplish the same end by chartering banks that issued notes? States had the right to grant incorporations, certainly—Hamilton and Jefferson had agreed on that—but the constitutionality of notes issued by a state-chartered bank was uncertain. President Jackson thought they were not constitutional.[53] But the year he left office, 1837, the U.S. Supreme Court ruled in *Briscoe v. Bank of Kentucky* in favor of state-bank notes. The decision fanned both the free-banking movement and popular resentment of shaky banks.

Hatred of banks added to the dysfunction of the nation's banking system. When Texas became a state in 1845, it became the first to ban banks absolutely.

Iowa and Arkansas followed suit when they became states a year later. Iowa farmers thought banking "mad," "the common enemy of mankind," a "swindle." One Iowa newspaper called banks a "vampire upon the body politic," "swindling," and "little monster." Lamented one Ohio newspaper: "There is not a single bank in the United States that is much better than a den of thieves, seeking an opportunity to 'fail,' to advantage and rob the people! How disgusting, then is the hypocritical jargon of the bank lackeys and slaves, about the recharter of the 'good banks,' 'sound banks!' Pish!—humbug! How can GOODNESS come out of HELL?"[54]

Iowa's constitution gave the state the authority to charter corporations except for banks, stating "the creation of this is prohibited" and establishing a penalty of one year in the county jail and a fine of a thousand dollars for anyone who engaged in banking or "creating paper to circulate as money." In a nation short on metal coins and awash in paper currency, one has to wonder how an offender might pay such a fine.[55]

But a hatred of paper money didn't stop people from needing a circulating medium, and Iowans turned to surrounding jurisdictions and to private lenders. Around the country, these lenders simply omitted "bank" from their titles and issued "certificates" or "notes" that functioned as money, as the New Hope Delaware Bridge Company in New Jersey did.[56] Money in Iowa became so scarce after the panic of 1837 that even fake paper was hard to come by. "The times are hard, and business of all kinds dull," lamented one newspaper. "Money, even counterfeit paper, and bogus, almost totally disappeared."[57] Free banking had indeed made banking more democratic, but also more chaotic, inflationary, and, as lax standards always do, attractive to con men and other crooks.[58] Counterfeiting was easy. A *Chicago Tribune* reporter in 1863 wrote, "It may be safely stated that the art, as pursued in the United States, is without parallel, and that without vaunt or hyperbole, we can 'beat the world' on this, our national specialty—counterfeiting."[59] By 1860 the country had about 1,600 banks, each issuing notes of various denominations, which meant, depending on how one counted, that between seven thousand and nine thousand different types of paper currency were in circulation, each note bearing the name of a bank that promised to redeem it in gold or silver coin. By one estimate, more than half of these were counterfeit.[60] But even the legitimate ones were hard to use.

"It was costly, of course, to return a note of, say, a Georgia bank received in New York to the bank in Georgia, so such notes circulated at discounts the farther they were from the issuing bank," writes Sylla. "Note brokers earned a living by buying bank notes at a discount and returning them *en masse* to the issuing banks for payment in coin."[61] Manuals gave shopkeepers the latest value of notes, and bank tellers could consult additional guides about which notes were counterfeit—guides that became outdated as soon as they were published. Such a fractious system hardly promoted commerce. Financial historians Robert Wright and David Cowen liken the situation to "trying to purchase an automobile or a refrigerator with a mix of yen, euros and Mexican pesos."[62] It could be done, but not easily.

4

The Civil War Tames Currency

AMID THE MONEY MAYHEM, WAR AGAIN INTERVENED. The Civil War demanded a uniform, trusted national currency that would enable the U.S. government to raise and borrow money easily. By the time President Abraham Lincoln took office in March 1861, seven southern states had seceded. The war formally started the next month.

Lincoln and his Treasury secretary, Salmon P. Chase, found the country financially unprepared. It was broke. Chase told Congress on July 1, 1861, that the Union would need $320 million to fund the war the next year—the actual amount would be $3.2 billion, or about $61 billion today—but that the Treasury had only $20 million available, all of it allocated many times over.[1] The government hadn't had a primary bank through which to borrow money since 1836, and it had no national currency nor real monetary system. Its tax system relied on tariffs, a woefully inadequate way to raise the funds for a full-scale war.[2] Gold and silver were becoming scarcer: even before the war, the public had begun to hoard specie on worries that conflict was coming and the North might not win. Chase and Congress made the shortage worse by requiring that $150 million in loans they had made to several of the nation's strongest state banks in 1861 be repaid in gold and silver rather than as notes.[3]

The sudden demands of war forced the government to resort to fiat money for the first time since the Revolution. In three installments beginning in 1862, it issued notes that the public quickly dubbed "Greenbacks." By war's end these Greenbacks, backed by nothing but the government's word, totaled about

$450 million. At the same time, the government imposed the nation's first income tax, which mitigated somewhat the Greenbacks' inflationary effect.

This wasn't enough to manage an increasingly complex nation. As Hamilton had argued at the end of the Revolutionary War, the government needed a bank to both issue a standard currency and provide credit, as well as a system for imposing and collecting taxes. With the ghost of Jackson and the public's mistrust of banks hanging over him, Chase could not propose outright a third bank of the United States. So he achieved the same end through an ingenious system that Congress adopted in several stages and that in effect created a stealth central bank. First, the Revenue Act of 1862 established the nation's first income tax. (It would be repealed ten years later before being reinstated permanently in 1913, with the ratification of the Sixteenth Amendment to the U.S. Constitution.) Then Congress passed the national bank acts of 1863 and 1864 to create a system of national banks that, properly considered, amounted to the nation's fourth central bank, after the Bank of North America and the first and second Banks of the United States. But out of a keen wish to avoid the tensions and disputes surrounding those previous banks, Chase's national bank system cleverly married the democracy of free banking—that of allowing many charters—with the essentials of a central bank: that of administering one standard currency for doing business with the federal government and of acting as the government's fiscal agent.[4]

Instead of one nationally chartered bank, the national bank acts created a new division within the Treasury Department, called the Office of the Comptroller of the Currency, to charter as many national banks as qualified. Each bank would issue national notes under a common standard, and the comptroller would control ("comptroller" is a fancy term for "controller") the stability of the nation's new national currency by regulating these banks' operations.

Chase and Lincoln hoped that many investors would be eager to own a national bank, and many did at first vie to open federally chartered banks in their cities, thus winning the right to call the institution the "First National Bank of [city]" or "Second National Bank of [city]." (One legacy of having "national" in a federally chartered bank's title is today's improbably named Fifth Third Bank of Cincinnati, Ohio, which was born from a 1908 merger of the Third National Bank and the Fifth National Bank.)

Each bank's investors had to buy U.S. bonds with a combination of Greenbacks and gold and silver coins, and each bank could issue only a set amount of national bank notes against those bonds. In this way, Lincoln and

Chase coaxed gold and silver from the hands of hoarders, boosted demand for federal bonds, established a national currency, and created a system of institutions that could once again lend the government money and serve as its banker at home and abroad.

The system also created the first federal insurance system for banks. Bank notes technically were liabilities of the issuing bank, but because they were backed by U.S. bonds, they functioned like "obligations of the federal government at one remove."[5] For that reason, "their value did not depend on the financial condition of the issuing bank."[6] Still, if a bank failed, these might not cover all the bank's losses, and the government had first dibs on the bonds held. To try to ensure that the losses didn't grow too big—that is, to ferret out bad banking as soon as possible—Congress gave the comptroller of the currency the right to examine national banks for safety and soundness.

The world, and most Americans, welcomed a national U.S. currency. According to the *London Times* in February 1863:

> By want of a paper currency that would be taken in every State of the Union at its nominal value the Americans have suffered severely. The different States were as to their bank notes so many foreign nations each refusing the paper of the other, except at continually varying rates of discount. . . . Only adepts and regular money changers could tell whether a note was current or not, the paper of broken or suspended banks remaining in circulation long after their value had departed.
>
> The Federal Government avoided loss by refusing all paper money of every kind. Its import duties were taken only in gold. . . . But the difficulties of the Government have compelled it to issue a paper that will pass current in any part of the territory. Through the evils of the war the people will at least gain that deliverance from the previous confusion of their currency which to Europeans appears a barbarism. If the social storm sweeps away the "wild cat" and bogus banks of the Union, it will have left some small compensation for the wreck of better things.[7]

In 1863 Chase listed his aims for the new national system, and they went far beyond funding the war: "the strengthening of the public credit; the strengthening of the bond of union; a safe currency for the masses; a uniform money, with some of which in his pockets a traveler who leaves San Francisco can pay for his breakfast on the Isthmus, for his dinner in New York, and for his supper in Liverpool."[8] He and others even blamed the lack of a national banking system for helping to cause the Civil War. "The revolted States could never have inaugurated rebellion without the currency of state-bank notes for circulation," said Representative Samuel Hooper of Massachusetts, who introduced the first National Banking Act in the House.[9]

Having created a camouflaged central bank, Chase expected state banks to convert to national charters in droves, ending the headaches of state-bank issued currency. That didn't happen. National banks were subject to stricter rules and more oversight to enforce those rules. State-chartered bankers didn't want more oversight. Banks began to practice what has become a time-honored practice in U.S. banking of "charter shopping." At the end of the nineteenth century, it involved institutions choosing to be state chartered to exploit looser standards.[10] Ever since, charter shopping has periodically encouraged a race to the bottom as regulators, whose budgets depend on fees from those they regulate, adopt looser and looser rules to entice banks to switch from federal charters to state charters or, nowadays, vice versa.

The Civil War and the popularity of a national currency overrode state bankers' objections to the federal system. But when state institutions wouldn't convert to national charters, Congress decided to tax their notes with the aim of driving them from the business of issuing currency.[11] State banks quickly sued, and the case went to the U.S. Supreme Court.

The issue was a mirror image of *McCulloch v. Maryland* nearly fifty years earlier, where the question was whether a state could tax the Bank of the United States. The ruling was the mirror image as well, with the Court finding that the federal government could tax the state-chartered banks. Presiding over the Court was none other than Salmon Chase, who had resigned as Treasury secretary and now was chief justice of the United States. Conflict-of-interest rules then were more lenient, and it wouldn't be the last time that Chase would rule on an issue he had been involved with. In 1870, in a case addressing whether the government had acted unconstitutionally by making Greenbacks legal tender for debts that predated the currency's existence, Chase ruled it had. As economists Milton Friedman and Anna Schwartz note, "Not only did [Chase] not disqualify himself, but in his capacity as Chief Justice [he] convicted himself of having been responsible for an unconstitutional action in his capacity as Secretary of the Treasury!"[12]

The tax worked for a time. Together, the national bank acts and the taxing of state-bank notes resulted in "303 bank closures and 879 charter conversions [to a national bank] between 1863 and 1869."[13] By 1865, three out of four banks in the United States were nationally chartered. The roughly 1,300 state-chartered banks in the Union at the beginning of the war had fallen to about 350, and nationally chartered banks had grown from none to nearly 1,300.[14] The ratio held until the 1880s, when the number of state banks began to grow again, surpassing national charters in 1892.[15] State bankers had discovered a loophole in the law: the federal tax meant to put them out of business technically applied only to their paper currency, their "notes," not to deposits, so state bankers began promoting deposit accounts that customers could draw on using checks.[16] America's dual-banking system was alive, if not necessarily well.

And a national currency, despite its advantages, didn't halt bank panics. Apparently customers didn't fully appreciate the federal government's implicit backing of notes. Or perhaps they worried that "deposits"—which the law didn't consider to be "notes"—weren't insured. Intermittent financial panics and bank runs, including some 850 bank closings, plagued the country from the time it restored the gold standard in 1879 through 1914, when the Federal Reserve System began operations.[17] Bank failures were a monthly occurrence throughout the late nineteenth and early twentieth centuries.

Nor did the national banks fulfill the public demand for currency. Circulating notes backed by U.S. bonds created a system that couldn't expand or contract as needed. Often it did the opposite. When better investments came along as the economy expanded—and needed more bank notes—banks might be inclined not to buy more government securities to issue more currency or credit, but instead to buy higher-yielding investments. Cash became scarcer during the fall harvest, for example, just when more cash was needed. "The currency was yoked to the finances of government, as reflected in the amount of its indebtedness, rather than to current demands of industrial and commercial enterprise," as a 1922 college textbook put it.[18] As an author of a 1910 report for the National Monetary Commission told Congress, "The sum of the whole matter is that under the existing system of bank notes based upon government bonds, normal and automatic expansion and contraction of the currency, in response to needs of trade, is flatly impossible."[19]

Under the national bank system, the thirty years from 1867 to 1897 was a period of sustained deflation. Falling prices particularly devastated American farmers and those who were tied to farming, which was most of the population. Falling prices, caused by a return to the gold system and the unresponsive national bank system, meant farmers had to sell their crops for less than they cost to produce.[20] Perversely, too few notes in some parts of the country, typically rural areas, led to too much idle cash and credit available at the biggest banks in money centers like New York and Chicago, where the nation's growing securities exchanges were located. Residents of these cities experienced an excess of available credit, that is, easy credit, a situation in which too much borrowed money chases too few good investments and invariably leads to unwise speculation. Investors with access to borrowed money sought riskier and riskier places to put it, in turn puffing up demand for enterprises that might not warrant funding. Easy credit alone can't cause a bubble, but manias can't happen without it. Leverage—borrowed money—typically makes a person more willing to take on more risk, more prone to gamble, than if she had to use her own money. Easy credit coupled with lax oversight brought one overly speculative cycle after another.

Speculators were ever present. During the relentless deflation of the last three decades of the 1800s, when prices fell "well more than 50 percent," the best known was financier Jay Cooke, financial adviser to Chase during the Civil War and in many ways de facto financier to the Union.[21] Cooke steered his bank into making too big an investment in the bonds of the era's high technology, railroads. Overextended, the bank lost the public's confidence, sparking a run that spread to others, creating the panic of 1873 and a deep recession. The next two decades were a time of successive downturns in the midst of overall deflation caused by the scarcity of circulating money. Economic instability bred civil unrest. The hardship these decades of deflation brought to farmers eventually resulted in the Nebraska Democrat William Jennings Bryan's famous "Cross of Gold" speech at his party's 1896 convention, which won him the first of three nominations for president. His argument, felt keenly by farmers, was that the gold standard had brought the continual impoverishment of rural areas, to the benefit of industrialists and financiers.

The recession of 1882 through 1885 followed a slowdown in investments in the railroads that in 1869 had physically united the country coast to coast. It included a bank panic in 1884, mostly in New York City, sparked in part when speculators' losses caused the failure of a large brokerage house. Then, after a smaller panic in 1890, came the panic of 1893, this one involving not only railroads but also the ongoing debate over whether to use gold or silver or both to underpin the nation's currency. Five hundred banks failed.[22] Still Congress could not be moved to reconsider having a bona fide central bank or otherwise change a decentralized central-bank system that amplified each economic turmoil.

In 1894, Ohio businessman Jacob S. Coxey led scores of protestors, known as Coxey's Army, in a march on the nation's capitol seeking relief from unemployment. Their demands included an increase in the amount of circulating money, just what the protestors in Shay's Rebellion had demanded a hundred years earlier. The government shut down Coxey and arrested his "army" for trespassing, but like Shay's, the protest reverberated among elected officials.

Cooke the speculator and Cox the cash-strapped bill payer showed that a national bank system hadn't resolved all of the country's banking issues. Federally chartered banks provided a uniform, stable currency, but they also provided easy credit for speculation even as they starved pockets of the country in need of more cash. And while a national currency united the country, when, where, and how to supply sufficient amounts of it were fraught questions.

Then came the panic of 1907, which though brief turned a downturn already under way into one of the country's deepest economic slumps. The crisis, which began with a failed attempt by speculators to corner the copper market and ended with the near failure of a huge New York financial institution, the Knickerbocker Trust, quickly spread to the national banks.[23] The Treasury was powerless against the contagion of mistrust. Its network of federally chartered banks had provided a uniform currency, but they couldn't act as a lender of last resort as a full-fledged central bank could.

That job fell to the financier J. P. Morgan, who stepped in to form a pool of bankers to provide liquidity to avert Knickerbocker's collapse. It wasn't enough. President Theodore Roosevelt instructed the U.S. Treasury to deposit $25 million in various national banks to help them meet withdrawals, coordinating with Morgan, who throughout acted as the nation's de facto central banker, empowered to decide which firms would receive cash and live. The additional cash eventually did soothe customers. But the federal government's inability to act on its own in the crisis, and its need to turn to a rich private banker, galvanized policymakers. It only added to the embarrassment that the U.S. economy was by then the world's largest.[24] Having a private citizen perform a government function also raised questions of fairness and conflicts: in deciding who would receive liquidity and who would not, was Morgan acting in the interests of the country, or of his friends and his own pocket?[25] The episode finally woke up the nation to the need for a better way.

Congress formed the National Monetary Commission, whose report in 1910 led to the Federal Reserve Act of 1913. As Congress negotiated the act, the memory of Jackson and the fight over the second Bank of the United States lingered. So did views of the very-much-alive William Jennings Bryan. Against this backdrop, President Woodrow Wilson and other central bank proponents, like Lincoln and Chase before him, did something clever: instead of creating a single central bank that could issue a more flexible national currency but would also stir up old passions, they created a federally chartered bank centered in Washington but with twelve regional Federal Reserve banks around the country, each incorporated as a private institution owned by local, member banks holding nontradable shares. The banks would be not-for-profit, but they would pay dividends to shareholders and, as important, give bankers around the country a voice in Washington.

This fifth attempt at a central bank—after the Bank of North America, the first and second Banks of the United States, and the national bank system—worked politically and practically for a large, growing economy whose prosperity was nonetheless still mired in an eighteenth-century debate about money and power. While giving a voice to those around the country, Congress structured the Federal Reserve Board in Washington as an independent central bank to minimize political pressure on monetary policy—pressure that Hamilton warned would always tempt the government to use the bank simply to create too much money. While the Federal Reserve System would be modified in the 1930s to strengthen its central board, the structure remains essentially as originally created. Today the Fed describes itself as "independent within the government."[26]

Uniquely structured as a system with both private and public elements, the Federal Reserve began operation in 1914, too late to avert yet another bank panic that caused 125 bank closings, but nonetheless a relief to many.[27] The opening words of the Federal Reserve Act set out the duties that have defined central banking since Hamilton's day: "An Act to Provide for the Establishment of Federal Reserve Banks, to Furnish an Elastic Currency . . . to Establish a More Effective Supervision of Banking in the United States, and for Other Purposes."[28]

Now the country had a central bank that could establish a monetary system that would adapt to economic cycles by adjusting interest rates as needed, and provide appropriate liquidity—both with short-term loans during normal times and as a lender of last resort to cash-strapped but otherwise sound banks when times were rough.[29] The Fed had potential conflicts of interest. It could provide liquidity to cover up problems at a badly managed bank that it should have overseen more carefully. Still, a bona fide central bank run by the government was a vast improvement, even if it sometimes seemed to be overly influenced by the private bankers who owned the regional banks, especially in New York.

With the creation of the Fed, the Treasury's Office of the Comptroller of the Currency lost the job of providing a national currency. Its name did not change, but its job became that of incorporating and supervising federally chartered banks. The Fed also joined with it as an additional bank regulator as the federal government tried, once again, to ride herd on state-chartered banks: state-chartered institutions that wanted to be part of the Federal Reserve system and take advantage of its check-clearing operations and other privileges would have to accept its oversight.

The importance of having a full-fledged central bank cannot be overstated. The Fed could act as a lender of last resort, stepping in to avert runs when few other lenders would or could, by offering cash in exchange for good assets pledged as collateral. Rather than having to sell assets at fire-sale prices, otherwise healthy banks could now borrow emergency cash from the Fed, albeit at a penalty rate to discourage misuse. No more would Wall Street bankers play this role—at least not without government oversight.[30]

In 1907, the nation had twenty thousand banks. By 1921 it had thirty thousand, half of which had been created after 1900. The growth rate of banks outpaced that of the U.S. population, and had been doing so for a half century.[31]

Why so many banks? The dual banking system led to the issuance of too many incorporations. After the Civil War, when Congress created the national bank system and taxed state-chartered banks out of the currency business, state banks had struggled and declined. But by 1900, the advent of checking accounts made state banks popular once again and their numbers grew, while growth in national banks slowed to a standstill.[32]

The competition between state-chartered and federally chartered banks now launched a race between state legislatures and the U.S. Congress to liberalize their charters. The race profoundly influenced the corporate form. State legislators in the 1800s and early 1900s had gradually made obtaining bank charters an easy administrative procedure while lengthening the charters' lifespans. In response, Congress in 1922 amended the Federal Reserve Act to extend to ninety-nine years what had been a twenty-year charter for national banks. In 1927, in the McFadden Act, it removed all limits to the life of federal bank charters.[33] Dual banking helped all corporations gain perpetual legal life.

Almost from the country's start, lawmakers and regulators have vacillated between granting bank charters according to the population's need or solely on whether owners met criteria for owning and running a financial institution, regardless of whether it could find enough customers. As a result, since the early 1800s the country has been periodically overbanked, which in turn has contributed to lax lending practices and economic instability. Despite the go-go headlines that characterized the 1920s, the rapid growth in the number of banks in the first two decades of the 1900s actually halted in 1921 and declined steadily through the rest of the decade as farming and other pockets of the economy faltered, taking their lenders with them.[34]

But with the creation of the Federal Reserve, 130 years of fits and starts to try to establish a central bank and national currency ended. A central bank wouldn't fix everything, but policymakers hoped it would end wild speculation and repeated runs and panics. No one had an inkling that the worst was yet to come.

5

Sunshine Charlie

IN THE SPRING OF 1929, WHEN PHRASES such as "wealth without work" and "permanent prosperity" were part of the popular lexicon, the financial editor of the *New York Sun* called Wall Street celebrity Charles Mitchell "the ideal modern bank executive." As head of National City Bank (precursor to Citibank), Mitchell had done more than any other banker to promote the consumer revolution of the 1920s. Colleagues at the bank, which vied with Chase as the nation's biggest, nicknamed him "Sunshine Charlie" for his optimism about the stock market and ability to persuade Americans to invest in it as never before. They also called him "Billion Dollar Charlie" for the hard-nosed sales approach behind that sunny outlook: over the decade, his coast-to-coast network of marketers had sold $20 billion in securities to retail customers. Journalist Edmund Wilson described him in the *New Republic* as "the banker of bankers, the salesman of salesmen, the genius of the New Economic Era."[1]

A few months after the *New York Sun* profile, the stock market crashed, beginning a continuous slide that, over the next three years, was accompanied by nearly eleven thousand bank and thrift failures and the biggest economic calamity in the country's history. Senator Carter Glass of Virginia, the cantankerous, revered, five-foot-four Democratic lawmaker known as the father of the Federal Reserve System, pronounced Mitchell "more than any 50 men . . . responsible for this stock crash."[2] Like the market, Mitchell's reputation had undergone a severe correction.

Mitchell had grown up in a suburb of Boston, the son of a produce dealer. He worked his way through Amherst College coaching others in public speaking and then, as a clerk at Western Electric in Chicago, took business courses at night. Contemporaries described him as a natural salesman. He had run his own investment house for five years by 1916, when, not even forty, he became head of the National City Company, the securities affiliate of National City Bank. He became president of the bank itself in 1921. Though the national banking acts of 1863 and 1864 had essentially prohibited banks and securities firms from mixing—a legacy of Jefferson's and Hamilton's worries about banks and speculators—National City bankers had found a way around that restriction by forming a state-chartered securities affiliate, National City Company, in 1911.[3]

The securities company tried to keep a low profile at first. Its formation by a commercial bank nonetheless sparked congressional hearings in 1912 to look into allegations that Wall Street bankers ran "money trusts," interlocking companies that engaged in anticompetitive financial practices. Shareholders of different companies had long created "trusts" by turning over control of their stock to groups of trustees, who then used a structure akin to a holding company to invest in and coordinate the operations of all the companies. They could thus create a monopoly beneath a surface appearance of competing companies, or control an entire supply chain behind a pretense of independent suppliers and purchasers. Creators of the trusts thought them legal end-runs around existing laws against monopolistic practices. The public had learned about trusts in oil, tobacco, steel, and railroads when, at the turn of the century, Presidents William McKinley and Theodore Roosevelt launched an era of "trust-busting" to dismantle these monopolies by rigorously applying the Sherman Antitrust Act of 1890 for the first time.

In the late 1800s and early 1900s, under a banner of making banking more democratic but actually intending to make these interlocking companies easier to form, Wall Street's financiers once again pushed states to loosen up their incorporation laws. New Jersey took the lead, earning the title "the mother of trusts" and "the traitor state" for helping to pioneer the holding company, a corporation with a structure that financiers found easier to use than trusts to own and control financial firms, railroads, and other companies.[4] Later, Delaware superseded New Jersey, and today it remains the premier state for corporation-friendly statutes.

The 1912 congressional money-trust investigation, known as the Pujo hearings after its chairman, Representative Arsène Paulin Pujo of Louisiana, produced a report in February 1913 entitled *Concentration of Control of Money*

Merely Recognizing a Fact, by S. D. Ehrhart, from *Puck,* January 6, 1911, depicting the
trusts of the time as "centralized wealth" that, to the detriment of the economy and
society, controlled major industries as well as credit. The baby Puck is saying to a
"Socialist orator" that he should "Sit down. You don't have to talk. This large person
[the man holding the candle snuffer labeled "Control of Credit"] is making socialists
faster than you can make them." Library of Congress.

and Credit. After detailing how national and state bankers and even the comptroller of the currency had thumbed their noses at the committee's requests for
documents, the report concluded that a "money trust" did exist, despite bankers'
denials. It found "an established and well-defined identity and community of
interest between a few leaders of finance, created and held together through
stock ownership, interlocking directorates, partnerships and joint-account
transactions and other forms of domination over banks, trust companies, railroads and public service and industrial corporations which has resulted in a
great and rapidly growing concentration of the control of money and credit in
the hands of these few men."[5] The "few men"—leaders of such well-known
banks as Morgan, National City, and Chase—thought they had found a way
around federal laws Congress had passed to dilute concentrations of power and
reduce conflicts of interest, laws designed to separate banking both from securities transactions and from nonfinancial commercial businesses.

The report didn't provoke immediate change, but the bad taste it left in the public's mouth helped catalyze the creation of the Federal Reserve that same year. Then World War I began, and attention turned to other things.

At the start of the 1920s, Mitchell, now at the helm of both the National City Bank and the "legally distinct but actually identical" National City Company, prepared to expand.[6] Starting with just a handful of branches, he opened scores of offices in nearly sixty cities, manned by an army of several hundred employees who made National City the leading pioneer in the new Wall Street niche of selling stocks and bonds directly to consumers. In 1927, Congress passed the McFadden Act, giving a boon to Mitchell and his imitators by enabling federally chartered banks to trade securities just as their state counter-parts could do. Reflecting the ongoing "dual banking" war between state and federally chartered institutions, the act is best known for barring commercial banks from interstate branching, and for allowing national and state banks to branch within a state on more equal footing—but it also helped stoke securities sales, including to retail customers, by federally chartered institutions.[7]

In a race to keep up with the states, national bank regulators had for years permitted national banks to use state-chartered affiliates to buy and sell stocks and bonds. This 1927 law now enabled Mitchell and other bankers to ramp up securities sales with a gusto that at once mirrored and helped propel the stock market's go-go growth. Securities trading and banking became inseparable as commercial banks moved beyond their traditional fare of offering short-term business loans and relied more and more for their profits on the sale and trading of stocks and bonds.[8] Mitchell and his competitors worked to create "financial department stores" that offered retail customers one-stop shopping for stocks, bonds, and more.[9]

Mitchell's children, Rita and Craig, sat for taped interviews in the 1990s in which they described the lavish life they lived, with dozens of servants in several homes, and how their father built National City from a few offices in New York to "the largest distributor of securities in the world" aimed at selling to "everyman." The concept was a mental shift for a public that had regarded the stock market as a professional's game, too risky for ordinary savers.[10]

During the aptly named "roaring" 1920s, America evolved into the urban-focused, car-centered, business-obsessed culture it is today. Not coincidentally, the decade also marked the start of the era of consumer debt. The optimism of the time, the adoration of electronic and four-wheeled inventions, the debate over religion and science, all sound familiar to modern ears, as do many of the scandals and excesses. Financially, however, it seems alien for its lack of accounting standards, transparency requirements, and anti-fraud or anti-manipulation laws. The decade's optimistic headlines overshadowed the persistent struggles of farmers and other struggling segments of the economy. A steady onslaught of bank failures, hundreds each year throughout the decade, destroyed many citizens' life savings and left many communities with inadequate credit. The Federal Reserve had given the country a workable national currency, but its creators' second aim—that it stabilize the banking system and dampen panics—remained unfulfilled. The Fed had the power to implement monetary policy and supply short-term loans to smooth out economic ups and downs, but having such authority is not the same as knowing when or how to use it. The Federal Reserve Board's mistake-riddled performance in the years leading up to the 1929 crash and in the years after it shattered the illusion that the Federal Reserve knew how best to loosen or tighten credit to keep the economy stable, or to bring out-of-control banks to heel. The banking crises from 1930 through 1934 dispelled any myth that having a central bank would magically rid the country of crippling bank runs.[11]

When New York Governor Franklin Delano Roosevelt took over as president of the United States, on March 4, 1933, the banking system was in tatters, and the nation had returned to the days of scarce currency, hoarded coins, and bartering or using informal credit to buy or sell. People in and out of government increasingly had proposed measures to expand oversight of banking and finance and, in the process, hold the government more responsible for the health of the American economy. It took the hardship of the Depression, however, to solidify this mindset.[12]

6

Radio, Rayon, and Retail Credit

AMERICA EMERGED FROM WORLD WAR I WITH a reasonably strong economy and an optimism that came to dominate the tumultuous, fast-paced 1920s, with its dancing "flappers," flagpole sitters, jazz music, and parade of household inventions that redefined modern life. For the first time in its history, America had a larger population living in its cities than on farms.[1] This was when the retail chain was born and ribbons of highway were built across the country. Electric devices, from refrigerators to air conditioners and electric hair curlers, became commonplace. Many items that had been around for years, such as the automobile, radio, and telephone, came into widespread everyday use, transforming America into a mobile, linked, and news-driven society. Facilitating the purchase of these items was installment debt, which also came into widespread everyday use. It revolutionized how Americans thought about and used credit and gave rise to another phenomenon that is familiar to Americans today: consumer advocacy for truth in advertising and for product-safety testing.

The era's marvelous innovations and advances touched nearly every aspect of American life. Alexander Fleming discovered penicillin in London in 1928. The decade ushered in nonstop intercontinental flight—the first by John Alcock and Arthur Brown in 1919, and the first solo by Charles Lindbergh in 1927. Women cast their first presidential ballots in 1920. Gary Cooper, Greta Garbo, Charlie Chaplin, Buster Keaton, and the Marx Brothers became stars. Hollywood introduced talking movies. Baseball slugger Babe Ruth and prize-fighter Jack Dempsey became national heroes. Radio stations grew from one in

1920 to 1,400 by 1924. Advertisers marketed on a new, mass scale. Cars led the way, followed by new products like rayon and deodorant. The anti-capitalist, anti-Semitic, and eventually pro-Nazi religious demagogue Father Charles Coughlin reached millions of listeners with his populist message via the new mass medium of radio. An ideological battle between science and religion played out in newspapers and over airwaves during the 1925 "Monkey" trial in Tennessee, where Darwin's theory of evolution was pitted in court against biblical creationism. *Time* magazine hit newsstands. The country's intolerance of immigrants skyrocketed, as did its phobia of communism, with a "Red Scare" at the start of the decade that left an indelible streak of anti-Marxist sentiment among Americans. Artistic revolutions flourished with the Harlem Renaissance and legendary musicians like Duke Ellington and Louis Armstrong. The writers Langston Hughes, Sinclair Lewis, F. Scott Fitzgerald, and Ernest Hemingway came into their own. A moral debate over alcohol, similar to today's over marijuana, led to Prohibition at the start of the decade and then its repeal thirteen years later, with speakeasies, bootlegging gangsters, and a not inconsequential disregard for the law in between.[2]

The first radio broadcast had aired in New York City on January 13, 1910, with tenor Enrico Caruso singing opera, but such transmissions meant little without appliances to receive them and audiences to listen.[3] Radio enthusiasts remained a small subset of the population until 1920, when the nation's first radio station heralded the device's spread to living rooms across America. In the presidential election of 1920, a Detroit station demonstrated how much faster than newspapers the radio could deliver news when it announced Harding's victory over Cox.[4] By 1923 there were 1.5 million radio receivers in American living rooms, and retail spending on radios rose from $60 million in 1922 to $842 million by 1929.[5] By the end of the decade, 40 percent of homes in America, and a much higher percentage of its well-to-do households, had radios.[6] Radio was the computer and internet of the era, transmitting news and commercials as well as being the industry whose stocks, principally those of the Radio Corporation of America, dazzled investors and speculators.

In 1900, perhaps 8 percent of U.S. homes had electricity; by the end of the 1920s, 68 percent did. Households with a telephone went from fewer than 10 percent in 1900 to more than 40 percent by 1929, with much of the growth since 1918.[7] Ownership of toasters, air conditioners, refrigerators, and washing machines followed a similar trajectory.

Many of these items were bought on credit. People always have borrowed money, but mass, retail consumer credit, especially for non-essentials, is a creation of the early twentieth century. Madison Avenue persuaded consumers that they could use the promise of future earnings to indulge sooner rather than later. That change in mindset, enabled by the advent of retail installment credit, ignited consumer borrowing on an unprecedented scale, bringing a massive change in the number of people who borrowed, and for what. And it started with auto lending. "The driving force behind this huge expansion of debt was, literally, the driver," writes credit historian Lendol Calder. Soon an expansion of credit made possible the mass buying of not just cars but also "radios, refrigerators, vacuum cleaners, fine jewelry and other expensive consumer durable goods." Large numbers of people went into debt to purchase and take home items that they once would have saved to buy or even felt fine doing without.[8]

Lenders, writes Calder, "accomplished what advertisers were powerless to do, which was to provide people with the means to turn expensive consumer dreams into instant realities. Credit, in short, made consumers of the millions." The middle class led this new trend; the working poor historically always had to borrow for necessities.[9] These new middle-class borrowers, by contrast, reflected an age of hope, a belief in "a new era" without recessions, in which a stream of new gadgets and wonders were within reach of the multitudes. "There was great hope," historian Robert Sobel said in a taped interview for PBS. "America came out of World War I [as] . . . the only strong country in the world. The dollar was king. We had a very popular president in the middle of the decade, Calvin Coolidge, and an even more popular one elected in 1928, Herbert Hoover. So things looked pretty good."[10]

Credit for the purchase of nonessential, non-income-producing goods grew so pervasive that it warranted comment in editorial cartoons. One from early 1926 shows a husband telling his wife that he paid the doctor who delivered their baby "another ten dollars on his bill," to which she responds, "Oh goody, only two more payments and the baby is ours."[11] But amid the optimism, many understood that credit meant debt, and debt could be trouble.

Debtor prisons—the work house—largely vanished in America in the 1800s, supplanted by more enlightened bankruptcy laws, but the shame of being in debt endured. Migrations in the latter half of the century from rural farming communities to cities, where people went to earn wages but often found the income meager and unreliable, gave rise to an informal industry of short-term lenders.[12] When wages fell short or were interrupted by illness or other misfortune, workers typically borrowed for a few days or weeks, trading in household items like furniture, cookware, or clothing and then buying them back until, a short time later, they repeated the cycle. The wage-earning poor often found themselves in a permanent cycle of debt to make ends meet. They would pawn goods, or worse, visit a loan shark; like payday lenders now, these lenders made loans on claims on a worker's next pay, charging unaffordable interest rates to the financially vulnerable, who too often eventually sank under such debt. Even borrowing to meet daily needs evoked shame. Pawnshops, the day-to-day bankers to the poor, provided booths for patrons to stand in when selling or buying back items so they wouldn't be seen by neighbors. This pervasive stigma against borrowing, which survived well into the 1920s, included an aversion to retail installment credit, which at first banks would not supply directly, preferring to lend to finance companies or retailers that then extended credit to customers.

As city populations swelled, mass advertising, mass marketing, and mass credit followed. Mainstream society condensed in city blocks, listened to the same radio broadcasts, and began to focus on outward appearances and trappings of wealth in a way that farm life, a more isolated affair, had not encouraged. Corporate America launched a battle to persuade consumers that they could be of sound morals and still buy now and pay later for a nonessential item like a radio or car. Borrowing for frills wasn't evil.

But it's also true that while people paid lip service to the myth of a golden age when Americans didn't borrow, many knew a different reality. "I have no doubt that some of you who read this book . . . are trying to get out of debt, a very ancient slough," wrote Henry David Thoreau in his book *Walden* in 1854. Satirists have long fed on this discrepancy between fiction and fact. The popular nineteenth-century humorist Charles Farrar Browne, known by the pseudonym Artemus Ward, wrote with his trademark misspellings, "Let us all be happy, and live within our means, even if we have to borrer money to do it with."[13]

In their 1873 book *The Gilded Age,* Mark Twain and Charles Warner created Colonel Beriah Sellers, a man who "could not keep from buying trifles every day that were not wholly necessary." He found "it was such a gaudy thing to get out his bank-book and draw a check," preferring to use "his old customary formula, 'Charge it'" with merchants. To "charge it" meant putting what was owed on a tab at a local store whose owner knew the customers and where they lived. The phrase "Charge it," perhaps inspired by Colonel Sellers, was the title of a popular novel in 1912, whose author preceded it with "Keeping up with Lizzie." The titles in turn helped inspire the "Tin Lizzie" nickname for the Ford Model T and the comic strip "Keeping Up with the Joneses."[14]

Henry Ford used electricity and new principles of quality control to revolutionize the assembly line, but he disapproved of new ideas about debt.[15] His belief that people should save up to buy a car was typical of how many Americans long had thought about debt, at least publicly: borrowing for income-producing goods, like a farm or a sewing machine, was okay, but borrowing for items that didn't help one make a living or that served one's vanity, such as jewelry or fancy clothing, was shameful.[16] Ford not surprisingly sold his cars to dealers for cash, but the reality was that most of the dealers' customers bought Ford cars on an installment credit plan provided by a finance company.[17]

Executives at Ford's rival, General Motors—cofounded by William C. Durant, who would play a lead role in stock market speculation in the 1920s—had a different view of the virtues of thrift. GM helped make the finance company respectable when, in 1919, it created its own banking unit, General Motors Acceptance Corporation, to extend credit to GM auto dealers and car buyers on a buy-now-pay-later installment plan. GM ads featured well-dressed men and women in upscale settings that often resembled banks. "Select the make and model that suits you best and buy it, if you choose, out of your monthly income," read a 1925 ad.[18]

Banks in the 1920s mostly didn't lend directly to consumers. Though some had begun to do so, most bankers thought consumer loans too risky. They preferred shorter-term loans to businesses, which provided a buffer from the masses. Banks by and large supplied credit to others, like finance companies, which then provided it to consumers.[19] "More than 2500 banks are cooperating . . . to finance the credit sales of General Motors cars and trucks," the GM ad explains, calling the plan "simple, sound, inexpensive."[20] The atmosphere shown in the ad evoked what it was really selling: respectability.

Forced to respond to the competition, Ford in 1923 put his save-to-buy credo into action by creating a layaway plan in which a Ford dealer would gather weekly payments from a customer and deposit them in a bank until the stash grew big enough for the buyer to pay cash for a car.[21] It was a flop. Why use layaway when installment buying let you drive the car home today? Within two years, with GM successfully challenging Ford's market dominance, Ford was forced to offer a company-sponsored installment plan. By the end of the decade, everyone selling in any significant way to the public had to do so.[22] A 1930 topic for high-school forensic debaters showed that the morality of installment borrowing wasn't entirely settled: "Resolved: That Installment buying of personal property as now practiced in the United States is both socially and economically desirable."[23] But the wording, which frames installment buying as a positive to be rebutted, shows that this kind of financing had become pervasive, if not universally accepted. The car companies hadn't just altered how America moved around: by introducing installment credit, they had altered how Americans bought just about everything.

Through most of the decade, 25 to 40 percent of car sales in a given year were cash transactions, but typically only wealthy buyers could afford that.[24] The rest of the car-buying public in the 1920s embraced installment buying. Car sales went from 2,500 in 1899 to 4 million in 1926, while the percentage of cars sold on credit went from zero to a solid majority.

Although advertising couldn't facilitate buying the way credit could, it helped shape how Americans thought about debt. The 1920s are when advertisers shifted from factual descriptions of a product to showing the person using it as happy, fulfilled, and sexually desirable. And those well-clad, appealing customers pictured buying new Buicks were a legacy of another novelty: the government's innovative sale of Liberty and Victoria bonds to finance World War I. To sell the bonds, the government had helped pioneer both mass marketing and the use of words that emphasized ideas—love of country and the need to win—over what a product did, which in the case of government bonds was to fund combat. The government sold the bonds directly to ordinary Americans through the twelve regional Federal Reserve Banks and through national banks, mostly in small amounts of fifty and a hundred dollars. It even sold the bonds on an installment plan, much as Hamilton had done in the sale of securities for the first Bank of the United States.[25]

The aim was to persuade as many Americans as possible not only to buy bonds but also to buy into the war, which had been unpopular. The government gave priority to smaller investors. When John D. Rockefeller wanted to invest $15 million in one round, for example, he was allotted just $3 million to allow those buying fifty and a hundred dollars' worth the chance to show their patriotism. Sales of the bonds were boosted by an unprecedented marketing campaign making an explicitly emotional appeal. One, combining love of country and a with-it use of technology, shows the Statue of Liberty talking into a telephone saying: "HELLO! This is LIBERTY speaking. Billions of dollars are needed and needed *NOW*." The campaigns proved a gigantic success. "By war's end, after four drives, twenty million individuals had bought bonds," writes historian Richard Sutch. "That is pretty impressive given that there were only twenty-four million households at the time. More than $17 billion had been raised."[26]

Marketers took notes, and among the first products to benefit were personal deodorants. Antiperspirant had been around since well before World War I, with advertisements touting what it did—stopping perspiration. To counter misconceptions that that was unhealthy, advertisers claimed that a doctor had developed the product to stop the "ailment" of underarm sweat. Popular sentiment forbade talking about body excretions publicly, making deodorants a hard sell. Even so, by the end of the war, about a third of women used them, including the "Odorono" brand that James Young, a former door-to-door bible salesman now at the advertising firm of J. Walter Thompson Co., was in charge of marketing. Young gained advertising immortality when he changed tactics and published ads to convince the other two-thirds of potential customers that their perspiration was something others would talk about publicly, but behind their backs.[27] "A woman's arm!" read the *Ladies' Home Journal* ad that Young ran in 1919. "Poets have sung of it, great artists have painted its beauty. It should be the daintiest, sweetest thing in the world. And yet, unfortunately, it isn't always." Ever since, ad executives have labored to convince Americans they can't be beautiful, happy, pleasant smelling, or cool without an endless list of items they once had never heard of.

Ads for credit were no different. One ad urging consumers to buy a GM car with an installment loan doesn't even picture a car, but the head of a well-groomed man wearing a tie next to the headline, "He makes only $3,000 a year . . . *but is worth* $112,290!" The ad says that even if "Jim" never gets a raise, he can use his future earnings—$112,290 over his lifetime—to purchase a car for himself and "Mrs. Jim." Corporate America realized that if it didn't sell consumer credit by selling confidence in the future, a competitor would.[28]

Household debt swelled. A great share of that increase went to durable goods, with cars leading the way, followed by radios and other household appliances, with a somewhat compensatory decline in expenditures on furniture, household furnishings, and jewelry. By the end of the decade, households were using debt to finance up to 90 percent of the purchase price of big-ticket items. Marketing historian Martha Olney convincingly argues that automakers' original motive for promoting the use of credit was to help dealers smooth out seasonal buying patterns—stopping and starting assembly lines was costly, as was holding inventory—and that marketers increased advertising because of favorable treatment under a 1917 tax law enacted to help pay war expenses. These incentives may have spurred the wider use of debt and advertising, but the success in luring in new customers sustained them.[29]

Average household debt, excluding mortgages and in constant 2016 dollars, climbed from $1,188 in 1900 to $1,336 in 1910, then stayed in the $1,000 to $1,130 range until the recession of 1920–1921, when it fell to $967. It then began to climb, to $1,427 in 1925 and $2,045 in 1929. After the 1929 crash it fell into the $1,300 to $1,400 range until 1935, when it began a steady and almost uninterrupted rise that continues today. (At the end of 2017, the average household credit-card debt was $15,983, which excludes of course mortgage, auto, and student loan debt. Add in all debt and the average was $133,568.) Olney found that from 1900 to 1920, debt as a percentage of income ranged between 4.40 percent and 6.96 percent, but rose to 9.34 percent by 1929, with most of that increase coming after 1925. Many households must have been far deeper in debt than the averages convey.[30]

All this modernization took place amid significant catastrophes and an economy that was, despite any of the Fed's stabilizing efforts, still rocky. On the heels of the 100,000 Americans killed and 200,000 wounded in World War I, the flu pandemic of 1918–1919 killed 20 million people worldwide, including 675,000 people in the United States (out of a population of 105 million).

A brief depression in 1920 and 1921 took a heavy toll. The war had increased demand for American goods, but after it ended in late 1919, a decrease in demand, coupled with the Fed's raising of interest rates, sent prices down and pushed unemployment as high as 19 percent. Rural areas, among the hardest hit, never fully recovered over the next decade. Between 1920 and 1932, roughly 25 percent of the nation's farms were sold to repay debt. Many of the sellers migrated to cities.[31]

Still, many people were prosperous and optimistic under Coolidge's tenure, from 1923 to 1929. That optimism, and the frenetic lifestyle that accompanied it, partly came from Americans' having more money in their pockets as the government retired its war bonds. Surely it also came from people's desire to forget the war, the pandemic, and the economy's underlying problems, reflected in the faces of farmers and sporadically laid-off industrial workers. Securities speculation became part of the frenzy. No group embraced the financial revolution in retail credit more than the denizens of Wall Street, and none among them was more eager than Sunshine Charlie. Irving Berlin's hit song "Blue Skies," with the line "Never saw things going so right," captured the mood of the time.[32]

7

If It Seems Too Good to Be True . . .

THE ARREST OF CHARLES PONZI IN 1920 provided a lesson in the danger of investments that seem too good to be true, though many paid no attention. An Italian immigrant and former vegetable dealer, waiter, and forger, Ponzi wasn't the first to perfect the swindle known as a pyramid scheme, but his $20 million fraud claimed the title as the biggest and best known at the time. Ever since, in dubious tribute, such swindles often are called Ponzi schemes. Ponzi promised investors big returns with little risk but then, instead of investing in a real product, he paid existing clients with money from newly recruited ones—and lived lavishly with the rest of the money. He took money in the front door, paid some of it out the back door, and stole the rest. The scheme is really an upside-down pyramid, starting small at the bottom and growing ever bigger as more and more customers and their money are needed to pay off those who entered before them. The exponential growth creates an inverted, top-heavy structure that eventually collapses.

After the recession at the start of the decade ended in 1921, the stock market began a rally that would run nearly uninterrupted for eight years. But it wasn't a full-fledged bubble until late in the decade, and it was preceded, as financial bubbles often are, by a real estate mania. This one began slowly in the early 1920s, in Florida, and rested on the premise that the state's sunshine and beaches would draw tourists from around the nation, now that they had cars and increasingly better roads to drive them on. But sometime around 1924, common sense, and any connection between prices and underlying dynamics, evaporated.

Descriptions of an undeveloped heaven on earth inflated land prices beyond reason. Like all speculative bubbles, this one was fed by easy credit. Lenders kept the spigot open too long because they stopped caring whether the upward trend in land prices correlated with the growth in tourist traffic or population.

Easy credit differs from ordinary credit in that it lacks underwriting. The financial equivalent of kicking the tires, underwriting—the formal acceptance of financial risk—requires that a company evaluate that risk before taking it on. Lenders do that by weighing the likelihood that a loan will be paid back. Similarly, insurers underwrite to determine when and how much they will likely have to pay for fire damage or unexpected death, so they can charge premiums that will cover their expected payouts and still earn them a profit. They can't predict which of their customers will need a payout, but using data gathered from experience and solid underwriting, they can tell with reasonable precision how many will draw how much in any given period. As part of their underwriting, insurers take care that the customers they accept create a pool that is large and diverse enough to make it probable that most won't need to draw on insurance. Securities underwriters in a public offering also assess risk: they purchase the stock shares or bonds of a company and offer them to the public, acting as a middleman by taking responsibility for the risks involved in selling them. With their money on the line, they have an incentive to perform a thorough due diligence on the company to help set the price of the offering appropriately, that is, so that the price reflects both the risk and the potential benefits of investing in that company.

In lending it's the same: underwriting requires assessing whether a borrower stands a reasonable chance of paying back a loan. A lender who underwrites wants to verify that a borrower—be it a company or a person—has a certain income or revenue. A lender wants to know where else the borrower owes money. Can he, she, or the company afford additional debt? How good has the borrower been at repaying past debt? Assessing a borrower's risk of defaulting also requires weighing the soundness of where and how a borrower is investing the money. Does the investment pose a big risk? Is it a sure thing, or might it take the shirt off the borrower's back? Even an otherwise creditworthy borrower can't repay a debt if a losing investment ruins him financially.

An investment that's underwritten is nonspeculative. That doesn't mean that the borrower won't default or the lender won't lose money, just that the odds of it happening are lower or, at least, better understood. Even the best underwriters

cannot foresee who specifically will default, but good underwriting helps minimize that risk. When lenders underwrite all loans, the overall default rate will be
less. They can't know which loan in a group will default, but they know that the
overall default rate will be lower if they have done their homework on each one.
They can't tell which person will die of natural causes at age eighty, but they
have a very good idea of what percentage of people in a given pool of eighty-
year-olds will. They can know statistically *about* a group with an exactitude not
possible person by person, or investment by investment, *within* that group.

A loan or investment that isn't underwritten is speculative, made in the hope
that past price increases will continue. It's a gamble that, at least for a time, is
self-perpetuating. Initial demand might be based on fundamentals. But once
demand starts going up solely because prices are going up—and absent any
assessment of whether a fundamental reason continues to justify the increase—
that demand will further raise prices by bringing in more speculators, and so on.
This begets an upward spiral of speculation. Inevitably the bubble bursts,
though often no one can say why the collapse happens on one day rather than
earlier or later. Suddenly everyone wants out. A reverse bubble ensues, in which
the price falls with every sale.

People are likelier to speculate on rising prices if they are betting with
borrowed money. When they use their own money, they tend to underwrite and
avoid risk. People using borrowed money typically are willing to take more
risk, particularly if they are in financial trouble and have nothing to lose and
everything possibly to gain, like a losing gambler doubling down on a bet. Easy
credit—too much money chasing too few good investments—flourishes when
lenders stop underwriting. So does the tendency of borrowers to take on more
and more risk, falling down a slippery slope of increasing losses.

Typically, lenders stop underwriting because making money, or appearing to
do so, causes blindness and amnesia. People forget past bubbles and tell themselves that "this time it's different." Phrases like that echoed through the 1920s,
during Ponzi's scheme, the Florida land bubble, and the subsequent stock
market mania. What seems too good to be true can be hard to resist. "The
United States is afflicted with 'new eras,'" economist John Kenneth Galbraith
said in an interview years ago about the crash of 1929. "Let us not think for a
moment that the illusion, the aberration of the 1920s was unique; it is intimately
a part of the American character. There's nothing unique about this. It is something which happens every 20 or 30 years because that's about the length of the

financial memory. It's about the length of time that it requires for a new set of suckers . . . a new set of people capable of wonderful self-delusion to come in and imagine that they have a new and wonderful fix on the future."[1]

In addition to easy credit, every bubble requires people willing to, as the saying on Wall Street goes, "drink the Kool-Aid," that is, to accept a premise that in hindsight is questionable or even ridiculous, and to do it on a scale that produces what Galbraith calls a "mass illusion." The phrase comes from the Jonestown cult of the 1970s, whose members drank poisoned Kool-Aid rather than be rescued by the authorities. Wall Street has appropriated it to mean an idea that is doomed but that a group of investors metaphorically drinks in, believes, or goes along with to profit from, or because of, peer pressure. Notions that "home prices never go down" or that badly run banks can "grow out of their problems" are examples of Kool-Aid. The former fueled the subprime mortgage crisis of 2007; the latter the thrift crisis of the 1980s. Bubbles end up not just deflated. They invariably also lead to scandal because crooks and those who skate near the edge are generally the first to see that a financial situation can be exploited because it lacks fundamentals or policing. In a bubble's aftermath, everyone wonders how otherwise seemingly sensible people behaved so foolishly.

When Ponzi got out of jail in 1925 for the fraud that became his namesake, he headed straight to Florida to make money ripping off gullible investors there. People around the country were so eager to get in on the Florida boom that many bought property by mail, sight unseen, putting money down on margin, that is, on credit for a fraction of the going price with a promise to pay the rest later. Miami billed itself as the "Wonder City" and the "World's Playground" and watched its population swell from 30,000 in 1920 to 75,000 by 1925. Similar influxes occurred around the state.[2]

"The good times . . . of high price almost always engender much fraud," observed nineteenth-century journalist Walter Bagehot. "All people are most credulous when they are most happy; and when much money has just been made, when some people are really making it, when most people think they are making it, there is a happy opportunity for ingenious mendacity. Almost everything will be believed for a little while, and long before discovery the worst and most adroit deceivers are geographically or legally beyond the reach of punishment."[3]

Compounding the trend in the 1920s was that many now-forbidden financial activities were legal. Bankers routinely manipulated markets. There was no federal requirement that companies disclose information, including risks, that a reasonable investor would want to know before putting down money, borrowed or not. Anyone trying to underwrite had to rely on the information that Wall Street deigned to release, which wasn't much.

During the Florida land bubble, people willingly believed that demand for homes and vacations in the state was boundless. But as prices were starting to fall, in 1926, two hurricanes literally knocked the stuffing out of already shaky developments. The boom collapsed, causing loan defaults that pushed nearly a hundred banks into failure over the next three years. Like many regions caught up in a real estate bubble, Florida eventually proved a lucrative investment, but not for decades. In the short term, mania fueled a rise in prices untethered to reality. The Marx brothers' movie *The Cocoanuts* made fun of those taken in by it: "Eight hundred wonderful residences will be built right here," Groucho Marx says in one scene, with palm trees in the background. "Why, they're as good as up, better. You can have any kind of home you want to. You can even get stucco. Oh, how you can get stucco."

Ponzi and the Florida bust didn't deter the investing public from entering the stock market, least of all Groucho Marx himself. He bet his life savings on stocks even as his film lampooned those taken in by the Florida bubble.[4]

By the end of the Florida land mania, middle-class America was used to borrowing money on a scale and on terms and for items it never had before—and not just new gadgets and inventions. America watched with fascination as a small group of men made fantastic amounts of money not by making a tangible item like steel or a railroad or a radio, but by trading pieces of paper representing slices of ownership in companies. This marked mainstream America's first love affair with a derivative, which, broadly defined, is any financial tool whose value is derived from something else. The stock market wasn't new, but the general public until the 1920s had largely regarded it as too risky for the likes of them. Cartoons and news stories at the turn of the century depicted year-end parties on the stock exchange as a raucous revelry. Editorial cartoonist W. A. Rogers regularly depicted the general public as sheep getting shorn by Wall Street's collaborating bears and bulls.[5] Now, as these traders in paper earned unimaginable sums, the public started to treat them as celebrities, almost royalty, as though their wealth reflected some inner brilliance rather than clever manipulation and luck. There was broker Michael Meehan, who

Great Activity in Wall Street, by W. A. Rogers, from the *New York Herald,* March 19, 1908,
depicts a raucous Wall Street doing an endless dance of bulls and bears, who made
money by preying on sheep, the public, who invariably lost money. Most Americans
considered participating too risky at the turn of the century, but that attitude would
change in the 1920s. Library of Congress.

specialized in trading RCA stock; speculator Jesse Livermore, who never did
anything but play the markets; and William C. Durant, cofounder of GM who,
unlike the others, once made money creating a product that people actually
used. By the 1920s, Durant made money solely by playing the market, backed
with money from those in the auto industry. And of course, there was Charlie
Mitchell.[6]

Then as now, some Wall Street investors created supply and demand by
underwriting, that is, by pricing securities based on the economy, interest rates,
population trends, future profit estimates, dividends, the soundness of a company's management, and so on. Speculative investors invested simply on gambles
that prices would go up or down. Then there were those, as now, who were

neither speculators nor nonspeculators but manipulators, making bets only after taking steps to make sure the outcome would be in their favor. These manipulators often focused on the stock of RCA, which sold the radios that swept the nation, that then brought into people's living rooms the news that helped hype the stock market and, eventually, filled those same living rooms with grim accounts of the economy's collapse.

After the Florida crash, Americans fixated on the ticker tape and the securities trading it represented. The cover of popular magazines pictured well-dressed men and women poring over the ticker. Bruce Fairchild Barton's bestseller *The Man Nobody Knows* described Jesus Christ as the father of modern business. Speculator John J. Raskob—a self-made millionaire who advised DuPont and General Motors, who chaired the Democratic National Committee from 1928 to 1932, and who would later help finance the building of the Empire State Building—declared in an interview in the *Ladies' Home Journal* a few months before the crash that "Everybody ought to be rich." Stock prices and the goings-on of market manipulators made front-page news and prime airtime. Best-selling books included titles such as *Beating the Stock Market* and *The Art of Speculation*.[7]

Manipulators could easily and legally rig the market, and now they had many more people to dupe: manufacturers and retailers had introduced Main Street consumers to installment credit for tangible items; Wall Street introduced them to installment credit for stocks and bonds. Buying securities on credit—known as buying on margin—let investors buy stock for as little as 10 percent down. For $1,000 a person could own $10,000 in stock. If the price went up, they could sell it to repay the other 90 percent, and take a profit. The risk was that if a stock fell in value by more than 10 percent, a stock broker would require the investor to put up more "margin" or would sell the stock to make up the difference. Selling put downward pressure on prices, resulting in more margin calls, which if unchecked could turn into a full-scale panic.

Everyone seemed to be investing, from the shoeshine man and grocery store clerk to Hollywood stars. Astrologer Evangeline Adams made headlines with predictions for clients such as Charlie Chaplin and Mary Pickford that share prices could rise "to heaven."[8] From his frozen camp on the South Pole, Commander Richard Byrd radioed buy and sell orders to his broker. The well-heeled passengers of the luxury ocean liner the *Berengaria*, on their way between New York and Europe in the summer of 1929, issued orders mid-ocean to their brokers via newly installed RCA radio equipment.[9]

Many small-time investors eagerly entered the market when values seemed to be rising, although often manipulators were artificially boosting the values. In March 1929, the broker Michael Meehan famously orchestrated one of the biggest manipulative pools of the time.[10] He and his friends began buying and selling RCA shares to each other to raise the price of the stock and create the illusion of rising demand. Members of the pool then began to "paint the tape" by planting favorable stories about RCA in the press. (Many such pools bribed reporters to write stories to make companies look exciting.)[11] In one week, from March 8 to March 17, investors pushed the price for RCA shares up 50 percent. Meehan and friends had stopped buying and now began selling, netting in 1929 dollars more than $13.5 million for one week's work. In 2017 dollars, that translates to more than $190 million.[12] An editorial cartoon after the stock collapsed depicted Meehan as a modern-day pied piper leading unwary RCA investors.

No one did more than Charlie Mitchell to bring stock brokerage to the masses. In June 1917, *The Magazine of Wall Street,* whose motto was "Fearless, Forward looking, Fortnightly," interviewed Mitchell, who correctly predicted that the war's main commercial benefit for Wall Street would come from the government's sale of Liberty bonds. Marketing the bonds to the middle class— getting them accustomed to buying securities—would lead, he said, to "the development of a large, new army of investors in this country" that he could sell to.[13]

Consumers purchased everything else on credit, why not securities? After all, professional investors put down a percentage of the price of a stock or bond, typically 20 to 50 percent, and borrowed the rest from the broker to buy it. The difference was that professional investors typically made such purchases on terms of three months to a year, and at low, fixed rates of interest. For retail investors entering the market, these "time loans" were replaced by much shorter ones in the "call market" that might last only a day.[14] Barton—the author who described Jesus as a salesman—interviewed Mitchell in February 1923 for *American Magazine* for a piece entitled "Is There Anything Here That Other Men Couldn't Do?," describing how Mitchell motivated salesmen by taking them to the top of floor of a "Bankers' Club," where they could look down on the streets of New York teeming with people. "There are six million people with incomes that aggregate thousands of millions of dollars," Mitchell would say. "They are just waiting for someone to come and tell them what to do with their savings. Take a good look, eat a good lunch, and then go down there and tell them." If the view didn't stir "a man's imagination" Mitchell said, "he's not big-league stuff."[15]

The lure of buying now and paying later began to chip away at the widely held belief that Wall Street routinely fleeced unsophisticated investors. Mitchell's retail outlets marketed this new view to amateurs eager to get rich, even as the lively, close-knit group of men who controlled and regularly manipulated Wall Street continued their financial escapades.

These amateurs might have questioned why the titans of Wall Street supplied such easy credit, but they were blinded by the prospect of easy money. A cartoon of the time depicts a nonprofessional "little investor" with a climbing pick in hand, warily walking a tightrope hooked on one side to "Wall Street," where he began, and on the other, far side to a mountain labeled "easy money" where he hoped to arrive.

Perhaps the public's favorable experience with war bonds had ignited, as Mitchell predicted, a willingness to broaden the buy-now-pay-later mindset to securities. Perhaps it was the extra money the retiring bonds had put into people's pockets. Perhaps headlines, radio briefs, and newsreels about the people who

Thar's Gold in Them Hills, a cartoon from Judge in the 1920s, depicts the public's increasing desire to speculate in the market, with retail credit fueling the boom of the "Little Speculator" taking big risks in the desire to make "easy money." Image courtesy of the Collection of the Museum of American Finance, NYC.

made millions buying and selling paper did it. Whatever it was, banks and brokerages succeeded in enticing a generation that had invested in war bonds to invest in bonds with no guarantee from Uncle Sam. Over the decade, the public's fascination with Wall Street grew into a national obsession.

Not everyone bought into the euphoria. During an interview from prison, Al Capone, infamous for the Valentine's Day Massacre of 1929, where he used a machine gun to eliminate competition in his bootleg liquor business, described the stock market as "a racket." "Those stock market guys are crooked. I won't play with them. I know lots better ways of investing my small change," he said.[16] He knew a rigged game when he saw one. Underwriting might have helped had due diligence been possible, but for outsiders information was scarce, suspect, and anything but uniform.[17] Dividends could be manipulated to hide problems even more easily than today; so could revenue and profit statements and predictions about future sales.

In early 1929, the respected banker Paul Warburg spoke out, saying the Federal Reserve had lost control of credit and had allowed the stock exchange to take charge. Stock prices, he said, didn't reflect "intrinsic value" but were artificially high, fueled by too much borrowed money. This was true, and even though the Federal Reserve had started to tighten up, it was too late. It should have acted sooner and more selectively so as not to punish the entire economy.[18] Economist Roger Babson repeatedly warned that a stock market crash was coming. Warburg and Babson suffered the typical fate of naysayers during a bubble: critics excoriated them, even calling them unpatriotic. Often, a telltale sign of a dangerous financial situation is that questions are met with anger and derision—especially by people who drape themselves in the flag. Such reactions suggest either that those in charge don't want anyone trying to understand the situation, or that they themselves don't understand it.[19]

Worries that investment had turned to widespread speculation dogged Federal Reserve Board members and newly elected president Herbert Hoover, sworn in on March 4, 1929. They understood that too much borrowed money was to blame, including money that banks had borrowed from the Fed at a low rate and then lent at a higher one to brokers, who in turn lent it as "call money" to small investors. This was not what the Federal Reserve Board's backers had envisioned. In 1928, Senator Carter Glass complained that banks were lending for "gambling in stocks and bonds, without regard to the need for money in legitimate industry," and threatened to overhaul the system.[20]

In fact, investors weren't as ubiquitous as people imagined. Despite the catch-phrase that "everyone's in the market," the majority of Americans felt safer watching from the sidelines. But many more ordinary Americans were investing than ever before, and banks lent the money to do it—not directly, but to brokers like Meehan, whose customers then borrowed it to buy on margin. How many Americans invested is hard to pinpoint, but all numbers point to a marked uptick by 1929 from the turn of the century. Historian Julia C. Ott concludes that less than 1 percent of the population owned stocks or bonds in 1900, or fewer than 760,000 people, but that about a third of the population purchased "some form of federal bond during World War I." By 1929, based on Ott's estimate that 25 percent of U.S. households invested in the market, at least 8 million Americans, or 6.5 percent of the population, held publicly traded stocks.[21] Not all who had bought war bonds later entered the market, but, as Sunshine Charlie predicted, many did. Economist Galbraith, using (possibly suspect) figures the industry supplied to the U.S. Senate five years later, estimated that active speculators "at the peak in 1929" numbered fewer than 1 million, with active margin accounts increasing by only 50,000 between the end of 1928 and the end of July 1929.[22] A more reliable gauge of the increase in speculative participation was the rise in call loans: early in the 1920s this market ranged from $1 billion to $1.5 billion, but by early 1926 it had risen to $2.5 billion, by 1927 to $3.5 billion, and by 1928 to $5.7 billion.[23]

Banks supplying the credit often borrowed from the Federal Reserve discount window at 5 percent. By the time the funds got to the retail investor, the rate could be 12 percent.[24] The Federal Reserve's board members hated but permitted this lucrative leveraging. Hoover and the board worried about it but felt unable to act for fear of being the catalyst that popped the bubble. They knew it would happen eventually, but they didn't want to be the immediate cause.[25] Hoover, correctly, blamed Federal Reserve officials for keeping interest rates low—thus keeping the availability of credit too high—during much of the 1920s to help war-ravaged Europe entice gold into its coffers with interest rates higher than those in the United States.[26] Coolidge made matters worse by proclaiming, shortly before leaving office, that stocks were "cheap at current prices." Hoover understood the danger far better and within two days of taking office urged the Fed to curb borrowing used to lend for speculation.[27]

The Fed had tightened credit a year earlier, in 1928. But this proved a very blunt instrument that didn't contain Wall Street's gambling. It unintentionally made matters worse by raising rates for the rest of economy, key parts of which, including the construction and auto industries, were already in recession by early 1929.[28] Farmers, who'd never recovered from the depression at the beginning of the decade, once again bore the brunt. Cracks in the economy abounded. Speculation continued unabated. The Fed had acted too little, too late, and in a manner that, by failing to be specific to banks, arguably worsened the overall situation.[29]

As 1929 progressed, reporters hung outside the Fed's constant closed-door meetings, which did little but cause anxiety because officials refused to say anything publicly. On March 26, 1929, borrowing rates on call loans reached 20 percent, making them too expensive for many in the already debt-burdened population. The stock market dropped amid mounting concern that, with call money out of reach, the bull market was over. Federal Reserve officials

"Somebody Had to Save Him from Himself," which ran on the front page of the *Los Angeles Times* on February 8, 1929, a few months before the crash, depicts "The Speculation Crazy Public" as a very fat restaurant patron and the waiter as the "Federal Reserve Board." The waiter yells "Don't you know when you've had enough?" and yanks the food from the table, creating a "withdrawal of speculative credit" but too late—the public is obese from overeating "stocks." Edmund Gale.
© 1929 Los Angeles Times. Used with permission.

maintained a "demoralizing silence."[30] Mitchell, who sat on the board of the Federal Reserve Bank of New York, wasn't having it. The next day he announced that National City Bank would provide $25 million for loans to brokers to lend in call loans. Afterward he justified this action by saying he had averted a liquidity crisis. Not only did Mitchell's action defy the Fed's policy of trying to rein in easy credit, it specifically provided funds to boost sales—to speculate— in securities of his bank or that his bank had an interest in. To Glass and others, the action underscored the absurdity of the phony demand created by easy credit. Worse, National City had been profiting by leveraging favorable rates on borrowings from the Federal Reserve. Glass declared that Mitchell had "slapped the Reserve Board in the face" and called for him to step down from the board of the New York Fed.[31]

The Federal Reserve and Hoover faced the classic dilemma during a bubble: calling out a problem and reducing money for loans would risk an abrupt, wrenching pricking of the bubble that would blast through the economy. Yet doing nothing would allow the problem to grow bigger and eventually implode, with costlier economic repercussions. "The real choice was between an immediate and deliberately engineered collapse and a more serious disaster later on," Galbraith writes.[32] Former Federal Reserve Board chairman Ben Bernanke, who is a scholar of the Great Depression, acknowledges the difficulty of diffusing an asset bubble, but says the Fed of the 1920s failed by not using its oversight of Federal Reserve member banks to curb excess lending in a targeted way. In other words, everyone would have been better off if the bubble had been curbed early and not allowed to grow into a massive problem.[33] Then as now, unrestrained bubbles raised the cost of the cleanup.

8

Crash and Contagion

THE CRASH OF 1929 BEGAN IN EARNEST over several days in October, with the twenty-fourth of the month now remembered as Black Thursday. No one knew at the time that it was the beginning of the most serious economic downturn in U.S. history. What we remember as the Great Depression would last until the end of 1941, when the United States entered World War II.[1] From the October crash, the stock market would continue to fall until 1932, by which time the economy would have contracted by a third. Unemployment peaked at nearly 25 percent, more than five times what it had been before the crash, and was still at 13 percent when the United States entered the war. On Black Thursday, farmers watched the price of wheat drop ten cents a bushel in a single day. From 1931 to 1932, prices overall fell by 10 percent. Stock prices fell 85 percent from their peak. Foreclosures soared, in the city and on the farm.[2]

Residential mortgages at the time were not the fifteen- to thirty-year fixed-rate and adjustable-rate models we know today, which if paid each month are extinguished by the end of the loan. They typically lasted for five to ten years and required monthly payments that mostly covered interest and then a huge balloon payment at the end of the loan. If the borrower could not make that final payment, the mortgage had to be refinanced. After the crash, with property values 50 percent lower than their peaks in the 1920s, banks wouldn't refinance, and a tidal wave of foreclosures hit the country.[3] Nonfarm mortgage debt fell from $30.2 billion in 1930 to $27.4 billion in 1932 as defaults escalated, despite efforts in at least thirty-three states to impose a moratorium on required payments or other relief for delinquent mortgage holders.[4] By 1934, half of all urban

Crowds panic in the Wall Street district of Manhattan due to the heavy trading on the stock market in New York City on October 24, 1929. Associated Press/Dennis Cook.

residential mortgages were in arrears. Deflation crippled the economy, leaving farmers and other debtors with steady obligations but depressed incomes.[5]

These troubles triggered a severe loss of confidence in the financial system, which in turn triggered more than 9,000 bank failures from 1930 through 1933. Nearly 40 percent of the industry disappeared, with 4,000 banks suspending operations in 1933 alone. More than 6,800 of the 9,000 failing institutions were state chartered, the vast majority of them having stayed outside the Federal Reserve System to avoid the oversight.[6] The point where the dam burst was Michigan, a state ever at the forefront of banking crises, where Henry Ford, though avowedly anti-bank, was nonetheless the largest depositor in a troubled Detroit institution whose troubles came to a head a month before Roosevelt took office as president. To avert the bank's collapse, the state's governor declared a bank holiday on Valentine's Day, an action that, instead of calming nerves as intended, only inflamed public fears and set off a bona fide contagion.[7]

After the 1929 market crash, an even worse slump in sales and rise in defaults on debt—including mortgages on homes and farms, and loans to buy securities—coupled with an increase in demand for cash, greatly accelerated bank failures.[8] All told, bank suspensions throughout the 1920s and the first four years of the 1930s totaled approximately 15,000 institutions. Of these, 85 percent never reopened.[9] The 9,000 failures from 1930 to 1933 cost depositors an estimated $1.34 billion, or $18 billion in today's dollars. That represents a loss of 22.5 percent of deposits in banks that suspended operations in those years. (Some 1,700 thrift failures cost depositors another $3 billion in today's dollars.) In just over a decade, the number of incorporated banks in the United States had declined 50 percent, from about 29,000 in 1920 to 14,000 by mid-1933.[10]

Debate continues on whether the Depression's effects could have been avoided or mitigated, but clearly the Federal Reserve's missteps worsened matters. These included a failure to act as a lender of last resort for at least some banks, which could have provided liquidity for otherwise healthy banks not just in big cities but in less populated areas, too. The Fed also did nothing to make unavoidable failures more orderly. Instead, after the crash and through FDR's inauguration in March 1933, the Fed continually raised interest rates, the opposite medicine it would prescribe today. Hoover wrote years later that his Treasury secretary, Andrew Mellon, summed up this way the reasoning behind what most economists today consider the era's misguided policy of tightening money and making prices fall during a recession: "Liquidate labor, liquidate stocks, liquidate the farmers, liquidate real estate. It will purge the rottenness out of the system." Whether or not Mellon actually said these oft-quoted, and to modern ears callous, words, they nonetheless sum up widely held thinking at the time: if there had been too much easy credit before the crash, the remedy was to tighten and force everyone to suffer back to health. This "liquidationist theory," according to Bernanke, held that "the Depression was unfortunate but necessary . . . [to] squeeze out all of the excesses that had accumulated in the economy in the 1920s." Today's central bankers would have put money into the system to cushion the fall in economic activity and try to keep credit from drying up.[11]

The global economy fared no better. Financial panics and mayhem lingering from World War I caused hardships and unrest that eventually gave rise to Hitler and World War II.[12] Economists Milton Friedman and Anna Schwartz, in their groundbreaking work *A Monetary History of the United States: 1867 to*

1960, set out what is now a central bank credo: avoid crises, or at least lessen rather than worsen them, by providing a "stable monetary background" as reflected, Bernanke says, in "low and stable inflation." So ingrained is this thinking among today's central bankers that Bernanke, in a speech to mark Friedman's ninetieth birthday, said, "I would like to say to Milton and Anna, 'Regarding the Great Depression, you're right, we did it. We're very sorry. But thanks to you, we won't do it again.' "[13]

The Depression caused political despair. Years afterward, Jesse Jones recalled the situation in his memoirs about his time as head of the Reconstruction Finance Corporation, a federal rescue operation that Hoover signed into law in early 1932. The RFC's mandate was to lend $50 billion of federal money to banks and industry to try to spark the economy, restore jobs, and, officials hoped, stop deflation in agriculture, real estate, construction, and finance.

> The then agonizing days and nights of fear and insecurity now seem a bad dream, now dimly remembered. In those dire days, between ten and fifteen million employable Americans disconsolately walked about without a means of livelihood. Other millions, whose income had been reduced, worked in daily dread of being dismissed or furloughed or of having to suffer still another cut in the necessities of life.
>
> The national income had fallen from $80 billion in 1929 to $40 billion in 1932. This meant very simply that the income of every individual in the United States, every farmer, businessman, industrialist, clerk, wage earner, or whatever, on the average had been cut in half. But many had no income at all because they had no work, and, in countless cases, family savings had been swept away in the collapse. Farm products had fallen to a starvation level, and the stocks of many banks, railroads and industrial corporations had dropped to less than 10 percent of their previous market value; some as low as 1 percent.[14]

The displaced set up tents in ramshackle encampments around the country known as Hoovervilles. Newspapers used as bedding by the homeless became known as Hoover Blankets, and a pocket turned inside out to show nothing inside was a Hoover Handkerchief. In May 1932, as many as twenty thousand desperate war veterans, some with families in tow, set up camp around the U.S. Capitol to demand early payment of wartime bonuses promised for 1945. The "Bonus Army" put out fliers protesting that a "winter of hunger faces the veterans" and decrying critics: "Heroes in 1917; They call us 'criminals' now," with "they" being, among others, Hoover, who also called them "communists." Organizers, "determined not to be bums," set out strict rules: "no alcohol, no fighting, no panhandling and no communists."[15]

Many people supported the veterans, and local residents brought them food, live music, and words of encouragement. The highly decorated, retired, outspoken Marine Corps general Smedley Butler, known for calling any but the most unavoidable war "a racket," told the protestors:

> I never saw such fine Americanism as is exhibited by you people. You have just as much right to have a lobby here as any steel corporation. Makes me so damn mad, a whole lot of people speak of you as tramps. By God, they didn't speak of you as tramps in 1917 and '18. Take it from me, this is the greatest demonstration of Americanism we have ever had. Pure Americanism.[16]

On July 28, 1932, police began to evict the marchers, and as the situation got out of hand, they shot two protestors. A panicked Hoover sent in the Army, led by General Douglas MacArthur, whose men set fire to all remaining encampments and ignited the ire of public opinion. Public protests broke out around the country. Workers in the Detroit area rioted at Ford Motor Company's River Rouge plant. A record drought, immortalized in John Steinbeck's *The Grapes of Wrath,* turned the prairies to dust. Farmers began blocking roads and ruining crops to raise prices. Some forcefully blocked foreclosures on neighboring farms. The governor of North Dakota advised farmers to "shoot the banker. Treat him like a chicken thief." A local judge in the northern plains was tarred and feathered.[17]

Desperate for food, several hundred farmers gathered in England, Arkansas, in January 1931 and threatened to stampede the stores, an action a Red Cross worker averted by figuring out a way to bypass paperwork and allot rations to the crowd. A *New York Times* front-page story ran with a headline "Reports of Invasion of England, Ark., by Crowd of Starving Farmers Stir Capital." Some in Congress called the farmers communists. Humorist Will Rogers pushed back, saying in a radio address that none of the protestors in the Arkansas town could be "reds": "A red can't live there because he can't eat." A prominent local lawyer, G. E. Morris, who had tried to calm the protestors, defended them, saying, "I knew the crowd to whom I spoke. . . . All of them were poor, illiterate Americans, having made share crops around England for years. They never heard that Russia had a revolution." Morris told a reporter, "It was pathetic to hear these men and women crying for food, telling us their children actually were starving."[18]

After meeting with merchants whose stores the protestors had threatened to raid, Morris warned that "unless measures for betterment of the situation are taken, the merchants must either put their stocks in the street or mount machine guns before their stores."

Amid the increasing chaos nationwide, some people called for more centralized control, through either a socialist or fascist dictatorship. Remarked Congressman Hamilton Fish, Jr. of New York, " 'I am trying to provide security for human beings which they are not getting. If we don't give it under the existing system, the people will change the system. Make no mistake about that.' " Fears rose that democracy could disintegrate.[19]

In a radio speech in February 1934, Huey Long, the powerful and divisive populist senator from Louisiana, proposed a "Share the Wealth" plan to tax the rich to provide a living wage for the poor.[20] Long, known for political stunts such as wearing purple pajamas during interviews with reporters, staunchly defended state-chartered banks, perhaps from a genuine belief that federally incorporated banks were an abuse of power but surely also from political expediency: his constituents mistrusted big-city financiers. In early 1933 a large New Orleans bank faced a liquidity crunch and feared that depositors would push it into ruin by descending en masse to demand their money when it opened on Saturday, February 4. Cash from other sources could not get there until Monday, so the bank needed to stay closed on Saturday while awaiting help. The governor could have declared a bank holiday, but that might have made the public worry. Long, his staff, and the local librarian searched through the night for a historical event the governor could use to declare a bank holiday but disguise as a bona fide holiday. All they could find was February 3, 1917, when the United States severed diplomatic ties with Germany in advance of World War I. Long "arbitrarily decided that so momentous a decision would have taken two days instead of one," says financial historian Susan Estabrook Kennedy. When the people of New Orleans woke up that Saturday, they found banks closed to celebrate the sixteenth anniversary of America's break with Germany, much "to the amazement of the local German consul." When a newspaper printed a story on the real reason for the holiday, "Long ordered the militia to take it over."[21]

Many feared the country was ripe for revolution. Historian Arthur Schlesinger writes that "a few hours before. . . . the inauguration [of FDR], every bank in America had locked its doors. It was not just a matter of staving off hunger. It was a matter of seeing whether a representative democracy could conquer economic collapse. It was a matter of staving off violence, even (at least some so thought) revolution. . . . Faith in a free system was plainly waning. Capitalism, it seemed to many, had spent its force; democracy could not rise to economic crisis. . . . Some looked enviously on Moscow, others on Berlin and Rome." Said Alfred M. Landon, Republican governor of Kansas, "Even the iron hand of a national dictator is in preference to a paralytic stroke." Years later, General Hugh S. Johnson, a World War I veteran and one of FDR's inner circle, said that no one would ever know "how close we were to collapse and revolution. We could have got a dictator a lot easier than Germany got Hitler."[22]

In December 1932, as the bank crisis escalated across the country, a conservative midwestern publication, the *North American Review,* ran an interview with Mussolini entitled "What a Real Dictator Would Do." It carried the odd assurance that "This article has been personally read and approved by Premier Benito Mussolini," and, as historian Benjamin Alpers observes, "openly packaged him as a model for the United States." The author of the piece described her meeting with the dictator in Rome: "I am asking the . . . creator of the Corporative State, what would be his solution of the problems of the world— what he believes is wrong with the world, how in his judgment government can best help business, how he would adjust capital and labour, what in his opinion should be done to meet the present crisis and to avoid depressions in the future." Mussolini ended by saying, "This is the world of the future, a world of more abundant life such as we have not known before. This is the new world that we are entering, where man will be more truly free for, well, as America defines it, 'life, liberty and the pursuit of happiness.' "[23]

Vanity Fair, in its June 1932 issue under the headline "Wanted: A Dictator," wrote of the country's economic decline: "There is only one answer to this predicament. Appoint a Dictator! Give to the next President the powers he would enjoy in time of war for the duration of the present emergency! At least one-third of Wilson's war-time measures were in a strict sense illegal and unconstitutional. They were taken because they were necessary. Similar measures are necessary now."[24]

On February 25, 1933, in a column entitled "Democracy and Dictatorship," journalist Walter Lippmann made the same argument, calling for Congress to give the president unprecedented powers to deal with the economic situation. The president needed a "concentration of authority" without which the country would find it "virtually impossible" to "carry out a program of recovery."

Lippman felt compelled to defend his suggestion by pointing out that Congress could revoke the authority at any time.[25]

Barron's business journal, in its February 13, 1933, issue, asked whether the newly elected Roosevelt would prove to be the "dictator" the country needed, saying that "more or less furtive suggestions of more or less dictatorship after [FDR is sworn in] continue to crop up here and there from time to time. Of course we all realize that dictatorships and even semi-dictatorships in peace time are quite contrary to the spirit of American institutions and all that. And yet—well, a genial and lighthearted dictator might be a relief from the pompous futility of such a Congress as we have recently had. . . . So we return repeatedly to the thought that a mild species of dictatorship will help us over the roughest spots in the road ahead."[26]

While these were not the majority view, Arthur Schlesinger notes, they were nonetheless "symptomatic."[27] By luck, he says, the election in the fall of 1932 provided an alternative, and a sentiment against any kind of dictatorship, either from the Right or Left, prevailed by decade's end. But Wall Street's excesses and the bank panics it helped trigger had spread a contagion that many felt imperiled American democracy.

As the Depression deepened on Hoover's presidential watch, he was increasingly worried by calls to abandon a free market and the U.S. Constitution. In his memoirs he recalled that "voices in the country vehemently demanded more violent action by the Federal government. Many of them were advocating collectivist ideas gleaned from the Socialists, the Communists, and the Fascists. Some even cried for dictatorship."[28] As an antidote, Hoover pushed Congress in 1932 to create the Reconstruction Finance Corporation.

The RFC quickly fell into controversy on charges of favoritism and conflicts of interest. Its first president, Charles Dawes, resigned after just a few weeks to try to rescue his Chicago bank, which had been destabilized by the collapse of a Chicago-based electric utility company built by businessman Samuel Insull from a stack of companies. (The failure of this byzantine structure resembled that of a subsequent energy company named Enron.) Insull's financial collapse wiped out tens of thousands of shareholders in the Chicago area, triggering defaults on loans that in turn endangered area banks. In the first of several loans to prominent Republicans, the RFC lent Dawes's bank $90 million; Democrats, starting their presidential convention in Chicago in June of that year, cried foul.

The scandal damaged the Hoover administration even though the RFC head who had approved it, Jesse Jones, was a Democrat and also would approve loans to companies headed by Democrats.[29]

Hoover didn't understand the politics involved. Rather than appreciate how the Dawes loan might look like favoritism, especially during such tough economic times, he complained that Congress had made the RFC's activities public. He unsuccessfully pushed Congress to ban publication of the agency's expenditures.[30]

When Roosevelt reopened many banks just a week after taking office and declaring a national holiday, people lined up to redeposit their money. FDR had soothed the nation the evening before, Sunday, March 12, 1933, with his first of more than two dozen radio addresses known as "fireside chats," promising that only sound banks would open and that "it is safer to keep your money in a reopened bank than it is to keep it under the mattress."[31] His masterful ability to communicate helped rebuild trust. Said Will Rogers of Roosevelt's description of the reopening, "He made everyone understand it, even the bankers."[32]

But the president's eloquence might have failed had it not been backed by the Emergency Banking Act of 1933 that Congress had just passed, on March 9. The economic crisis had sent gold to cookie jars across the country and also to hoarders abroad, depleting the Federal Reserve's supply. To act as a lender of last resort, the Federal Reserve needed to supply troubled banks with cash that was backed by gold. The Fed didn't have that gold, leaving it no leeway to issue more currency. On top of that, officials at the Federal Reserve's twelve regional banks, who would be delivering the cash, worried that the collateral that national commercial banks would pledge in exchange for that cash had been made worthless by economic conditions.[33]

The emergency legislation surmounted these hurdles by permitting FDR to take the country off the gold standard. The Federal Reserve could issue cash backed by Treasury securities or a host of other items in lieu of gold. Then, in a series of steps over the following months, Roosevelt took the United States off the gold standard even more completely, ordering that domestic currency could no longer be redeemed for bullion. For the first time since the Civil War, the country was using fiat money. (Nixon and Congress took the country off gold officially in the early 1970s. The United States has used fiat money ever since, with the country's stability and strength, its laws and its military—in short, people's faith—standing behind the dollar. Symbolically, in 1977 the House banking committee dropped the word "currency" from its official title. The comparable committee in the Senate had done so seven years earlier. These name changes signaled that a long-running chapter had closed in the nation's tumultuous history of trying to establish a national paper currency, at least for a majority of Americans.)[34]

FDR also interpreted the emergency act as allowing him to promise the regional Federal Reserve banks that the federal government would protect them against loss, and he said so publicly in a telegram to the head of the Federal Reserve Bank of New York on March 11, 1933. In effect, he put the full faith and credit of the U.S. government—of taxpayers—behind the collateral being given the Fed as lender of last resort. This effectively was deposit insurance, because it guaranteed the value of assets on the books of America's banks.[35] FDR's soothing words to the public worked, backed by moves that made more cash available and protected the Federal Reserve system against loss. Going off gold made it possible.

As for the Reconstruction Finance Corporation, officials quickly realized that having it lend money to beleaguered banks wouldn't work. The banks were already over-leveraged. So, in a move that anticipated federal regulators' response to the mortgage crisis of 2007, Congress authorized the RFC to inject capital by taking ownership stakes in banks rather than asking for collateral.[36] Some institutions fought the idea, fearing that Roosevelt wanted to take over the nation's banking system.[37] And some regulators provided reason to worry. For example, in the midst of the crisis, Albert Agnew, general counsel of the Federal Reserve Bank of San Francisco, called the nation's dual system of state and federal charters "a hodge-podge" that had thwarted the creation of any rational, nationwide banking policy. He warned that "either the bankers of this country will realize that they are guardians of the moneys committed to their charge, and will conduct themselves accordingly, or banking will cease to be a private enterprise and will become a purely government function."[38] Mostly, however, companies welcomed federal money, and the RFC successfully helped the economy recover. It eventually wound down in 1957.

Other Hoover actions would have a longer-lasting impact on banking and securities trading. President Hoover pushed, and in July 1932 Congress passed, the Federal Home Loan Bank Act. It established a new federal agency, the Federal Home Loan Bank Board, to create and oversee nationally chartered versions of state-chartered savings and loans. Savings and loans, also called thrifts, were essentially commercial banks specializing in home loans. In addition, and more important for the history of financial bubbles, the act established a system of twelve Federal Home Loan Banks around the country that, with implicit taxpayer backing, would borrow money at low rates that thrifts could borrow in turn and then lend out in mortgages. Hoover's short-term aim was to refinance the stalled home-lending industry, which had become mired in defaults and foreclosures. Longer term, the twelve banks became one of the founding agencies that established a housing policy of massive federal subsidies to promote home ownership in the United States. Today, many elected officials have little idea the Federal Home Loan Banks exist, much less that they play a central role in supplying credit. Yet they would be a major source of easy credit in the crises that led to the two biggest bailouts in U.S. history, of the savings-and-loan industry in 1989 and of Wall Street banks in 2008.

The second of Hoover's actions that has significantly affected financial services ever since were his repeated requests, starting in 1929, for more oversight of the banking system. This included his recommendation to Congress in December 1931 that it "should investigate the need for separation between different kinds of banking." That same year his Treasury secretary, Ogden Mills, warned in an annual report to Congress that the "dual system" of federal and state-chartered banks created "unsound practices" that were exacerbated by a mingling of "the functions of commercial and investment" banking—all of which had created a "problem calling for remedy."[39] Hoover, in a letter sent two weeks before his term ended to his friend and magazine publisher, Arch W. Shaw, lamented the pitfalls of dual banking, writing that "we cannot endure 49 separate regulatory systems which are both conflicting and weakening," by which he meant the forty-eight state regulators at the time and the federal government. "We must accept the large view that the mismanagement, instability and bad functioning of any single institution affects the stability of . . . other financial institutions. Therefore there must be cooperation within the financial system enforced by control and regulation by the government. . . . We cannot endure that men will either manipulate the savings of the people so abundantly evidenced in recent exposures."[40] Senator Carter Glass put it more bluntly, calling dual banking "the curse of . . . this country."[41]

Hoover's call for more congressional oversight of both Wall Street and dual banking had profound consequences. Increasingly during his presidency, he worried about short-sellers, traders who borrowed stock, sold it, then bought it back more cheaply to return to the original owner, while pocketing the difference. This works, of course, only if the stock's price falls after it is sold. Hoover believed that short-sellers' bets on falling prices too often became self-fulfilling prophesies: they sent signals to the market about key players' expectations. Given the unruly, unregulated, and often manipulated markets of the 1920s, he had reason to be suspicious. He pleaded with Wall Street executives to stop short sales, with no effect. So in early 1932 Hoover persuaded the Senate to hold hearings into short-sellers' practices.[42]

In what proved to be a monumental decision, Congress expanded the scope of these hearings to take a broader look at Wall Street's traders and bankers. The testimony that ensued, first in early 1932 and then again in early 1933, shocked the public and led to a series of groundbreaking legislation that forever changed the rules governing finance in the United States. U.S. senators asked questions and heard answers that recalled the Pujo hearings into the money trusts twenty years earlier, when details about how a small group of men controlled banking and credit had angered the public and helped win support for creation of the Federal Reserve. Now new Senate hearings solidified the idea that the stock market was rigged and in need of reform, as were the nation's banks and bankers, who Father Charles Coughlin, in his increasingly popular radio broadcasts, called "banksters." The phrase caught on.

A page-one story in the *New York Times* on April 27, 1932, carried a photo of three men lugging a trunk up the steps of a U.S. Senate office building. Two were plainclothes police officers. The other was U.S. Representative Fiorello H. LaGuardia, a progressive Republican who supported women's right to vote and laws against child labor, and who the next year would be elected mayor of New York. LaGuardia was about to testify at the Senate banking committee hearings that had morphed into a broad probe of Wall Street. The trunk held documents to illustrate his testimony.[43]

In his opening statement, LaGuardia described information he had obtained as a member of the House Judiciary Committee. "It has been stated by responsible officials of the New York Stock Exchange, before our committee, and I believe also before this committee," he said, "that the exchange as such, and the membership of the exchange, had absolutely nothing to do with the promotion of stocks, with the ballyhooing of stocks in order to raise prices; that they were simply brokers to buy and sell for their customers. Any such statement made by any member of any stock exchange is deliberately false, is a misstatement, and is made knowing that it is a misstatement. And the peculiar part of the stock business as it has been developed in this country is that misstatements are profitable."[44]

Having built up suspense by keeping the documents secret and then ceremoniously carting them up the steps, LaGuardia now theatrically opened the trunk to show senators the paper trail of A. Newton Plummer, a publicist who had written scores of checks totaling $286,279 during the 1920s bull market to financial journalists at leading newspapers, including the *New York Times* and the *Wall Street Journal*. (The *New York Times* story about the hearing was careful to note that the reporter on its staff who had received the checks no longer worked there.) The journalists, La Guardia showed, then printed favorable "fake" stories about stocks that Plummer and his colleagues, including RCA specialist Michael Meehan, had manipulated through dozens of pools. Plummer, LaGuardia said, had been indicted and was awaiting trial in New York in state court on charges that he had forged securities documents.

"Now, if our friends on the New York Stock Exchange say that Mr. Plummer is not a reputable, honest man," LaGuardia told the committee, "then I submit that they were using Mr. Plummer for 15 years to write their stuff on their stocks. So they may take their choice on that. But here are these checks which will tell the story."[45]

Today, a U.S. Senate website describing the hearings says these sessions made "little progress" in exposing the workings of stock mania. That isn't accurate. The continuation of the hearings a year later, in early 1933, would make bigger headlines and be better remembered, particularly as a driving force behind passage of America's securities and banking law, but the hearings in early 1932 sparked public anger over the murky dealings of Wall Street and influenced the legislation's eventual passage. The details of Plummer's widespread bribes were one startling revelation from that year's hearings, as were details of the RCA pool Meehan had put together that had made millions in one week.[46]

"Not only do brokers rig the market," said La Guardia, but they also "speculate in stocks in which they are directors." These practices, he pointed out, contradicted New York Stock Exchange President Richard Whitney's recent testimony that brokers had not inflated stock values in the 1920s and that the public had only itself to blame for that.[47] (Whitney, scion of a Boston banking family who attended Groton and then Harvard, served as head of the New York Stock Exchange from 1930 to 1935, before being convicted of embezzlement and sent to the federal prison in Ossining, New York, known as Sing-Sing, where his fame caused jailers and fellow inmates alike to seek his autograph.) At the hearings, Senator Glass compared pools' operations to "playing in a card game with a card up your sleeve." After breaking for summer and the fall presidential election, the hearings would not resume until the next year, but public disclosure of Wall Street's inner workings, set against the backdrop of the stock market crash and ensuing recession, had had its effect.

On the Senate floor, Glass reiterated his long-held belief that investment banking, which specialized in the creation, sale, and trading of securities, should operate separately from commercial banking, which specialized in taking deposits and making loans to businesses. Operating these activities in a "financial department store," he said, created conflicts of interest and in any case was illegal under the banking acts of 1863 and 1864. As proof he held up and waved a memo dated November 6, 1911, by a top U.S. Department of Justice official, U.S. Solicitor General Frederick W. Lehman, explaining exactly that point. By brandishing the "Lehman memo" and accusing Presidents Taft and Wilson of purposely burying it, Glass made page-one news, though he later apologized for the assertion that they had purposely concealed it.[48] The truth was that the legality of National City's and other banks' activities in securities had been questioned from the start. The twenty-year-old Lehman memo would make an even bigger splash when the hearings resumed a year later.[49]

Shortly before they did resume in early 1933, Hoover, in a letter to his friend Shaw, worried, like many, that the nation's economic plight would be democracy's undoing: "The last four years have shown unquestionably that it is . . . finance . . . which has failed and produced by far the largest part of the demoralization of our systems of production and distribution with its thousand tragedies which wring the heart of the nation. . . . The credit system . . . should be merely a lubricant to the systems of production and distribution. It is not its function to control these systems."[50]

"Democracy cannot survive unless it is master in its own house," he went on. "The economic system cannot survive unless there are real restraints upon unbridled greed or dishonest reach for power. . . . For an outraged people may destroy the whole economic system rather than reconstruct and control the segment which has failed in its function. . . . Failure means a new form of the Middle Ages. . . . The next effort before the country is to reorganize the financial system so that all this will not happen again."[51]

This was from a man who resolutely opposed FDR's New Deal as too great a government incursion into the running of business. In opposing the banking industry's call for a hands-off approach—more of the laissez-faire policies that had prevailed under President Coolidge—Hoover clearly embraced a role for government. "We have three alternatives," he wrote: "unregulated business," which described Wall Street and the banking system at the time; "government-regulated business, which I believe is the American System"; or a "government-dictated business, whether by dictation to business or government in Business. This is the New Deal choice. These ideas are dipped from cauldrons of European Fascism or Socialism."[52]

Hoover and Roosevelt disagreed on much, but they shared a fear that the financial crisis could undo democracy. Hoover hated Roosevelt's New Deal, but for Roosevelt it was a way to prevent a breakdown of American democracy, not a move toward totalitarianism. "Men may differ as to the particular form of governmental activity with respect to industry and business, but nearly all are agreed that private enterprise in times such as these cannot be left without assistance and without reasonable safeguards lest it destroy not only itself but also our processes of civilization," Roosevelt told the country in a September 1934 radio chat. "Demoralization caused by vast unemployment. . . . is the greatest menace to our social order."[53]

Roosevelt believed that his landslide election victory gave him a mandate to make big changes, albeit not until his swearing in on March 4, 1933. As the new year began and the country waited for the change in command, the Senate hearings into Wall Street resumed, and the final and most severe wave of 1930s bank failures unfolded across the country.

Since the November election, a global depression, the Fed's mishandling of monetary policy, and a severe loss of confidence had pushed the country's economy down. The Michigan bank crisis set off rampant hoarding nationwide, a point emphasized by officials at the Reconstruction Finance Corporation with this anecdote: a South Dakota couple buying a farm that had been foreclosed on brought a tin can of money to the closing at the bank, only to find that when they counted it out, it contained just ten thousand dollars, two thousand dollars short of the price. "With a look of disgust the husband remarked, 'Well, Mama, I guess you brought the wrong can.' "[54]

In this atmosphere, industry, while decrying government intervention in business, looked longingly to Washington and U.S. taxpayers for relief. In February, as the Senate hearings were under way again, Thomas Lamont, acting head of JPMorgan & Co., wrote to president-elect Roosevelt, explaining how serious the banking panic had become and begging him to "save the country from a disaster." He warned, "Urban populations cannot do without money. It would be like cutting off a city's water supply. Pestilence and famine would follow; with what further consequences who can tell?"[55]

In a May 1934 newspaper column, Will Rogers poked fun at businesses' dual personality of wanting the government to leave them alone—until they got in trouble and sought taxpayer money, with no strings attached. Under the headline "Mr. Rogers Makes Public a Little Inside Stuff," he wrote:

SAN FRANCISCO, Cal., May 2.—See where the U.S. Chamber of Commerce are gathered in Washington again. It's the caviar of big business.

Last time they met I happened to be in Washington and was the guest of Jesse Jones (head of the Reconstruction Finance) at their dinner.

Now the whole constitution, bylaws and secret ritual of that Orchid Club is to "keep the government out of business."

Well, that's all right, for every organization must have a purpose, but here was the joke:

They introduced all the big financiers—the head of this, that and the other. As each stood up Jesse would write on the back of the menu card just what he had loaned him from the RFC. (got that menu card yet.)

Yet, they said, "keep the government out of business."

Yours,

Will Rogers.[56]

The hearings resumed with a new chief counsel, Ferdinand Pecora, whose uncanny memory and prosecutorial prowess commanded so much attention that, rather than being named for the legislator who chaired them, the proceedings became known as "the Pecora hearings." Despite the sensational revelations produced by the first set of hearings, bankers had largely refused to comply with requests for documents. Pecora, armed with an expanded congressional mandate, used the committee's subpoena power to obtain documents and compel testimony. The hearings continued off and on through November. What had begun under Hoover with a narrow, limited purpose now changed not only America's financial industry but also how Congress conducted investigations. Pecora's use of subpoenas became common practice by congressional committees, making refusal to turn over information a thing of the past. Pecora's treasure trove of newly produced documents riveted the nation.

J. P. Morgan Jr.'s father had helped rescue the nation after the banking panic of 1907. That episode and the revelations from the Pujo hearings convinced Congress that the nation's financial system had grown too big and complex to be left in the hands of any private individual. Now Jack Jr. squirmed under Pecora's questions about Wall Street and its commercial and investment banks.

Senator Glass, a frequent critic of the financial industry but nonetheless a fan of the house of Morgan, derided the hearings as a "circus," saying to laughter and applause that "the only things lacking now are peanuts and colored lemonade."[57] A week later, as if to oblige, a savvy public relations man for the Ringling Brothers circus brought to the hearing thirty-two-year-old Lya Graf, twenty-seven inches tall. The publicist, who billed her as the smallest woman in the world, helped her climb onto Morgan's lap. Pictures of the world's smallest woman sitting in the lap of the world's richest man ran in newspapers around the country and remain among the best remembered photos from the hearings and the era. The publicity stunt embarrassed them both. Graf eventually returned to her home country of Germany, where the Nazis declared her "a useless person" and sent her to her death at Auschwitz.[58]

Pictures of Morgan holding a tiny woman were a bizarre distraction but couldn't eclipse details of how his friends and associates had won favorable stock deals or how Morgan had paid no income tax for the past three years, largely because of losses in the stock market. He hadn't broken the law, but the revelation played poorly before a financially struggling public, and he resented the ordeal.[59] "Pecora has the manner and the manners of a prosecuting attorney who is trying to convict a horse thief," he complained. "Some of these senators remind me of sex suppressed old maids who think everybody is trying to seduce them."[60]

The biggest blockbuster testimony came from National City Bank's Mitchell. A heavy-set man known for a daily exercise routine that included walking from his Fifth Avenue townhouse to work in downtown Manhattan, Mitchell arrived for the Washington, D.C., hearings with an entourage of lawyers and staff, his self-assurance buttressed by his imposing stature—*Time* magazine described him as having "neck, biceps and calves as toughly muscular as ever."[61] But he was soon rattled by Pecora's questions. He conceded, for example, that he had made over $1 million in 1929 but had not paid income tax that year, evading it by using a scheme called "a wash" in which he created a temporary loss by selling stock to his wife and then buying it back. The hearings revealed that others, including Albert H. Wiggin of the Chase National Bank, had also paid no income tax.[62]

But Mitchell's time in the spotlight was the most memorable. Pecora juxtaposed Mitchell's testimony with that of Edgar Brown of Pottsville, Pennsylvania, who had invested over $125,000 with National City in 1928 after selling a string of theaters. Brown had hoped to move to California and retire on the money. National City salesmen proceeded to invest his money in increasingly risky bonds that the bank needed to unload—a long list that included investments in Cuban sugar and operations in Brazil, Chile, and Peru.[63] Brown understood none of this. He told the senators that every time he tried to get National City to cash him out, a salesman talked him out of it. He said that any time he mentioned selling his holdings, especially National City Bank stocks, he was made to feel "in the category of the man who seeks to put his own mother out of his house. I was surrounded at once by all of the salesmen in the place and made to know that that was a very, very foolish thing to do." Now forty, deaf and ill with tuberculosis, Brown needed the money. Committee members and the public presumed that if National City treated Brown this way, it had done the same to thousands of others.[64]

"Did you get anything back out of your investments?" asked Pecora, his last question of the day. "Not a cent," Brown replied.[65]

A group of National City Bank employees tried to blow the whistle on the bank in a letter to President Roosevelt, claiming that what the hearings brought to light was just the beginning, and that "while 'the Senate Committee meant well,' its members 'did not know what to ask questions about.'" The letter suggested that the bank didn't sue to recover loans to officers "for fear of what might be revealed in the courtroom," including irregularities in bonds for Panama "with full knowledge of officials of the State Department" and in "postwar airplane contracts."[66] Self-dealing, conflicts of interest, unloading less-than-attractive securities onto an unsuspecting public—all the elements of shady dealing were there. One bank official testified that National City Company was the largest trader in National City Bank stock, a violation of the spirit if not the letter of federal and state law. The overlapping ownership of the two companies allowed "for the disposal of securities which the bank was forbidden to sell."[67]

Further questioning of Mitchell focused on the memo written by U.S. Solicitor General Lehman addressing the legality of the relationship between National City Bank and National City Company. The memo, which Glass had waved in the Senate a year earlier, showed that the Justice Department had concluded many years earlier that National City and similarly structured banking firms violated the law.[68] Pecora added the Lehman memo to the hearing record in its entirety, calling special attention to the following portion:

> The agreements and arrangements in question were means of enabling the bank to carry on business and exercise powers prohibited to it by the national banking act[s].
>
> I have reconsidered the question with care . . . and have reached the conclusion that both the bank and the company, whether considered as affiliated or as unrelated, are in violation of the law.[69]

No record exists of any action by President Taft or President Wilson to implement changes based on the memo's conclusions. The original memo has never been found, only mimeographed copies.[70] Its import, however, was clear: the operations of the nation's biggest banks and their securities affiliates during the 1920s were illegal under Civil War–era law, and this was an open secret at the highest levels of the U.S. government. The revelations, startling for the disregard for the law they showed, underscored a recurring issue for Wall Street: regulation, and by inference deregulation, has two parts, law and enforcement of law. That the law means nothing if not enforced was not lost on Senator Glass and his powerful counterpart in the House, Representative Henry Steagall, Democrat from Alabama. They and others began crafting and arguing over legislation to regulate banks and securities markets. The Lehman memo and National City's activities convinced many policymakers not only that laws against illegal practices needed to be enforced but also that some legal practices, such as market manipulation, ought to be banned.

Leaving aside that the national bank acts of 1863 and 1864 were routinely violated by financial firms with both securities and bank businesses, lawmakers could have asked, and fifty years later would ask, whether financial empires that engaged in both could have done so fairly for the public and more safely for the economy if they had been properly supervised by federal regulators.

That question didn't seem to be on the table. That Charlie Mitchell and his colleagues engaged in practices that ignored the law and looked unethical at best led to only one question: how should the practices be effectively outlawed?

In the first two months of 1933, as Congress and the White House pondered these questions, bank failures continued at a record pace. "The credit structure of the U.S. is a disgraceful failure, our entire banking system does credit to a collection of imbeciles," said Senator William McAdoo of California, formerly Treasury secretary under President Wilson. He called for banning state banks altogether. Eugene Meyer at the Federal Reserve told the Senate he agreed.[71]

The media, reflecting public sentiment, focused on the Senate hearing's findings. The previous decade's admiration of Wall Street titans transformed overnight into fascination with their fall. They turned out not to be geniuses after all, but artful dodgers. Only when the tide went out, as the saying goes on Wall Street, could one see who'd been swimming naked, and it seemed like everyone. Articles such as "Big Bankers' Gambling Mania" in *Literary Digest* and "Banksters Must Go" in *Colliers* captured the mood. "If you steal $25, you're a thief," declared the *Nation*. "If you steal $25 million, you're a financier." The *Commonweal* claimed that Al Capone's exploits paled in comparison.[72] As lawmakers pondered how to curb the speculation, self-dealing, and public deception that had spawned the crash, the hearings helped solidify support for government action against speculation. Even so, a schism remained between those who viewed state-chartered banks as unneeded and disruptive and those, like Huey Long, who believed that little banks protected the citizenry from the kinds of misdeeds the big banks specialized in. This latest clash of big versus small in American politics, of Jefferson versus Hamilton, played out over another key financial issue: should the Federal Reserve Board's power in Washington be strengthened, and the powers of its regional reserve banks curbed, to make the Fed better able to operate day to day and more nimbly in responding to a crisis? Bankers, of course, opposed centralizing power in Washington because they feared increased oversight.[73]

About Mitchell, however, opinion was unanimous. He resigned from National City Company and National City Bank before the hearings ended. Pecora later recalled watching from a Senate office building as the fallen banker walked toward the train station to return to New York. In contrast to his bravura entrance at the hearings, he walked "completely alone," shoulders "stooped. . . . The impression it made on me was of a person going into exile."[74]

Mitchell was arrested the next month. He was eventually found not guilty of criminal tax evasion but paid $1 million to settle with the Internal Revenue Service. Unlike many of his peers who fell from grace after the crash, he returned to Wall Street, paid off several million dollars in debt, and become a respected if less celebrated banker until his death in 1955.[75]

National City, Chase, and other banks failed to build successful one-stop, financial "department stores," but they earned the dubious distinction of becoming the recipients of the first federally financed bank bailouts, courtesy of the Reconstruction Finance Corporation. National City and Chase shut their securities affiliates in 1933 and received RFC money by the end of the year. According to legal and banking scholar Arthur E. Wilmarth, Jr., National City's securities affiliate had recorded "profits of $25 million during the boom years from 1925 to 1929 . . . [but] suffered more than $100 million of losses from the end of 1929 through the end of 1932." The reversal weakened the entire bank, which "after earning total profits of more than $85 million between 1925 and 1929 . . . recorded almost $170 million of losses from January 1930 through January 1934." This "wiped out two-thirds of National City's shareholders' equity. Many of National City's losses resulted from bad loans that the bank made to support . . . activities" of its securities affiliate.[76]

9

Tickled with Poverty

INAUGURATION DAY, SATURDAY, MARCH 4, 1933, FELL in the midst of a full-fledged bank panic. President Roosevelt addressed the issue head on, telling the nation in his first radio address, "Practices of the unscrupulous money changers stand indicted in the court of public opinion, rejected by the hearts and minds of men." He outlined his plan to fix the situation: "We require two safeguards against a return of the evils of the old order; there must be a strict supervision of all banking and credits and investments; there must be an end to speculation with other people's money." By that afternoon, all forty-eight states had declared bank holidays. The national bank holiday Roosevelt declared on Monday, March 6, merely sanctioned a fait accompli.[1]

Americans reacted good-naturedly. Churches in Chicago saw an increase in paper money offerings—not coins. Studio cafes in Hollywood let movie stars buy food with IOUs, with Cary Grant reportedly even leaving an IOU tip. The governor of California postponed the execution of two men, saying it was no time to hang a man.[2] Said Will Rogers, "I Never Saw a Nation So Tickled with Its Poverty."

1933 BEVERLY HILLS, Cal., March 8.—It's surprising how little money we can get along on. Let the banks never open. Let scrip never come. Just everybody keep on trusting everybody else.

Why it's such a novelty to find that somebody will trust you that it's changed our whole feeling toward human nature. Why never was our country so united, never was a country so tickled with their poverty.

For three years we have had nothing but "America is fundamentally sound." It should have been "America is fundamentally cuckoo."

The worse off we get the louder we laugh, which is a great thing. And every American international banker ought to have printed on his office door "Alive today by the grace of a nation that has a sense of humor."

Yours, Will Rogers.[3]

Even the exiled Russian revolutionary Leon Trotsky predicted a good outcome for the United States, saying the government would centralize banks and emerge financially stronger than ever.[4]

A week after FDR declared the holiday, on March 13, banks in bigger cities began to reopen, but the question of how to restore lasting confidence remained. Congress went to work, passing legislation to fix housing, securities markets, and banks.

In housing, Congress took steps that had far-reaching consequences for the nation's housing market and ultimately the entire U.S. economy. In 1932, alongside the Reconstruction Finance Corporation, Congress had created twelve Federal Home Loan Banks, overseen by a Federal Home Loan Bank Board. Now under Roosevelt, Congress created the Home Owner's Loan Corporation and put it under the oversight of the Federal Home Loan Bank Board. The new corporation's purpose was to help homeowners who were in danger of defaulting on their mortgages because the credit squeeze had prevented them from refinancing.

The Home Owner's Loan Corporation revolutionized home lending. It bought short-term balloon mortgages typical of the time and exchanged them for fixed-rate twenty-year loans that were "self-amortizing," with monthly payments reducing interest *and* principal so that the loan would be fully paid off by the end of its term. There was no balloon payment, which so often had forced borrowers to refinance. This was new, and people liked it. It helped one million homeowners who had been in default stay in their homes.[5] These twenty-year loans would evolve into the now-familiar thirty-year, fixed-rate mortgages, helped along by two pet projects of FDR's that also involved housing.

The first was the Federal Housing Administration, or FHA, which Congress created in 1936 to promote home ownership by guaranteeing mortgages to riskier borrowers, thus giving lenders more confidence in making loans to people who were creditworthy but not well-to-do. The other was the Federal

National Mortgage Association, now known as Fannie Mae, which Congress created in 1938 to buy up FHA loans from lenders, giving them an additional reason to feel good about making FHA loans—they wouldn't have to hold them on their books.

Fannie Mae created what's known as the secondary mortgage market: the large-scale buying of mortgages from primary lenders. Over the years, Congress has told Fannie Mae and its competitor, created in 1970 and known as Freddie Mac, to buy a much broader array of mortgages. Fannie and Freddie now dominate the gigantic secondary mortgage market for non-FHA, prime mortgages—those to people with the best credit. By providing this liquidity for home loans, Fannie and Freddie lower the cost of borrowing for middle- and upper-class home buyers.

Following the stock market crash and the revelations from the Pecora hearings, resistance to reform melted away. The Chamber of Commerce applauded FDR's programs to help industry, though it still opposed giving the government any say beyond that. "Those who are best equipped to solve the problems of industry are those who themselves are engaged in industry," read a resolution passed by the chamber's members.[6] It was the old refrain: Give us your money, not your oversight.

Congress didn't listen. The elected officials whom Morgan had compared to old maids understood public sentiment: two days after Pecora's inquiry revealed that twenty Morgan partners, as well as other high-profile players on Wall Street, "had not paid a penny in income taxes in two years," the Senate unanimously passed legislation separating commercial banking from investment banking.[7] It was part of a packet of laws intended to curb misdeeds in securities trading, which Americans had long mistrusted as the dark side of banking. One, the Securities Act of 1933, was meant to ensure that any person or company selling stocks or bonds to the public provide investors with all significant information, financial or otherwise, that might affect a buyer's decision. It prohibits "deceit, misrepresentations and other fraud in the sale of securities."[8]

Related legislation, passed the next year, was the Securities Exchange Act of 1934, creating the Securities and Exchange Commission (SEC) and giving the agency broad power to set and enforce rules governing securities markets, the investment community, and public companies, including how and when important information must be made public. Market manipulation and insider trading—trading on information not publicly available—became illegal. Under these new laws, no more could Meehan use investor pools to rig the market. Even privately held companies could come under the SEC's disclosure and enforcement rules if they borrowed from the public, and under the agency's scrutiny if they engaged in illegal activities such as manipulating a stock price. Many key aspects of investing that modern business takes for granted stem from these laws, which implement basic protections for investors: requirements that those who sell securities be vetted and licensed; that advertisements be truthful and not misleading; that securities sold to an investor be in his or her best interest—or at least mostly so; and that the person selling them provide complete information, including disclosures of any conflicts of interest.

In addition to the securities acts of 1933 and 1934, Congress took a third major step to ride herd on securities markets and ensure that Justice Department memos about securities and banking would no longer be ignored. It separated investment banking from commercial banking in the Banking Act of 1933, popularly known as Glass-Steagall, forcing banks to decide to be one or the other. Investment banks would be regulated by the SEC, commercial banks by the federal bank regulators.

Congress also strengthened the Federal Reserve Board's power in relation to the twelve regional banks, to make it clear that decision-making rested with the board. And it sharpened the three tools that the Fed uses to keep the economy steady and maintain credit at appropriate levels and, as part of that mission, to keep the nation's money and financial system sound: it bolstered its authority to implement monetary policy, supervise banks, and provide liquidity. A key goal of these changes was to eliminate the in-fighting between Washington and the Federal Reserve Bank in New York that had contributed to the Fed's failure to act more responsibly in setting interest rates and curbing risky bank practices before and after the crash.[9]

In 2016, the Chamber of Commerce described the Federal Reserve Board's regulatory role as an afterthought of Congress, a job that lawmakers have given it "ad hoc" during crises. This is not true. Bank oversight has never been a last-minute assignment but an essential component in the arsenal of central banks in all their incarnations in U.S. history, and certainly from the Federal Reserve's founding.[10]

From the start, lawmakers expected the Fed to set monetary policy, act as a lender of last resort, and regulate banks. Though the three are inextricably intertwined, it's useful at times to think of the first two—adjusting interest rates and lending in emergencies—as duties squarely in the purview of a central banker, and the third, policing banks, as a duty the Fed shares with other bank regulators: the comptroller of the currency and the federal agency that insures commercial bank deposits.[11] Congress also gave the Fed, as a bank regulator, the additional duty of keeping commerce and banking separate, a role lawmakers bolstered in 1956 by making the Federal Reserve the regulator of bank holding companies, a corporate structure banks had adopted in lieu of trusts to try to get around such restrictions. The Fed failed to use its dual, overlapping roles of central banker and bank regulator in the decade leading to the 1929 crash, when companies like National City showed that a bank's affiliates can cause as much damage to a bank's credit markets as the bank itself. As lawmakers in the 1930s pondered how to fix this they faced a familiar problem: many state banks were outside the Fed's reach.

(In 1977 Congress gave the Federal Reserve another job: a so-called dual mandate to keep employment as high as possible and prices stable. It was mostly symbolic. Employment has more to do with fiscal policy and hence with what the White House and Congress do. As for price stability and low inflation, that essentially was always the Fed's mission, even if it fell short.[12] This "dual mandate" should not be confused with the two hats the Fed wears as central banker on the one hand and bank regulator on the other, even though all these roles are related.)

FDR's White House, along with Senator Glass and others, aimed not only to remedy the immediate crisis but also to bring all state banks under federal oversight, something they saw as a lasting solution to the nation's "hodge-podge" of dual banking. A 1933 report for the Senate from Federal Reserve Board Chief Counsel Walter Wyatt describes state and national regulators engaged in a race to the bottom, outdoing each other to lower standards. Wyatt wrote that as states lifted restrictions and oversight, Congress would relax safeguards in the original national bank acts of the 1860s. "Such competition between the federal government and various states," he said, "has led to more and more laxity in bank regulation and supervision." He recommended formation of a unified national bank and included a legal analysis on the constitutionality of eliminating state banks.[13] He didn't win the day, but the decades since he wrote his report have proved his point: failure to coordinate state and federal bank oversight repeatedly has created a race to the bottom among regulators and helped to fan financial crises.

But Congress did agree to cap the interest rate that banks could pay on deposits on the theory that unhealthy competition for depositor funds had helped cause the bubble that led to the crash. Congress reasoned that many banks had overpaid for deposits, which forced them to compensate by making loans that carried higher rates of return, but also more risk.[14] Or perhaps an eagerness to invest in high rate but high risk loans came first, making banks willing to pay too much to lure deposits into their coffers. More likely, it was both. Either way, instead of making more money to pay higher expenses, many banks fell further down the slippery slope of financial loss. In a phenomenon akin to doubling down in gambling, the slippery slope in finance occurs when losers take bigger and bigger risks—and increasingly have nothing to lose by doing so—to try to make up for past losses or rising obligations. Congress wanted to limit the means—borrowed, depositor money—for engaging in such behavior. Congress also had another reason to limit interest payments—doing so left banks with more money to pay premiums as part of lawmakers' next big undertaking: federal deposit insurance.[15]

By far the most contentious debate in financial reform was over the creation of federal deposit insurance. The Glass-Steagall Act, which had separated commercial and investment banking, also temporarily created the Federal Deposit Insurance Corporation, or FDIC, for commercial banks, but only after much sturm and drang. In 1935 Congress made it permanent, having already added, in 1934, a similar system for thrifts, the Federal Savings and Loan Insurance Corporation, or FSLIC. The question of whether to guarantee commercial bank customers against loss on some or all of their deposits was tied up with equally contentious questions about bank branching, a subject that might make modern readers yawn, as surely many did at the time, but that proved a perennial life-or-death issue among bankers.

The scourge of bank failures since WWI had shown that those with only one branch, especially in remote rural areas, could withstand a run less well than a bank with several branches. Not all customers in a state would participate in a run, the thinking went, so a branch besieged by depositors could be helped with cash from a sister branch. A bank with branches was also less likely to be tied to one industry. If this were so, expanded branching powers might make deposit insurance unnecessary. People with this view tended to favor fewer, more centralized banks with more branches. Opponents of branching included states-rights advocates in the Jeffersonian tradition, who feared that branching would create just the sort of large urban money centers they had long mistrusted. These advocates favored deposit insurance as a way of preserving small rural banks. The fight over branching and, by extension, deposit insurance was a much more visceral issue than the question of whether to separate commercial and investment banking, which had almost unanimous support. Arguments over insurance and branching, by contrast, threatened to torpedo all of Glass-Steagall.

As bank runs and closings accelerated in the winter of 1933, proposals to use deposit insurance to protect savings and thus avert runs gathered more support than motions to expand branching. The national and state bank holidays, coupled with snags in the Fed's role as lender of last resort, accelerated calls for some kind of permanent guarantee for depositors. Deposit insurance addressed a central paradox of banking: when people think they can get their money, they don't want to. If they think they can't, they do. Branching would help with this, but a federal guarantee was more concrete, and in many cases it would make a lender of last resort unnecessary. Deposit insurance had many opponents, but its star ascended when the Fed failed to act as lender of last resort from 1930 to 1933.[16]

The idea of insurance wasn't new. New York State had experimented with deposit insurance in 1829, and between 1886 and 1933, Congress considered 150 deposit insurance proposals. None went anywhere. After the panic of 1907, seven states —Oklahoma, Kansas, Nebraska, Texas, Mississippi, South Dakota, and North Dakota—guaranteed deposits at state-chartered banks, but these plans were overwhelmed by the massive number of bank failures in the 1920s. The state funds failed not just because so many banks went under at once, but also because too many had been given coverage without sufficient screening to weed out weaker, poorly run firms.[17]

Beyond these failed efforts, deposit insurance proved controversial for another good reason. Although insurance calmed depositors, it also made them indifferent to how their bank was run. Depositors' indifference is an instance of what economists call "moral hazard," a situation where someone receives the benefits of a financial action or decision but is shielded from any downside. Insured depositors, for example, would get their money if a bank prospered or failed. People in this or similar financial situation, opponents of insurance argued, would be not only indifferent to risks, but encouraged to take bigger and bigger ones in the knowledge that others would pay the price. Deposit insurance would be like allowing a gambler to keep all winnings and be reimbursed for any losses. A person in this situation would gamble all day long.

The concept of a federal insurance program thus faced powerful opponents. Executives at the nation's big banks opposed it, arguing that it would promote laxity in how banks were run and put an unfair burden on larger institutions if funding was based on fees assessed on deposits. Depositors would accept a lower interest rate on deposits in exchange for the security of a government guarantee, making it cheaper and thus easier for bankers, including bad bankers, to raise money to take risks. Deposit insurance, in short, could provide easy credit—too much borrowed money relative to good investments—for bankers.[18] That interest rates would be capped didn't seem to assure opponents—what if caps were lifted?

Not all but many smaller, state-chartered banks also opposed deposit insurance because they believed—correctly—that it would subject them to greater federal oversight.[19]

Still others opposed it on principle. The president of the New York–based Chemical Bank and Trust Company, Percy H. Johnston, told Congress deposit insurance was unnecessary "unless we are going to guarantee all elements of society against misfortunes and evils of all kinds. Of course, if we are going to have socialistic government, then we ought to guarantee everybody against all manner of things."[20] The American Bankers Association repeatedly asked its members to contact President Roosevelt and members of Congress to express opposition, up to the day that FDR signed the Glass-Steagall Act, on June 16, 1933.[21]

Democratic Representative Steagall and Republican Senator Vandenberg, whose state maintained its tradition of banking upheaval, championed federal deposit insurance. Although many bankers didn't support it, many others, who understood the stability that having the government's name on the door would bring, did, along with farm groups in states where local bank failures were endemic.[22] Vandenberg, and eventually even Senator Long from Louisiana, thought deposit insurance would preserve dual banking by putting small banks on equal footing with money-center banks during crises. Little institutions were far more often doomed by runs than their bigger, better-known city counterparts, where a well-known name like "Morgan" could alone stabilize a bank.[23]

President-elect Roosevelt and Senator Glass, despite wanting more uniform oversight of banks, particularly state-chartered ones, nonetheless agreed with the big banks that deposit insurance would make depositors indifferent to risk-taking by bankers. In October 1932, Roosevelt wrote in a letter to John E. Emmons of Bethel, Ohio, that any proposal to have the federal government guarantee deposits "would be quite impossible. It would lead to laxity in bank management and carelessness on the part of both banker and depositor." That laxity would translate into a loss for taxpayers: "I believe that it would be an impossible drain on the Federal Treasury to make good any such guaranty. For a number of reasons of sound government finance, such a plan would be quite dangerous."[24]

Roosevelt, in short and correctly as it turned out, worried that deposit insurance would create moral hazard by privatizing gains and socializing risks: depositors got to keep interest earned in normal times, and society—taxpayers— would have to pay up in a crisis. Free markets are, in theory, the mirror image of moral hazard. When someone makes an investment or other financial bet, he or she reaps the rewards but also must shoulder the consequences. Companies that make a profit stay in business; those that lose money fail. With deposit insurance, depositors would incur all the upside—their money would be guaranteed against loss—but none of the bad. If a bank was badly run or otherwise ran into trouble and fell short on funds to repay deposits, depositors wouldn't care because the insurance fund—and ultimately taxpayers—would step in. On March 8, 1933, in his first press conference as president, Roosevelt threw water on the idea, saying:

> The general underlying thought behind the use of the word "guarantee" with respect to bank deposits is that you guarantee bad banks as well as good banks. The minute the government starts to do that the government runs into a probable loss. . . . Any form of general guarantee means a definite loss to the government. The objective in the plan that we are working on can be best stated this way: There are undoubtedly some banks that are not going to pay 100 cents on the dollar. We all know it is better to have that loss taken than to jeopardize the credit of the United States government or to put the United States government further in debt. Therefore, the one objective is going to be to keep the loss in the individual banks down to a minimum, endeavoring to get 100 percent on them. We do not wish to make the United States government liable for the mistakes and errors of individual banks, and put a premium on unsound banking in the future.[25]

Security for depositors did create a risk for taxpayers, but deposit insurance had an undeniably big benefit: it would reduce runs by restoring depositors' confidence. Yes, taxpayers would have to cover any shortfalls from the sale of a failed bank's assets. But when depositors knew their money was safe, society would suffer fewer such disruptions. Yes, deposit insurance reduced free-market discipline. But it also reduced the rough and indiscriminate aspects of the free market that sparked panics and exacerbated them.

As the bank failures mounted between the election of FDR and his swearing in, those in favor of deposit insurance grew to include President Hoover. The three weeks before Roosevelt took office were dire, particularly the last one. In response, likely during that time but possibly earlier, Hoover drafted a "plan for government guarantee of bank deposits" that called for a "100% government guarantee" of many deposits.[26] Hoover presented the idea to the Federal Reserve Board just days before his presidency ended, but on March 2 the board rebuffed the idea. Hoover asked them to reconsider, and the board again declined. As tensions rose around the country, the staffs of the president and president-elect talked nearly constantly, but FDR wouldn't agree to a coordinated announcement. He would act only after he was sworn into office.[27]

For Hoover, the deposit guarantee was simply a way to avert catastrophe. But as a lame duck president, he felt he could take little action without the incoming president's approval, which FDR wouldn't give. FDR's refusal to join with Hoover, even to assure the public, worsened the banking crisis. As Hoover feared, FDR waited until he was sworn in to take action, either because he didn't understand the severity of the situation before then or because he wanted to take full credit for fixing it.[28] But Hoover hurt his own cause by contradicting himself. Even as he pushed behind the scenes for deposit insurance and urged FDR to make a joint public statement, he simultaneously argued that the public's dislike of Roosevelt's policies was the cause of sagging confidence and that FDR should disavow those policies—a peculiar stance given that Hoover had just lost the election to FDR in a landslide.

Hoover spelled out his alarm in a letter to FDR on February 18, 1933, two weeks before the inauguration, which he had hand-delivered by the Secret Service for fear "it's misplacement would only feed the fire and increase the dangers." Deploring "proposals to abrogate constitutional responsibility by the Congress with all the chatter about dictatorship," he wrote: "The major difficulty is the state of the public mind—for there is a steadily degenerating confidence in the future which has reached the height of general alarm."[29]

Hoover wrote again ten days later, "It is my duty to inform you that the financial situation has become even more grave and the lack of confidence extended

further than when I wrote to you on February 18th." The new administration
would have to take immediate action upon taking over the White House in four
days, he said, warning ominously of "contingencies in which immediate action
may be absolutely essential in the next few days." Roosevelt's staff met with
Hoover's and presumably grasped the seriousness of the situation, but Roosevelt's
response remained maddeningly noncommittal. Possibly it was public expectation that FDR would abandon the gold standard that raised fears and panic before
the swearing in—even though when he effectively did so shortly after taking
office, the economy responded favorably, demonstrating, in Hoover's view, "the
not uncommon phenomenon in economics that the expectation of a devaluation
can be highly destabilizing but that devaluation itself can be beneficial."[30]
Whatever the worries and despite Hoover's untenable requests that FDR repu-
diate the Democrats' election platform, Roosevelt's inaction before his inauguration likely did deepen the panic.[31]

Moral Hazard

IN THE END, DEPOSIT INSURANCE WON THE DAY. As runs spread, public opinion forced opponents and supporters to come together, which they did, but for different reasons.

In exchange for supporting deposit insurance, FDR and Glass demanded more federal oversight of banks. Glass favored giving this job to the Federal Reserve Board. Overlooking the Fed's shortcomings during the 1920s, he instead heaped criticism on the Comptroller's Office, which he said "has not done its duty—its sworn duty—and has permitted this great number of banks to engage in irregular and illicit practices, with the result that they have endangered the whole banking community and not only the whole banking community but have pretty nearly paralyzed the whole business community of this country."[1]

Farmers, however, saw the Federal Reserve as the problem. Along with many state bankers, they worried that tying deposit insurance to federal oversight was a disguised plan to kill dual banking, which it was. Representative William Lemke, a Republican populist from North Dakota who supported some of FDR's New Deal initiatives, nonetheless spoke for many during debate in the House:

> It was the Federal Reserve bank that, during the war, increased the money in actual circulation—doubled it—and then in 1920 and 1921 contracted it—virtually cut it square in two. I mean the money that was actually in circulation at that time . . . the people know that it was the Federal Reserve octopus that contracted the currency in the nation as a whole, and at the same time, increased it in the large

cities—increased it for the gamblers in stocks, bonds and the necessities of life. The people know the Federal Reserve octopus loaned . . . to the gamblers of this nation in 1928 some $60 billion of credit money—bank money—hot air—to gamble with in domestic and foreign stocks and bonds. . . . No nation, no industry, can survive such an expansion and contraction of money and credit. Give to me the power to cut square in two at will, and I can keep you in bondage. That is exactly what the Federal Reserve banking system has been doing for the American people—it has taken their homes—it has filled the penitentiaries with its victims—it has caused self-destruction and suicides by the thousands.[2]

Representative John D. Dingell (D-Mich.) took the floor minutes later to chastise bankers themselves:

The myopic banker as an adviser should receive about as much consideration at the hands of the House as a braying jackass on the prairies of Missouri. They proved by their inability to maintain their own business that they have absolutely no right to advise the House . . . I believe in preparing the medicine and forcing it down the throats of the few oppositionists who remain. Reactionary bankers opposed all progressive regulatory or safety laws. . . . As a matter of fact, recent developments in the field of American banking convinced the people that America had no bankers and much less a banking system. We discovered that what we believed to be a bank system was in fact a respectable racket and so many connected with it only cheap, petty loan sharks and Shylocks.[3]

Both sides had to compromise. State banks agreed to more federal oversight in exchange for a federal deposit insurance sticker on the door. Glass agreed that oversight needn't be by the Federal Reserve but that state banks could choose to be overseen either by the Fed or by the insurance fund instead.[4] Deposit insurance was voluntary but as a practical matter compulsory. Who, after the banking crises the nation had just been through, would put money into an uninsured bank? This is when Congress also gave the Fed authority to cap the interest rates that federally insured institutions could pay on deposits, thus effectively imposing the ban on state and federally chartered banks alike.

With the new law, the federal government could finally claim oversight of all commercial banks, albeit through three different agencies and to varying degrees. But dual banking survived, which meant that America's banks, while more unified, fell short of the single system Roosevelt and others wanted.[5] America now had its three main federal bank regulators: the Federal Reserve, the Treasury's Office of the Comptroller of the Currency, and a new federal agency, the Federal Deposit Insurance Corporation (as well as, to a lesser degree, the federal insurance fund for thrifts, though that would eventually be folded into the FDIC). This trio are known as the nation's prudential regulators, or safety and soundness regulators, or systemic (not "systematic") regulators. Of all the reforms of the 1930s, even more than the separation of investment and commercial banking, it was the creation of the FDIC and the institution of federal deposit insurance that would change the dynamic of financial rules and oversight. The FDIC put American taxpayers into the equation.

A Pulitzer Prize–winning editorial cartoon from 1931 by John T. McCutcheon of the *Chicago Tribune,* entitled *A Wise Economist Asks a Question,* shows a man down on his luck sitting on a park bench labeled "victim of bank failure." A squirrel asks, "But why didn't you save some money for the future, when times were good?" The man answers, "I did." Depicting depositors as bankers' victims fit popular sentiment. Many politicians believed—or knew they should say they believed—that smaller savers deserved better. Most policymakers, however, understood that helping depositors was a means to an end. The ultimate purpose of deposit insurance was not to shield individual depositors from loss but to stop runs and so preserve the system.[6] For that reason, Congress never guaranteed all deposits, only enough to quiet fears. Limiting coverage was key to winning support from many members of Congress, even though the limit of $2,500 in 1933 entirely covered most accounts. (That's also true with today's $250,000 limit, which consumers can stretch to higher coverage by opening more than one account.) With the advent of federal deposit insurance, failed banks wouldn't file for bankruptcy but instead would be taken over by the FDIC to preserve depositors' immediate access to insured funds. The FDIC would then work to sell off or manage the institution's assets to repay the uninsured and other creditors as much as possible. (In practice, especially in times of crisis, the FDIC effectively has insured all deposits by transferring them to another institution or by keeping the failed institution open with massive injections of cash.)

That deposit insurance was a means to the end of stabilizing the economy by preventing the failure of solvent but cash-short banks meant that stricter oversight was neither a punishment nor an afterthought. Regulators became surrogates for depositors, providing some semblance, in theory, of the market discipline that the safety net had eliminated. With deposit insurance rendering

A Wise Economist Asks a Question. John T. McCutcheon of the *Chicago Tribune* won a Pulitzer Prize in 1932 for this depiction of the damage caused by widespread bank failures. The "wise economist," a squirrel, asks a "victim of bank failure" who is sitting on a park bench, "But why didn't you save some money for the future, when times were good?" The man answers, "I did." Photo courtesy of the *Chicago Tribune* © 1931 Chicago Tribune. All rights reserved. Used by permission and protected by the copyright laws of the United States. The printing, copying, redistribution, or retransmission of this content without express written permission is prohibited.

depositors indifferent, regulators now sat at the table on behalf of taxpayers to ensure that banks weren't gambling with public money.[7] Regulators were to be the antidote to moral hazard.

The response by Congress and the White House to the unprecedented upheaval of the Great Depression, especially their establishment of the FDIC, altered the public's expectation of federal leaders' responsibility for the economy. The Roosevelt administration understood this new reality: though the FDIC mimicked a private-sector insurance company funded by premiums, a crisis would show it to be 100 percent government-backed. The fund's title included "Federal" for a reason. "The Insurance Corporation's interest in the sound operation of banks," Leo T. Crowley, chairman of the brand-new Federal Deposit Insurance Corporation, told senators in 1935, is more tangible and more vital than that of any [other] supervisory authority. . . . [it] has a financial liability to these depositors. Its interest in the sound operation of these institutions is one of dollars and cents. . . . The Insurance Corporation . . . can be a charitable institution which will pay for the mistakes, bad banking and dishonesty of bankers, in which case the cost of the insurance must be set so high that it will be an injustice to every sound bank. Or, by being placed on a sound basis, the Corporation may be used as an instrument to improve the standards of bank management. . . . The latter course, which I prefer, requires that the standard of bank supervision throughout the country be improved, that the Corporation be given the right to protect itself against excessive risks, and, finally that the Corporation be not handicapped by taking into the fund banks which are unsound.[8]

Crowley said it would be calamitous to force the FDIC to accept bank evaluations from examiners at other agencies. "You cannot hope to keep this Corporation solvent unless you either give it tremendous income, or unless you give it supervisory powers and the right to correct unsound practices. If the government is going to insure deposits, and really this is a government fund . . . it should try to centralize the control of these banks."[9] He worked with the comptroller and the Fed to ensure that FDIC examiners could walk into any insured bank, federal or state, and demand to see its records.

Glass pushed back, maintaining that the FDIC was not a government guarantee but a government-sponsored insurance program privately funded by "assessments on banks." This insistence on the distinction between a federal guarantee and a bank-funded insurance program, which he shared with Representative Steagall, had been key to winning Congress's support for creating the FDIC.[10] Crowley agreed that in normal times that was the case, but he reminded the senators that they had created deposit insurance precisely to encourage such normal times by maintaining confidence. Maintaining trust required preventing runs, and that required weeding out unsound practices and institutions. Allowing a crisis to develop would require the government—that is, taxpayers—to step in. "If we are going to have to pay the same proportion of losses in the future as the depositors suffered in the past," he said, "I don't think the banks can finance that fund themselves." Stressing the point that in a crisis tax funds would be at risk, he added, "Banks can finance this plan provided the Corporation is given the power to protect itself, particularly in not permitting [states] to indiscriminately charter new banks and make the Corporation take them into the fund."[11]

Deposit insurance immediately quelled the panic. Even the free-market econo-mists Milton Friedman and Anna Schwartz, in *A Monetary History of the United States, 1867–1960,* lauded its success: "Federal insurance of bank deposits was the most important structural change in the banking system to result from the 1933 panic, and . . . the structural change most conducive to monetary stability since state bank notes were taxed out of existence immediately after the Civil War."[12] Former Fed chair Ben Bernanke agrees. "We went from liter-ally thousands of bank failures annually to zero. It was an incredibly effective policy."[13]

By 1941, the number of banks had fallen to just over 14,400. More than 9,300 were still state chartered, but now at least they were federally policed.[14] FDR enraged Republicans by taking credit for deposit insurance.[15] The Republican National Committee in 1936 complained to the *New York Times* that Roosevelt's October 1932 letter denouncing deposit insurance proved that he "not only had nothing to do with bringing about effective deposit insurance, but that the prop-aganda department of the New Deal National Committee, through handbills, franked mail paid for by taxpayers, and statements is engaging in a deceitful effort to give him credit for what he didn't do."[16] The RNC claimed that the Republican senator from Michigan Arthur Vandenberg deserved the real credit, having fought both FDR and the big banks to get insurance passed. That was true, though plenty of Republicans had opposed it, just as many Democrats, led by Steagall, had pushed for it. But there's no denying that Hoover and other key Republicans had backed it against stiff opposition from key Democrats, including FDR.

The race to take credit for a policy that overnight stopped the nation's bank panic amounted to a financial Rorschach test, with each side seeing what it wanted. For Vandenberg and Hoover, it restored public confidence. For Roosevelt and Glass, it would rid the system of the worst of dual banking's loose standards and the resulting speculation.[17] Advocates of dual banking thought it put small banks on equal footing with big ones in times of crisis.[18]

Neither the president, Glass, nor most bankers wanted deposit insurance, but there it was, changing finance forever. The irony, wrote Galbraith, is that "the anarchy of uncontrolled banking had been brought to an end not by the Federal Reserve System but by the obscure, unprestigious, unwanted Federal Deposit Insurance Corp."[19]

Contrary to intentions of foes and friends, the FDIC created a safety net that would evolve into a larger, even more dangerous instance of moral hazard: a government policy that viewed certain Wall Street banks as "too big to fail" and that often, especially in the 1980s, encouraged keeping sick institutions afloat, only to have them grow into costlier problems for taxpayers.

As for the professional speculators of the era, Mitchell made his comeback, but others fared less well. In 1936, GM founder William Durant filed for bankruptcy, listing the clothes he wore, valued at $250, as his only asset. He talked of a comeback until he died, in 1947, but none of his many ventures, including selling a cure for dandruff, amounted to anything. Jesse Livermore, a speculator through and through, couldn't adjust to the new rules prohibiting pools and insider trading. In 1940, the day before Thanksgiving, he entered a men's washroom and shot himself in the head.[20]

And the general public? Investing in the securities market regained popularity after WWII. Today more than half of the nation's 126 million households invest in it, many through retirement plans such as a 401(k). The financial scandals continued as well.

PART TWO

A WONDERFUL LIFE: SOCIALISM FOR THE RICH

Zombie Banks

CITICORP VICE CHAIRMAN HANS H. ANGERMUELLER SAT before Congress in May 1986, complaining that federal red tape made a nightmare of buying a special type of bank known as a savings and loan or thrift. "So why bother?" he asked lawmakers.[1]

He was posturing. Citicorp, the nation's largest banking holding company, did want to bother with those kinds of banks, very much so. Even as Angermueller complained, his colleagues a few blocks away were wrestling with oil billionaire Gordon Getty over the right to buy the second biggest S&L in the nation's capital. The bank in question might have seemed like an odd prize because it was on the brink of failing. Federal regulators wanted to sell it for that very reason, hoping a deep-pocketed buyer would spare the government the cost of closing it and having to pay off depositors. Thrift regulators had thousands of such sick banks across the country. Any chance to avoid paying off depositors was worth taking if it meant not having to draw down funds from the Federal Savings and Loan Insurance Corporation, or FSLIC, which like the FDIC for commercial banks, Congress had created in the 1930s to insure deposits at thrifts. FSLIC, pronounced Fizzlick by insiders, was nearly insolvent.

Angermueller, Getty, and executives at scores of other companies wanted to buy ailing thrifts in the mid-1980s as desperately as the government wanted to sell them. For the government, selling a sick thrift rather than closing it maintained public confidence while requiring less upfront cash, which was in short supply. Buyers had to agree to absorb some of the losses of the thrifts they were buying, thus reducing the government's—and ultimately, taxpayers'—burden to depositors. Buyers agreed to do this because they could use thrifts to create financial supermarkets like the one that Citicorp's predecessor, National City Bank, had created under Charlie Mitchell in the 1920s. Sixty years later, buying a savings and loan and assuming some of its liabilities was the easiest way around the regulatory barriers to such department stores—barriers erected in the 1930s, largely because of Mitchell, that disallowed the selling of banking, securities, and insurance products under one roof.

Regulators and members of Congress, however, had relaxed the rules in the late 1970s and early 1980s to give S&Ls privileges that commercial banks didn't have—to cross state lines, to sell a full array of financial products under one roof, and to be owned by or own any type of company, financial or not. Regulators hoped the relaxed rules would allow thrifts to diversify out of the home lending business that they had specialized in and, in the process, restore health to an industry that had sunk into financial hardship. But deregulation, poorly executed, had made the industry sicker, and by the mid-1980s, federal regulators no longer held out deregulation as a cure for thrifts but instead offered it as a lure to any buyer who would take the money-losing institutions off the government's hands.

An estimated nine of every ten thrifts were losing money in early 1981 and, if liquidated, the group would have had a negative net worth of $100 billion, meaning their liabilities exceeded their assets by that amount. The federal deposit insurance fund for thrifts couldn't cover the shortfall. Tens of billions of dollars from taxpayers would be needed to close these hundreds of insolvent institutions and fulfill the government's promise to pay off depositors. By mid-decade, thrifts had grown even sicker because the White House of President Ronald Reagan, aided by both parties in Congress, had kept them open, allowing losses to grow. Acknowledging that a taxpayer bailout was needed would have been political suicide for an administration that had swept into office promising lower taxes, less government, and a smaller deficit.

So Reagan, as soon as he was sworn in, needed to sell as many ailing thrifts as possible and to employ myriad accounting tricks to keep others open to hide the industry's worsening plight—and the inevitable bailout—from the public eye as long as possible, at the very least until after the next election, when he hoped his vice president, George H. W. Bush, would win the White House. Firms as diverse as Citicorp, the insurance company American International Group, Ford Motor Company, Nordstrom, and Merrill Lynch eagerly lined up to purchase tickets into the world of deregulated finance. Executives and politicians knew that customers wouldn't care if an institution were called a commercial bank or a thrift, or if it were insolvent or not, as long as deposits were federally insured. As FDR predicted, deposit insurance had made depositors indifferent to whether the firm holding their money was well run or bankrupt.

Savings and loans were banks that for well over a century had specialized in making home loans. Since the 1930s, the government had let S&Ls pay more interest on savings than it had allowed commercial banks to offer, enabling thrifts to attract longer-term deposits that complemented the maturity dates of longer-term investments, specifically residential mortgages. Commercial banks, by contrast, had focused on shorter-term deposits in checking accounts—which thrifts weren't allowed to offer—and on shorter-term loans to businesses.[2]

This arrangement, underpinned by federal deposit insurance, provided relative stability in finance for several decades. Each sector of finance—commercial banks, investment banks, thrifts, insurers, real estate firms—operated reasonably happily within its own sphere—that is, until the 1970s shattered that tranquility. Computers revolutionized credit, and the Vietnam War and spikes in oil prices fueled inflation.[3]

Computerized information technology was as groundbreaking as the transcontinental railroad had been in 1869. It enabled financial executives to sell, lend, and keep track of loans and deposits easily and quickly across the nation. The commercial paper market—companies borrowing and lending directly to each other, bypassing commercial banks as intermediaries—took off. This trend toward "disintermediation" sent commercial banks in search of new lines of business, and they set their sights on consumer lending, particularly residential mortgages.

Consumers, their wallets ravaged by double-digit inflation and interest rates that climbed past 20 percent, sought higher earnings from their savings than the puny interest the government allowed banks and thrifts to offer. Federally insured institutions suffered as depositors—a key source of funding from which to make loans—abandoned them for the money-market accounts aggressively advertised by Wall Street's investment banks. The investment banks too were eyeing the consumer lending market, including home loans, and seeking loopholes around barriers to entering commercial banking.

To help banks and thrifts compete, Congress voted in 1980 to phase out the caps imposed in the 1930s on the interest rate they could pay depositors. As further lure to help federally insured thrifts and banks, the same legislation also raised deposit insurance 2.5 times, from $40,000 to $100,000.[4]

For thrifts, the root of their problem was that, as inflation continued to soar, with their concentration in home loans, they found themselves squeezed by an interest-rate mismatch: the thirty-year mortgages they held on their books earned single-digit interest rates, but they had to pay depositors double-digit rates or lose them to competitors. Lifting interest-rate caps, it turned out, had backfired. Inflation transformed once complacent savers into fickle shoppers hypersensitive to even small differences in rates. Long-term depositors overnight became short-term. Yet these same people, as homeowners, refused to pay double-digit rates on mortgages. Funding long-term assets like mortgages with short-term liabilities like deposits is a risky formula, and in an environment of high inflation, it made insolvency quick and inevitable. Thrifts' costs to raise money exceeded their returns on their mortgage investments. Commercial banks also suffered, but less so, because they had a wider array of investments, with varying maturities. The changing financial environment ruined the "3–6–3" business model that had served thrift executives well for decades: pay 3 percent on savings deposits, charge 6 percent on mortgages, pocket the difference, and play golf at 3:00.

So in 1982 Congress tried another fix, this time on the asset side of the thrift industry's balance sheet. It allowed S&Ls to diversify out of home mortgages and into such investments as commercial real estate and credit-card lending, which might yield higher profits in a shorter time. Lawmakers overrode state usury laws that limited the interest that lenders could charge for home loans. They also overrode state laws that barred "due-on-sale" clauses. With those clauses nullified by the federal government, banks could demand full repayment of their loans when a home was sold. That meant home sellers could no longer transfer low-interest mortgages to buyers—often a strong selling tool— and buyers would be forced to take out higher-cost mortgages. Congress also overrode state laws that prevented mortgage lenders from offering adjustable-rate mortgages. Each of these changes shifted more and more of the interest-rate risk inherent in mortgage lending from thrifts onto home buyers.

The premise underlying all these changes—the Kool-Aid of the S&L crisis— was that deregulation of markets, coupled with federal preemption of state consumer protection laws, would let thrifts grow out of their $100 billion insolvency. Thrifts couldn't survive forever with liabilities exceeding assets, but, with luck, giving them more time and new lines of business would enable them to realign their balance sheets. That presented the Reagan White House with a conundrum: when a federally insured institution nears insolvency, the law requires that regulators close it and shut off insurance to additional depositors. But the White House couldn't afford to close all insolvent thrifts without a massive taxpayer infusion, which would violate Reagan's pledge to keep taxes low. To keep them open—and avoid (in reality, delay) burdening taxpayers—the government sought to sell as many thrifts as possible to healthy buyers and to use accounting tricks to make those that remained, which Wall Street dubbed "zombie banks," appear solvent. These tricks let thrifts and regulators appear to be in compliance with the law while keeping a mounting taxpayer liability off the U.S. budget and thus, to the unsuspecting public, largely hidden from view.

In 1978, more than 80 percent of the thrift industry's assets were home loans. After Congress loosened the rules in 1982, with the Garn–St. Germain Act, that fell to 56 percent, and then, for many, to zero.[5] In 1982, California State Assemblyman Patrick Nolan, a Los Angeles Republican who received $154,000 in campaign contributions from thrifts in the 1980s, went the last mile, sponsoring a bill to permit California S&Ls to invest their assets however they wished. California thrifts now didn't have to put a dime of their federally insured deposits into home loans; 100 percent of their lending could and did go into wind farms, junk bonds, restaurants, even a Nevada brothel.[6] That wasn't all. Thrifts not only could now invest in anything from shopping centers to high rises by lending to others, they could now also take direct ownership positions in such projects. That still wasn't all. Despite all the loosening of restraints, lawmakers allowed thrifts to keep the tax breaks and other benefits—like the ability to borrow cheaply from the Federal Home Loan Banks—that they had been given over the years in exchange for focusing on lending to homeowners.

Yet, as thrifts diversified, so did other types of financial service companies, with home lending often at the center of their strategy. A race began among banks, thrifts, investment banks, insurers, and real estate firms as each tried to enter the others' businesses. All embraced deregulation with a vision of crafting a financial department store that could finance home construction, sell homes, provide the mortgages to buy them and the credit cards to furnish them, and issue insurance policies in case of fire.

Immediately after the president's inauguration, as Congress and regulators busily cut rules governing thrifts, the Reagan White House, with Vice President

Bush actively overseeing finance policy, set out to deregulate by also cutting the number of people overseeing the industry. It was part of Reagan's and Bush's election pledge to shrink government. Thrifts, armed with deposit insurance that made depositors indifferent but with fewer rules and less oversight, plunged headlong into new businesses without sufficient know-how or incentives to act cautiously and underwrite properly. By the middle of the decade, what had been an interest-rate mismatch in 1980 had turned into a bad-asset problem, caused by all the bad judgment involved in investing without underwriting—that is, without assessing risks and the likelihood of repayment. Instead of growing out of a problem, thrifts had grown into a new, more expensive one.

At his 1981 swearing-in, Reagan declared, "Government is not the solution to our problem. Government is the problem." Yet the S&L industry's woes already had caused him to break his campaign pledges to shrink government and taxes. The actual taxpayer bailout of the thrift industry began as soon as the government permitted federally insured, bankrupt institutions to stay open, regardless of whether the White House formally recognized the cost on the budget. No one in the administration doubted that the promise to pay insured depositors had to be honored. Failure to do so would have caused mayhem at thrifts and commercial banks and possibly the country's entire financial sector. The only question for Reagan and Bush was not if they would tell taxpayers, but when.

Because of deposit insurance, Reagan White House officials did not worry that closing hundreds of thrifts would disrupt the economy with panics, only that making taxpayers cover the cost would anger voters. Closing insolvent thrifts would even have benefits: evidence suggested an industry dedicated to mortgage lending and supported by tax breaks and other subsidies was no longer needed. The country had too many banks. Having fewer might give more business and a stronger balance sheet to those that remained. Bush would prove that in early 1989, when, as the nation's new president, he unveiled a bailout plan to close hundreds of thrifts beyond the hundreds that already had disappeared since 1980—all told, a third of the industry by 1994—with little effect on the economy. For now, mid-decade, the question was how to hide the mounting tax liability until after the 1988 election. Reagan and Bush knew deposit insurance would help them do that. As long as their money was guaranteed, depositors didn't care if a bank was insolvent. In fact, they eagerly put their money into the sickest thrifts, which, with interest caps lifted, tended to offer higher-than-market rates in a desperate bid to lure cash in the door to remain liquid and invest in high-risk ventures that might help them dig out of their troubles. This was, of course, not the intended purpose of deposit insurance.

Citicorp eventually won the bid for the D.C. thrift, agreeing to put up nearly $52 million to offset part of the sick institution's $80 million deficit. It was Citicorp's fourth purchase of a thrift in as many years. For decades, commercial bankers had scorned S&L executives as their hayseed cousins. Now they gladly became thrift executives so they could evade banking restrictions with the government's blessing. Many laws from the 1930s, and some going back to before the Civil War, made it hard for commercial banks to cross state lines, to sell securities or insurance or real estate, or to own or be owned by a non-bank. Congress hadn't saddled thrifts with all these restrictions because no one thought this sleepy backwater of community-based home-loan banks would ever aspire to do any of these things. Now thrifts were the hottest ticket in town, a loophole through which any company—commercial bank, investment bank, car manufacturer, or clothing retailer—could offer every kind of banking or other financial service under one roof.[7]

Charles Keating, an anti-porn crusader from Cincinnati, Ohio, epitomized the go-go mentality of 1980s thrift executives. Keating had entered the savings-and-loan industry by purchasing a California thrift, Lincoln Savings, in 1983, just a few years after settling securities fraud charges with the SEC. Citigroup's entrance into the thrift industry symbolized the changes gusting through financial service markets. Keating's entrance brought something else: fraud.

The thrift industry was centered in California, just as commercial banking and finance were centered in New York. Many of the nation's biggest thrifts were headquartered in San Diego, Los Angeles, and San Francisco, where their executives had moved to finance homes for the hordes of Americans migrating west after World War II.

Keating planned to grow Lincoln in California and surrounding states. Little of his business plan centered on the home lending that had been the justification for tax breaks and other benefits that Congress had given to S&Ls, however. Instead, in five years Keating steered Lincoln from a company with $1.1 billion in assets, 30 percent of them in home loans, to one with $6 billion in assets, the bulk of them in risky ventures like land development and low-grade high-risk bonds, including $11.8 million in the junk bonds of the Circus Circus casino and in a six-hundred-room luxury resort in Phoenix, built at what regulators believed was a record cost of $500,000 per room.[8] These investments were funded in part by federally insured deposits, and thus, implicitly, taxpayers.

Like many S&L executives at the time, Keating sought out high-risk, potentially high-return investments in commercial real estate and jumped into a newly hot sector of the securities market, junk bonds, to do it. Michael R. Milken, an investment banker with no-holds-barred tactics and a bad toupee, earned himself the sobriquet "junk bond king" by popularizing these high-risk deals. Among Milken's avid clients were thrift executives whose insolvent institutions gave them little to lose and everything to gain by rolling the dice.

The investment bank Milken worked for, Drexel Burnham Lambert Inc., filed for bankruptcy in February 1990 after pleading guilty to six felony counts of fraud and agreeing to $650 million in criminal and civil fines. The government banned Milken from the securities industry after he pleaded guilty to criminal charges and paid hundreds of millions of dollars in fines in what remains one of the largest securities fraud settlements ever.

In 1993, Keating was convicted of selling $200 million in junk bonds without disclosing their risk, including to customers of his failed thrift, who were persuaded to put their federally insured deposits into the higher-yielding bonds on the false promise that these were also federally insured. He served nearly five years of a twelve-and-a-half-year prison sentence before the conviction was overturned because the jury had received improper instructions. Among those who asked the court for leniency was Mother Teresa, moved by Keating's donations to her charities.[9]

Keating's troubles exposed a trail of lobbying and campaign contributions to state and federal officials, most notoriously to five U.S. senators known as the Keating Five: Republican John McCain of Arizona and Democrats Dennis DeConcini of Arizona, John Glenn of Ohio, Alan Cranston of California, and Donald Riegle of Michigan. Asked whether his $1.3 million in contributions to these men influenced them to intervene with thrift regulators on his behalf, Keating replied, "I want to say in the most forceful way I can, I certainly hope so."

In retrospect, regulators should have expected that someone like Keating would enter the S&L world. Crooks pop up when fraud is easy to execute and poorly policed. Like many financial crises, the thrift industry's problems didn't start with crooks. But when the government allowed hundreds of insolvent

Charles H. Keating, founder of American Continental Corp., lashes out
at federal regulators at a press conference on April 17, 1989, in Phoenix, Arizona,
a week after his company filed for bankruptcy. AP Photo/Jeff Robbins.

banks to stay open, the illness of those institutions encouraged risk-taking that
spread financial contagion, luring in lawbreakers and letting them prosper.

By the time Main Street America had its first inkling of trouble in the S&L
industry, the crisis was five years old. In March 1985, the SEC closed down a
small, fraud-ridden government securities dealer in Fort Lauderdale, Florida,
called ESM Government Securities. ESM, in turn, couldn't repay millions of
dollars it owed to an Ohio thrift, Home State Savings Bank of Cincinnati. When
the *Cincinnati Enquirer* broke news of Home State's losses on March 6, depositors lined up at its door, panicked that its collapse would deplete the state-run
deposit insurance fund, which had just $130 million to cover deposits at seventy
of Ohio's three hundred thrifts. (The rest had federal deposit insurance from the
FSLIC.)

Unlike commercial banks, which had a single, federal deposit insurance
system, state-chartered thrifts still had a few state-sponsored insurance funds that

ran alongside the federal FSLIC. And now, in the 1980s, state-run insurance for thrifts failed for the same reasons those for commercial banks had failed decades earlier: the pool of insured institutions was too small to provide sufficient premiums, and the firms covered were too often badly run and supervised. Now, as lines formed in Ohio, state and federal officials worried that the panic would spread to other states, even to federally insured thrifts and commercial banks.

Commercial banks had their own crises. From 1980 to 1994, bad management and slumps in oil prices caused 1,600 banks insured by the Federal Deposit Insurance Corporation to fail or effectively fail, saved only with government help. Though serious, these accounted for 9 percent of the industry, in contrast to the 1,300 thrift failures during the same period, which wiped out 32 percent of all S&Ls.[10] When the Penn Square bank in Oklahoma City failed in 1982, large institutional investors lost tens of millions of dollars in deposits above the $100,000 limit that applied at the time, even though the government decided to protect deposits of retail customers greater than that amount. The FDIC's decision to cover some but not all deposits above the insured limit caused controversy, but regulators hoped the losses for large depositors, mostly other banks, would induce them to be less indifferent to where they deposited funds.

Penn Square's troubles helped trigger in 1984 the biggest failure until then, that of Continental Illinois National Bank and Trust Company. The FDIC bailed out Continental with $4.5 billion, prompting congressional hearings in which Comptroller of the Currency C. Todd Conover articulated a new federal policy: the government would not let the nation's largest eleven banks fail. Industry and policymakers immediately dubbed it the "too big to fail" doctrine. It was a policy of protecting any bank whose demise would threaten the financial system and hence damage other banks and financial institutions. The government's rescue of Continental meant the bank's $3 billion in insured deposits were safe, but so were $30 billion in uninsured liabilities, including billions of dollars in uninsured deposits, those above the $100,000 limit. It was the first time since the Great Depression that federal officials had rescued a bank to prevent systemic damage.[11]

Throughout the 1980s, Mexico and other Latin American countries struggled to repay tens of billions of dollars to U.S. banks. In response, the United States organized a consortium of commercial banks, central banks, and the International Monetary Fund to act as an international lender of last resort to extend billions of dollars in loans and other aid to the debtor nations. This amounted to a backdoor bailout of U.S. banks. Regulators also let banks delay reporting billions in losses, an action that likely "weakened market discipline and encouraged excess risk-taking in subsequent decades."[12]

Then in the early 1990s Citibank nearly collapsed from bad commercial real estate loans and entered into a two-and-a-half-year hand-holding program with the Federal Reserve, raising renewed questions about why big banks received special treatment.[13] While dramatic, these episodes didn't threaten the existence of the FDIC or require a permanent taxpayer bailout. That at least was the perception, and in banking, perception can be everything.

Ohio's regional crisis drew attention to the nation's ongoing—and worsening—thrift crisis. The White House pulled Federal Reserve Board Chairman Paul Volcker off a United Airlines flight in San Francisco so that Ohio Governor Richard Celeste could tell him personally that the state was about to declare the first broad-scale closure of banks since Roosevelt's national "holiday" in 1933. Celeste intended to shut dozens of shaky, state-insured thrifts. As the nation's central banker, Volcker needed to maintain public confidence in the financial system. After decades of relative calm in banking, Volcker worried about what people would do if they couldn't get their money right away out of the dozens of thrifts Celeste was temporarily closing, and how the public would react to televised images of depositors lined up around the block. Who knew what other panics might ensue? A story that in an earlier era might have played out for days in the newspaper or over the radio would now be seen on the evening news by millions, including many who had lived through the Great Depression.

Since the Depression era, American finance had become a benchmark of financial safety worldwide. Regulators and policymakers would not tolerate even a remote prospect of rattled confidence. Volcker's advice to Celeste was simple: "The system can stand one failure. It can't stand a second." He didn't mean this literally. He assumed that more problem thrifts could surface. But if Celeste mishandled the situation by projecting anything other than confidence and control, he would spark fear and more runs. Volcker's message was clear: Celeste had to avoid causing any unnecessary failures. Volcker pledged support in the Fed's capacity as lender of last resort to ensure that the state's thrifts had cash to meet withdrawals and thus sidestep avoidable insolvencies. Even so, the dollar plunged overnight on news of Ohio's problems as investors grew anxious about the security of the U.S. banking system.[14]

Most of the seventy Ohio thrifts that had state-regulated insurance stayed shut for several weeks longer than the twenty-four hours the governor intended. The Ohio legislature backed deposits with taxpayer money. Volcker publicly vowed to provide reopened thrifts with any needed cash. Confidence was restored.

Nationally, top thrift executives downplayed events in Ohio, as did the White House. When asked, President Reagan said: "This is not a major threat to the banking system. There is no other problem of that kind anyplace else in the country that we're aware of." Reagan's staff, led by Vice President Bush, were meanwhile scrambling to contain that threat.[15]

Ohio's problems soon spread to Maryland. On April 13, 1985, it was Volcker's turn to place an urgent call, to Maryland Governor Harry Hughes. Old Court Savings and Loan of Baltimore had borrowed unusually large sums of cash from the Fed, a telltale sign, Volcker told the governor, that the institution had a run on its hands. As often happens when a bank gets into trouble, some people, usually industry insiders or eager customers with deposits greater than the insured limit, had detected that trouble before the regulators did. No depositors stood in lines. Instead a silent run took place as depositors sitting in front of computers withdrew sums that in aggregate totaled some $630 million. If news of these massive withdrawals leaked out, a full-scale run, with customers lined up at the door, might ensue, providing television cameras with a powerful image that was the first requirement of any story vying for airtime.

The situation, Volcker said, could blow up any day—no matter that Maryland's thrift regulator, Charlie Brown, and the head of the state insurance fund, Charles Hogg, had assured the governor and members of Congress just days earlier that the state faced no threat in the wake of Ohio, despite also having a state-run insurance fund. For Governor Hughes, the message was clear. The central bank was worried, and he should be, too.

Old Court's willingness to pay above market rates on deposits—almost always a red flag and in this case a full percentage point above—should have tipped off state officials that the bank was in trouble. Some, like Hogg and Brown, did know it, but when a depositor asked, they lied, saying the thrift could pay better than competitors because it had "eliminated the middle-man" in real estate deals and was less vulnerable to changes in local housing markets.

Because the federal government didn't bear direct responsibility for state insurance systems, thrift regulators at the Federal Home Loan Bank Board, which oversaw the federal insurance system for thrifts, felt they were off the hook and offered Maryland little assistance. Volcker's staff knew better. A loss of confidence in banking anywhere in the country fell in everyone's lap. So the Federal Reserve, to Maryland officials' lasting gratitude, stepped in to help.

Old Court had been purchased in 1982 by Jeffrey Levitt, a young Baltimore lawyer whose behavior, like Keating's, was emblematic of the swindlers who had moved into the S&L industry across the country after regulators decided in the early 1980s to let insolvent savings-and-loan banks stay open. Still, it's curious that the state allowed Levitt to safeguard other people's money because when he bought Old Court, he had, like Keating, a history of encounters with the law: a report on Maryland's thrift scandal found Levitt "was well known as the person responsible for a major portion" of trouble at another of the state's thrifts, where he had been a lawyer and, state prosecutors charged, stolen funds to buy Old Court.[16]

When he was fresh out of law school, Levitt had been thrown off the state parole board—an almost unheard-of sanction—for soliciting business from inmates during prison inspection tours. He also had received a one-year suspension from practicing law for lying in a Baltimore City Superior Court hearing, and as a slum landlord he violated housing codes so often that Fridays in Baltimore housing court were known as "Levitt Days."

As owners of Old Court, Levitt and his wife, Karol, lived like royalty. For three years they used depositors' money to buy, among other things, $400,000 worth of jewelry, an $18,000 putting green at their Florida house, three thoroughbred race horses, two Ocean City condominiums, an apartment in New York City, seventeen automobiles, a Rolls-Royce golf cart with a TV and tape deck (very fancy at the time), and dozens of sterling silver serving trays, prompting a *Washington Post* columnist, in a profile of the couple, to ask, "Who did they think would come over for dinner, the Sixth Fleet?" Their conspicuous consumption reached absurd levels. A waitress in a Baltimore restaurant reportedly watched Jeffrey and Karol eat a full dinner and then six desserts each. In total, Levitt stole nearly $15 million from depositors.[17]

A month after Volcker's call to Hughes, state officials seized Old Court and began a criminal investigation. The state's attorney general, Stephen Sachs, had to choose between sunshine and secrecy: make the bank's problems public and thus stop it from continuing to cause harm but possibly spark panic that would aggravate the situation short term; or say nothing and, though not upsetting the public now, allow the problem to fester and almost certainly grow worse and costlier to fix. He decided to close Old Court and charge Levitt with fraud.[18]

This choice did in fact ignite runs at thrifts around the state, with depositors withdrawing cash at a rate of $4 million an hour until the governor limited withdrawals to $1,000 per person per month. In the following months more than a dozen of the state's savings and loans were seized, with access to billions of dollars in deposits limited or frozen while state and federal officials sorted out the mess. Officials booted dozens of thrift executives from their jobs, many for out-and-out thievery but also some for gross incompetence. Managers at one thrift, for example, didn't know how to process individual retirement accounts. So they just put IRA applications and checks in a brown grocery bag next to a staff refrigerator, unprocessed and uncashed.

But no one epitomized mismanagement like the Levitts—and their regulators, Hogg and Brown. Even after Old Court was taken over by the state, Hogg and Brown let it continue offering above-market rates on deposits. The thrift's ads didn't mention that it was on a slippery slope to becoming ever more insolvent: paying high rates because it was desperate for cash to invest in high-risk ventures in an attempt to make up its losses, which increasingly were due in part to paying such high rates. Like a gambler who doubles down, insolvent thrifts that were allowed to stay open had nothing to lose. They kept investing in riskier, potentially higher-returning projects, but instead of climbing out of a hole, they almost always slid further into it.

When Attorney General Sachs heard an Old Court radio ad still offering the high rates, he telephoned Hogg to say, "You'd better get that fucking stuff off the air or I'm going to sue you." Hogg argued that pulling the ads would undermine consumers' confidence. Sachs held his ground: it was a sham to ask depositors to pour money into such a shaky institution. It was bad enough that Hogg and Brown had hidden the mess for so long from the state's top officials. But now the governor knew. Such shenanigans had to stop. The ads were pulled, but not before scores of new depositors had been lured inside the sick thrift.[19]

In September 1985, a second S&L shock hit Maryland and rippled through the nation: a subsidiary of a state-chartered thrift, a real estate tax shelter company called Equity Programs Investment Corporation, or EPIC, filed for bankruptcy. EPIC's collapse shook the nation's housing market. Its business plan was to buy homes and lease them back to builders, then bundle the contracts into limited partnerships that functioned as investments, providing tax shelters for investors all around the country. None of the investors ever expected to see the property EPIC owned. Neither did the thrifts or banks from coast to coast that lent it millions of dollars.

When EPIC collapsed, lenders were left owning hundreds of condominiums and houses built only as tax breaks, not as homes people wanted. Many of them were in oversupplied cities, such as Austin, Dallas, and Denver. EPIC's failure forced the third-largest private mortgage insurer in the country, Ticor Mortgage Insurance of Los Angeles, to file for bankruptcy, sending wider ripples of disruption through the thrift and mortgage industries.

As Jeffrey Levitt shuffled in and out of the Baltimore courthouse during his arraignment in late 1985 for bank fraud and theft, bystanders spit on his squat 230-pound body, hissing and shouting like a lynch mob. He appeared for sentencing wearing yellow pants, a madras shirt, and docksiders without socks, an outfit more suited to a backyard barbecue with young Republicans than a

Jeffrey Levitt, president of the failed Old Court Savings and Loan Association, exits a sheriff's van as he arrives for sentencing on theft and misappropriation charges in Baltimore on July 2, 1986. Levitt pleaded guilty to stealing $14.6 million from savings and loan depositors. He was sentenced to three years in prison and fined $12,000. AP Photo/Bill Smith.

court hearing. The humiliating leg irons that checked his gait were no doubt a gratuitous concession by state officials to appease the angry depositors who filled the courtroom. "If I did what the public wanted, the Levitts would be hanging from the rafters in front of the courthouse," a judge in the case said. Jeffrey pleaded that he was a first-time offender. "The biggest first offender the state has ever seen," the judge replied.

In a curious way, Levitt's flamboyancy did consumers a favor. The longer that thrift abuses went undetected, investigators said, the more expensive the cleanup bill would have been. Consumers, however, failed to see the silver lining. They picketed the legislature in Annapolis and heckled the governor across the state, voting him down in his bid for the U.S. Senate in 1986. The bill presented to Maryland taxpayers for repayment to depositors eventually reached $185 million, a hefty sum but not the $7 billion originally feared.

Though thrift executives condemned Attorney General Sachs for blowing the whistle on Old Court, Sachs said he'd do it again. "All the arguments that say, 'Well, you don't recklessly make moves because the financial markets are sensitive,' of course, that's all true," he said. "But it doesn't gainsay any of that to say that when you see a cesspool, you should try to clean it up."[20] Maryland's official report on the crisis, by a special counsel appointed by the state legislature, concluded that while Sachs may have sparked a few runs, he saved taxpayers millions of dollars over the long haul. Voters didn't see it that way. Sachs lost his bid for governor in the fall of 1986.[21]

Maryland's report on the crisis concluded that it had occurred despite a robust economy because S&Ls, as is often the case in financial services, exerted too much control over regulators and lawmakers, who "consistently enacted legislation created by industry-dominated boards or commissions and often bowed to the influence of special interest groups representing the . . . industry." Lawmakers, it said, focused more on loosening rules for the industry than on the safety of depositors.

In the 1980s, executives at nationally chartered thrifts cited looser state rules to persuade federal regulators and Congress to loosen their regulations. Then state-chartered thrifts argued they could not compete unless they could do what federally chartered institutions could. State-chartered thrifts threatened to switch to a federal charter, and vice versa, to get relief, in a merry-go-round of ever-weakening rules. Regulators, whose budgets rely on the fees from those they oversee, obliged by loosening rules, setting off a competition between state and federal officials to see who could be the most lenient. This phenomenon of "regulatory capture" or "charter shopping" exposed a race-to-the-bottom weakness in the nation's dual banking system, same as ever. S&L executives viewed the relaxed rules as government-insured licenses to gamble—just as Leo T. Crowley, the first head of the Federal Deposit Insurance Corporation, had warned would happen if lawmakers granted deposit insurance without proper oversight.

Maryland provided another cautionary lesson. Though regulated by state officials, its insurance fund, like its federal counterparts, was financed by member institutions. Rather than giving industry participants an incentive to weed out bad players, as Glass and others had expected, industry funding made executives arrogant, insistent that insurance officials worked for them, not for taxpayers. That's why Maryland's insurance fund chief, Hogg, and chief regulator, Brown, viewed themselves as more beholden to the industry than to the public.

Maryland's report on the crisis cited three major causes: no oversight, lax rules pushed by industry, and executives who could and did take money for their own use. This was the blueprint that it turned out thrifts followed nationwide. The report also made special mention of the bankers' professional enablers: lawyers, accountants, appraisers, credit-reporting agencies. For example, the respected Baltimore law firm of Venable, Baetjer, and Howard—nearly ninety years old when the Maryland crisis struck—advised the state insurance fund on rules and regulations even as it advised thrifts that violated them. In 1987 the firm paid Maryland $27 million to settle a $450 million lawsuit claiming that its malpractice and conflicts of interest had helped spark the crisis.[22]

Maryland played out, in a microcosm, the thrift crisis occurring nationwide. The state's tourism slogan at the time was "America in Miniature," and so it was.

The American Home: Safeguard of American Liberties

BEFORE LEVITT AND KEATING GAINED NOTORIETY, America's most famous thrift executive was George Bailey, who, with his uncle Billy in Frank Capra's film *It's a Wonderful Life,* runs the Bailey Brothers Building and Loan in the mythical American town of Bedford Falls. By taking in customers' deposits and lending them out to homebuyers, the brothers finance the construction of the town's middle- and working-class houses, steering the tiny thrift through the troubled years of the Great Depression. One day George, played by Jimmy Stewart, faces a run on his thrift as crowds of worried customers demand their money. Capra made the film in 1947, but the era it depicts doesn't appear to yet have deposit insurance. It's up to George to restore trust. "You're thinking of this place all wrong, as if I had the money back in a safe," Bailey frantically tells those lining up to empty their savings accounts. "The money's not here. Why, your money's in Joe's house . . . and a hundred others. You're lending them the money to build and then they're going to pay it back to you." Acting as lender of last resort, Bailey takes two thousand dollars he has saved for his honeymoon and gives cash to any customer who remains unconvinced. The tactic works.[1]

S&L executives and lobbyists cultivated Bailey's image as their own. Like all bankers, thrifts acted as middlemen, matching people with excess cash with those needing to borrow. Commercial banks in the nineteenth and most of the twentieth centuries made comparatively few home loans. The home loan market in the United States was dominated by savings and loans until at least the 1970s—and especially the 1980s—when banks lost much of their short-term commercial lending business to the commercial paper market, forcing them to focus more on consumer lending, from home loans to credit cards. The thrifts' forerunner, called a friendly society or building and loan, was a model America imported from Britain, even though it was not without problems. Established to attract savings from commoners, British thrifts proved so vulnerable to embezzlement by owners and managers that in 1825 Parliament established a special committee to investigate.[2]

The first S&L in the United States, formed in 1831 during Andrew Jackson's presidency, was established near Philadelphia by textile workers to pool their money to help one another buy homes. Depositors owned and operated such early thrifts, and codes of conduct were strict. One firm fined its treasurer fifty cents for every board meeting he missed. For the next hundred years, scores of similar institutions sprang up. In 1869 a 109-page book entitled *Workingman's Way to Wealth* described, in the most enthusiastic terms, building and loans and how to use them. An 1876 article in *Scribner's* magazine entitled "A Hundred Thousand Homes: How They Are Paid For" included a typical building and loan advertisement:

FOURTH OF JULY! INDEPENDENCE DAY! Young man and Woman, stop and reflect! The money you fritter away uselessly will make you independent. Today sign the magna charter of your independence, and, like our forefathers, in about eight years you will, in a great degree, be independent by saving only thirty-three cents each day. In that time you will realize $2,000, or have a home and be independent of the landlord. Let this, indeed, be your day of independence, by subscribing for shares in the new series, now issued, in the State Mutual Savings Fund, Loan and Building Association.[3]

Some thrifts lent only to their own depositors, making borrowers and lenders one and the same pool. Others lent to anyone who was creditworthy. Most were started by groups of immigrants but eventually grew to where lender and borrower didn't know each other. Still, like the customers of the Bailey brothers, depositors and lenders invariably lived within the same community.

As politically sophisticated businessmen began to enter the thrift business at the turn of the twentieth century, they saw that the image of S&Ls as vital to the nation's well-being could pay off in favorable treatment by the government. By the 1890s, the thrifts' chief lobbying group, the U.S. League of Savings Institutions, had at least one member thrift in every congressional district and boasted political clout second to none. Its letterhead and business cards carried the motto "The American Home: The Safeguard of American Liberties." Said the group's founder, "The future of the Republic depends upon the question whether we can make this nation a nation of home-owners or not." The winning entry in the group's contest in 1897 to draw the ideal American Home, showed, in the words of the *Omaha Bee* newspaper, "a comfortable modern home surrounded by a large lawn in which children are at play. A mother with a baby carriage stands in front of the house, while a little daughter runs to greet her approaching father." A church and the flag are in the background.[4]

The Russian Revolution of 1917 aided the thrifts' cause, as Americans resisted the challenge to free-market capitalism. Their executives understood how to couple a unified voice in Washington and state capitals with the political clout of small local banks waving the American flag and selling the American dream of home ownership. It was pro-America, anti-communist, and in keeping with the founding fathers' view that owners of private property made the best citizens; they would protect democracy because they were free to vote in their best interests, not those of a landlord or others to whom they were beholden.[5]

The federal government, led by Herbert Hoover as secretary of commerce under Presidents Harding and Coolidge, took up the cause of promoting private homeownership. Hoover started an "Own Your Own Home" campaign because, as realtors proclaimed, "socialism and communism do not take root in the ranks of those who have their feet firmly embedded in the soil of America through homeownership."[6] The number of thrifts reached an all-time high of 12,500 in 1925, though even then they still totaled less than half the number of commercial banks.

More than 1,700 thrifts failed during the Great Depression, costing depositors $200 million ($3 billion today), a third the value of their deposits, and leaving far fewer dollars for home loans. Presidents Hoover and Roosevelt, aided by an alarmed Congress and a downtrodden public, gave the S&L industry new legislation designed to increase funds for housing—Hoover the Federal Home Loan Bank System, and Roosevelt the Federal Housing Administration and Fannie Mae.

But the two presidents didn't have the same goals in mind.[7] Hoover, representing the party of free markets and big business, opted in the name of homeownership to favor the interests of S&Ls over competition. Roosevelt, representing the party dedicated to helping the little guy, favored harnessing government power to foster competition in housing finance.

Hoover successfully pushed Congress to create the Federal Home Loan Bank System: twelve regional banks—known derisively during Roosevelt's tenure as "Hoover creations"—to borrow money from the government at cheap rates and lend it to thrifts at below-market prices. Thrifts were to pass the savings to customers. Congress intended the regional banks to subsidize healthy thrifts at times when thrifts found attracting new deposits hard, and to thus supply cash for mortgages in good times and bad.

Roosevelt, hoping to increase mortgage lending in rural areas, pushed to create the Federal Housing Administration, an agency that insured mortgages to low-income borrowers. With his eye on a broader housing policy, FDR horse-traded with the thrift industry: if its executives supported—or at least stopped opposing—the FHA, he would support deposit insurance for thrifts via the Federal Savings and Loan Insurance Fund, or FSLIC. It worked. After FHA-backed loans failed to catch on among lenders, however, Roosevelt pushed through additional legislation in 1938 to create Fannie Mae to buy FHA loans. Fannie held on to the loans or sold them to other financial institutions, establishing a secondary market in FHA loans that enabled them to be traded across the country.

Roosevelt also pushed thrift legislation in 1933 to empower Hoover's Federal Home Loan Bank Board to charter and regulate federal S&Ls. Up to that point, thrifts had existed alongside commercial banks through state law. The move to federal charters created a dual system for thrifts like the one for commercial banks, and with just as many headaches.

Taking advantage of the bad name that commercial banks had earned from the 1929 crash, S&L executives billed themselves as bankers to Main Street. The thrifts themselves were relatively small: in 1935 the nation's 10,825 savings institutions had $16.9 billion in assets, while the nation's 15,488 commercial banks had $48.8 billion. Thrifts gave themselves names like "Dime" and "Emigrant," seeking to attract small, steady savers of the working and middle classes.

When it came to obtaining government subsidies, thrift lobbyists had a more hard-boiled view of life. They pushed for tax breaks, arguing that such support wasn't socialism but essential to promoting the American Dream. Government should deliver entitlements, they argued, and then leave the industry to run its affairs. Any attempt at regulation really *was* socialism, they said. Any politician opposed to these views was targeted as anti-homeownership and therefore un-American.

Thrifts won the special treatment and became hooked on it. They loved deposit insurance and federally subsidized borrowing from the twelve regional Federal Home Loan Banks, as well as another S&L perquisite: since the late 1890s, savings and loans had been exempted from any excise or income tax. They remained tax-exempt until 1951, but even when some taxes were imposed, their burden was lighter than that of banks and other companies. The differential narrowed but continued for decades. In return, S&Ls were supposed to sell one product, home loans. And their clients weren't expected to be Rockefellers.

By 1945 the number of thrifts in the United States had fallen to 6,700 and commercial banks to 14,000, both about half their pre-crisis peaks. The decline reflected the many failures during the Depression as well as the mergers that had ensued as the turmoil tapered off, the economy stabilized, and banks and thrifts adopted more conservative business strategies. Then good times reigned. For the next twenty years, beginning with a veteran-driven home-buying boom after World War II, the thrift industry prospered, especially as the population moved west.

There were some problems. California officials granted too many S&L charters, causing several big thrift failures in the state in the 1960s. In 1967, Robert Gene ("Bobby") Baker, who had been the top aide to Lyndon Johnson when LBJ was Senate majority leader, was convicted of tax evasion, theft, and conspiracy to defraud the government in connection with $99,600 that he had received from California S&L executives. The government claimed Baker was transporting stolen money, while thrift executives claimed the money was for campaign contributions. Baker went to jail; the thrift executives did not. They tightened their control in Congress and over their regulators at the Federal Home Loan Bank Board, which oversaw the Federal Home Loan Bank System.

Thrift executives had never liked Fannie Mae or FHA loans, which they thought of as competition. But in the 1960s and 1970s, inflation and other changes forced thrift executives to seek government help in expanding their businesses out of local communities, where the flow of new deposits might be too low to support the demand for new home loans, while in another region of the country, deposits might exceed demand for mortgages. Thrifts needed a way to tap into regions where they could provide more loans or find more deposit money. They began to pine for a government-sponsored corporation like Fannie to create a secondary market for non-government guaranteed mortgages from which they could buy and sell loans. Having fought the creation of Fannie, thrift executives now asked Congress for a similar corporation, but one dedicated to buying home loans only from thrifts.

Some in Congress suggested a logical move: expanding Fannie's charter to allow it to buy and sell not just FHA loans but all types of home loans, including those from thrifts. That didn't suit thrift lobbyists. They wanted a corporation controlled by the three-man Federal Home Loan Bank Board in Washington, the same board that supervised the regional Federal Home Loan Banks, the thrift insurance fund FSLIC, and nationally chartered thrifts. Industry executives reasoned that putting the corporation inside the bank board system— which they effectively controlled—would add to the thrift industry's political and economic clout.

In 1970 Congress granted the request of industry lobbyists at the U.S. League, creating the Federal Home Loan Mortgage Corporation, known as Freddie Mac, to be run by the Federal Home Loan Bank Board. Freddie would buy and sell conventional home loans from thrifts only. Somewhat oddly, the same legislation simultaneously expanded Fannie's charter beyond government-insured mortgages so that it too could buy conventional home loans—those not insured by the federal government as FHA loans were. Fannie soon abandoned FHA loans, leaving them for another federal agency—Ginnie Mae—to buy, and rushed into the conventional home-loan market. With the stroke of a pen, Congress established twin federally chartered companies with the same function, that of keeping the mortgage markets liquid by creating a secondary market that would maintain a steady demand for home loans. The two companies had to buy mortgages in good times and bad, thereby steadying the housing market and, because that market is so large, the economy.

Like Fannie Mae, Freddie Mac bought home loans with federally subsidized money that came not just from the Federal Home Loan Banks: the two companies' perceived federal status allowed both to borrow in the general credit markets at near government rates. They used the cash to buy mortgages from lenders, giving the lenders fresh funding to make additional loans. The biggest difference between Fannie and Freddie was that Freddie was owned by the Federal Home Loan Bank system, while Fannie had been made into a publicly traded company in the late 1960s because Congress wanted to keep it off the U.S. budget as President Lyndon Johnson struggled to finance the Vietnam War. It remained a government-sponsored enterprise, or GSE, created and overseen by the federal government, but now shareholders owned it, converting it to a footnote in the U.S. budget.

Congress exempted Fannie and Freddie from state and local taxes, from the Securities and Exchange Commission's financial disclosure rules, and from the SEC's registration requirements (and fees) for offering bonds. Wall Street saw these exemptions and the two entities' federal charters as signals that Uncle Sam would never let them fail, making them virtually risk-free as borrowers. Their special status and privileges saved the two companies billions of dollars each year. Fannie and Freddie's securities stated in big letters that they were not guaranteed by the United States, but Wall Street didn't believe it. The result was that the two companies could borrow more cheaply than anyone else except the U.S. Treasury itself. No matter how creditworthy a potential competitor was, Fannie and Freddie could always borrow for less and thus outbid any other company for the purchase of conventional mortgages. That gave them a monopoly in the secondary market for conventional home loans. No law prevented Wall Street bankers from entering. Economics did. With these advantages, Fannie and Freddie built a secondary market that, by taking mortgages off lenders' books, mitigated some of the interest-rate risk that home lenders faced.

Fannie Mae and Freddie Mac worked just fine, but the economy didn't cooperate. Inflation continued to climb during the 1970s, outpacing the relief that the regional banks, or Freddie Mac, or any other division of the Federal Home Loan Bank System or other government subsidy could bring to the S&L industry. A thrift holding a home loan yielding 6 percent would sell it to Freddie, relend the proceeds for a home loan yielding 7 percent, only to find that the market rate had risen to 8 percent. By 1979, when Volcker decided to raise interest rates to contain inflation, the thrifts' situation became critical. Market rates rose to double digits. Fannie and Freddie dampened the effect on thrifts but couldn't erase it. Raising deposit insurance to $100,000 in 1980 and simultaneously phasing out interest-rate caps was supposed to help but didn't bring relief fast enough and brought a new set of problems: thrifts now were forced to pay double-digit rates for deposits to remain liquid yet earned lower rates on existing home loans, putting the industry in an interest-rate squeeze.

As thrifts lobbied to expand out of home loans and into shorter-term, more profitable investments, market forces brought more competition. Merrill Lynch and other Wall Street brokerages tried to steal customers from both thrifts and commercial banks by marketing mutual funds and money-market accounts that offered consumers not only higher interest, but also interest-earning checking accounts which banks by law couldn't yet offer (and couldn't fully offer until 2011). Depositors pulled hundreds of billions of dollars from banks and put the money into securities industry accounts. For the first time, banks and thrifts faced a battle for deposits from outside the banking business. Brokerage firms were beating them.

Inflation, however, was only one engine of change. Computer technology, which moved sophisticated, complex transactions with a speed and ease unimaginable only a few years earlier, empowered companies to borrow easily and directly from each other for short periods, issuing IOUs known as commercial paper and bypassing the banks altogether. The commercial-paper market became a major player in finance almost overnight. This was good news for business borrowers, who could raise money more cheaply, but it was a disaster for bankers, who lost many of their best borrowers. In 1992 dollars, the commercial-paper market totaled $35 billion in outstanding loans in 1970. By the mid-1980s it was $330 billion and by 1990 about $559 billion.[8]

Squeezed between money-market accounts luring their depositors and the commercial-paper market taking their loan customers, commercial banks scrambled for new business and found it in home mortgages. Thanks to Fannie, they no longer worried about the risk of an interest-rate squeeze, which historically had been one reason they kept largely away from the mortgage business. At the same time, the rise in companies offering private mortgage insurance by the 1970s had virtually eliminated the already low risk of home loan defaults. Two of the main risks in home lending—interest-rate swings and defaults—could now be effectively managed, if not eliminated.

So banks entered the mortgage business with a vengeance, with the goal of winning more than just home loans: they wanted to capture the entire consumer credit market. Once they gained a captive client with a thirty-year mortgage, they envisioned selling him everything from a Visa card to a revolving line of credit on a checking account. Banks also began to eye the real estate industry and two other areas from which they were largely legally excluded: securities and insurance. In addition, they looked to expand beyond state boundaries, where federal and state laws had penned them.

Computers helped. Without previous experience, a New York bank could create a securities division, letting computers do much of the work of assessing risks in the new market. Moreover, it could easily set up a loan office across the country, say in California, that technically didn't qualify as a bank under federal law because it didn't accept deposits.

Banks were not alone in wanting to expand their financial products. Real estate companies, insurance companies, and securities firms longed to move into every aspect of each other's businesses to offer one-stop financial shopping. Instead of having to bear the expense of setting up a new office or of having to hire consultants, a company could sell insurance or real estate or make business loans by installing a desktop computer with the proper software.

High interest rates also lured companies that were not traditionally in the finance business. Retailers like Nordstrom wondered why they couldn't make money charging interest on credit-card purchases as banks did. Sears, Roebuck hoped to offer banking products in its department stores. Ford Motor Company wanted to sell—and finance—everything from cars to credit cards to home loans. One-stop shopping became the holy grail of finance in the 1980s, just as it had been in the 1920s.

Laws restricting such activities became Swiss cheese as lawyers found loopholes in statutes that mostly restricted commercial banks but not the rest of finance. The laws restricted what commercial banks could sell, where they could sell it, and who would pocket the profit. Now the combination of inflation and technology, by creating incentives and tools to blur once-clear distinctions among banks, thrifts, and other financial institutions, produced de facto deregulation. That inevitably led to a call for the formal tearing down of the restrictions—but not the benefits, such as deposit insurance—erected in response to the crash of 1929.

As banks ventured more aggressively into mortgage lending and thrifts increasingly sought special treatment to remain afloat, some regulators and industry leaders began to ask whether the federal government still needed to subsidize the housing industry. Had market innovations made government subsidy an anachronism? And what about all those other restrictions? Were they dinosaurs, too?

In 1979, Fed Chair Paul Volcker picked higher interest rates as his weapon of choice to battle inflation. The stability provided by the cap on interest rates that banks and thrifts could offer, known as Regulation Q, soon began to work in reverse: savers flocked to put their money into unregulated and uninsured but higher-yielding money market and mutual fund accounts. These accounts had held only $3 billion in 1977, but they jumped to $50 billion in 1979, $100 billion in 1980, $200 billion in 1981, and $233 billion in 1982. Today the mutual fund industry holds $18 trillion in consumer savings. Congress could have extended the caps on interest rates to unregulated accounts, but instead, caught up in a growing enthusiasm for deregulation, it took a giant step to deregulate finance by lifting the caps for all. President Jimmy Carter signed interest-rate deregulation into law on March 31, 1980, touting its benefits to small savers. No mention was made of a need for tighter oversight amid this lifting of rules.

Six years later, President Reagan told a White House conference of small business owners that the government's old, misguided view of the economy could be summed up in a few words: "If it moves, tax it. If it keeps moving, regulate it. And if it stops moving, subsidize it." Now, he said, "We've turned all that around."[9]

Under the guise of promoting homeownership and deregulation simultaneously, members of the U.S. House and Senate banking committees, eager to keep the thrift lobby's campaign contributions coming, granted thrifts permission to expand into new areas: credit cards, commercial and general consumer lending, and interest-bearing checking accounts. Permitting the thrifts to venture far outside mortgage lending broke the social contract that justified the many federal subsidies the industry enjoyed.

The biggest bone, however, proved too big for the system to swallow safely. Congress voted to raise deposit insurance to $100,000 from $40,000 per account for both the FSLIC, which insured thrifts, and the FDIC, which insured commercial banks. This increase not only far outstripped the rise in inflation but signaled that S&Ls were abandoning their role as banker to the little guy. Depositors with $100,000 tended to be better-to-do investors who often had professionals managing their money. Main Street had ventured onto Wall Street once again, a change that would be expensive for taxpayers.

In spite of sunshine-in-government laws, the decision resulted from a backroom deal made by lawmakers on both sides of the aisle of the House and Senate banking committees. These lawmakers also ignored bank regulators, who cautioned the increase was ill-advised, and instead bowed to industry executives, particularly from California, who had lobbied hard for the $100,000 limit. California thrifts had a batch of $100,000 certificates of deposit nearing maturity, and they worried that customers would move their money if it wasn't fully insured. The executives believed—correctly—that consumers would accept a lower interest rate in return for an increased federal deposit guarantee.

Consumers will always accept a lower interest rate in exchange for that assurance. That's how deposit insurance provides easy credit for banks.

Another beneficiary of the change was Merrill Lynch, which used the $100,000 threshold as a wedge into offering insured accounts just as banks could, despite laws intended to bar the securities industry from such transactions, and even though Merrill didn't pay deposit insurance premiums to the government insurance funds. Thrifts and banks offered their highest rates to deposits of $100,000 or more—and now could offer federal deposit insurance on top of it. Many people didn't have $100,000, so Merrill—investment banker to the retail customer—hatched a solution: brokered deposits. Merrill collected whatever people had to invest, pooled it into blocks of $100,000 in accounts in its own name, and then pulled that cash in and out of FDIC- and FSLIC-insured banks and S&Ls to earn the highest insured rate they offered, moving funds to gain even a few hundredths of a percentage point. Soon these brokered accounts earned the nickname "hot money" for how fast they moved in and out of institutions.

Merrill and copycats had found a way to offer the highest possible rates in federally guaranteed accounts offered only at banks and thrifts. It was a brilliant use of a loophole. With the increase in deposit insurance, brokers no longer needed to fret when a bank or thrift offering a high rate for $100,000 was in shaky condition. The securities industry was in full moral hazard mode. Thrifts, insolvent and desperate for cash, quickly became addicted to brokered deposits. "Few appreciated the potential adverse consequences of deregulating an industry that was deeply in the red and had nothing to lose," noted William S. Haraf, a visiting scholar at the American Enterprise Institute. In retrospect, he had put it mildly.[10]

13

Financial Cocaine

ALTHOUGH RONALD REAGAN OPPOSED GOVERNMENT BAILOUTS for any industry, his transition team arrived in Washington in January 1981 circulating a memo among themselves about thrifts. "The new Administration," it warned, "may well face a financial crisis not of its own making. . . . Confidence in the entire financial system could evaporate."[1] The conundrum was: could Reagan fulfill the promise to pay depositors at sick thrifts without raising taxes?

Reagan's Treasury secretary, Donald Regan, came from Wall Street, and thrift executives knew that he and his colleagues at Treasury considered S&Ls small-town yahoos given to polyester pants and government subsidies. If a bank wanted to specialize in home loans because of market demand, fine. But Regan and his free-market acolytes viewed specialization via government subsidies as inefficient and unnecessary now that the nation's secondary mortgage markets—led by Fannie and Freddie—were so large and robust they made it easy for commercial banks to compete in home lending. Many in the Reagan White House thought a federally subsidized thrift industry was obsolete. "The whole idea that we need specialized institutions to deal in home mortgages probably deserves re-examination," chirped the *Wall Street Journal*'s editors in June 1981.[2] Still, Regan needed to deal with a sagging industry, one that had big campaign contributors to Reagan. In May 1981, he asked his newly hired assistant Treasury secretary for domestic finance, Roger Mehle, to find a solution. Mehle soon had a eureka moment: S&Ls were insolvent—balance-sheet liabilities exceeded assets—but the deregulation of interest rates coupled with deposit insurance kept them liquid, enabling them to raise plenty of cash, at least for a while, so they could meet withdrawals, pay their electric and phone bills, and keep their doors open and depositors calm.

The simple solution lay in the difference between net worth, which is a balance sheet problem, and cash flow, which is all about liquidity. With interest rates deregulated, thrifts—no matter how desperate—could raise rates until cash came in the door. Depositors, protected by insurance that made them indifferent to how poorly an institution was run, would flock to get the higher rate regardless of whether the thrift operated in a risky manner. The industry was like a college student with zero savings, a maxed-out credit card, and thirty dollars in his pocket. He owed more than he could pay, but he could still use the cash that night to go to dinner with friends. The thrifts could party on as long as regulators didn't pull the plug or their depositors didn't demand their money all at once and reveal the embarrassing truth that the thrifts' obligations far exceeded their assets. Allowing sick thrifts to offer high rates might be unsafe—to pay them, the thrifts would need to make commensurately risky investments—but obliging regulators at the Federal Home Loan Bank Board, appointed by the free-market president, could be counted on to look the other way.

Once interest rates came down, Mehle argued, the pressure would ease and profitability would return to much of the industry, helping restore its net worth and lower the taxpayer liability. Until then, the cash influx bought the administration time to embark on a longer-term solution to the industry's interest-rate mismatch. The root of the problem? Regulations required the industry to concentrate in home loans—long-term lending—when its source of cash, deposits, had become short-term and highly volatile. The solution: a regimen of deregulation enabling the industry to diversify out of home loans and thus become less vulnerable to interest-rate swings. Thrifts, in short, could become commercial banks. "This is an earnings problem, not a cash flow problem," Mehle said.[3] The White House loved his plan.

Deposit insurance law demanded that regulators of either a thrift or a commercial bank close insolvent institutions, a requirement that tacitly recognized the need to limit taxpayers' liability. So, to keep insolvent thrifts open, regulators, with Congress's help, used accounting tricks to make the balance sheets of sick thrifts look healthy. Government officials could thus be in technical compliance with the law. At the same time, the White House, with Congress's help, embarked on an aggressive strategy to diversify thrifts out of home loans. This included selling them to buyers with the promise of allowing the buyers to diversify into all manner of financial services, and letting the thrifts themselves enter any and all new businesses. They hoped that together these schemes would erase the lines of a distinct S&L industry that was so vulnerable to interest-rate swings.

The centerpiece of the accounting trickery was paper: federal certificates— IOUs issued by the Federal Savings and Loan Insurance Corporation, first on its own and then with congressional approval—that thrifts could count as capital and which the insurance fund promised to redeem for cash if needed. If a thrift's obligations to depositors and other creditors exceeded its assets by $1 million, for example, FSLIC would issue a note for $3 million. The institution now would appear to have the resources to meet its obligations and still have $2 million left over. In exchange, the thrift would build up reserves until the IOU was no longer needed and could be torn up.

The problem was that until they were torn up, the notes were a taxpayer obligation, and as such they would have to appear on the federal budget, increasing the U.S. deficit. That would defeat the purpose of the plan. So the White House, overruling its own accountants in the Office of Management and Budget, decided that because the notes were not cash outlays, they would not be included in the budget. Only FSLIC's cash transactions would be included.

The U.S. government (mostly) uses accrual-basis accounting, with money owed to and by the government recorded as obligations occurred, regardless of when any cash changes hands. Using cash-basis accounting just for the IOUs was classic apples-to-oranges accounting tomfoolery. The Reagan White House employed other tricks as well. When two sick thrifts merged, for example, the resulting bank was allowed to book the resulting larger negative net worth as an asset to be written off slowly over time. None of this accounting chicanery of "spending without counting" fooled Wall Street, which found the accounting for IOUs ridiculous. Quipped an investment banker to the *Wall Street Journal*: "They'd issue a piece of paper that says I owe you some money if you need it, and I'm doing it this way because I don't have enough money. How dumb do they think people are?"[4]

In the wake of the 1929 crash, Congress intended accounting principles to provide investors—and regulators—with a standard they could use to compare firms and judge business performance. While generally accepted accounting rules aren't perfect, and no company's books are 100 percent accurate at any given moment, they are reasonably so, in part because generally accepted

accounting principles, or GAAP, require firms to be consistent in the application of the rules. Consistency ensures that investors can gauge a company's
performance over time and compare it to that of peers and other industries. That
would be impossible if companies switched the rules they used each quarter
according to what cast them in the best light. Now that GAAP presented political problems, however, the White House changed the rules. It called its new
bookkeeping "regulatory accounting principles," or RAP, to distinguish it from
GAAP. Wall Street promptly called it "CRAP." Said one S&L merger specialist,
"I've never seen a government agency undertake such hokum with such relish."[5]

Mehle's plan, while expedient, turned regulatory thinking on its head. As a
rule, bank regulators consider it safe to allow solvent institutions long on net
worth but short on cash to stay in business via loans from the Federal Reserve.
But the Federal Reserve frowns on supplying cash for liquidity to institutions
with little or no net worth—in the patois of Wall Street, "lending into a hole."
Officials there know that unless dealt with quickly, financial sickness tends to
worsen and infect other financial firms. That's why the deposit insurance law
effectively requires regulators to close federally insured institutions when they
approach insolvency—a net worth of zero. It's a financial quarantine, to prevent
illness from spreading. If unchecked, it will inevitably spread to taxpayers.

Keeping dead thrifts alive reversed that principle, maintaining institutions
that had lots of cash but no or even negative net worth. As a policy it also
amounted to a bailout of the executives who ran these zombie institutions,
creating moral hazard for those in charge because they continued in their high-
paying jobs, suffering no pain as their banks fell into insolvency. Moral hazard
encouraged reckless behavior. Executives with nothing to lose and everything
to gain took bigger and bigger gambles and fell further down the slippery slope.
This magnified moral hazard for depositors: they not only didn't care whether
federally insured thrifts were well run; they wanted to put their money into
those paying the highest interest, which under the Reagan White House's new
forbearance plan were the sickest of the sick.

Estimates of the industry's negative worth quickly shot up to $178 billion,
giving Federal Reserve Board Chair Volcker a coughing fit as he accidentally
inhaled his cigar smoke on hearing the figure. The FSLIC had only $8.5 billion
to back thrifts with deposits of $600 billion to $700 billion. But, asked Office
of Management and Budget Chief Lawrence Kudlow (now Trump's National
Economic Council director), what good was talking about it?[6]

It only added to the disaster that the White House pressed banking agencies to reduce their examination staffs as part of the president's promise to shrink government. From 1980 to 1984, at the height of the deregulatory frenzy, everyone complied but the Federal Reserve Board. Now there were fewer rules *and* fewer police. The examiners who remained, often recent college graduates earning $14,000 a year or less, had little experience with the complexities of financial fraud and incompetence, especially as practiced by those with expensive suits and six-figure salaries.

White House officials, meanwhile, unwittingly furthered the lobbying goals of the industry they disdained. Thrift executives would have preferred a direct, no-strings-attached taxpayer bailout that would rescue even the sickest thrifts, but they eventually warmed to Mehle's stealth version of the same thing. Zombie thrifts and their lobbyists even became addicted to his plan, with some dubbing the accounting tricks and IOUs "financial cocaine." Keeping dead thrifts alive strengthened the S&Ls' numbers and thus their lobbying might. Industry executives used that power—and FSLIC's continuous funding shortage—to keep their lucrative jobs and taxpayer-subsidized advantages by slowing the Treasury's efforts to dismantle insolvent thrifts. Government help wasn't socialism, they argued; it was an endorsement of home ownership. In addition to keeping the dead alive, however, Mehle's plan came with a bonus: it gave the thrifts more freedom than their commercial banking rivals had, allowing savings and loans to zip ahead of competitors in the race to offer consumers a full suite of financial products. A full-fledged bailout at the start of the 1980s might have lacked that advantage.

Federal law mandated the closing of insolvent thrifts. FSLIC officials interpreted the law to mean they could either sell insolvent institutions, merge them with healthy companies, or close them and pay off depositors. FSLIC officials took this to mean they could choose whatever option was cheapest for the government, and they slanted the math in favor of mergers and sales. They might inflate the cost of an S&L shutdown by ignoring the money the government would recover from the sale of the closed institution's assets, or they might fail to figure in the cost if a merger later failed. Such calculations led to very few closings at a time the government could ill afford any.[7]

From 1934, when deposit insurance was created, until 1980, the Federal Home Loan Bank Board had had to resolve only 165 problem thrift cases.[8] In

Reagan's first two years in office, a thousand S&Ls disappeared. Many were merged or bought privately with the government's blessing but with no federal aid, with buyers happily chalking up the cost of resuscitating a dead bank as the price of admission to a fully deregulated financial business. But nearly half were transferred to new owners with help from the thrift deposit insurance fund, often with IOUs in lieu of cash.

As thrifts expanded their offerings but shrank in number, they and their cousins in commercial banking underwent another change. Their profitability relied increasingly on income from fees—from ATMs, bounced checks, and credit cards—rather than on income from loans, that is, from the difference between what it cost to borrow money to make a loan and what a loan earned. This applied to Fannie and Freddie too. They had earned a profit from the difference between what a mortgage they owned paid them in interest and the interest they paid to borrow money to buy that mortgage. But with inflation rates higher than interest rates on mortgages, Fannie and Freddie were losing money, even with their comparatively low borrowing costs. They were threatened by the same interest-rate mismatch that bedeviled thrifts. Soon after its creation, in 1970, Freddie Mac found a solution. It stopped holding on to the mortgages it bought from thrifts and instead bundled them into collateralized bonds called mortgage-backed securities, which it sold to investors. Freddie's profits came from the fees it charged investors to guarantee against default the loans collateralizing the bonds. As a result, it was relatively unaffected by the interest-rate squeeze. Not so Fannie, whose borrowing costs, though cheaper than any private company could match, soon reached double-digit rates that overshadowed the single-digit returns it earned on the home loans it owned. As the thrift industry bled, Fannie bled too. By the start of the 1980s it was losing $1 million a day. It soon embraced Freddie's model.

Armed with this new business model of creating bonds backed by mortgages and earning a fee for insuring the underlying mortgages against default, Fannie and Freddie brought efficiency to the secondary market while supplying fresh cash to lenders. This made more money available to home buyers, lowering their borrowing costs. By helping lenders manage the interest-rate risks associated with home loans, it also enticed more lenders into the residential mortgage business. An efficient market should have lowered the profit that any single institution could make on home loans and led to fewer institutions with larger market share. The administration's misuse of accounting and deposit insurance did the opposite by keeping sick institutions alive.

Richard F. Syron, special assistant to Fed Chair Volcker, wrote to Mehle in August 1981: "Expanding the powers of savings and loans raises a number of difficult and complex public policy questions, including the treatment of the industry in relation to other financial institutions and whether specialized lenders should continue to be a feature of our financial structure."[9] In other words, the policy of deregulating thrifts might be doing more harm than good, and not just to taxpayers.

Robert McCormick, an Oklahoma banker who was president of the lobby group representing small and medium-size commercial banks, wrote to Treasury Secretary Regan on June 23, 1982: "If anything, giving thrifts these powers will diminish the safety and soundness of these troubled institutions over the short term as they scramble for on-the-job training in the slipperiest of economic times; times in which the origin of sound, profitable commercial loans is far from easy."[10] Thrifts, he warned, had not yet "digested" the new powers they were granted in the 1980 law. More than anything else, he and his peers in commercial banking were angry that the unfair competition from the zombie thrift population had been created and sustained by a Republican president who professed laissez-faire capitalism.

President Reagan made matters worse by pushing through Congress in 1981, as his first major legislative effort, a massive tax shelter for real estate investments. This shelter fueled a financial frenzy as thrifts, banks, and insurance companies competed to lend money for shopping centers, condominiums, and other developments built to take advantage of the tax break, not to respond to consumer demand. The tax change artificially pushed up real estate prices, prompting calls for further deregulation so thrifts could take direct ownership positions in these seemingly lucrative projects. At the same time, thrift executives assumed that oil prices would continue rising and fuel a never-ending economic boom. From 1975 to 1981, oil prices had shot from $7.64 to $35.53 a barrel. Many thrift executives, thinking they would go as high as $100 a barrel, approved loans on that basis, violating a basic tenet of banking: never lend on the expectation that prices will rise.

Oil prices fell instead, as the balloon of speculation was pricked. In Dallas, one thrift had built condominiums on I–30 as fast as construction crews could work, even though half the completed units were vacant. Cars were towed from a junkyard and parked in empty driveways to create an illusion of financial health, but this was contradicted by the signs of desperation motorists could see from the highway: NOW LEASING! TWO MONTHS FREE RENT! THREE MONTHS FREE RENT! NO DEPOSIT! LOW RENT! Row after row of apartments stood empty.

Regulators tried to assure themselves that no one would purposely run his or her own company into the ground. They soon learned that many people end up doing just that for short-term gains. The risk was especially high in publicly traded firms, where the money at stake was someone else's. Behind the I–30 disaster stood Danny Faulkner, whom the *Dallas Morning News* described as "one of Dallas society's most colorful characters . . . [he] transformed himself from an illiterate Mississippi house painter into a high-roller known for traveling by Rolls-Royce and helicopter." His exploits "bankrupted five savings and loans and eventually cost the U.S. government $1 billion." They also landed him in jail for fraud.[11] One eccentric Austin thrift owner, Stanley E. Adams, became so enthusiastic about growth that he filed an application to open a branch on the moon, picking as a site a crater in the Sea of Tranquility. Back on Earth, he talked of building the tallest office building in China.

When the bottom fell out of the real estate market in Texas, California, and Colorado, oil cities suddenly found themselves glutted with homes. Some had a ten-year oversupply of office space. Texans converted the interest-rate squeeze into a joke about an Aggie gas station owner who bought fuel at fifty cents a gallon, sold it for forty-five cents, and hoped to make up the difference on volume. Thrifts that regulators had encouraged to expand into new ventures became epicenters of loss in every region. In the oil patch, many thrifts had perfected the art of "daisy chains," the repeated selling of loans to one another to inflate their price and with the goal of preventing regulators from realizing how many loans were in default. Executives at Empire Savings and Loan of Mesquite, Texas, bought land for $1 million in 1982 and sold it six months later for $16 million. Over two weeks in November 1982, investigators found, Empire and its partners used repeated sales to each other to inflate the price of another parcel of land from $3.2 million to $96 million.

Another Dallas thrift, Sunbelt Savings, was controlled by Edwin T. McBirney, nicknamed "Gunbelt" for his Wild West business style. Described by the *Los Angeles Times* as "high strung and jet fueled," McBirney had a reputation as a gambler in his social life as well, making frequent trips to the casinos of Las Vegas, often with an entourage of executives and Sunbelt clients. Sunbelt operated a fleet of seven airplanes and paid tens of thousands of dollars for McBirney's limousine bills. Texans in the financial services industry talked about his parties for years afterward, like the Halloween party at his palatial home in 1984, when McBirney dressed up like a king, served lion and antelope meat to hundreds of guests, and hired a pair of disco singers known as Two Tons of Fun to provide the entertainment. Sunbelt picked up the tab. Even the downturn in oil prices didn't deter McBirney, who in March 1986 flew several dozen executives and other guests to Las Vegas for a weekend at the Dunes. Recounted in lurid detail in *Texas Monthly* a year later, the party's entertainment on Saturday night began when "four women came into the room and began a strip-tease act. Once disrobed," according to the article, "they proceeded to perform sexual acts on some of the businessmen." Except for the cost of the prostitutes, which McBirney's lawyer insisted was paid from McBirney's and others' pockets, the outing was billed to Sunbelt. By that June, Sunbelt had gone from one of Texas's fastest-growing S&Ls to the sixth costliest failure of a federally insured institution ever (as of 2018), at a cost of nearly $3.8 billion.[12]

The 1981 tax law hadn't just exacerbated the thrift crisis. Budget counters saw that within a few years it would produce a deficit four times larger than the highest deficit during the Carter administration. With a budget hole of his own making, not one he could blame on Democrats, Reagan pushed Congress in 1986 to end the real estate tax break, turning off the spigot as abruptly as it had been turned on five years earlier and closing off a source of funds that sick thrifts had become addicted to.

Soon, the industry's losses from an interest-rate mismatch became losses on bad assets. Losses—and taxpayer liability—rose, as did fraud. That's when Keating entered, with the help of the five senators and the future Fed chair but then private-sector economist and consultant Alan Greenspan, who wrote letters to regulators praising Keating's business skills. As for "the Keating Five," a Senate Ethics Committee probe turned up little, and the senators denied wrongdoing, saying they didn't trade favors for money but merely acted for a constituent who claimed that regulators had unfairly targeted him. But the link to Keating hurt all five senators' reputations and dogged them for years, as late as John McCain's presidential bid against Barack Obama in 2008. Keating died in 2014.

Interest rates that had peaked at 21.5 percent in December 1980, began to fall in 1982, but not far or fast enough to help the thrifts. The phony accounting that had bought time had made the situation worse: Instead of growing out of their interest-rate mismatch, the industry grew into a costlier problem of bad assets.

A *Washington Post* editorial in July 1985, commenting on an internal report written for federal thrift regulators, provided the first public acknowledgment that the Reagan administration's policy of allowing insolvent institutions to stay open and diversify was increasing the scope and cost of the thrift industry's problem. "The cause is no longer high interest rates, but high-risk loans going sour," wrote the editors. "It's Congress that is going to have to answer the basic questions. Should the regulations be enforced, and should the weakest S&Ls be forced to fold? The right answer is yes."[13]

As the Maryland and Ohio thrift catastrophes made headlines in the mid-1980s, White House officials realized they had to take drastic action if Vice President Bush were to win the presidency in 1988. The situation had so deteriorated that they would have to close an estimated 400 of the worst of the worst thrifts before the election, and eventually as many as an additional 1,000. These 1,400 or so represented 40 percent of the industry and held 43 percent of its assets. But closing several hundred would do until after the election. The solution: a $10.8 billion bailout that administration officials knew was a band-aid, but which they cheerfully called a "recapitalization" of the insurance fund.[14]

In a scheme worthy of Rube Goldberg, the Federal Home Loan Banks would donate $3 billion from their profits, which the government would use to buy twenty- and thirty-year Treasury bonds that, on maturity, would be worth $10.8 billion. Then, through a new federal entity constructed so that its obligations would not appear on the budget, the government would use the Treasury bonds as collateral to borrow $10.8 billion from the private sector over five years. Interest on this debt would be paid from the regular fees the FSLIC charged the S&Ls it insured. Under this arrangement, spending would go up only as the deposit insurance fund spent the $10.8 billion to close insolvent thrifts, offsetting income registered by the fund when it received the money, for a net deficit impact of zero.

Authorizing the scheme, President Reagan signed the Competitive Equality Banking Act into law on August 10, 1987, saying, "From the outset, our guiding principle in working with the Congress on this bill has been to avoid a taxpayer bailout—as was the case in both Ohio and Maryland—for an industry that has the wherewithal to help itself. This legislation vindicates that principle. The Congress is clearly on notice that industry resources are to be relied upon to finance the [thrift deposit insurance] operations, now and in the future." It was more fiction to buy time.

President Ronald Reagan greets President-elect George H. W. Bush, *left,* upon his arrival to the White House on November 10, 1988. AP Photo/Charles Tasnadi.

In addition to the mini-bailout, the new law eroded the rules even further. It closed a loophole that had allowed a nonfinancial company to act as a bank by making loans but not also taking deposits, thus evading the legal definition of a bank. Wall Street had called these creatures "non-bank banks." But it allowed existing non-bank banks to stay open. More important, by prohibiting new non-bank bank entrants, it made the thrift charter even more valuable—now it was the only game in town for a company, financial or not, that wanted to offer a full range of financial products under one roof. It also blew a hole through restrictions on crossing state lines, on what products could be sold, on who could own a thrift—all rules that still applied to commercial banks. By this time thrifts were identical to commercial banks in all but name, but they played ball on a field that was anything but level.[15] Commercial banks and others scrambled over the next decade to own thrifts. Meanwhile, as Reagan reassured the public there was no national thrift crisis, his staff scrambled to contain it and plan for how Bush would resolve it once he became president. The one certainty was that it would be the largest bailout taxpayers had ever seen.

To keep depositors calm amid this mini-bailout, Congress included language in the new law saying that the "full faith and credit" of the United States stood behind all federal deposit insurance. This had been true from the start, as the first FDIC head, Leo Crowley, tried to explain to Senator Carter Glass fifty years earlier. Premiums paid by the banks and thrifts funded the federal insurance system, but in times of stress and panic, when the calming effect of deposit insurance was most needed, premiums would not cover the full potential cost of keeping the system solvent. The 1987 bailout law now stated explicitly that the United States would make up any shortfalls.

Another drama was also unfolding. To keep the IOUs issued by the thrift insurance fund off the U.S. budget, the Office of Management and Budget had said they were not backed by the federal government. Wall Street—and the buyers of ailing thrifts who accepted the IOUs in lieu of cash—didn't believe it and proceeded as though the notes were backed by taxpayers. But as the debate over the 1987 law unfolded, the public statements by the White House and thrift executives that $10.8 billion would be enough to solve the industry's woes became less credible. People in the know worried that the notes were in fact worthless. The OMB, to admit reality and restore confidence in its own integrity, reversed itself and said the notes *did* have the full faith and credit of the government and therefore had to be included in the deficit—though OMB officials cleverly used a loophole in how the budget was scored to keep the notes from actually appearing on the budget until the next fiscal year, after the election. The OMB's decision, coupled with the bailout legislation, produced a remarkable result: a provision in the legislation exempted Reagan's chief thrift regulator, M. Danny Wall, chairman of the Federal Home Loan Bank Board, from OMB control over his issuance of IOUs to sick thrifts. With the OMB's decision now tying those IOUs directly to taxpayer dollars, Wall had the power to draw directly from the U.S. Treasury without limit, interference, or permission from anyone. It was a first in U.S. history. Many Republicans and Democrats expressed horror but none seriously tried to stop it; the direness of the situation and the complicity of both Republicans and Democrats made that impossible. One high-ranking Treasury official described the scheme as "a printing press out of control," though his colleagues had lobbied for it. "What the Federal Home Loan Bank Board has come to symbolize is the corruption of our constitutional process," said Rep. Jim Leach (R-Iowa). Rep. Henry B.

Gonzalez (D-Tex.) asked, "How can it be that an individual or an agency would have the power to commit the Treasury to [tens of billions of] dollars without going through the authorization and appropriation process, which even the President can't do?"[16]

To obtain industry's support for the bailout legislation, which the White House had to have to get it passed, Reagan's team very reluctantly agreed to give the thrifts $800 million to reimburse them for an increase in insurance premiums they had paid to help shore up the fund. So angry was the White House at what they considered blackmail that they insisted the funding in the bill be stated as $10.8 billion rather than a round $11 billion in the hope historians ever after would ask "why .8?" and be reminded of the industry's behavior.

Winning passage of the $10.8 billion mini-bailout required support from Democrat Fernand St. Germain, who headed the House Banking Committee, and Republican Jake Garn, who headed the Senate Banking Committee. The two had little in common. St. Germain, a self-proclaimed protector of the little guy, had a taste for prostitutes—S&L lobbyists made sure he had professional lady companions at all business outings. Lobbyists joked the securities industry took care of him on Mondays, Wednesdays, and Fridays, and thrifts took over on Tuesdays, Thursdays, and Saturdays. "And on Sunday we all rested," quipped a former thrift official. Garn, a champion of business and free enterprise, preferred to have his ego stroked, so for him industry funded the Garn Institute in his home state of Utah to examine finance issues; the *Wall Street Journal* called it a "magnet for S&L money" and "influence-peddling" to curry favor with Garn and others in Congress. The two lawmakers did share one belief: the thrift industry needed help.[17]

The two lawmakers had led Congress to pass the Garn–St. Germain Act of 1982, sanctioning the use of IOUs and further relaxing restrictions on what thrifts could sell while protecting the industry's tax breaks. The 1982 act was the third and final step in deregulating the thrift industry during the early 1980s.

The first step had been the 1980 law that phased out interest-rate caps, increased deposit insurance coverage to $100,000, and permitted thrifts to exercise broad new powers similar to those of commercial banks.

The second step occurred as federal thrift regulators relaxed the rules. Lawmakers in the 1930s had not anticipated that an industry that lobbied for tax breaks and other subsidies in exchange for focusing on home lending would ever stray from that mandate and want to sell credit cards, commercial loans, securities, and insurance; open additional branches within states and across state borders; and be owned by clothing retailers or motorcycle manufacturers. Though Congress had to loosen laws to allow some of these kinds of diversification, federal regulators often simply unwrote rules that their predecessors had put in place to mimic for thrifts the legal restrictions Congress had placed on banks.

The third step came when President Reagan signed the Garn–St. Germain Act. At the Rose Garden signing ceremony, he commented, "I think we've hit the jackpot." Thrifts now could invest 30 percent of federally insured funds in consumer loans, up from the 20 percent permitted in the 1980 law. They could invest 40 percent in nonresidential mortgages, up from 20 percent permitted in 1980; 10 percent in loans to business, up from zero; and 10 percent in leasing activities. The law thus enabled an industry created to specialize in home lending to invest 90 percent of its assets in activities other than residential mortgages.

How did the thrift industry fare so well legislatively after the dimensions of the crisis and the industry's outsized abuses became clear? Money. As with all financial lobbyists then as now, most of the industry's political action committees (PACs) gave to both parties and often to both candidates in a single race. PACs formed by thrifts or their lobbyists contributed $4.5 million to House and Senate candidates between 1983 and 1988. Members of the Senate and House banking committees, including Garn and St. Germain, were the top beneficiaries.

14

Cover-Up and Bailout

AT A NOVEMBER 1987 BREAKFAST MEETING IN New Orleans hosted by the junk bond specialists at Drexel Burnham Lambert, several prominent thrift executives, unaware that a reporter was in the room, openly discussed the need for a taxpayer bailout, even though they were publicly insisting no such action was needed. The executives talked of a secret fifty-page plan they had prepared that called for four new federal agencies to spend billions of taxpayer dollars to warehouse bad real estate until prices recovered; an oil import fee to subsidize the distressed economies of the oil-producing states; and reinstatement of the 1981 real estate tax break. The industry's strategy was simple: it would lobby against any bailout plan that required major funding from the industry. They hoped to buy time until the cost of resolving the crisis grew so big no one would expect healthy thrifts to pay for it. Only the taxpayers would have pockets deep enough.

Federal Home Loan Bank Board Chair M. Danny Wall colluded in the deception. Wall, a former chief of staff to Senator Garn, told Congress in mid-1988 that the federal thrift deposit insurance fund would accumulate $42.5 billion in premiums over the next ten years, while bailing out problem thrifts would cost just $30.9 billion. A *Washington Post* story revealed that Wall had discounted the costs by a large percentage—called a net-present-value calculation—without also discounting, by the same amount, the funds available to handle them. This made the costs to resolve the problem seem smaller and the resources to handle it appear larger, especially relative to one another. Good accounting requires either that both numbers be discounted—and by the same percentage—or that neither be. Wall's assistant Karl Hoyle defended the calculation, saying, "That may not be the way to do it, but that's the way we do it." Wall never used the method again. His task was to hide the problem, not become even more of a laughing stock.[1]

Wall found his unlimited draw on the U.S. Treasury enormously helpful in issuing IOUs to entice people to acquire failing institutions. From January through August of 1988, the bank board closed, merged, or sold 101 thrifts, with half the actions taken in the last three weeks of August. The deals were cemented by nearly $10 billion in IOUs for those buying the thrifts. By issuing most of the notes after mid-August, Wall helped the administration comply with the Gramm-Rudman-Hollings Balanced Budget and Emergency Deficit Control Act, which required automatic spending cuts if the federal deficit exceeded a stated target; a quirk in the law allowed notes issued after August 15 to not count in the 1988 deficit.

In late September, Senate Banking Committee Chair William Proxmire (D-Wisc.) became the first elected official in Washington to say publicly that a huge taxpayer bailout was needed. But industry and White House efforts to obscure the size of the problem had worked: the thrift mess didn't become an issue in the 1988 presidential campaign. The Democratic nominee, Michael S. Dukakis, brought up the issue once to blame Reagan and Bush for pushing S&Ls into disastrous investments. Democrats urged Dukakis to drop the issue, knowing that congressmen like St. Germain and speaker of the House Jim Wright of Texas were also to blame. Political reporters, largely uninformed about the thrift crisis and bored by it, didn't pursue the issue.

Just before voters went to the polls, the thrift industry held its annual convention, this time in Hawaii, with lavish dinners that even some executives thought inappropriate given the industry's finances. Bob Hope, who often traveled to cheer military troops under fire, regaled a packed audience of convention-goers. "I know the savings and loans are in trouble," he joked. "My checks show a picture of my branch manager standing on a ledge." The crowd loved it. At the end of his performance Hope asked for a show of hands for Dukakis supporters. He counted a dozen or so. He asked for a show of hands for Bush, and the room went wild. "Banking," said Hope. "That's Republican."[2]

By election day in November, Wall had not closed the hundreds of sick thrifts he needed to close by year's end, when tax breaks and other subsidies for investors provided in the 1987 bailout legislation would expire. So he conducted a flurry of negotiations with Wall Street titans, and between December 20 and December 31, struck deals for nearly sixty institutions. The buyers included Revlon cosmetics billionaire Ronald Perelman, Texas oil billionaire Robert Bass, and bond legend Lew Ranieri, who had earned millions of dollars for the investment banking firm of Salomon Brothers under a federal law that enabled thrifts to receive big tax breaks by selling money-losing mortgages to Wall Street for cents on the dollar.[3]

Wall painted the deals—dubbed McDeals—as far better for taxpayers than they were. Including tax breaks, for example, the government promised to give Perelman $6 billion in federal aid for the thrift he bought, not the $5 billion Wall publicly announced. The deal with Bass cost at least $4.8 billion in government subsidies, not the $1.7 billion Wall first estimated. Congressional auditors found the government would have been better off waiting for Congress to supply the necessary funding to shut the thrifts. Wall's estimate that the deals cost taxpayers $40 billion soon rose to $95 billion. As he crafted deals and insisted that a taxpayer bailout wasn't in the offing, Treasury officials worked with the Bush transition team to craft a plan to solve the thrift crisis once and for all, with what would be the costliest taxpayer bailout in U.S. history. Even the 2008 bailout during the Great Recession, though nominally much bigger, would end up being largely repaid and thus costing taxpayers less. At the Republican convention that August, Bush declared, "Read my lips: no new taxes." He did so even as his staff was crafting a bailout that would be paid for with deficit spending.

Bush's staff coordinated with the Federal Reserve on the plan, which Treasury officials printed on plain paper rather than official stationery so they could disavow it if it leaked to the press. The new president would unveil it as soon as he took office, in the hope that voters would forget about it by the next election. The plan's architects were two Harvard professors, Robert Glauber and David Mullins, known as the Brady Boys after Nicholas Brady, who had hired them and who would become Bush's Treasury secretary.

Glauber and Mullins had met Brady when he chaired the investment bank Dillon, Read & Company. A good friend of Vice President Bush, Brady had been asked by President Reagan to head a commission to study the stock market crash of mid-October 1987. Glauber and Mullins wrote the commission's report, concluding that the crash had been caused by computerized, indexed trading that relied on unregulated options and other derivatives. A *Fortune* article captured the reaction to their handiwork: "Though the Brady Commission's final report was unwieldy, sometimes confusing, and laced with calls for regulation that appalled both the Fed and laissez-faire-minded Reaganites, it was highly regarded for its revelations about how markets behave. The commission established for the first time that the stock, futures, and options markets acted together."[4]

Choosing Mullins and Glauber to lead a major administration initiative was ironic, given that during the campaign, Bush had derided Harvard University as a hotbed of mushy-headed liberalism. (He had graduated from Yale.) And the two unabashed elitists clearly lacked political sense, a naïveté that worked in their favor: they crafted the bailout package they considered best for the country, without regard to what would play in Congress. Coordinating the Treasury's S&L bailout efforts with those of the banking agencies was Richard Breeden. A graduate of Stanford University and Harvard Law School, Breeden had been a securities lawyer at the white-shoe firm of Cravath, Swain & Moore. As a top aide to Vice President Bush, he had written a report on how to reform financial services. Breeden was one of the most knowledgeable officials in Washington on the thrift crisis, and his approach was more sophisticated and realistic than that of many others in the administration. He understood that moral hazard accompanied deposit insurance and that its guarantee of tax dollars required a government role in overseeing the financial system. As Breeden saw it, that role was to make sure banks operated fairly and safely and that the gamblers who ran them risked their own money before tapping taxpayers'.

On the sunny morning of February 6, 1989, reporters filed from the West Wing of the White House into elevators and down corridors to an auditorium in the Old Executive Office Building. There President Bush stood before television cameras to announce to the public what many Reagan and Bush administration officials had long known was inevitable: the thrift industry faced a $90 billion problem, he said, and taxpayers would have to contribute $40 billion to fix it. Even this greatly understated the size of the problem: Bush's aides knew the actual cost would be many multiples bigger. "Nothing is without pain," Bush said.[5]

Within weeks, the estimated total cost, including interest, had risen to $126 billion, then $157 billion, then $166 billion. Even these calculations were suspect: the White House would not say whether it assumed a thirty- or forty-year payoff; who would pay interest charges; or even what discount rate it used. Republican and Democratic lawmakers alike put the cost at $300 billion or more. With interest, the tab could exceed $500 billion in ten years, or, if interest rates rose significantly, more than $1 trillion over several decades, enough by some calculations at the time to add $13 billion a year in interest—forever—to the national debt.[6]

Headlines of rising cost estimates prompted White House officials to think how to minimize the burden on taxpayers. Mullins and Glauber suggested forcing customers of banks and thrifts to pay a tax on deposits. Intellectually the proposal had merit because the people who used the service—deposit insurance—would pay for it. Politically, it was dead on arrival. The two professors hadn't briefed the chair of the Federal Deposit Insurance Corporation, L. William Seidman, an Ivy Leaguer whose unpretentious straight talk gave him a unique facility with the press. Typical of his no-nonsense style, he bicycled to work from Georgetown in a uniform of tan chinos, dark blue blazer, and loafers.

When Seidman learned of the proposal from a *Washington Post* reporter, he dubbed it the "reverse toaster theory," a reference to the days when interest rates were capped so thrifts gave away small appliances to lure depositors from competitors. The "toaster" line made headlines nationwide, instantly killing the idea but also informing the general public that one way or another, the average working person was going to pay for the mess. "I think it is ironic that in the first week of the new administration, they came up with a new tax," said thrift executive Ross Towne. "I don't care what they call it, it's a tax. Whatever happened to all that 'Read my lips' stuff?"[7]

Before the toaster story broke, mention of the S&L debacle put the average citizen to sleep. Afterward, *Saturday Night Live* did a skit on the S&L mess, and Phil Donahue devoted an entire show to it. One of his outraged guests drew cheers when he asked, with no hint of irony, "Why can't the government pay for these debts instead of taxpayers?"[8]

Four-fifths of the nation's S&Ls experienced net withdrawals in January, a loss one government economist attributed entirely to the toaster stories. The hoopla embarrassed Mullins and Glauber, but their political flat-footedness raised awareness, mitigating the political clout of the thrift industry and making the bailout more palatable to Congress. Once everyone understood that the bankers—or more precisely, their depositors—would be rescued with tax dollars, voter anger trumped the lobbyists' campaign contributions and efforts to stop the plan, and the Bush White House had an easier time getting the legislation passed. "It was great," Glauber said. Brady gave Glauber and Mullins commemorative toasters. Glauber kept his in his office. Mullins brought his home, boasting it was the first home appliance he ever owned.[9]

For others, voter anger had a less pleasant outcome. In late spring both Speaker of the House Wright and the majority whip, Tony Coehlo (D-Calif.), were forced to resign because of a House Ethics Committee probe into their financial relationships with thrifts and, in Coehlo's case, to junk-bond king Michael Milken. Republican Newt Gingrich, then a back-bench House member from Georgia, pestered the committee to undertake the probe, despite warnings by GOP consultants that doing so would backfire because Republican closets also held plenty of S&L skeletons. (In 1997, the same ethics committee reprimanded Gingrich, who had by then become House speaker, and required him to pay an unprecedented $300,000 fine after he admitted breaking House rules by "failing to ensure that financing for two projects would not violate federal tax law and by giving the House ethics committee false information."[10])

Bush's bailout bill called for hundreds of thrifts to be closed and for the Federal Home Loan Bank system to be dismantled. The function of chartering and overseeing federal thrifts would be transferred to a new agency, the Office of Thrift Supervision, housed within Treasury on an equal footing with the Office of the Comptroller of the Currency, which chartered and oversaw federal commercial banks. The law also merged the thrift deposit insurance fund into the FDIC and essentially banned the bogus accounting the S&Ls had used. It spun off Freddie Mac into a congressionally chartered, shareholder-owned company just like Fannie Mae. And in a change that would supply easy credit for the new millennium's housing bubble, it allowed commercial banks as well as thrifts to borrow from the regional Federal Home Loan Banks if the money funded home loans. The twelve regional banks would be regulated as Fannie and Freddie were, that is, as government-sponsored enterprises, or GSEs. The law also created a new agency, the Resolution Trust Corporation (RTC), to sell loans and property that the government would inherit from the failed thrifts it closed. The RTC's mission was to sell the assets for as much as possible, but to do so without either flooding the market with properties and depressing prices, or artificially withholding properties and inflating prices.

The bailout bill included several million dollars to beef up law enforcement to put crooks who looted S&Ls in jail. It increased the fine for defrauding a financial institution to $1 million per person, per day, per violation. It required all thrifts and banks to have federal insurance, and all institutions with federal insurance to have a federal regulator. President Bush signed it into law on August 9, 1989. Questioned about having hidden the problem from taxpayers, he said, "I'm not inclined to go into any personal blame, simply to say that we've got to solve this problem and we're on the path to doing that." He distanced himself from Wall, refusing to personally thank the man who had done so much of the dirty work to keep the crisis under wraps.[11]

By 1991, the Bush administration had abandoned any pretense of limiting taxpayer liability. "We certainly are concerned about additional costs, and it seems clear there will be higher costs than originally estimated," a White House spokesperson said. "We don't have agreement on how much they will be." In 1996, the General Accounting Office of Congress estimated the final cost of the thrift industry bailout, including interest, at nearly $400 billion, most of it paid by taxpayers.[12] It wasn't the $1 trillion some feared, but it was far greater than the original $40 billion Bush had estimated taxpayers would pay.

Bush hoped that once the bailout package became law, the public would lose interest. But House Banking Committee hearings, televised on C-SPAN in November 1991, provided embarrassing details of how the Reagan-Bush White House had handled the thrift crisis, including the failure of Silverado Banking, Savings and Loan of Denver, where Bush's son Neil had been a director. Neil Bush, lampooned on late-night television, became the literal poster child for the S&L debacle when a political group plastered his face over downtown Washington with demands he be jailed. The Banking Committee hearings shed light on why Silverado was not closed until after the 1988 presidential election: Kermit Mowbray, the regional Federal Home Loan Bank Board regulator for the thrift, testified under oath that Wall's Washington staff had ordered him to wait, even though field examiners had been recommending the action for months. Mowbray signed the letter ordering the seizure of Silverado on November 9, 1988, the day after the election.

The hearings also focused on how lawyers and accountants had aided fraud at S&Ls by allowing executives to "opinion shop" for a professional who would approve whatever the thrift wanted. U.S. District Court Judge Stanley Sporkin had raised the issue, as had Representative (and now Senator) Ron Wyden, a

Democrat from Oregon, who said, "Elephants were walking through the living room and the accountants missed them."[13]

In 1989 the General Accounting Office found that six of eleven auditors it studied—all of them among the nation's biggest—had signed off on inaccurate financial reports, making troubled thrifts look healthier than was the case. It referred several for disciplinary action by regulators and professional audit groups. "They didn't do enough work, period," said the report's author.[14] Keating, for example, hired at least two accounting firms in five years for Lincoln before he found one, Arthur Young, pliant enough to report the financial results he wanted, even if in defiance of reality. Silverado officials told federal examiners in 1986 that they had switched auditors because the new firm, Coopers & Lybrand, was cheaper. In fact, the decision was based on what transactions Coopers would require the thrift to count as losses. In 1985 Silverado reported a loss of $20 million. In 1986, despite a downturn in Colorado real estate, it posted $15 million in profits and its executives pocketed $2.7 million in bonuses.

In 1992 the Cleveland law firm Jones, Day, Reavis & Pogue settled a malpractice suit brought by the FDIC for $16.5 million and agreed to pay $24 million to settle with bondholders in Keating's American Continental Corporation. The law firm of Sidley & Austin settled a malpractice suit with federal thrift regulators for an undisclosed amount, said to be $7.5 million, for its work for Keating. Despite the culpability of lawyers and accountants, the Bush bailout had too many other oxen to gore to include a cleanup of the practices of all of these enablers. That had to wait for the next crisis, involving a company called Enron.

Once lawmakers had dealt with the long-overdue closing of hundreds of thrifts, they focused on barring regulators and politicians (themselves) from ever again hiding insolvencies of federally insured institutions or allowing the cost of resolving them to balloon at taxpayers' expense. In 1991, Congress passed the Federal Deposit Insurance Corporation Improvement Act, requiring regulators and the FDIC to close or resolve problem institutions as soon as possible and at the least cost. Coupled with reforms in the 1989 bailout bill, that meant, in theory, no more zombie banks; in other words, no more IOUs not scored on the budget or other accounting trickery. Still, the new law gave regulators room to keep a sick institution open if doing so would avert a loss of trust in the system and so prevent other runs.[15] Any threat of systemic risk trumped efforts to avoid taxpayer liability.

The U.S. deficit for fiscal 1992, just before Bush's presidency ended, was $290 billion, by far the largest up to that time and more than four times what President Reagan and Vice President Bush inherited in 1981.

One lasting impact of the S&L crisis is that it led Reagan and Congress to dismantle decades-old commercial banking laws. Today, people often think the deregulation of financial services occurred in 1999, when the Gramm-Leach-Bliley Act made it easier for Citibank and Traveler's Insurance to merge. In fact, that law merely gave congressional blessing to changes that Reagan had already put in place, at first so he wouldn't break his campaign promises but then, as the Mehle plan failed, to hide the cost of the S&L bailout until Bush could win the White House. Reagan and Bush lifted geographic, product, and ownership restrictions on thrifts and in the process forced regulators and Congress to allow the rest of the financial services industry to bypass such restrictions and become one-stop financial shops too.

Commercial bank regulators, for example, had barred Sears, Roebuck, from owning a full-service commercial bank, the theory being that Sears might use the bank to unfairly withhold credit from its competitors or provide itself dangerously easy credit terms. But the law said nothing about whether Sears could own a thrift, and S&L regulators permitted it to.

Closing the hundreds of dead thrifts across the country at any time during Reagan's presidency would have bankrupted the thrift insurance fund and required taxpayer money. But closing them sooner rather than later would have made the cost much less. The interest-rate mismatch that defined the first phase of the S&L crisis would have required perhaps $30 to $60 billion in tax dollars to fix. The bad assets of the crisis's second phase cost ten times that.[16]

The savings-and-loan crisis also plowed the ground for financial crises over the next thirty-five years: the Reagan-Bush legacy of hiding the S&L problem to win office upended the 1930s social contract. In their rush to deregulate, policymakers forgot or purposely ignored that taxpayer-funded safety nets require them to police the corporations that profit from using those safety nets.

Once Bush won office, his White House, to his credit, crafted a new philosophy in its bailout bill that recognized regulation as consisting of both rules and oversight, and that the looser one is, the tighter the other must be. White House officials could not talk too loudly about this insight, however, for fear of rebuke from free-market colleagues in the GOP. And Wall Street undermined the idea at every turn. As the thrift crisis evolved from an interest-rate squeeze to a bad-asset problem, Wall Street busily created, with congressional help but little media attention, two new securities—over-the-counter derivatives and mortgage-backed bonds—neither of which had adequate oversight. Both were intended to mitigate the risks of the interest-rate squeeze that had plagued thrifts. Instead, they would amplify those risks to an almost unimaginable degree, largely due to lack of oversight.

15

Russia Defaults

IN SEPTEMBER 1998, BANKERS FROM MORE THAN a dozen Wall Street firms crowded for much of the day in a wood-paneled room in the New York Fed's fortress-like, Renaissance-style building in lower Manhattan. With its proximity to Wall Street, the Federal Reserve Bank of New York interacts daily with the nation's most powerful financial companies, making it second in importance within the sprawling Federal Reserve System only to the Federal Reserve Board in Washington. But on this day, New York Fed President William McDonough took second place to none in confronting what he, Federal Reserve Board Chairman Alan Greenspan, and U.S. Treasury Secretary Robert Rubin considered the biggest threat to the nation's financial system in fifty years.[1]

It was the first day of autumn and an official day of reckoning for the investment and commercial bankers in attendance: they stood to lose billions of dollars in loans and other investments in a giant hedge fund, Long-Term Capital Management. The partners who owned Long-Term, known as "quants" for the complex quantitative formulas they used to analyze markets, had placed huge financial bets on the assumption, among others, that Russia would never default on its bonds. They had bet wrong, and now these partners lacked the money to pay up. The bankers who lent Long-Term money had known for a few weeks that the fund was in trouble, but until a few days earlier they had not understood the enormity of its problems and its potential to bring down not just the firms meeting at the New York Fed that day, but the entire U.S. economy. If Long-Term ran out of money to pay its obligations, it would cause massive losses at other firms, which in turn would be unable to pay their obligations. Losses would ricochet through the financial system.

Only at the meeting did the attendees learn how much Long-Term had borrowed from each of them and, worse, that they might have multiple claims on the same collateral, mostly Treasuries or related securities. They also now understood that if everyone sold whatever collateral they could lay claim to, they would create a market glut that would sink the assets' value and with it what each could recover. The crisis bound each bank's fate to that of the others.[2]

Fed officials had been just as much in the dark, having learned about Long-Term's problems only at the beginning of September, when Bloomberg published a letter the fund had sent to its investors alerting them to its mounting losses. How did Long-Term blindside everyone in the financial elite?

Hedge funds have no legal definition. They are investment pools—typically private partnerships—for the wealthy, essentially lightly regulated mutual funds for the rich.[3] True mutual funds, which are legally defined and more heavily regulated, are investment pools for rank-and-file retail investors. Hedge funds supposedly cater to more sophisticated investors, especially institutional ones such as insurance companies, pension funds, and the firms represented at the New York Fed that afternoon—theoretically savvier financial players who could withstand bigger losses than the average person and who understood full well the risks of investing. Hedge funds like Long-Term operated in the shadow-banking world, where an expanding group of financial institutions do many of the things banks do—borrowing, lending, investing—but are largely unregulated. Shadow banks then as now depend in many ways on federally regulated companies that own federally insured banks. They enjoy—some might say exploit—the benefits of the regulated, taxpayer-insured system without being subject to all of its rules or oversight.

Hedge funds employ many strategies. Long-Term relied on complex formulas, executed by computers, to prowl the markets "to ferret out temporary market price anomalies" in historic relationships among various instruments such as bonds, stocks, and currencies.[4] Because the discrepancies typically were small and short-lived, the hedge fund used derivatives—financial contracts that derive their value from an underlying commodity, security, or currency—to place bets quickly and in large volume. Using derivatives as a proxy, Long-Term could place bets on an asset's future price—such as the Japanese yen's exchange rate with the Russian ruble—without having to buy or sell yen or rubles. By the time one could invest in actual currencies, discrepancies that might be worth a wager would be gone. Derivatives enabled Long-Term to place bets very fast but also, because of the fund's high leverage, in huge dollar amounts.

A derivative is a contract between two people or entities. Sometimes it is between someone who wants to buy an item—say, corn—and another who wants to sell it. These people are hedgers. They use derivatives to manage risk by locking in future prices on a commodity they actually want to buy or sell. Doing so gives them a better idea what their future costs and revenues will be. These buyers and sellers can also take out a derivative on that first derivative, to cushion them in case the price they locked in proves later to be too high or too low.

Not everyone who uses derivatives is a hedger. Often, one or both parties in a contract is a speculator, a person or entity that doesn't want to own or sell the underlying item but wants to bet on its future price pure and simple. Though scorned by Thomas Jefferson, speculators, as Hamilton understood, play an important role in keeping markets liquid. Speculators do this for derivatives by ensuring that there are plenty of buyers and sellers willing to take the other side of a given contract, including and ultimately for true hedgers.

U.S. derivatives markets started in earnest after the Civil War in Chicago, mainly for trading farm products. By the later twentieth century they had grown to include contracts on financial products like stocks and bonds. Myron S. Scholes, who with Robert C. Merton and Fischer Black pioneered what is now called the Black-Scholes mathematical model for valuing derivatives, defines them broadly: "The purest among us might argue that any security is a derivative if its price dynamics depend on the dynamics of some other underlying asset or assets and time."[5] The notion that a financial instrument could be proxy for something else is exactly what unsettled Americans about paper money two centuries earlier. Now it was cutting-edge finance.

The derivatives Long-Term often used were traded "over the counter," Wall Street parlance for an unregulated security, one not traded on an exchange, as stocks or futures are. Over-the-counter derivatives were just private contracts between two parties. Traded "off exchange," these contracts made up an unregulated, "dark" market that was mostly off any financial regulator's radar. By making over-the-counter derivatives easier to value, the Black-Scholes model fueled an explosion in these contracts, enabling the assets underlying these instruments to grow ever more esoteric—derivatives on derivatives on derivatives.

People have long recognized that securities markets need speculators, but also that having too many can turn healthy risk-management into pure gambling and even a rigged game. In 1936, as deflation trapped farmers between low prices and high debt, Congress passed the Commodity Exchange Act, which along with the Securities Exchange Act of 1934, required buyers and sellers of securities and commodities futures contracts to trade in the open, on exchanges that all could see. Such transparency, lawmakers thought, made it harder for traders to manipulate prices. "It should be our national policy to restrict, as far as possible, the use of these exchanges for purely speculative operations," President Roosevelt told Congress. The laws should be "for the protection of investors, for the safeguarding of values, and so far as it may be possible, for the elimination of unnecessary, unwise and destructive speculation."[6] Of course, pure speculation was the raison d'être of hedge funds like Long-Term, which used unregulated derivatives as their tool of choice. The derivatives were unregulated essentially because of a linguistic sleight of hand: Wall Street simply refused to call them "futures," which with few exceptions had by law to be traded on an exchange. With next to no oversight, hedge funds and over-the-counter derivatives lacked the ground rules set in the 1930s for fair, competitive markets. They lacked "all the fundamental templates that we learned from the Great Depression are needed to have markets function smoothly," derivatives lawyer Michael Greenberger said in an interview on *Frontline*.[7] They weren't bound by rules requiring they be traded on an exchange to make prices transparent. They weren't bound by rules requiring record-keeping or that entities making bets first demonstrate they have the financial wherewithal to pay up if needed. The over-the-counter market was the Wild West of finance. Wall Street loved it.

Anyone could play, and over-the-counter speculators proliferated. The over-the-counter derivatives market grew from virtually nothing in the 1980s to $80 trillion by the end of 1998, rivaling its exchange-traded and regulated cousins. (By 2016, the over-the-counter market was worth $500 trillion.)[8]

Long-Term owed its presence in this dark market to creditors and counterparties who lent the hedge fund too much money without knowing, much less challenging, the premises on which it based its trades: that Russia would never default on its debt; that interest rates would move in certain directions; that the International Monetary Fund, as the world's central banker, would resolve financial problems in Asia and Brazil and elsewhere around the globe.[9] And while the hedge fund's trades were diversified among markets, diversity provided little protection in the worldwide financial crisis that hit all markets when Russia did the unthinkable and defaulted in August 1998. Investors the world over ran to safety, shedding riskier securities in favor of safer ones, especially U.S. Treasuries, and destroying Long-Term's precise mathematical predictions.[10] Unease begat unease in a biblical unfolding that became a self-fulfilling prophesy: people thought prices would fall in one security, so they sold all of their holdings in that security, making prices fall. Selling collateral to recoup losses only made markets slide further.

As the turmoil spread, Treasury and Fed officials realized with queasy stomachs that financial relationships that the markets and Long-Term's staff had assumed were uncorrelated suddenly had become highly correlated. In a worldwide crisis of confidence, they moved in unison, and always against Long-Term's favor.

That fall day in 1998, the assembled bankers realized that Long-Term's impending trillion-dollar collapse gave them no choice but to act together in their collective self-interest by keeping it afloat. They would have to put more money into the fund, take ownership of it, and wind down its operations in an orderly way to minimize both their own losses and a wider market disruption that would make those losses even bigger. Greenspan insisted to Congress that "no individual firms were pressured to participate" in this bailout and that the Fed just helped them see that doing so "served their mutual self-interest and avoided possible serious market dislocations." But a suggestion from the nation's central bank officials to take action that they deemed necessary to save the system was like being asked to volunteer at gunpoint. So it was that, after days of resistance, disagreement, and failed alternative plans, fourteen of the fund's largest creditors and counterparties assembled that fall afternoon agreed to ante up $3.65 billion for a privately funded but federally orchestrated bailout of Long-Term. Investment bank Bear Stearns alone refused, which, it's worth noting, no one ever forgot.[11]

McDonough, in coordinating the effort, assumed the role that J. P. Morgan had filled ninety-one years earlier, when the nation still had no real central bank, to avert a cataclysmic domino effect from the failure of the Knickerbocker Trust Company. Federal Reserve officials, as Morgan had done decades earlier, now orchestrated a plan of cooperation among competitors who, especially in an emergency, were more inclined to push each other out of the way in their dash for a lifeboat. McDonough, aided by Rubin and Greenspan, didn't focus on helping any specific bank but on containing the risk to the system.

McDonough used his position at the Fed to act as a neutral, trusted, though not disinterested third party that he hoped could avert the worst outcome of a philosophical puzzle called the "prisoner's dilemma." The dilemma demonstrates that in certain circumstances, if each member of a group acts in his or her best interest, they can paradoxically produce the worst outcome for all. In the Long-Term crisis, if each of the banks sold all the collateral it could get its hands on, the resulting deluge of sales would substantially devalue that collateral and widen everyone's losses. McDonough's message was simple: Don't rush to the emergency exit. Don't dump collateral. Sit tight and help each other by putting up more money.

As Greenspan told Congress a week later, such an agreement served "their mutual self-interest," an ironic concept for a sworn disciple of libertarian Ayn Rand, who believed that markets always get it right because everyone acting in his own best interest yields the best outcome for all. He usually advised government to get out of the way. But the coordinated effort, he told the lawmakers, was not only in the best interest of each firm but in the market's best interest too, because it would avoid wide-scale mayhem. Having patiently explained to Congress many times why a hands-on policy to prevent crises made no sense, Greenspan now told lawmakers why a hands-on effort to contain and clean up a problem after the fact was necessary.[12]

Greenspan so radically opposed government intervention to *prevent* problems that he thought federal regulators should not police markets or banks even against fraud, even though as a bank regulator he had sworn to uphold the law, including anti-fraud statutes. Yet he justified Fed action *after* problems emerged to avoid "unacceptable risks to the American Economy." Stock market investors appreciated that Greenspan was hands off until markets ran into deep trouble. Indeed, they counted on him to ease up on monetary policy when markets went amok, dubbing his predictable willingness to do so the "Greenspan put," a policy the *Economist* visualized in a cartoon depicting Greenspan as a lifeguard on the beach.[13]

Now Greenspan and McDonough insisted publicly that the Fed had done nothing in the Long-Term crisis but provide a neutral, private—that is, secret— place where fierce competitors could put down their swords, come together, and avert a catastrophe. All but one of the assembled Wall Street officials, however, took the Fed's advice as a command, and a justified one: McDonough worried that Long-Term's demise would cause some markets to "cease to function for a period of one or more days and maybe longer," a throwback to the chaos following the 1929 crash that was unthinkable in modern times.[14] Bear Stearns alone refused and enjoyed a free ride to safety only because no one else did.

To the *Wall Street Journal*'s editorial board and to much of the country, the bailout had "the smell of $3.5 billion worth of moral hazard." The newspaper noted that "high-flying" Long-Term, headquartered in the wealthy suburb of Greenwich, Connecticut, and employing two hundred people to serve just one hundred well-heeled, supposedly sophisticated investors, had earned returns of 17.1 percent, 40.8 percent, and 41.8 percent in the previous three years. If government let them keep the up side but protected them against loss, why shouldn't they act irresponsibly again? Tails they won, heads someone else lost.

In addition to raising moral hazard issues, Long-Term's plight took regulators to the novel territory of cobbling together a privately funded, government-orchestrated bailout. The 1907 bailout had been aided by government money but privately implemented. Now the size of the bailout, the threat to the economy, and the federal government's arm-twisting grabbed headlines: how could a hedge fund run by two Nobel Prize winners and myriad other brainiacs—including a mastermind of George H. W. Bush's S&L bailout, David Mullins, who had then become vice chairman of the Federal Reserve—collapse and threaten to take with it all the storied banks in the room, not to mention the U.S. economy?

With equity of $4.8 billion and next to no oversight, Long-Term had borrowed $125 billion—a debt-to-equity ratio of 25:1—then parlayed that $125 billion into $1.4 trillion of bets in over-the-counter derivatives.[15] That such smart people had created such a mess startled regulators and the public. But even more startling was how irresponsible Long-Term's lenders were. Why did supposedly smart bankers learn only shortly before the September meeting— for the first time—how deep in debt Long-Term Capital was?[16] These titans of finance hadn't done basic underwriting before investing billions of their share-holders' dollars in Long-Term. Instead, they took it on faith—in the academic and professional reputations of Long-Term's partners—that the fund was a good risk. They drank the Kool-Aid. Congressional investigators called it the "halo" effect.[17] Bankers considered Long-Term's partners so brilliant and savvy at managing risk that proper underwriting wasn't needed. Anyone wanting more information was afraid to ask, for fear of seeming foolish. The result of Wall Street's failure to do its homework was that it provided the hedge fund easy credit, allowing it to borrow more money than it could responsibly invest.

Lenders did require collateral for much of their exposure, yet hadn't bothered to understand how much other collateral Long-Term Capital had pledged, what would happen to its value if all of it had to be sold at once, or whether circumstances such as bankruptcy could trigger rival claims. Selling collateral en masse would dilute its value, or possibly even make it temporarily worthless if markets froze. If the fund filed for bankruptcy in the Cayman Islands, where it was chartered, officials there could block claims on collateral in the United States. In short, the assembled bankers painfully acknowledged that day that they had not taken even the most elementary steps to assess the chances they would be repaid. The kicking-the-tires exercise they failed to execute also should have included some stress tests of the borrowers' investment assumptions to determine what would happen if those proved wrong.[18] But Long-Term wouldn't disclose that information, and its bedazzled lenders didn't press the issue.

Now it was too late. That bankers were only now learning of the fund's total exposure astonished regulators, even though they themselves had dropped the ball. Wall Street's bankers, who justified their multimillion-dollar paychecks on grounds that they were uniquely talented and smart, hadn't assessed Long-Term's ability to repay loans by, among other criteria, finding out who else it owed money to and on what terms. Lehman's Dick Fuld, Goldman Sachs's Jon Corzine and John Thain (later CEO of Merrill Lynch), as well as Citigroup's Sandy Weil—the A-list bankers in the room—had each failed to monitor the risk his firm and his shareholders faced.

Regulators had behaved just as irresponsibly. They failed to police the bankers to guard against their lending on such lax terms, with so little underwriting. Until Long-Term threatened the entire economy, Fed officials knew nothing— some might say purposely looked the other way so they would know nothing— about how it had used over-the-counter derivatives to turn $4.8 billion into $1.4 trillion in risk.

To understand how Long-Term got into such a mess requires looking back to the legendary bond-trading firm of Salomon Brothers, which the press in the mid-1980s crowned the "King of Wall Street."[19] Long-Term's founder, John Meriwether, had helped ruin Salomon, and if he hadn't been booted out as a result, events might have unfolded differently.

In April 1991, a young trader named Paul Mozer confessed to Meriwether, then Salomon's vice chairman and Mozer's boss, that he had submitted an illegal bid during the auction for U.S. securities.[20] The market in those securities, which funds the federal government's borrowing needs and is the biggest in the world, is the domain of an elite group of Wall Street banks and brokers that the New York Fed designates as "primary" dealers. Primary dealers must participate— and are the sole participants—when the New York Fed buys or sells Treasury securities, the principal mechanism it used at the time to set interest rates. (Since 2015, the Fed has also set interest rates by adjusting the rate it pays banks on reserve balances with the Fed or by selling securities, usually Treasuries that it agrees to repurchase at a set price at a set time to primary dealers and others in what's called a "reverse repurchase agreement" or "reverse repo.") Treasuries fall into three categories: bills, which have a maturity of a year or less; notes, which have a maturity of two to ten years; and bonds, which have a maturity of more than ten years, often thirty years. When the Treasury issues new securities, individuals and other firms also can bid to buy them directly from the government, but only primary dealers can make bids on behalf of themselves *and* of clients. As such, they are the market's biggest participants, the major cog in the machinery by which the federal government borrows money.

U.S. Treasuries are the world's benchmark of financial safety, and the government expects primary dealers to protect their integrity. With advance knowledge of the government's borrowing and buying needs and of what many in the market will want to buy or sell, primary dealers naturally obtain information sooner than the general public. Both the Fed and Wall Street expect that they will not misuse that knowledge or their unique position.

A violation of auction rules raised eyebrows even within the rough-and-tumble culture of Salomon and even about a market that was relatively unregulated and that tolerated many practices in which participants "squeezed" competitors a bit. Mozer told Meriwether he had stepped over the accepted threshold, using an illegal bid to unfairly buy up more shares, but that it was his sole offense.

Many at Salomon held Meriwether in awe, revering him for the big profits his team of orderly, quiet math-oriented PhDs generated on the firm's otherwise rambunctious and unruly trading floor. Michael Lewis, in his now classic book about Wall Street, *Liar's Poker,* had chronicled how the firm's frat-boy, "big swinging dick" culture made it king of Wall Street's bond jungle. The hijinks of Salomon traders, led by their boss, the equally revered Lewis Ranieri, included replacing vacation attire in a colleagues' suitcase with ladies' underwear, burying a trader's desk in garbage, and convincing a new trader that the SEC was investigating him for stealing hot dogs from the firm's cafeteria.[21]

Against Salomon's crude culture, which had historically valued gut instinct over refined analysis, Meriwether had assembled the rocket scientists of the bond markets, a set of Harvard- and MIT-trained mathematicians and economists whose aloofness set them apart from the rest of the Salomon trading floor, earning respect but also resentment. Meriwether almost single-handedly brought to bond trading "quants," analysts who believed that math could predict market behavior better than instinct could.

Meriwether immediately reported Mozer's revelation to those above him, including Salomon's chairman, John Gutfreund, and its chief counsel, Donald Feuerstein. All three knew this was serious, possibly even criminal, but, inexplicably, they didn't report it right away to officials at the Treasury or the Federal Reserve.[22]

A few weeks later, in May 1991, following a $12.5 billion Treasury auction, traders at competing firms complained to Treasury officials that Salomon had unfairly tried to "corner the market," making Treasury notes scarcer and therefore more expensive for competitors.[23] The officials launched an investigation, as did Salomon Brothers, though less heartily.[24] The beginning of the end of Salomon Brothers came a few weeks later, on June 10, 1991, when Gutfreund traveled to Washington to meet with U.S. Treasury Undersecretary Robert Glauber about the government's inquiry. In one chair sat Gutfreund, an Oberlin College English major who ten years earlier had changed Wall Street forever by converting Salomon from a partnership to a publicly traded company, one of the first investment banks to do so. He had refashioned Salomon from a scruffy outsider into an investment bank titan. In another chair sat Glauber, who with Mullins was one of the Brady Boys who had secretly crafted Bush's S&L bailout plan. Before entering government, Glauber had been a finance professor for twenty-five years at the Harvard School of Business. In government, he maintained a friendly, professorial air that belied a no-nonsense attitude.

As Gutfreund talked, looking Glauber in the eye, he failed to mention that he and other top officials at Salomon had known for nearly two months that one of the firm's top traders, and possibly others, had been making illegal bids at Treasury auctions since the beginning of the year, including purchases in clients' names without authorization and a $1 billion bid that was submitted, the firm later claimed, as a "joke."[25]

When Salomon finally reported the violations in early August 1991 and disclosed them publicly, Glauber hit the roof. He was incensed at the firm's failure to report the problem as soon as possible. Equally damning was Gutfreund's silence in his face-to-face with Glauber. It smacked of a cover-up, and the arrogance of it infuriated Treasury officials.

Mozer's illegal action turned out not to be a unique event: he had lied about that. Eventually he was sentenced to four months in prison, fined $30,000, and barred from the securities industry for life. The SEC also brought civil charges against Gutfreund and Meriwether for failing to properly supervise Mozer, whom they had kept on the job for weeks after he confessed to Meriwether. They paid fines of $100,000 and $50,000, respectively. Mozer's sentence was unavoidable, but if Gutfreund and Meriwether had reported the problem immediately—and taken Mozer off the job—they might have avoided charges and kept their jobs and reputations—and saved Salomon. As often happens when business and government collide, the cover-up proved worse than the crime. Any firm can have a bad actor like Mozer, but Gutfreund's silence called the entire firm's integrity into question. It caused Salomon's share price to plunge, threatened the firm's credit rating, which would raise its cost of borrowing, and threatened its ability to participate as a primary dealer in U.S. Treasury auctions, an area it had dominated.

Government regulators tend to respond favorably when company executives self-report wrongdoing. Instead, Gutfreund and Salomon's top managers failed to disclose key information and came clean only when investigators closed in.[26] Gutfreund announced his departure from Salomon within weeks of his ill-fated meeting with Glauber.

Salomon's biggest investor, Warren Buffett, reluctantly stepped in. Dubbed the Oracle of Omaha for his business acumen and preference for his home state of Nebraska, Buffett has an avuncular, unpretentious demeanor that enables him to hold forth with confidence, often clutching a cherry coke while wearing suits shiny from wear and glasses occasionally held together with duct tape. Armed with integrity and lack of affectation, Buffett functions as the deus ex machina of the nation's financial scandals and crises, often arriving on stage just in time to avert catastrophe. He's the billionaire everyone respects, a widely trusted third party routinely asked to step in to restore order and confidence. So it was with Salomon.

Gutfreund, despite the harm he had caused, stuck to his bare-knuckle approach to the end, telling Salomon's managers as he resigned and introduced

Buffet as the firm's new chairman, "I'm not apologizing for anything to anybody. Apologies don't mean shit."[27]

Buffett ran Salomon for less than a year, but he remained its largest shareholder and retained close ties with management. The company never recovered its former glory. It was bought by the insurance giant Travelers Group in 1997 and folded into Travelers' investment banking division; the insurer then merged with Citicorp in 1998 to form Citigroup, which quietly dismantled what remained of Salomon's testosterone-fueled culture. Within a decade it was all but gone.[28] Such was the end of the storied bond-trading house of Salomon Brothers Inc.

By the time a rogue Salomon trader distorted Treasury markets to the detriment of competitors and U.S. taxpayers, David Mullins had become vice chair of the Federal Reserve. In that role, he responded to the Salomon scandal by recommending not more rules for the relatively loose Treasury markets, but more cops. In a masterstroke of ironic understatement, he told Congress in September 1991, a month after Gutfreund resigned, "It is clear that tightening up on enforcement would be efficacious."[29]

"The Board of Governors," he went on, "considers the U.S. government securities market to be the most important securities market in the world. It is important for at least three reasons. First, market conditions there determine the cost to the taxpayer of financing U.S. government operations. Second, this market serves as the foundation for other money and capital markets here and abroad, and as a prime source of liquidity for financial institutions. Finally, and for us perhaps most important, the U.S. government securities market is the market through which the Federal Reserve implements monetary policy and thus this market must be an efficient and reliable transmitter of our monetary policy actions."[30] In short, taxpayers, world markets, and the U.S. economy depended on the integrity of the Treasury markets. Testifying to Congress again a few months later, he underscored the seriousness of Salomon's misdeeds: "Although many aspects of the Salomon Brothers admission of wrongdoing and the results of the subsequent investigation cause concern, one is particularly unsettling: Because of the falsification of bids at auctions, the Treasury was the direct counterparty in attempts to manipulate the market."[31]

The scandal forced the publicity-shy Meriwether to leave Salomon Brothers in 1991, but Wall Street still revered his trading intelligence and talent. By 1994

This 1989 photo of John Meriwether, the publicity-shy, legendary bond trader at Salomon Brothers, was taken two years before his forced resignation led him to create Long-Term Capital. Associated Press.

he had founded Long-Term as a replica of his corner of the Salomon trading floor. The math nerds he'd lured to Salomon were now ensconced in his hedge fund's posh headquarters in Greenwich, Connecticut. He also attracted academic and market luminaries such as Scholes and Merton, whose formula for valuing derivatives had facilitated the proliferation in over-the-counter securities in the mid-1980s.[32] While at Long-Term, Merton and Scholes received the Noble Prize for that work. The hedge fund, making trades and taking positions premised on their models, would implode less than a year later.

Meriwether also lured Mullins to Long-Term Capital from his seat at the Fed, where he had been appointed in 1990 by President Bush as a reward for helping him get elected. Enticing Mullins to Long-Term Capital four years later was a feather in Meriwether's cap and, some thought, a partial vindication for Meriwether's having been forced out of Salomon. Mullins had been the Federal Reserve's point man on the Salomon Brother's scandal. How bad could Meriwether's role have been if a high-ranking Fed official would join him as a business partner?

The irony was that Long-Term, like all hedge funds, had been set up to avoid just the kind of oversight "to control speculation and financial leverage" that Mullins and Glauber had advocated for in their report on the 1987 market crash.[33] With all this history, when it came time in September 1998 for Long-Term to alert the Federal Reserve Bank of New York that the hedge fund faced collapse, Meriwether and Mullins made the telephone call together. One lesson they took from the Salomon scandal, which they had learned sitting on opposite sides of the table, was to tell the government of trouble as soon as possible.[34]

Days after the Long-Term bailout was announced, Greenspan took a chauffeured car from his office to Capitol Hill to explain to lawmakers that the fire sale of the Long-Term collateral lenders held would have been okay "18 months ago," when markets were stable, but was unacceptable now, when markets were fragile and shaky.[35] This statement was true but also nonsense. The market fragility and shakiness that undid Long-Term revealed as useless its investment assumptions and strategy and the very assets that were supposed to be ballast in rough weather. Exactly when lenders would want to sell such collateral is exactly when they could not. Eighteen months earlier, they would not have wanted to sell because the hedge fund didn't seem to be in trouble. In stable times, creditors and counterparties wouldn't want to sell off collateral. In bad times, selling off so much of the same type of collateral all at once would further erode prices and add to instability. The real issue wasn't the downturn but that Long-Term and its creditors had done a lousy job of stress testing their assumptions and otherwise insulating themselves from it. But double-talk is a central banker's stock and trade. "If I've made myself too clear," Greenspan once quipped, "you must have misunderstood me."[36] Contradictory translations abounded after any Greenspan utterance, as headlines from a random date—July 14, 1988—show:

"Greenspan Sees Stable Rates" (*New York Times*)
"Greenspan Signals Higher Interest Rates" (*Wall Street Journal*)
"Greenspan Warns of Inflation" (*Washington Post*)
"Greenspan Expects Growth, Low Inflation" (*Baltimore Sun*)[37]

Meriwether, Scholes, Merton, Mullins, and the rest of the crew at Long-Term erred in thinking that their formulas were stronger than mass emotion. In many ways, the rough-hewn Salomon traders who bought and sold by the seat of their pants had it over the quants in times of trouble. They had a better grasp of psychology. Greenspan's extreme laissez-faire philosophy that markets police themselves suffered from the same limitation. That approach works in the long run, but as the country saw during the 1929 crash, the pain of getting there can be extreme. Short-term emotion often makes markets irrational. Yale economist Robert Shiller won a Nobel Prize in 2013 for his pioneering work showing how human emotion can make markets inefficient, particularly in the here and now.

Long-Term's stress tests said the most it could lose in one day was $35 million. The fallout from Russia's default gave it daily losses closer to $500 million. The market acted rationally on information that Long-Term hadn't allowed for, and that plunged the fund into chaos.[38] So by that fall day in 1998, as Long-Term's creditors and counterparties gathered in a staid conference room at the New York Fed, they had surely felt their astonishment give way to incredulity about their having so stupidly allowed their star-struck attitudes to replace sound underwriting. Just as the hedge fund relied too much on market history, so creditors and counterparties paid too much attention to the partners' past and too little to what Long-Term was actually up to. When Meriwether and others at the hedge fund told creditors they wouldn't give details about their strategies and investments, the bankers didn't flinch.[39] "We had no idea they would have trouble—these people were known for risk management. They had taught it; they designed it," said one Merrill Lynch risk manager, Dan Napoli, who loved to golf in Ireland with Meriwether. "God knows, we were dealing with Nobel Prize winners!"[40]

Long-Term was a cautionary tale of hubris and easy credit: bankers lent it too much money without doing any homework to assess whether it could pay them back. Instruments like over-the-counter derivatives that could mitigate risk instead amplified it when misused, especially when economic forces took a downturn. That's what Warren Buffett meant when he called derivatives "landmines" and "time bombs." The very smart partners at Long-Term understood all this, but their arrogance had made them stupid in practice.[41]

After a long day at the Fed, and after a brief interlude in which the ubiquitous Buffett made an unsuccessful offer to buy Long-Term, fourteen banks agreed to pony up $3.6 billion and take a 90 percent ownership stake in the fund. Bear Stearns, saying it had already lost enough money on Long-Term, refused, causing much resentment. The deal left Meriwether, Mullins, and the other partners with a 10 percent stake, and that only in exchange for the humiliation of having to accept a salary to help the banks wind it all down. It was a classic Wall Street maneuver in a crisis: leave those who caused the trouble in place—and pay them—because they are presumed to be the only ones who understand

the tangle they've made well enough to unravel it. Two years later, all the partners had left and the fund was "liquidated."[42]

Once the bankers had anted up the bailout money, taken over the fund, and
restored order, Greenspan and Rubin proceeded to lobby hard on behalf of
President Bill Clinton's White House against any regulation of over-the-counter
derivatives. A handful of America's biggest commercial banks—all of them
major Long-Term investors—dominated the over-the-counter derivatives
market, where they acted as middlemen, matching parties for each side of a
contract. Markets perceived these banks as too big to fail and thus a low credit
risk; that and the advantage of having tax-subsidized deposit insurance enabled
the banks to borrow money to fund their over-the-counter derivatives operations more cheaply than competitors. After the Long-Term crisis, these banks
wrote off $445 million in credit losses on derivatives in the third quarter of
1998, a nearly fivefold increase over the $94 million they had written off in the
second quarter. Profits on these contracts in the third quarter fell to $614 million,
down from $2.6 billion in the second.[43]

On February 15, 1999, not quite six months after the Long-Term bailout,
Time magazine's cover pictured Fed Chairman Greenspan, Treasury Secretary
Rubin, and Deputy Secretary of the Treasury Larry Summers, the MIT-trained
economist and soon-to-be president of Harvard known for his acerbic personality. The magazine titled its story "Committee to Save the World" and promised "the inside story of how the Three Marketeers have prevented a global
economic meltdown—so far."

The Committee to Save the World

THE THRIFT CRISIS UNFOLDED ON George H. W. Bush's watch as vice president and president, but it wasn't the S&L bailout—a tax by another name—that undid his re-election bid. What angered voters and helped Bill Clinton defeat him in 1992 was the 1990 budget deal, which more obviously to the public violated his famous campaign pledge, "Read my lips: no new taxes."

On taking office in January 1993, Clinton set several milestones. He was the first post–Cold War president and the first baby-boomer president. He would deliver the first balanced budget in decades and would become the first Democrat since FDR to win a second term in office. He also became the second president, after Andrew Johnson, to be impeached. In 1998 the U.S. House of Representatives initiated impeachment proceedings on grounds that Clinton had lied to a grand jury and tried to obstruct justice in a federal investigation into his two-year affair with a twenty-one-year-old White House intern. The Senate, as it did for Johnson, voted not to convict.

Amid headlines about a semen-stained dress and Clinton's ruminations on "what the meaning of *is* is," two other Washington dramas unfolded in the 1990s that helped set the stage for the next decade's subprime mortgage bubble and implosion. Both involved questions about how to regulate financial markets, and in both instances, the Clinton administration's answer was "very lightly."

First, Federal Reserve and Treasury officials campaigned to discredit a prominent securities lawyer named Brooksley Born who, as head of the federal agency overseeing exchange-traded derivatives, warned about the growing risks of over-the-counter derivatives and proposed oversight of them. Second, the same officials prodded Congress to formally deregulate financial services, in a bid to catch up legislatively with what industry had already done in practice over the last twenty years. The legislation that eventually passed, the Gramm-Leach-Bliley Act of 1999, in theory called for more rational and orderly oversight of a finance industry whose rules had been much relaxed.

In August 1996, two years before the Long-Term meltdown, Clinton had named Born to head the Commodity Futures Trading Commission (CFTC), which Congress created in 1974 as an independent agency in the executive branch to oversee exchange-traded derivatives called futures—agreements to buy or sell a commodity such as wheat or orange juice at a set price and time.

Born had undergraduate and law degrees from Stanford, where she was the first woman editor of the law review, and she had a law practice at the prestigious Washington, D.C., law firm of Arnold & Porter focusing on derivatives. Futures contracts and options, exchange-traded derivatives that appeared in earnest more than a decade before the Civil War, had been regulated since the 1920s. By the mid-1990s, most still involved agricultural goods but soon included Treasury securities and foreign currencies. When Born came to the CFTC, the off-exchange market of OTC derivatives had begun to rival that for exchange-traded ones. She asked her staff to collect information on the OTC market, about which regulators knew almost nothing.[1]

What little they did know came from private lawsuits. Losses on over-the-counter derivatives, for example, had forced Orange County, California, to file for bankruptcy in 1994, with Merrill Lynch paying $400 million four years later to settle charges that it had given the county "reckless" advice in selling it the investments. In 1996, Bankers Trust agreed on a nearly $200 million settlement with its former client Procter & Gamble, which had sued claiming the bank purposely misled the company about the risks of investing in derivatives. Taped conversations emerged of Bankers Trust traders "boasting of how much money they were making from these deals and how little Procter & Gamble understood they were at risk." Said one trader, "It's like Russian roulette, and I keep putting another bullet in the revolver every time I do one of these."[2]

When the facts in these suits emerged, the Fed, the SEC, and the CFTC (before Born) launched investigations, and the federal government eventually fined Bankers Trust $10 million.[3] Born began to wonder what else was out there. What scared her, she told her staff, was that if not for the lawsuits, regulators would not have known about even these frauds. Soon after she arrived at the CFTC, however, she learned that Greenspan, for one, didn't want to know. He told Born at a luncheon meeting that he was so against financial oversight that he didn't believe regulators should police for fraud, even though the law requires them to. This was as radical and outside of the mainstream thinking on financial oversight as one could get. All this worried Born. Her interest, in turn, worried Wall Street, which liked nothing better than to be left alone.[4]

Born's Wall Street adversaries—the over-the-counter derivatives industry, led by JPMorgan and the law firm of Cleary Gottlieb—immediately launched a campaign with the press and lawmakers to paint—and taint—Born's efforts as a turf war with the Securities and Exchange Commission over which agency would oversee this growing market. In fact it was not clear whether jurisdiction over non-exchange-traded derivatives resided with the CFTC or the SEC, although in retrospect Born and her lawyers likely were correct that the authority to peer under the tent resided with her agency. Previous heads of the CFTC, like its former chairman Wendy Gramm, wife of powerful senator Phil Gramm (R-Tex.), had chosen not to exercise the agency's oversight authority, and Wall Street bankers didn't want the question tested in court for fear Born was right. When her counterpart at the SEC, Clinton appointee Arthur Levitt, clearly would not take action to shed light onto the OTC market, Born decided she would.

Leading the crusade in government on Wall Street's behalf against regulation in general and by Born in particular was the "Committee to Save the World": Greenspan, Rubin, and Summers.

The actor playing Summers in the movie *The Social Network* deftly captured his well-known arrogance and prickly personality. Summers became president of Harvard in 2001 but resigned five years later amid a brewing faculty revolt, partly incited by his apparent suggestion that women lack the ability to be scientists. He was a hands-on president, leaving "nothing . . . on auto-pilot," as a *Boston Globe* reporter put it. "His dominating personality" was "unafflicted . . . with self-doubt in matters of finance," and he meddled in a manner that ignored advice contrary to his own view and, as it turned out, common sense. For example, he helped persuade Harvard to take several billion in funds from what was the equivalent of its checking account—its cash account, essentially—and invest it in over-the-counter derivatives. When the market fell amid the mortgage crisis in 2008, Harvard lost $1.8 billion on the investment, causing a cash crunch that left it scrambling to borrow money to pay daily expenses, despite owning the largest endowment of any university (though that, too, lost considerable value during the downturn). *Forbes* magazine likened it to the "homeowner who takes out a second mortgage in order to pay off credit card bills." Harvard recovered, and more people than just Summers were involved in the decision, but he nonetheless bears a major responsibility.[5]

Greenspan, Rubin, and Summers agreed completely on regulation of markets: they wanted as little as possible, even as they happily offered other types of government intervention and subsidies. Throughout the 1990s, the three flew around the world to quell myriad economic crises. They negotiated with leaders, and sometimes supplied money from the International Monetary Fund, to contain a series of international problems as contagion rocked Mexico; then Asian countries; then Russia, Brazil, and South America. By decade's end, according to *Time* magazine's adulatory cover story about the three, "40 percent of the world's economies" had been "tugged from robust growth into recession or depression."[6] These crises, which included Long-Term, were of a new kind. Unlike, say, the Latin American debt crisis of the 1980s, in which the fallout was concentrated in a few big commercial banks, these new problems hurt a broader swath of the market, spreading risks among a growing and increasingly interconnected investment community of hedge funds, mutual funds, and investors. The relatively new over-the-counter market in derivatives greatly augmented that connectedness.

The three regulators saw unregulated over-the-counter derivatives as tools for mitigating risk by spreading it among finance companies, including federally insured institutions, and thus diffusing its concentration in any single firm. Born's decision to flex some oversight muscle now galvanized the three, who argued that if she oversaw the industry it could call into question the legality of the over-the-counter market.[7] Their rather contorted reasoning that in retrospect seems disingenuous, went like this: the CFTC oversaw exchange-traded derivatives, so if it regulated over-the-counter derivatives, it might be forced to define them out of existence—or declare them illegal—because they were not traded on an exchange, and it could regulate only exchange-traded derivatives. They knew Born had never suggested declaring over-the-counter derivatives illegal, only in need of oversight. What actually worried Wall Street was price transparency, which would increase competition and lower costs, cutting into its profits. But the scare tactic worked.[8]

After Long-Term, powerful members of Congress on both sides of the aisle, such as Representative Jim Leach (R-Iowa) and Senator Paul Sarbanes (D-Md.), saw Born's point. But they lost the debate. After a ferocious battle, the Committee to Save the World, on Wall Street's behalf, persuaded Congress in 1998 to impose a moratorium that barred Born's agency from regulating over-the-counter derivatives.[9] The action usurped her authority, and she soon announced she would step down. They had succeeded in running her, figuratively, out of town.

"I know of no set of supervisory action we can take that would prevent people from making dumb mistakes," Greenspan told Congress on October 1, 1998, just days after his colleagues in New York had orchestrated the bailout of Long-Term. "I know of no piece of legislation that can be passed by the Congress which would require us to prevent them from making dumb mistakes. I think it's very important for us not to introduce regulation for regulation's sake." This was the straw-man argument Greenspan and others trotted out when anyone suggested more oversight. Mischaracterizing those who favored oversight as wanting rules for no reason created a position that was easy for purported free-marketers to knock down.[10]

Greenspan told lawmakers that government intervention in Long-Term was necessary even as he, Rubin, and Summers told those same lawmakers that oversight of the tools the hedge fund had used to cause trouble was not. They pooh-poohed Born's suggestion that preventive steps might avert such crises. In reality, Born advocated nothing more radical than making the over-the-counter market observe the safety measures that Congress had imposed on the stock and bond markets in the 1930s: transparency, record-keeping, and prohibitions against manipulation.

Once they obtained a moratorium on regulating OTC derivatives, Greenspan and Summers, who moved up to secretary of the Treasury in mid-1999, when Rubin left to join Citigroup, set to work making the ban on regulation—euphemistically called "legal certainty"—permanent. The result was the Commodity Futures Modernization Act of 2000, which barred both the SEC and the CFTC from regulating over-the-counter derivatives. The law also relaxed oversight for exchange-traded futures. In a peculiar twist, it required the SEC and the CFTC to police some over-the-counter securities against fraud, but then prevented them from using the tools necessary to do so, expressly prohibiting either agency from

"imposing reporting, record keeping or disclosure requirements or other prophylactic measures designed to prevent fraud" in these markets.[11] Financial lobbyists
felt their campaign donations had been money well spent. (One of the few fights
they lost on this issue was a push to win approval to sell all types of over-the-
counter derivatives, called swaps, to the general public, defined as people with
less than $10 million in assets. Instead the new law required the major Wall Street
regulators to study the issue. They did, issuing a report in 2001 that generally
recommended against such sales.)[12]

The Clinton White House and top Senate Republicans, including Finance
Committee Chair Phil Gramm (who was also a key player on the Senate
Banking Committee), pushed for the legislation. Gramm even slipped in what
became known as the "Enron Loophole," which excluded derivatives based on
oil and gas commodities from federal or state oversight no matter how they
were traded, on or off exchange; while the loophole helped Enron, it also benefited Koch Industries, owned by the oil billionaire Koch brothers, who are large
derivatives traders. Clinton's White House went along, even though exempting
energy futures went squarely against the recommendation of the President's
Working Group on Financial Markets. The group, set up eight years earlier in
the wake of the 1987 stock market crash, included the heads of the financial
agencies—the Fed's Greenspan, the Treasury's Summers, the SEC's Levitt, and
the CFTC's William J. Rainer, who replaced Born. In November 1999 it issued
a report recommending against regulating financial over-the-counter derivatives because they were "not susceptible to manipulation," but advocating *for*
regulating derivatives for nonfinancial commodities like metals and energy
because their prices were easy to manipulate, to the detriment of retail and
wholesale consumers.[13]

A few months earlier, in April 1999, another report by the group had recommended that hedge funds be required to make "meaningful" information public.
The rest of the recommendations, however, amounted to saying that companies
should do a better job of underwriting and regulators should do a better job of
encouraging them to do so. Born signed her name, knowing that the "three
marketeers" prevented her from doing much else. She'd already announced she
would step down and had one foot out the door. As for making hedge funds
more transparent, in 2006 a federal appeals court ruled in favor of industry and
against an effort by the SEC to make them more open.[14]

17

Dysfunctional Oversight

EVEN AS GREENSPAN, SUMMERS, AND RUBIN FOUGHT for legislation putting the over-the-counter market off-limits to federal regulators, they fought for Congress to officially deregulate financial services generally. The legislation was a delayed addendum to the deregulation that already had taken place and would make it easier for the financial industry to do what it had figured out how to do through the aggressive use of loopholes over the previous twenty years. The result, the Gramm-Leach-Bliley Act of 1999, formally repealed sections of the 1933 banking act known as Glass-Steagall that had separated commercial and investment banking, and sections of a 1956 law separating banking and insurance. Now the same holding company officially could house investment and commercial banking, securities brokerage services, and insurance under one roof.[1]

Greenspan's Federal Reserve provided the impetus for passing the bill by temporarily allowing the insurance giant Travelers Group to merge with banking behemoth Citicorp to create Citigroup. Without formal congressional okay, the merger would have been more difficult, though not impossible.[2] Lobbyists nicknamed Gramm-Leach-Bliley the "Citicorp-Travelers bill," but in fact Citigroup executives said that if the legislation again didn't pass (variations of it had been pushed for a decade), they could fold their bank charter into one of their thrift charters, which permitted a broader array of activities. They might have had to shed some divisions to stay within the law, but the essence of the merger wouldn't be threatened.[3] Still, lawmakers did not want to have to explain the bill's failure to the financial services companies that had been so good about writing campaign checks. Typically, the financial services industry made (and still makes) more in federal campaign contributions than the healthcare, energy, defense, agriculture, and transportation industries combined.[4] Lawmakers coveted seats on the House and Senate Banking Committees for this reason. Some companies even suspected that the committees delayed final passage of a deregulation bill for decades just to keep the checks coming. They may have been right.

Members of the financial services industry, having spent decades fighting to enter each other's turf even as they lobbied to keep would-be competitors out of their own, had finally joined hands. It was only practical. Commercial banks had won entry into investment banking and insurance via loopholes and court decisions.[5] Investment banks had dug tunnels through Glass-Steagall to connect investment and commercial banking. Merrill Lynch had used certificates of deposit to offer banking services to clients even as it fought efforts by banks to sell securities. But by 1999, commercial and investment bankers had made peace. A series of court cases and changes in financial demographics that seemed to favor one-stop shopping for banking, investments, and insurance won over most players. The last holdout—retail insurance brokers—finally decided to hop on the bandwagon or risk having the commingling of all financial services happen without their having any say in crafting the bill.[6]

Many in Congress viewed Gramm-Leach-Bliley as the law that, at long last, would bring rational oversight to an already deregulated financial system. Two decades of ad hoc deregulation had left a hodge-podge system to police increasingly large, complex companies selling all manner of financial goods. This was a chance for lawmakers on both sides of the aisle to bring rationality to the chaos through "functional regulation," as staffers on congressional banking committees called it. Financial-service holding companies would be permitted to own a range of companies, each regulated by the agency with the best expertise. Securities regulators at the SEC would regulate investment banking activities within the holding company, while bank regulators at the Office of the Comptroller of the Currency, the Fed, and the FDIC would oversee commercial bank activities. Insurance activities would continue to be largely overseen by state insurance commissioners. And the Federal Reserve would become the uber-regulator, overseeing the holding company.

Functional regulation assumed that the 1929 crash was not caused by the comingling of commercial and investment banking in and of itself but by a lack of commonsense rules and oversight to enforce them. There had been no required recordkeeping or reporting of information, no ban on fraud, and—this was key—no enforcement of *existing* bans on mixing commercial and invest-ment banking, bans that National City had flouted for decades. Lawmakers crafting the bill embraced the Bush-era mindset that regulation—or deregula-tion—consisted of both rules and the policing of those rules, and that efforts to regulate or deregulate required a clear articulation of which of the two was being loosened as well as a review of whether a commensurate tightening of the other was needed. That was the theory. In practice, functional regulation proved wildly ineffective.

The lawmakers and staffers who crafted functional oversight assumed that regulators would see eye to eye and coordinate. They didn't anticipate that territorial claims could make one agency's regulators touchy that those in another agency might step on their toes. They also didn't take into account differences of style that translated into very different practices depending on who was in charge. Nor did they anticipate the havoc that would result from concessions that let the five biggest investment banks evade oversight. But in the beginning, as Clinton signed the bill in November 1999, regulators favored the idea of fewer rules, as long as it came with more oversight. That was the idea, anyway.

Among the most aggressive advocates for the deregulation of commercial banking was Jerry Hawke, a Washington lawyer considered a preeminent expert on finance. Clinton named him Comptroller of the Currency in late 1998, over objections of some Democrats on the Senate Banking Committee. Hawke performed as his skeptics anticipated: as comptroller, he fought off efforts by states to force nationally chartered banks and their holding companies to follow state consumer protection laws. Under his direction, the OCC ruled that most of those state laws didn't apply to national banks, and even in the rare instances when they did apply, only federal regulators, not states, could enforce them. After winning this argument in court, federal regulators proceeded to do nothing to curb abuses by national banks in retail mortgage and credit card lending, where many of the worst consumer banking practices occurred. Roy Cooper of North Carolina summed up the frustration of state attorneys general across the country when he complained to Hawke in 2003 that by telling states to shut up and sit down the comptroller had taken "50 sheriffs off the job during the time the mortgage lending industry was becoming the Wild West."[7]

Hawke's tenure as comptroller was also marked by his office's failure to uncover money laundering at Riggs Bank, which was headquartered literally across the street from the U.S. Treasury. With a reputation for serving global thugs, Riggs helped Chilean dictator Augusto Pinochet hide millions of dollars in assets from international prosecutors while he was under house arrest in Britain. Riggs's problems predated Hawke's time as comptroller, and rumors persisted in Washington for decades that the bank had deep connections to the CIA. Still, when Riggs's practices became public, they created controversy for Hawke.[8]

Hawke was given the appointment as comptroller as a reward for decades of work pushing commercial banking law to the edges and, more immediately, for being Treasury Secretary Rubin's point man at Treasury in 1998 during the fight for final passage of Gramm-Leach-Bliley. Hawke stepped down as comptroller in 2004, after ten years in government, to rejoin his law firm of Arnold & Porter. On his office wall today hangs a picture of Clinton signing the Gramm-Leach-Bliley Act, with a personal message to Hawke scribbled in pen: "Jerry, You started all this. It would not have happened without you.—Larry Summers."[9]

President Clinton's signing of the Financial Services Modernization Act of 1999, the formal name of Gramm-Leach-Bliley, marked a milestone in the two-decades-long march of financial deregulation, which eliminated many key measures that Congress put in place seven decades earlier to safeguard U.S. markets. Interest-rate caps imposed in the 1930s had been lifted more than a decade earlier. Also long gone were the geographic restrictions preventing federally chartered banks from crossing state lines. The sale of thrifts during the 1980s' S&L crisis had torn down that wall, and Congress followed with formal recognition in 1994 by effectively removing barriers to interstate banking and branching. The result was a set of mergers that yielded a 27 percent decline in the number of banking institutions.[10] The ideological descendants of Thomas Jefferson, Andrew Jackson, and Huey Long had lost the states' rights argument against interstate banking, but they proved correct in warning that removing geographic barriers would lead to enormous concentrations of power. Interstate banking brought convenience for consumers, efficiencies of scale that cut operating costs, and geographic diversification that freed institutions from the vagaries of one region's economy. It also led to unprecedented bigness, as in Bank of America's growth from a regional bank in California to a coast-to-coast presence as the nation's biggest financial firm.

These developments thrilled Greenspan, who had argued for years that America needed banking giants that could compete internationally. The president of the Federal Reserve Bank of Kansas City said in a 2009 speech that from 1994 to 1999 the nation's "largest 20 institutions grew from controlling about 35 percent of industry assets to controlling 70 percent."[11] Interstate branching reduced bank failures, but when bigger banks did fall into trouble, they posed a bigger risk. The too-big-to-fail phenomenon that began with federal deposit insurance was now systemwide thanks to behemoth, one-stop financial companies.

By the time Congress debated Gramm-Leach-Bliley, only one big philosophical question remained: Should deregulation extend to permitting a nonfinancial company like Target to own a bank, or vice versa? Should the trend adopted during the S&L fiasco, to allow such a comingling of commerce and banking, be allowed to continue? Or should the door once again be shut?

Many lawmakers intended Gramm-Leach-Bliley to close the door, saying they wanted to return to the traditional policy of separating commerce and banking, which state and federal officials followed out of a mistrust of bigness and power and of potential conflicts of interest.[12] But that division has never been absolute. Exceptions have abounded. In early America, incorporated banks were authorized to undertake public works such as building sewer or water systems. In the early twentieth century, the money-trust bankers influenced industrial America by extending credit to companies, raising money for them on the securities markets, and sitting on their boards.

To circumvent any rules that did exist, bankers created more than a hundred holding companies in the 1940s and 1950s to expand through affiliates into forbidden enterprises, mostly into financial services such as investment banking, insurance, and real estate but also into nonbanking enterprises. One bank holding company owned an enterprise "for catching, processing and selling fish" and another that engaged in "metals manufacturing."[13]

Congress intended the Bank Holding Company Act of 1956 to thwart these forays by applying to holding companies the laws separating commercial banking from investment banking and from nonbanking operations. Excerpts from the *Congressional Record* regarding the passage of the 1956 act capture debates of the same issues that had occupied many Americans since colonial days. The Senate version of the bill, while noting that holding companies are not necessarily "evil," sums up the philosophy behind the legislation:

Adequate safeguards should be provided against undue concentration of control of banking activities. The dangers accompanying monopoly in this field are particularly undesirable in view of the significant part played by banking in our present national economy. . . . The bill's requirement for divestment of nonbanking assets will help to keep bank ventures in a field of their own. The committee was informed of the danger to a bank within a bank holding company controlling nonbanking assets, should the company unduly favor its nonbanking operations by requiring the bank's customers to make use of such nonbanking enterprises as a condition to doing business with the bank. The bill's divestment provisions should prevent this fear from becoming a reality.[14]

Concerns about money, credit, and power remained very much alive. Resolving them remained a work in progress.

In practice, breaches of this separation continued. Reagan and Bush aggressively allowed them during the S&L crisis to entice buyers for ailing thrifts. The 1987 bill that provided a $10.8 billion band-aid during the crisis, the Competitive Equality Banking Act, allowed non-bank companies to keep banks they had created by exploiting a loophole in the legal definition of a bank. Congress allowed these existing combinations to continue, grandfathering them in, even though it prohibited creation of new ones. Sears, Roebuck kept its bank, as did Merrill Lynch.[15]

Many hoped that Gramm-Leach-Bliley, through a bipartisan effort led by Representative Jim Leach of Iowa and Senator Paul Sarbanes (D-Md.), would halt more mixing of commerce and banking. Compromise was essential, however. Lawmakers ended up saying that commercial entities such as Sears and Ford could keep the thrifts they'd acquired during the crisis, but that once the law passed, no more thrifts could be purchased by nonfinancial companies. Further, any group allowed to keep a thrift it already had could not expand its ownership of banks and could sell its banking divisions only to other financial service companies.[16]

Thus did the expanding trend toward mixing commerce and banking halt— sort of. Critics such as Hawke, Senator Gramm, and John Dugan, a bank lobbyist who would eventually replace Hawke as comptroller of the currency, argued such restrictions were meaningless because thrifts could open branches at will in many states. But enough lawmakers and policymakers, including even Greenspan and Rubin, stood firm, at least until financial services fully digested financial deregulation.[17] With the door closing, in late 1998 and early 1999, before the bill became law, nearly seventy companies—including retailer Nordstrom and insurance giant American International Group—raced to apply for federal approval to buy or start thrifts. Such charters, they reasoned, would hedge their bets if the bill that passed was not to their liking. One major retailer mistimed its application and missed its chance to start a thrift—and to enter banking: Wal-Mart. Its executives have been kicking themselves ever since.[18]

Within a few years, most of nonfinancial corporate America's appetite for banking began to wane. Ford and Sears, for example, sold the thrifts they'd fought so hard to get. But the issue of mixing commerce and banking didn't die. The Gramm-Leach-Bliley Act completed under Clinton what the Reagan and Bush White Houses had begun twenty years earlier on ideological grounds and to help win an election. Still, the irony of the situation—the Clinton White House pressing for more rational oversight of finance even as it worked to preempt any policing of a huge slice of the securities markets (over-the-counter derivatives)—wasn't lost on onlookers. To Senate investigators of the mortgage meltdown ten years later, Rubin would say he actually agreed with Born that derivatives should be regulated, but that Wall Street's opposition was too great to fight.[19] His claim draws skeptical looks from those involved in the debate at the time.

As Gramm-Leach-Bliley was crafted, a few people voiced concern that with looser rules, financial holding companies needed more oversight. In many ways, simply divvying up regulatory duties by function only preserved the status quo. In theory, lawmakers increased oversight by expanding the Federal Reserve's duties to oversee the holding companies of these new behemoths, but in practice the Fed performed the same duties it had before, and how aggressively it exerted what oversight it had depended on the will of its chair.

The upshot was that the new law explicitly sanctioned mingling taxpayer-backed depository institutions—commercial banks—with all other financial companies and, though in a more limited way than before, with nonfinancial ones as well. Some people raised concerns that this newly sanctioned world posed problems for the safety net of federal deposit insurance. In an annual report three years earlier, the president of the New York Federal Reserve, E. Gerald Corrigan, fretted over even a limited mixture of banking and other industries: "Can the official safety net apparatus—including liquidity support from the central bank—be available to part of a firm without, at least by implication, it being available to the firm as a whole?"[20] The former chair and chief executive of Citicorp, Walter Wriston, voiced similar fears: "It is inconceivable that any major bank would walk away from any subsidiary of its holding company. If your name is on the door, all of your capital funds are going to be behind it in the real world. Lawyers can say you have separation, but the marketplace is persuasive, and it would not see it that way."[21] Gramm-Leach-Bliley gave only a perfunctory nod of an answer to the knotty issue that Corrigan and Wriston raised.

Even as Clinton signed the new bill on that fall day in 1999, the next domestic financial crisis was unfolding.

18

Enron: The Emperor's New Clothes

KENNETH LAY DIED IN 2006 AT THE age of sixty-four, likely escaping years of jail time. Six weeks earlier, he had been convicted on federal charges of conspiracy and fraud in one of the nation's biggest corporate scandals, the collapse of the Houston-based energy company Enron. Lay established Enron in 1985 and grew it into the country's seventh largest company by market capitalization before it fell apart in 2001. The jet-fueled executives he hired convinced the world they were leaders in the trading of natural gas and electricity. Their real talent as it happened was fraud and manipulation.

Enron started out unremarkably, delivering gas to customers from its pipelines. By the new millennium, it was leading the way in energy deregulation and innovation, or so it seemed. Through a series of acquisitions, big projects, and bold derivative plays, it rode high into the 1990s, becoming by 2000 a Wall Street darling whose annual revenues had shot to $100 billion, more than three times what they had been two years earlier.[1] Investors loved the predictability of Enron's earnings growth, and few asked why they were so very reliable. At its all-time high, in August 2000, Enron stock reached ninety dollars a share—several times the earnings of its competitors—before falling to fifty cents within a year.[2] In reality, though Enron executives publicly denied it, the company had become a derivatives trader in unregulated—over-the-counter—energy futures. Wall Street called it "the Goldman Sachs of energy trading." Lay had planned to add weather futures and internet broadband futures.[3]

Enron cultivated its image as a new-age energy company that thought more creatively than competitors. Its executives also created a cut-throat culture that left no room for admitting mistakes. Employees got the message: hide problems. Workers who didn't earned lower grades from colleagues and managers and fell in employee rankings. Each year, those who hit the bottom 20 percent of the rankings were fired. This rank-and-yank system gained fad popularity in corporate America in the 1980s and 1990s, until it was seen as a factor in Enron's undoing. Holding workers accountable, corporate governance gurus realized, was not the same as provoking anxiety through a stratified system that encouraged deception and made firings inevitable, frequent, and capricious.

A broader euphoria fueled Enron's popularity on Wall Street. In the lead-up to the tech bubble of the late 1990s, the phrase "new economy" at first denoted a service-based economy based on technology, in contrast to "old-economy" bedrocks like manufacturing. As the tech bubble grew, "new economy" came to mean an era no longer plagued by recessions. The public's infatuation with all things tech grew delusional, much as it had in the 1920s. Analysts and investors took to saying and no doubt some actually believed that new tech companies didn't need to be making any earnings before going public, as long as revenues were growing.

Traditional, GAAP accounting under this mindset came to be seen as stodgy. Companies, especially those without earnings, complained that "generally accepted accounting principles" unfairly penalized them in the public's eye by making their revenues appear too volatile—or puny. Public companies still had to file financial reports with the SEC using these accounting principles, but in press releases and when speaking to reporters and investors, they touted balance sheets using rules they hand-picked to boost and smooth out their financials. They called these custom-tailored balance sheets "pro forma." It was a serious-sounding name for clap-trap.

Such customized accounting has a place. Analysts, for their own use, often refigure balance sheets and income statements to highlight various aspects of a company's numbers. But as a routine way to report earnings, pro forma financials are bogus—and since Enron's collapse, effectively banned by Congress. That's because alternate accounting practices undermine the point of the standardized rules that regulators have developed since the 1930s to replace the gobbledygook that passed for disclosure before then. While many companies peddled pro forma disclosures in the 1990s, smart investors never bought into the notion of a new era, much less one that justified accounting manipulation and a belief—Kool-Aid—that tech stocks could only go up.

Yet as the dot-com frenzy of the 1990s went bust in the spring of 2000, Enron didn't miss a step. Investors, eager for steady results after the tech bloodbath, pushed Enron's stock to its apex that August. Sixteen months later the company would file for the biggest bankruptcy the country had yet seen. It remains among the top ten.[4]

The person credited with opening the public's eyes to Enron is Bethany McLean, who, as a reporter at *Fortune* magazine, performed the financial equivalent of pointing out the emperor wasn't wearing any clothes. In an article on March 5, 2001, she asked: "How exactly does Enron make its money?" She says she was just reflecting rumblings she was hearing in the market, particularly from Jim Chanos, a short-seller who runs Kynikos Associates, *kynikos* being the Greek word for cynic. Short-sellers profit by betting that a stock will decline in price. At *Fortune,* McLean had the megaphone and the courage to ask aloud the question many investors were afraid to voice publicly for fear they would appear stupid or incur the wrath of Enron executives. As McLean put it in a 2005 interview with C-SPAN:

> We've all been in a situation where you don't really understand something but you say you do because you don't want to ask a stupid question. And for a lot of people—it sounds hard to believe, but for a lot of people, that's what happened with Enron. They didn't really understand, but they didn't want to ask. So then, I think, when something is published in a major magazine like *Fortune* saying, "nobody gets this," I think people became a little bit . . . freer to voice their concerns.[5]

Intimidation made Enron possible. Its managers proclaimed themselves the smartest guys in the room, and no one would admit to not understanding their master plan.

But often the smartest person in the room is the one willing to ask the dumb question. And McLean is no slouch. A math and English major at Williams College, she worked first at Goldman Sachs, a place whose culture and demands she says she wasn't prepared for but from which she learned much, including the invaluable skill, especially as a reporter, of reading a financial statement. Enron's were intentionally complicated, and even seasoned Wall Street players had trouble keeping up. One of the more remarkable aspects of McLean's piece

was the response she got from analysts, even those bullish on Enron stock, to
her basic question about how the company made money: "If you figure it out,
let me know," S&P credit analyst Todd Shipman told her. "Do you have a
year?" said Fitch analyst Ralph Pellecchia. Goldman Sachs analyst David
Fleischer summed it up: "It's very difficult for us on Wall Street with as little
information as we have."[6]

The Kool-Aid of the Enron scandal was the idea that the company's executives knew more than anyone else. The reality was that Enron, formerly a business, had become a bubble, divorced from reality and, most important for
investors, from real earnings and profits.

When McLean asked Enron her now famous question, and the follow-up question of whether its money came from derivatives trading, executives went berserk.
"We are not a trading company," the firm's chief financial officer, Andrew Fastow,
insisted: Enron was mostly an energy supplier. CEO Jeff Skilling belittled her.
"People who raise questions," he told her, "are people who have not gone through
[our business] in detail and who want to throw rocks at us."[7] Skilling's bluster
was typical of those in finance who either don't understand something or, more
likely, don't want others to. McLean's questions cut to the heart of the problem,
and Enron's response provided a red flag.

Fortune published her story. It was a journalistic triumph and, for Enron, a
prick that caused its balloon to deflate quickly and completely. Another telltale
event occurred a few weeks later, on a conference call in April 2001, in which
analysts talked with Enron executives about the company's first-quarter earnings. When a short-seller named Richard Grubman pressed Skilling for a
balance sheet statement to accompany the income statement the company had
just released—a reasonable request by any measure—Skilling balked, becoming
increasingly annoyed until he called Grubman an "asshole."[8] His words took
many aback. Veterans of Wall Street, known for foul-mouthed speech, understand that a public business call about a Fortune 500 company's—or any
company's—earnings is no place for crass behavior. Enron employees, listening
to the call via a piped-in link, broke into applause and refashioned the company's motto, "Ask why," into "Ask why, asshole."[9] But to outsiders, Skilling's
response raised hard questions.

So did events four months later, in mid-August, by which time the company's stock had fallen into the low forty-dollar range, less than half its value a
year earlier: Skilling suddenly announced he was leaving the company. "I am

resigning for personal reasons," he said, insisting that his departure was unrelated to Enron's performance. It was the classic "spend more time with my family" departure that always sends up another red flag. Smart investors hearing these words brace for the other shoe to fall.

Shortly after Skilling's announcement, on September 11, 2001, terrorists attacked the United States, and the nation briefly forgot Enron. Soon, however, the company was back in the news, announcing a $618 million loss in mid-October. In early November it announced that it had to restate earnings for the previous five years, reducing them by $600 million, or 15 percent, and warning more bad news might come.

The restatement revealed that the company had pushed billions of dollars of debt off its books through a series of complicated partnerships arranged and controlled by company officials in what appeared—and turned out—to be egregious conflicts of interest.[10] At the end of November, a potential merger with a rival energy company fell through, and other firms stopped doing business with Enron. Its deteriorating situation over the year had pushed its stock price down, which triggered requirements to repay loans or put up more money in those partnerships, simultaneously worsening its debt obligations and cash shortage, which pushed the stock down further. The merger was its last hope. On December 2 Enron filed for bankruptcy.

The bankruptcy, when it finally happened, hardly stunned markets. A few weeks earlier, federal regulators had finally started to take a hard look at the company, only to find that its claims of innovation were nothing more than accounting chicanery. The tight friendship that Enron's Ken Lay enjoyed with George W. Bush, who became president in January 2001, suddenly embarrassed the White House.[11]

A few analysts, notably John Olson at Merrill Lynch, had tried to ask tough questions even before McLean or the short-sellers had. But Enron officials pressured Merrill's president, Herb Allison, to push Olson out. Allison, who had been a leader in coordinating Wall Street's bailout of Long-Term, did just that, in the summer of 1998. He acted after two Merrill employees complained that Enron had shut them out of "lucrative" Enron stock underwriting deals because Olson was too critical of the company when speaking to reporters.[12] Like other investment banks at the time, Merrill pretended to have a firewall between those who analyzed stocks and made buy or sell recommendations to the public, and those who actually bought and sold securities or businesses. They didn't, which made anyone paying attention suspicious of the stock recommendations that firms like Merrill Lynch made to the public. Smart money knew not to rely on such recommendations, even if retail stock buyers, scorned by Wall Street as suckers, didn't.

Just weeks after Enron collapsed, lawyer and derivatives expert Frank Partnoy told congressional investigators how Enron's executives had relied on derivatives to devise twisted transactions internally and with customers, and used partnerships "to generate false profits and to hide losses." The company, he said, "has been compared to Long-Term Capital Management," which, he reminded lawmakers, "lost $4.6 billion on more than $1 trillion of derivatives" and had to be bailed out. He agreed that "there are similarities in both firms' use and abuse of financial derivatives. But the scope of Enron's problems and their effects on its investors and employees are far more sweeping. . . . In short, Enron makes Long-Term Capital Management look like a lemonade stand."[13]

Federal investigators found not only that Enron had engaged in accounting fraud, but also that it had made an energy shortage in California worse by manipulating markets there, causing rolling brownouts and higher prices. The state's cost for electricity rose from $7 billion in 1999 to $27 billion in 2000, the climb starting just after Senator Phil Gramm pushed through Congress the Enron-Koch exemption allowing companies to trade energy derivatives with virtually no government oversight.[14]

Enron's eventual collapse from accounting fraud, bad management, and market manipulation caused millions of people to lose billions of dollars. Many of the losers were small investors with life savings at stake. Yet, in contrast to what happened when the Long-Term fiasco hit, no one called for a bailout of Enron or any of its shareholders. The only money that Enron's investors recovered came from criminal and civil cases—and it ended up being cents on the dollar. The company's failure hurt individuals, eroding trust in corporate America and the accuracy of its financial disclosures, but it didn't threaten the system. Enron, in short, was the exception that proved the rule: thrifts, banks, and a giant hedge fund that threatened a system underpinned by deposit insurance were bailed out; companies that simply hurt investors were not. Deposit insurance and the too-big-to-fail safety net it engendered helped the individual only as a means to an end, instilling public confidence so the little guys in aggregate wouldn't rattle the financial system with runs. If a small investor lost his money to unscrupulous business executives, however, he was on his own.

Lawmakers did, however, recognize that the scandal had sufficiently angered the voting public that they needed to take action. First, the government focused on putting those responsible in jail. Fastow, Enron's chief financial officer, pleaded guilty to conspiracy to commit securities and wire fraud. He was sentenced to ten years in prison and forced to forfeit more than $29 million. Former CEO Skilling, considered the leader of the fraud, had to forfeit $42 million and served fourteen years in jail.

Lay, after being convicted of fraud, died suddenly of a heart attack. After growing up poor in rural Missouri, Lay had built a life of riches and relative fame, becoming a friend to President Bush and, eventually, an Enron apologist who denied to the end his own culpability in the company's demise.[15] Even his remorse over Enron's bankruptcy seemed more for himself than for the millions of people who lost tens of billions of dollars. "I'm sure there's absolutely nothing in my life, including the loss of life of many of my loved ones, that even comes close to the same level of pain, and the same enduring pain, that has caused," he told a jury.[16]

Lay and other Enron officials, including board members, argued throughout their legal ordeal that they were victims of bad information they had received from outside gatekeepers such as their auditor, Arthur Andersen, and lawyers at Vinson & Elkins. SEC and Justice Department investigators didn't buy it. An Enron vice president, Sherron Watkins, won fame and a *Time* magazine cover by coming forward as a whistleblower. Watkins wrote a seven-page letter to Lay and the auditors at Arthur Andersen in August 2001, alleging fraud at Enron. "I am incredibly nervous," she wrote, "that we will implode in a wave of accounting scandals. My 8 years of Enron work history will be worth nothing on my resume, the business world will consider the past successes as nothing but an elaborate accounting hoax."[17] Watkins clearly knew about the partnerships created to hide losses and debt. Though many lauded her actions, others questioned her motives. By August 2001, the damage was done. *Forbes* magazine questioned her timing in a piece headlined, "Sherron Watkins Had a Whistle, But Blew it." Was she covering for herself, and possibly Lay and others, by trying to make it seem that he didn't know about the fraud? Or was she sincerely trying to alert higher ups? She cautioned Lay that some unhappy workers knew enough about the company's accounting chicanery to get Enron in trouble. Enron didn't fire her, but she said she faced retaliation and was made a pariah.

McLean thinks that while many at Enron clearly knew about the fraud, Lay himself was likely clueless to its true extent. She doesn't think that gets him off the hook, nor has she sympathy for former executives' arguments that they relied on other professionals. Lay had a pattern of looking the other way, as he did in 1987 when he learned that Enron traders were cooking the books to generate profits. He took action only when they started losing money. "I don't understand how a CEO can take hundreds of millions of dollars in compensation from a company supposedly because of the great job [he is] doing running that company, and then when things go bad, say, 'not me, I didn't know, not my fault, not my responsibility,'" McLean said. "That just to me is an incredible shirking of responsibility. And I think if that sort of attitude is allowed to stand, it says something pretty frightening about corporate America."[18]

Congress agreed. In July 2002, just eight months after Enron filed for bankruptcy, lawmakers passed legislation to address two key problems in corporate America the incident had exposed: conflicts of interest in the accounting profession, and serious shortcomings in corporate governance.

The accounting industry's problems had been glaringly evident in the savings and loan crisis, but the Bush White House didn't address the issue in its thrift bailout and reform law in 1989. It could take on only so many industries at a time. As for the second issue, since the thrift debacle, investors had become increasingly concerned about the tendency for boards of directors to serve management, not shareholders, despite laws and lip service to the contrary. Enron's failure aroused enough anger—and financial loss among voters—to enable lawmakers to enact long-needed reforms in both areas. The result was the Sarbanes-Oxley Act of 2002, or SOX, named in the tradition of Congress for the bill's main sponsors, Senator Paul Sarbanes (D-Md.), chair of the Senate Banking Committee, and Representative Mike Oxley (R-Ohio), chair of the House Financial Services Committee. While the bill was being drafted, Oxley sided with industry and repeatedly tried to derail it or water it down, but public sentiment ultimately forced him to back it. At one point he sheepishly suggested that his name be left off the bill, an offer Sarbanes graciously declined. Oxley's name is forever on one of the most important pieces of legislation on accounting and corporate governance in U.S. history, despite his best effort to kill it.

The bill reformed accounting. It created the Public Company Accounting Oversight Board to ensure that accountants apply generally accepted accounting principles (GAAP) properly. Those rules are developed by the Financial Accounting Standards Board, or FASB, a self-regulatory organization, or SRO, run by the accounting industry under authority of the Securities and Exchange

Commission. SOX also ended a huge conflict of interest among accountants by barring firms from both auditing a company and providing consulting services to it. Of the $52 million in fees Enron paid Arthur Andersen in 2000, for example, more than half came from consulting. Andersen projected that the growth in consulting fees could yield two or three times that amount in a few years, far outpacing prospective earnings from audits. "There's no way that you could have a client which is that huge and important to you and not be tempted to turn your head away from problems," Dan L. Goldwasser, a lawyer who advises accountants, told the *New York Times*. "If the audit partner who's on the Enron account lost that account, they were history."[19]

Sarbanes-Oxley largely banned companies from giving executives personal loans and required them to more fully disclose companies' off-balance-sheet activities that affect financial performance. Lawyers representing publicly traded companies now have stricter requirements to report improprieties up a company's hierarchy, including telling the CEO or chief counsel and, if there is no action, members of a board's audit committee or the full board. The act requires chief executives and chief financial officers to certify in writing that financial statements are accurate, with penalties of up to $1 million and ten years in prison for unintentional mistakes and up to $5 million and twenty years in prison for intentional ones. In short, top officials can no longer deflect blame for fraudulent or inaccurate financials by saying, as Lay and other Enron executives did, that they relied on information from lawyers or accountants. The act also requires that companies demonstrate they have internal controls in place to make falsifying financial statements harder. If your workplace requires you to change your password every six months, thank this provision of the Sarbanes-Oxley Act.

The act bars reporting financials on a pro forma basis unless a company also reports them according to GAAP and describes how the two sets of numbers relate to each other. This requirement effectively ended bogus pro forma statements. Members of a company's audit committee must be independent directors, that is, they must have no official position in the company or other ties to it. The audit committee must hire and deal directly with a company's outside auditor. And at least one member of the audit committee must be a financial expert with an understanding of accounting and how to read financial statements. Audit committee members must also provide a way for employees to tell them anonymously of any accounting or auditing concerns. In addition, the act sets out penalties of up to twenty years in jail for anyone destroying documents in a legal investigation, and it provides some protection to whistleblowers against retaliation by employers.

SOX also spurred the New York Stock Exchange and other exchanges to tighten rules for publicly traded companies, leading to a requirement, for example, that a majority of board members be independent and, coupled with an additional law, that all members of a company's compensation committee be independent.

Yet Sarbanes-Oxley left a glaring issue untouched: unregulated derivatives.

The over-the-counter derivatives market grew wildly in the 1980s, but it hit a bump in 1990 when a court ruling in New York created uncertainty over whether energy derivatives were futures contracts that fell under the oversight of the Commodity Futures Trading Commission.

Well before Clinton appointed Born to head the CFTC in 1996, Ronald Reagan had appointed Wendy Gramm, the wife of Senator Phil Gramm, to the post in 1988. Gramm still held the job in 1992, when Congress gave the CFTC the power to clear up the confusion from the court ruling. Gramm led the drafting of rules to do just that, clearly exempting energy contracts from CFTC oversight. The commission approved the rules a few days before Gramm left office, in January 1993. Five weeks later, she joined the board of directors of Enron, which had pushed for and was very pleased with the commission's decision. She sat on the board's audit committee, along with Robert K. Jaedicke, a former dean of the Stanford Business School. Enron paid her as much as $1.85 million during her tenure, which lasted from 1993 to 2001.[20] Among the more outrageous actions the company took during her time on the board was creating a fake trading floor to make the firm's energy division look busy to visitors.[21]

In 1999, while an Enron director, Gramm became head of a research group at the Mercatus Center at George Mason University, in the Virginia suburbs of Washington, D.C.[22] Mercatus, a think tank that advocates for deregulation, including of energy markets, was founded and largely funded by the Koch brothers and heavily influenced by them via Richard Fink, a cofounder and Mercatus board member. Fink served as a vice president and member of the board of directors of Koch Industries, as well as chairman and CEO of the Koch unit that lobbies on behalf of the company and its affiliates.[23] In a neat arrangement, Enron and its chairman donated tens of thousands of dollars to Mercatus when Wendy Gramm, who holds a Ph.D. in economics from Northwestern, held spots at both institutions—and just as her husband was slipping language into legislation to further exempt energy futures from federal oversight.[24]

At Mercatus, Gramm wrote in favor of deregulation. She cowrote, for example, a public comment in June 2000 to regulators at her former agency, the Commodity Futures Trading Commission, about types of trades and trading platforms that Enron wanted to do and that were at the heart of the over-the-counter derivatives bill her husband was then cosponsoring in the Senate.[25] In December 2003, two years after Enron filed for bankruptcy and as investigations swirled over what responsibility she and other directors played in its collapse, she coauthored a comment on a proposed SEC rule intended to make directors more accountable to shareholders. "Clearly," the authors wrote, "some boards of directors (and firm managements) have made decisions with their own rather than the shareholders' best interests in mind."[26] In neither comment did she mention her connection to Enron.

Gramm and the other Enron directors never faced criminal charges.[27] But they did pay $13 million out of their own pockets to help settle shareholders' suits alleging they had failed to perform their duties. Enron's insurance company paid an additional $155 million.[28] If the directors had been found guilty of criminal wrongdoing, the insurer might have tried to renege on making payments, and shareholders might have lost even more of each dollar they had invested. It is not clear whether federal investigators took that into account in deciding not to press criminal charges.

Before its demise, Enron was a major contributor to Senator Gramm's political campaigns. Enron and Koch Industries executives can only have been pleased when Gramm led the charge to exempt by law not only over-the-counter derivatives from federal oversight but *all* energy futures from oversight. Without that exemption, as *Barron's* pointed out in an article about the Gramms entitled "Mr. and Mrs. Enron," the CFTC might well have decided to regulate Enron's trading operations as an "organized exchange" overseen by the agency. Ditto for the Kochs' energy trading business. Emails in the fall of 2000 discussing strategy to get the bill passed included some written by lobbyists employed by Enron and Koch Industries: they discussed how and when to get Lay on the phone to Senator Gramm and noted that at one point, Fed Chair Greenspan had urged the senator to push the bill through Congress.[29]

Enron's demise is as much a board failure as it is an accounting fraud. Senate investigators concluded that the directors as a group had neglected their duty to shareholders, but they saved their harshest criticism for the audit committee, because Gramm and its other members had approved all the off-balance-sheets partnerships so rife with conflicts of interest, including partnerships with the company's CEO, Skilling, and its chief financial officer, Fastow.

The Sarbanes-Oxley Act was not passed soon enough to head off a series of high-profile accounting crimes that emerged in Enron's wake. Less than a year after Enron filed for bankruptcy, telecommunications giant Worldcom became engulfed in an equally sensational scandal. Its bankruptcy filing in 2002 eclipsed Enron's as the biggest up to that time. Several WorldCom executives pled guilty to fraud charges, and the company's chief executive, Bernard Ebbers, was sentenced to twenty-five years in prison. The disgraced CEO of conglomerate Tyco was convicted of looting the company of millions of dollars to pay for such items as a $5 million wedding ring and several mansions, one of which had a $6,000 shower curtain.[30] There were other examples of wrongdoing as well. TV celebrity Martha Stewart, charged with covering up insider stock trading, was convicted of obstructing justice and lying to federal investigators about a well-timed sale of stock. She served five months in jail and five months of house arrest, then was on probation for two years. Fans of Stewart, who built a business empire showing viewers how to make impossibly cute crafts, quickly forgave her.

Many other companies, worried lest they be charged with fraud, reviewed their accounting practices and announced earnings restatements, hoping to stay ahead of any perceived wrongdoing. A memorable chapter in the Enron scandal was the role of the energy trader's auditor, Arthur Andersen. Employees in Andersen's Houston office destroyed documents in the fall of 2001, as the company's troubles escalated and the SEC and Justice Department launched probes. Destroying potential evidence is never a good idea when a company runs into trouble, but it's a criminal offense to do so once government investigators get involved—which they did in October amid revelations of Enron's earnings—if the intent is to hide key information.

Andersen reported the document shredding to the Justice Department, denying criminal intent. Self-reporting often earns less severe punishment from regulators, but not this time. The Justice Department charged Andersen with obstruction, and a federal jury convicted it, leaving the firm unable to audit the books of companies registered with the SEC. But Andersen was ruined simply by being charged with criminal wrongdoing, well before any determination of guilt. Many clients, hoping to distance themselves from any taint, fired it for that alone. The U.S. Supreme Court eventually set aside the conviction, determining that a lower court judge had given the jury improper instructions, and the government elected not to retry the case. Andersen had salvaged its reputation, to a degree, but too late to save itself or hundreds of employees.

One of the companies that fired Andersen once criminal charges were filed was mortgage giant Freddie Mac. Freddie's new auditor did what every newly hired auditor does: it reviewed the company's books to throw out any questionable accounting treatments so that it would not, and could never, be blamed for them. Scrutiny was especially tough because, in a bizarre twist, an anonymous person had written to officials at Freddie's competitor, Fannie Mae, alleging accounting improprieties at Freddie. Fannie gave the letters to Freddie officials, and the Freddie board launched a probe. Freddie ended up restating its earnings for 2000 to 2002, cutting them by $5 billion.[31] Among several questionable practices, Freddie had misapplied accounting rules for its use of over-the-counter derivatives, which despite being unregulated were nonetheless subject to accounting rules. Those rules set out that derivatives must be marked periodically up or down on financial statements to prevailing market prices.

Following accounting rules on derivatives could make earnings look volatile from quarter to quarter, something Wall Street analysts abhorred and that Steady Freddie—the company's nickname for itself—avoided by simply applying whichever rule was more favorable each quarter. Such arbitrary and inconsistent application of accounting rules, needless to say, violated GAAP.

After the revelation of Freddie's mistakes, investors—and members of Congress—started to wonder if Fannie had done the same thing. Fannie's chairman, Franklin Raines, swore it hadn't, insisting that the battering the company's stock was taking was unjustified collateral damage from Freddie's accounting woes. In a confrontation with Congress, Raines testified that he would welcome scrutiny of how Fannie scored its derivatives. "After a thorough review of all the facts, if it is determined that our company made significant mistakes," he said, "our board and our shareholders will hold me accountable. And I'll hold myself accountable."[32]

Accountants at the SEC reviewed Fannie's books and determined that it had indeed violated accounting rules. The company was forced to restate its earnings from 1998 through 2004, reducing them by $10.6 billion. Raines, who had been

Former Senator Phil Gramm, *center*, and his wife, Wendy, *left*, in August 2008.
Barron's dubbed the couple "Mr. and Mrs. Enron" in 2001. AP Photo/Mary Altaffer.

President Clinton's budget director before going to Fannie, and the company's chief financial officer, Timothy Howard, were ousted in 2004. Raines paid nearly $25 million to settle federal civil charges, and Howard paid $6.4 million. But they won a victory of sorts in 2012 when a judge dismissed, for lack of "direct evidence," a shareholder suit alleging they had manipulated earnings to meet goals that triggered multimillion-dollar pay packages.[33]

Other crises emerged after the stock market's tech bubble burst in early 2000. Coupled with Enron's collapse and other accounting misbehaviors, they left no corner of Wall Street untouched by scandal.

A congressional investigation led by senators Carl Levin (D-Mich.) and Susan Collins (R-Maine) in 2002 detailed how bankers at Merrill Lynch, Citigroup, and JPMorgan Chase had joined accountants, lawyers, and other enablers to help Enron cook its books, creating complex deals to hide debt and show borrowed money as income. "Our investigation indicates that Enron could not have engaged in the extent, and to the extent, of the deceptions that it did without the knowing assistance and participation of major financial institutions," Levin said.[34]

Fannie Mae Chairman and CEO Franklin Raines, *left*, and CFO Timothy
Howard prepare to testify before the U.S. House Financial Services Committee on
October 6, 2004, following an auditor's report critical of accounting practices
and management policies. AP Photo/Dennis Cook.

In April 2003, in an agreement with regulators led by New York State
Attorney General Eliot Spitzer, nearly a dozen Wall Street firms agreed to pay
$1.4 billion to settle charges of conflicts of interest like the one Merrill Lynch
had when it ousted a stock analyst after Enron complained about him. As part
of the deal, the firms agreed to separate their securities research departments
from their investment banking businesses and ensure that no one from the
investment banking side could influence the compensation of, or reports by,
stock analysts. No more could an analyst or company recommend that the
public buy stocks without disclosing whether they owned shares in the company
they were recommending or had other potential conflicts of interest. (Congress
relaxed this agreement in 2012, in legislation intended to jump-start the
economy after Wall Street's mortgage meltdown.)[35]

Spitzer also exposed widespread conflicts of interest and wrongdoing in the
mutual fund industry. Among the problems: fund managers allowed wealthy
hedge funds' clients to profit at the expense of ordinary retail investors, and
they steered retail customers into expensive, inappropriate products in exchange
for higher commissions. These extra payments—kickbacks, really—are legal
only if customers are told about them.[36] Spitzer's exposé yielded tens of millions
of dollars in fines and restitution, and it galvanized the SEC to vow better

policing of the investment community. (The congressional probe by Levin and Collins also lit a fire under the SEC to probe the connections between Enron and its bankers.) But Wall Street got a moment of revenge: in 2008, federal investigators caught Spitzer with a paid escort in the Mayflower Hotel in Washington, D.C., eliciting the popping of champagne corks on the floor of the New York Stock Exchange. The man who had brought so much of Wall Street's dirty laundry to light was himself exposed.[37]

In 2003, news broke that New York Stock Exchange Chair and CEO Dick Grasso received a pay package of nearly $140 million, approved by the exchange's board of directors, whose members headed the Wall Street firms Grasso was supposed to be policing. Since its inception, the SEC has allowed some key Wall Street institutions to police themselves, despite the obvious, inherent conflicts of interest that created. These "self-regulatory organizations," or SROs, of which the New York Stock Exchange was one, in theory can conduct business while also monitoring member firms and their executives for wrongdoing. Although the arrangement had been in place for years, the sheer size of Grasso's pay package—and that it was paid by the firms he was supposed to police—grabbed the attention of investor groups and members of Congress. Grasso was forced to resign, but he kept much of the money. Embarrassment over how few disciplinary actions Grasso or the SEC had taken over the years, a record in sharp contrast to all the problems that had emerged, did however prompt long-overdue structural changes. The roles of chair and CEO at the exchange were split, for example, and independent directors were added to the board. But many considered the changes insufficient.[38]

To recap: In 1989, the biggest taxpayer bailout up to that time resolved the worst of the S&L crisis, making good on the fifty-year-old promise of a federal safety net for depositors, though at a cost many times higher than would have been necessary had action been taken years sooner. In 1998, the government orchestrated a privately funded multibillion-dollar bailout of Long-Term Capital Management to protect the financial system from chaos.

Then a string of accounting and other scandals followed the collapse of the dot-com market bubble in 2000—notably at Enron, Worldcom, Fannie Mae, and Freddie Mac—revealing widespread fraud, corruption, and conflicts of interest in corporate America and the securities markets. The scandals shook public trust, but because they didn't threaten the financial system, they yielded new law but no bailouts.

Yet a much bigger scandal was already percolating, largely unnoticed, in the market for subprime mortgages: home loans for people with less-than-perfect credit. As the Sarbanes-Oxley Act attempted to reform accounting and to hold executives of publicly traded companies accountable, a key corner of the securities arena remained unregulated: over-the-counter derivatives, a market that approached $100 trillion when Enron collapsed and would reach seven times that amount by 2008. A handful of commercial banks dominated the business, with the five largest accounting for a whopping 97 percent of the over-the-counter derivatives market. By 2016, it was hardly more democratic, with four banks controlling 91 percent and the largest twenty-five banks nearly 100 percent. The business of selling instruments to spread risk has always been highly concentrated, as use of these securities in the subprime mortgage market would demonstrate.[39]

PART THREE

ILL-GOTTEN GAIN: BOOM, BUST, AND THE GREAT RECESSION

19

Tent City

IN MARCH 2009, SEVERAL HUNDRED PEOPLE CAMPED in tents in downtown Sacramento, California, capital of the state that the thrift industry during the 1950s and 1960s had made into a flagship for homeownership. Now, families who had recently lost homes to foreclosure had settled in a makeshift, ramshackle community where a lack of toilets and fresh water had health officials worried about an outbreak of cholera or other illness. The tents symbolized the plight of people in California and across the nation. A housing boom that started in the 1990s had turned into a bubble by 2003 and then imploded in 2007, gutting the economy and costing millions of Americans their homes, jobs, and retirement money. Two years later, amid the biggest recession since the 1930s, TV images of the shantytown put faces to the crisis.[1]

By 2009, an estimated 5 percent of all mortgage holders were in foreclosure nationwide, more than triple the previous record, 1.5 percent, set during the recession of 2001. If you added in seriously delinquent loans—ninety days or more past due—the rate doubled to nearly 10 percent, four times the rate of the prior downturn. Unemployment hit 10 percent, more than double what it had been two years earlier and the highest in a quarter century, as 8 million jobs "were swept away." Home prices nationally had fallen 30 percent since their peak in mid-2006, losing $5.5 trillion in value. Major banks and financial firms teetered on the edge of bankruptcy. Credit markets froze. The value of retirement plans plummeted.[2]

The federal government would spend or pledge to spend some $24 trillion to bail out Wall Street, try to unfreeze credit and commerce, and restore confidence. By luck, most of that money was either repaid or never used. But matters easily could have played out differently. And the price of the bailout doesn't capture the estimated $20 trillion in lost economic activity, including "underemployment, long-term unemployment, foreclosures, homelessness, underwater mortgages, bankrupt businesses large and small, lost savings, deferred or denied retirements, educations cut short, and so much more" that will never be recovered.[3] Even those with jobs and savings lost out: the Fed's policy of setting interest rates near zero to try to resuscitate the economy gave banks "free deposit money" at the expense of depositors, who lost an estimated $250 billion a year in interest income.[4] (The general public's losses would have been greater still had industry succeeded in its push in 2000 to sell credit-default derivatives (swaps) to the public or had President George W. Bush been able to privatize Social Security, as he tried to do in 2005.[5])

The housing bubble officially lasted from mid-2003 to the end of 2007, but home prices had already stopped rising by 2006 and had even fallen in some areas.[6] When the bubble finally did burst, the deluge of mortgage defaults it unleashed "was without parallel, save perhaps for the Great Depression."[7] The downturn, dubbed the Great Recession in a tip of the hat to the 1930s downturn, was the longest since World War II and officially ran from December 2007, when the expansion ended, to June 2009, when the next expansion began.[8] But many Americans suffered fallout before and long after those bookends, with consequences that sparked protests on the Right and Left and residual anger that influenced the outcome of the presidential election seven years later.

In 2003, before the housing boom was a full-blown bubble, 1 of every 46 mortgage holders was in foreclosure or seriously delinquent. By the end of 2009, when foreclosures reached their peak, they numbered 1 in 10. Not until 2016, at 1 in 34, did the numbers approach normal levels, a testament to the decade or more a consumer needs to recover financially from a home foreclosure. With consumers accounting for 60 to 70 cents of every dollar spent in the economy, the lesson was clear: hobble consumers, hobble the economy. Recovery came slowly and unevenly. Economists Atif Mian and Amir Sufi found that in the "20 percent of counties that were hardest hit" by the crash, the average unemployment rate jumped more than 2.5 times, to 13 percent, and remained above 10 percent for at least three years after the official end of the recession; other research suggests the fallout lasted much longer, at least six years.[9] Long-term unemployment, defined as being without a job for

twenty-seven weeks or more, was "notable" compared with previous recessions, according to the Bureau of Labor Statistics. The mortgage lenders of
Wall Street had crippled the housing sector and, in the process, it turned out,
themselves. Bailing out those who had caused the crisis was repugnant. Not
bailing them out would have made the economic damage even worse. But the
rescue that federal officials concocted was fundamentally flawed: it failed to do
enough to help Wall Street's customers, the people in the tents, the people
behind the nation's consumer spending.[10]

Presidents Hoover and Roosevelt worried that civil unrest during the 1930s
Depression would undermine democracy. The Bush White House had the same
fear seventy years later as it grappled with the mortgage crisis, as did the Obama
White House when it inherited the mess.

Ben Bernanke, chairman of the Federal Reserve Board during the Great
Recession and, by coincidence, a scholar of the Great Depression, was ever
mindful as the mortgage meltdown unfolded that "the Federal Reserve . . . failed
its first major test in the 1930s" by remaining "passive in the face of ruinous
deflation and financial collapse." The resulting global downturn brought "bread-
lines. . . . 25 percent unemployment in the United States and the rise of fascist
dictatorships abroad."[11] In the fall of 2008, Bernanke and Treasury Secretary
Hank Paulson faced the calamity of hundreds of thousands of people losing their
jobs as "companies of all kinds" cut "costs and capacity." Tim Geithner, who
served as president of the New York Fed during the crisis and then as Treasury
secretary after Paulson, describes the anguish that federal bank regulators felt as
the downturn destroyed "$15 trillion in household wealth," pushed 9 million
people below the poverty line, and caused 5 million homes to be lost: it was "a
stress test of the American political system, an extreme real-time challenge of a
democracy's ability to lead the world" in the face of such economic loss.[12]

As Treasury secretary, Paulson felt a "jolt of fear" as Lehman Brothers, the
nation's fourth largest investment bank, collapsed in mid-September 2008.
Watching the problems of Lehman and then of insurance giant AIG's "spiraling
out of control. . . . I could see credit tightening, strapped companies slashing
jobs, foreclosures rising ever faster: millions of Americans . . . [losing] their
livelihoods and their homes [and it] . . . would take years for us to dig ourselves
out from under such a disaster." He stole a moment to call his wife. "What if the
system collapses?" he told her. "I am really scared."[13]

As credit markets froze in 2008, hundreds of businesses, from small firms to giant General Electric, were thrown into a liquidity crisis. Commercial bankruptcies reached 61,000 in 2009, triple the number in 2006. Depositors started runs on uninsured money-market accounts, on investment banks, and even on certain federally insured banks rumored to be in trouble. The week before federal regulators shut down what was then the nation's largest thrift, Washington Mutual, depositors withdrew more than $2 billion a day, nearly $17 billion in all, because they were worried about delays in getting their money or about losing amounts above the insurance limit. A "fog of a panic," as Geithner termed it, caused lenders to mistrust other lenders and companies on the fear that assets they listed on their books as performing would turn out to be bad mortgages. "It was the worst financial panic in American history," Bernanke recalled a decade later.[14]

The government faced a dilemma: intervene, including with a liberal use of tax dollars for bailouts, or let giant institutions fall, sending crippling ripples across the economy at home and abroad. Reluctantly, President Bush agreed that the government needed to jump in to pledge federal guarantees for the multitrillion-dollar markets in commercial paper, money-market funds, and any new bank debt; seize and run two of the world's biggest financial firms, Fannie Mae and Freddie Mac; and spend tens of billions to bail out the world's biggest insurance firm, AIG. None of it seemed to work. Bernanke, Paulson, Geithner, and Federal Deposit Insurance Corporation Chair Sheila Bair scrambled to set the right course. Republicans quickly dubbed Paulson "Comrade" for his role in orchestrating the government intervention, which shielded Wall Street from the consequences of its own actions, although they spent little time asking why the two biggest taxpayer-funded bailouts in U.S. history—the S&L crisis and now this—took place under two avowedly free-market presidents, George H. W. Bush and his son, George W. Bush.

Despite the moral hazard of bailouts, government officials had no choice but to step in. Letting bad actors suffer the consequences of their behavior works during normal times, but in a crisis it fans the fires—and would have repeated the mistakes the government had made after the 1929 crash. Absent government action, "We would have been eating grasshoppers and living in tents. Things could have been that bad," an energy company executive hyperbolically but not inaccurately told members of the Financial Crisis Inquiry Commission, created by Congress in 2009 to study the causes of the fiasco.[15] The commission's report, which runs to 550 pages—not counting the index, thousands of supporting documents, and hours of recorded interviews—encyclopedically details every twist and turn of the crisis and the financial and political forces that created it. But while the report captures facts, it doesn't fully capture the anxiety those in charge felt as the crisis unfolded. Its mission was to defog events.

As regulators struggled to see through the mist, they found themselves too busy reacting to the tidal wave of mortgage defaults engulfing the economy. Starting in early 2007 they faced a nonstop parade of major bankruptcies and financial disruptions, any one of which in normal times would have been monumental. Their fear that economic mayhem would lead to civil upheaval cannot be overstated.

To the public, the crisis seemed to begin suddenly, in the summer and fall of 2008, as Lehman failed. In fact it had been unfolding for eighteen months. One telltale jolt followed another, including one that Paulson received on a trip to China in August 2008 for the Olympics in Beijing. Top Chinese officials told him the Russian government had approached them to propose coordinating the sale of "big chunks" of each country's billions of dollars in Fannie and Freddie securities, a move that would have destroyed U.S. markets (and very possibly also the world's). Although the Chinese "declined to go along with the disruptive scheme," Paulson recollects, the national security threat from the financial crisis became clear.[16] But it took Lehman's collapse to make Bernanke, Paulson, Geithner, and others comprehend the full scope of what was happening.[17]

Slow as federal regulators were to see the big picture, once they did they worked tirelessly to keep the devastation from being even worse than it was. Double-digit unemployment was hard, but it was still less than half the rate seen during the Depression. The panic, however, was unparalleled.

How did such a massive crisis develop? The short answer is that lenders, flush with money made cheap by events and by the federal government, aggressively coaxed millions of borrowers to refinance mortgages without assessing whether those borrowers could repay the new loans, which carried very onerous terms. Worse, the lenders intended that most wouldn't be able to repay and would have to refinance into new loans that were also unaffordable. This process would produce an endless cycle of refinancing fees for the lenders—so long as home prices rose forever and borrowers stayed afloat. Regulators looked the other way and ignored those who sounded warnings. Most members of

Congress, blinded by the largesse of lobbyists, did too. Credit-rating agencies, over-the-counter derivatives dealers, lawyers, and accountants enabled each step of the mad scheme of excessive risk-taking.[18] Doomed to implode, the process of forcing customers to refinance over and over into increasingly bigger loans created a bubble that made bankers and their enablers billions while it lasted.

Easy credit greased the wheels. After the crash in technology stocks in 2001, and then the terrorist attacks of September 11, consumer confidence collapsed, sparking a recession. Federal Reserve Board Chairman Alan Greenspan feared that deflation would trigger spending cuts and layoffs, further dampening the economy. He reacted by cutting interest rates to the low single digits, reigniting a housing boom that had been in progress before the dot-com bubble imploded.

At the end of 1980, the prime rate, the benchmark interest rate that banks use to charge their most creditworthy customers, had peaked at 21.5 percent, not returning to single digits—9.5 percent—until mid-1985.[19] At the beginning of 2001, it was 9 percent. As the Fed responded to the terrorist attacks that September by lowering rates, by mid-2003 the prime rate had fallen to 4 percent, triggering a refinancing frenzy among prime mortgage holders eager to lower their monthly payments.

In the 1980s, the interest rate for a thirty-year, fixed-rate mortgage was in the high teens. By 2000 it had fallen below 10 percent. After the 9/11 attacks, it hit 5.25 percent, then hovered at or below 6 percent until 2006. Interest rates on adjustable mortgages fell even further, below 4 percent in 2003, and stayed at or below 6 percent through 2007.[20] Some 1.75 million prime mortgage borrowers refinanced in 2000. In 2003, the number reached over 12.6 million. Subprime borrowers—those with dented credit—also refinanced mortgages in greater numbers, but the uptick was less dramatic: subprime borrowers accounted for 586,522 in refinanced loans in 2000 and over 1.2 million in 2003.[21]

For Wall Street and the rest of corporate America, the Fed's decision to lower interest rates made cheap money even cheaper—so cheap that interest rates on loans fell below the rate of inflation. Another key benchmark rate—what banks charge to borrow from each other—plunged from 6.5 percent at the beginning of 2001 to 1 percent by Memorial Day 2003, a level not seen since the Kennedy administration. By 2003, companies with the best credit could borrow money for ninety days in the commercial paper market at an annual rate of 1.1 percent.[22] Then in 2004, the Securities and Exchange Commission lowered Wall Street's cost of borrowing even more by allowing investment bankers—including Paulson, head of Goldman Sachs at the time—to borrow more money without having to hold more capital as a cushion against potential losses. Now so fully awash in cheap, borrowed money, Wall Street faced a problem: as funds to invest proliferated, good places to invest had grown scarcer. The dot-com crash and the terrorist attacks had sent the economy into a slump—except for housing, thanks to the refinancing boom. Then in 2004 Greenspan pulled back, raising rates a percentage point or so, not too much but enough that demand for refinancing among prime mortgage holders significantly ebbed. As the 2003 refinancing boom for prime borrowers slowed, mortgage lenders wondered how they might keep the fee-income bonanza going. At the same time, Wall Street bankers wondered where they could invest so much easy credit. The two groups found the same answer: subprime mortgage borrowers. These borrowers were riskier than those with prime credit ratings, but, for that very reason, also paid higher returns.[23] In finding the same answer, mortgage lenders and Wall Street also found each other, and they embraced like newly smitten lovers.

Investors had long loved the idea of investing in mortgage lending. Home borrowers seldom defaulted, even in tough times, and home prices generally had risen steadily since the Depression. Prices had slumped in regional pockets occasionally but nationwide hadn't fallen in a single year for many decades. Subprime mortgage holders, despite posing a higher risk of default, made their monthly payments almost as reliably as prime mortgage holders did if the loan was properly underwritten and priced. Investors now made a fatal miscalculation. They assumed low default rates would continue to be the norm even when the terms of subprime loans, and how they were underwritten, fundamentally changed. Wall Street financiers encouraged this assumption even as they began to structure subprime mortgages to force borrowers to refinance over and over and into bigger and bigger loans, an unsustainable cycle that would ultimately leave consumers overwhelmed with debt.[24]

That mortgage holders would eventually collapse under the weight of so much borrowing didn't deter Wall Street. The idea of interacting with individual borrowers did, however. So the prospect of borrowing cheaply to invest in what historically had been the relative safety of mortgages, and ones that yielded a higher return than in the prime market, required another ingredient to make subprime home loans appealing to investors. It was the same innovation that made investing in prime loans through Fannie and Freddie so alluring: securitization, that is, the pooling of dozens, hundreds, even thousands of consumer loans as collateral for bonds that investors could buy and sell.

Securitization magically muted the most unattractive feature of mortgage lending—dealing with borrowers individually—while preserving its low-risk profits. As Wall Street investor and former bond trader Lew Ranieri put it, a home loan was an "ugly object" that securitization "dressed up" for investors. Bonds backed by subprime mortgages were called "private-label mortgage-backed securities," or PLMBS, or simply "private label." This distinguished them from Fannie and Freddie's bonds, mostly for the prime market, which are called "agency MBS," or "GSE MBS" because the two companies are "government-sponsored enterprises." The assembly line that created private-label securities—brokers, lenders, credit-rating agencies, over-the-counter derivative sellers, Wall Street bankers—started slowly in the 1970s, picked up steam in the mid-1990s, and had started to kick into high gear by the end of the decade. By 2003, Wall Street and subprime mortgage lenders were ready to rev the engine of private-label securitization for subprime borrowers full throttle. Regulators like Greenspan heralded this as a democratization of credit, dismissing any abuses as inconsequential anomalies.[25]

Easy credit and securitization, coupled with see-nothing, know-nothing regulators, created the ideal climate for a bubble in subprime lending. Just as important, however, was a change in the corporate governance structure of Wall Street banks. Before 1970, the nation's major investment banks were organized as partnerships, with a firm's partners sharing profits but also losses. Partners watched each other carefully, as people tend to do when their own money is at stake. The New York Stock Exchange even barred its members—investment banks—from being publicly traded, changing its policy only after some firms complained because they wanted to cash in by selling shares of themselves to the public that could be traded on the big board.[26]

As partners, investment bankers had been betting their own money. Former partners at Lehman Brothers and Morgan Stanley describe the firms' cultures before going public as low-key and ultra-serious, with executives sitting in a room together "not to socialize but to 'overhear, interact, and monitor' each other. They were all on the hook together." Because "they were personally liable as partners, they took risk very seriously." They were well compensated, "but the big payout was 'when you retire,'" which kept them focused on the long term.[27]

When investment banks converted to a stockholder model, they began to reward their executives for quarterly and yearly results, regardless of long-term consequences. Merrill Lynch went public in 1971 and by the end of the 1980s, only Goldman Sachs remained a partnership, waiting until 1999 to follow the rest of the pack.[28] As partnerships, investment banks focused on helping companies raise money through the sale of stocks or bonds. As publicly traded firms, they started to focus on proprietary trading, investing not for clients but for the firm. If their bets paid off, the bankers received huge bonuses; if not, shareholders bore the loss, and bankers typically still pocketed huge bonuses. This gambling with other people's money had worried Jefferson and Hamilton, and it worries banking experts like former Fed chairman Paul Volcker today.

From the end of World War II to the mid-1970s, executive pay in financial and nonfinancial industries increased in tandem and modestly, at about 0.8 percent a year. In the 1980s, however, yearly increases began to rise faster, hitting 10 percent between the mid-to late 1990s, with the financial sector driving the quickened pace. And driving the financial sector were the investment banks under their new stockholder model. Such divergence hadn't been seen since the 1920s. By the mid-2000s, average compensation for all employees in the financial sector was $102,000, compared with $58,666 for nonfinancial businesses. Financial executives' pay averaged $3.4 million a year in 2005, higher than in any other sector. The top executives earned many times that, with compensation packages worth tens of millions of dollars. Merrill Lynch Chairman and CEO Stanley O'Neal earned more than $91 million in 2006, a year in which the firm bet heavily on subprime mortgages. When he was fired, in 2007, his severance package was $161 million.[29]

Debt—borrowed money—held by the financial sector also soared, from $3 trillion in 1978 to $36 trillion in 2007, and more than doubled as a percentage of GDP. From 1980 to 2006, the financial sector's share of corporate profits nearly doubled, too, from 15 percent to 27 percent.[30] Finance wasn't just a lubricant for the engine of commerce anymore but a main component of the engine itself.

William McChesney Martin, the Fed chairman under Presidents Truman, Eisenhower, Kennedy, Johnson, and Nixon, famously said a central banker's job was to "take away the punch bowl just when the party gets going."[31] Alan Greenspan, Fed chairman before and during the bubble, didn't see his job that way.

Neither did lawmakers. In the housing boom of the 1990s, home prices went up because demand for housing and home renovations increased. In the 2000s, prices went up because people were investing in housing solely because prices were going up. The dog was chasing its own tail. Elected officials and regulators took no action, allowing too many people at too many corporations too much access to other people's money with virtually no policing.

20

Financial Magic

LEW RANIERI SITS IN HIS OFFICE ON Manhattan's East Side amid a clutter of mementos from a decades-long career on Wall Street, where he's been a fixture since his glory days at Salomon. Known for his love of ballet, rumpled attire, loud mouth, and keen mind, he has an outsized persona as a practical joker. At Salomon he was known to prowl hallways brandishing a sword from his collection, and he once set a colleague's pants on fire with a Bic lighter. Now, a decade after the mortgage crisis, the college dropout who rose from Salomon mail clerk to financial tycoon speaks about a less tangible legacy: his reputation in the wake of the biggest economic catastrophe since the 1930s, thanks to securities he helped reinvent.[1]

Wall Street has long designated Ranieri the godfather of "securitization," a term he says he coined during an interview with a Wall Street reporter to describe the conversion of consumer debt into tradable bonds. He once relished getting the credit for securitization but has since become less proud of it. "I do feel guilty," he told a *Fortune* magazine reporter in 2009. "I wasn't out to invent the biggest floating craps game of all time, but that's what happened." He has also insisted that securitization wasn't meant to take "away the thrifts' primary business of home lending," but rather be an "adjunct" to it.[2]

The truth is that neither Ranieri nor his contemporaries on Wall Street killed the thrift industry. Interest-rate swings and government policy did that. Nor did they invent securitization. Ranieri's Wall Street predecessors had done it decades before, in the 1920s. By 1925, bonds backed by real estate loans comprised nearly a quarter of all corporate debt. With little oversight, the market became rife with abuse and defaults, and resulting losses for the investing public galvanized states to pass laws requiring the registration of bonds backed by mortgages and restricting how they were sold. Fast forward fifty years, and the federal government—not Ranieri or Wall Street—became the first to successfully rediscover the 1920s practice of pooling mortgages to collateralize a bond. This remake, issued in the 1970s, differed from its predecessor by being federally subsidized. It's this federally backed version that became the model for modern mortgage-backed securities, both those in widespread, proper use today and those so widely misused during the mortgage bubble of the new millennium.[3]

What Ranieri did was help create a private-sector version of what the federal government had rediscovered, and thus reinvent a securitization market that, because it was divorced from government, looked much like the one that operated so robustly five decades earlier, until it went bust and states essentially banned it. Ranieri led the charge to persuade Congress to preempt those state laws. After federal lawmakers agreed to override state rules governing the registration and sale of private-label mortgage bonds, Ranieri then pushed to change federal tax law, which had disadvantaged investors who bought them. Both changes were essential to the creation of private-label mortgage-backed securities, including those at the heart of the mortgage bubble.

Other marquee names on Wall Street helped reinvent private-label securitization, but no one pushed harder than Ranieri to bulldoze the twin roadblocks of state law and federal taxes.[4]

The first attempt at a modern, private-label bond collateralized by mortgages was in 1977 by Bank of America and Ranieri's boss at Salomon at the time, Robert F. Dall. It flopped because all but fifteen states had investor protection laws that prohibited or made difficult the sale of such private-label mortgage-backed securities. Tax law too at the time was punitive. The flop galvanized Ranieri into action.

The circumstance that led the federal government and then Wall Street to rediscover securitization was the same one that had killed the thrift industry when it was borrowing short from depositors and investing long in mortgages: interest-rate risk, specifically an interest-rate squeeze.

Mortgage securitization—the creation of bonds collateralized by home loans—actually helped the thrift industry survive for longer than it otherwise would have. Thrifts were able to remove low-yielding mortgages from their books by selling them to Fannie and Freddie, who then bundled and sold them to investors the world over. Securitization transformed long-term consumer credit that institutional investors normally wouldn't touch—and that trapped thrifts in an interest-rate whip-saw—into bonds that investors now craved. It also transformed securities markets. Once the process proved successful for home loans, Wall Street applied it to all manner of debt, from consumer credit cards to commercial real estate loans. But as Ranieri, Wall Street, and the American public would learn, the alchemy of securitization also could work in reverse. Used correctly, securitization mitigated risk. When misused, it amplified it.

To understand securitization, start with Fannie and Freddie. Nobody does it better. Fannie and Freddie are essentially giant, wholesale thrifts—banks specializing in home loans. By congressional mandate, they don't sell home loans to consumers—the "primary" mortgage market—but instead buy home loans from primary lenders, creating the "secondary" mortgage market. As government-sponsored entities or GSEs, they are required to buy loans in good times and bad, supplying retail lenders with new cash to make additional mortgages. This makes mortgage markets more liquid and thus lowers the cost to consumers of borrowing to buy a home.

The high-interest-rate environment of the 1970s ravaged Fannie and Freddie just as it did thrifts. The loans they bought from lenders performed. Borrowers paid on time. Nonetheless, Fannie and Freddie were losing money. The loans were yielding single-digit returns when inflation had bumped the cost of borrowing into the double digits. Because of Fannie and Freddie's ties to the government, the investment community treated them—and securities they issued—as being federally guaranteed. Credit markets, believing the government would never let either company fail, allowed them to borrow more cheaply than any other entity except the U.S. Treasury itself. Still, this advantage over the private sector didn't save them from an interest-rate squeeze in the 1970s and 1980s: even their relatively low cost of borrowing was higher than the yields on the mortgages they bought. By the early 1980s, the interest-rate mismatch was costing Fannie $1 million a day in losses. Freddie had been smarter: shortly after Congress created it, it began pooling its mortgages to collateralize bonds that it sold to investors, thus removing the loans from its books. Fannie soon caught on.

The first modern, mortgage-backed securities arrived in 1970, not from Wall Street but from Ginnie Mae, a federal agency Congress spun off from Fannie Mae in 1968. Ginnie Mae guaranteed bonds collateralized by home loans that in turn were guaranteed by the Federal Housing Administration (FHA) and Veteran's Administration (VA). The act that created Ginnie Mae also made Fannie Mae a shareholder-owned company to help President Johnson make the deficit seem smaller during the Vietnam War.

Fannie Mae's purpose remained that of creating a secondary market in VA and FHA loans, but the 1968 law gave it several advantages over other publicly traded firms that caused it to soon abandon that loan market. It gave Fannie Mae a multi-billion-dollar line of credit with the Treasury and exempted Fannie from state and local taxes and from SEC registration fees when the company issued debt. And federally insured banks were allowed to hold Fannie Mae's debt and preferred shares without limit, just as they could Treasury securities. This contrasted sharply with much stricter limits on the concentration of securities banks could hold in other publicly traded companies. After splitting Ginnie Mae from Fannie, the law authorized both to create bonds collateralized by mortgages and, to facilitate the sale of these bonds nationwide, exempted both from state laws governing such securities.[5]

Then in 1970, the thrift industry persuaded Congress to create Freddie to buy its conventional mortgages—"conventional" meaning those not insured by the FHA or VA. The same legislation also freed Fannie to buy conventional mortgages. Congress thus created identical mortgage-finance twins, Fannie and Freddie, that began in earnest to build America's secondary-mortgage market for conventional mortgages. (Freddie would be owned by the thrift industry until 1989, when Bush's thrift bailout package spun it off into a shareholder-owned, publicly traded company just like Fannie.)

Securitization found traction with Fannie and Freddie. Freddie adopted it first, and Fannie soon followed, leaving VA and FHA loans to Ginnie Mae entirely and focusing, as Freddie did, on buying up conventional mortgages to prime borrowers, those with the best credit.[6] Together, Fannie and Freddie plunged into the business of buying loans and pooling them to back bonds they could sell to Wall Street, thus selling off the mortgages on their books and shielding themselves from the interest-rate snare that had decimated the thrift industry. By statutory mandate Fannie and Freddie had to buy mortgages day in and day out, but now they could act as middle men, immediately selling off those mortgages to the investing public. Thanks to securitization, low-yielding loans in a high-rate environment no longer threatened to kill them.

Securitization soon revolutionized the financing of all consumer debt. Securitization enabled lenders to tap capital markets—investors—for funding instead of relying so much on federally insured depositors. For investors, securitization transformed consumer debt into bonds that they could buy and sell without having to take responsibility for, or even understand, the underlying loans, much less the people who held them.

Investors didn't want direct ownership of an individual consumer's mortgage. They didn't want to process payments, get stuck if interest rates rose, or have to repossess a house and resell it if the borrower defaulted. But investors did want safe places to put their money to work, especially places whose security was nearly as reliable as a U.S. Treasury bond but with a higher yield. That's what Fannie and Freddie, with their perceived government backing, offered: an investment with the safety of Treasuries but with the higher return of mortgages. Fannie and Freddie's mortgage-backed securities were a hit.

Ideally, an investor matches the maturity of the funds he or she borrows to make an investment with the maturity of the investment, locking in an interest-rate spread that pertains even if prevailing rates change. Mortgages make that hard to do. They are a long-term proposition, particularly in the United States, where the market is dominated by the thirty-year variety that came into being in the 1930s. But thirty-year funding is as scarce as thirty-year mortgages are common. So most mortgages are funded with money that must be repaid more quickly.

Securitization dampened this risk. It pooled mortgages to back a bond that could be sold to investors, who would be repaid as home buyers in the pool made monthly payments. Because bond prices rise and fall inversely with interest rates, investors could always adjust the price of these bonds (mortgage-backed securities) to mitigate—not eliminate but manage—the first pitfall of mortgage lending: interest-rate risk. Mortgage-backed bonds shielded lenders and investors alike from the risk of being stuck holding a low-yielding investment at a time of rising rates. If interest rates rose, bond holders could always sell at a lower price, so that the yield for the buyer would match prevailing rates. The seller would thus get cash he or she could invest at the higher rates. A mortgage-backed security was the solution to an interest-rate mismatch.

In theory, the same end could be reached if mortgage lenders sold home loans directly to the public by lowering or raising prices similarly. But for institutional investors, that would be cumbersome and risky. More important, selling loans individually wouldn't address the two other risks of mortgage lending: prepayments and defaults.

Take prepayment risk. Mortgage holders, on average, stay in a home from seven to ten years, repaying their loan early because they are moving for a job or into a bigger or smaller house or, often, to refinance to take advantage of lower rates. Prepayments often upset a lender's profit calculations: consumers like to refinance into lower-priced mortgages when rates fall, exactly when a lender wants them to keep paying on their higher-priced loans. (Likewise, consumers like to hang on to their lower-cost loans when rates rise, which is exactly when lenders want them to refinance into higher-cost mortgages.) Prepayments dash an investor's assumed rate of return. They create a risk that makes buying individual mortgages unappealing.

To help lenders—especially those in the thrift industry—shift some of this risk onto consumers, Congress in 1982 preempted state laws that had allowed home buyers to assume a seller's home loan. Now lenders could insist that borrowers pay off their loans when they sold their house. This due-on-sale provision helped lenders when rates were rising because home sellers would have to extinguish their lower-yielding loans, and buyers would have to borrow at the higher rates. While this change aided lenders somewhat, it did little for investors, who still didn't want to bear the prepayment uncertainty of owning individual mortgages.

That's where mortgage-backed securities—bonds backed by pools of well-underwritten home loans—come in. If investors use sound underwriting to learn enough about a sufficiently large number of mortgages, then they can estimate statistically how many mortgages within a pool backing a bond will likely prepay under various interest-rate scenarios. Fannie and Freddie are such investors. They have decades of data from millions and millions of mortgages. They don't know which specific borrowers will repay, but they can estimate, with great accuracy, the percentage within a group who will. A sudden drop in rates can upset even the best models, but drastic shifts are rare. The result is that pooling allows the finance industry to make sophisticated estimates of what prepayments will be, and thus what the ultimate, blended yield on any group of mortgages underlying a bond will be. Investors like that relative certainty.

This is what Ranieri meant when, as he was creating the mortgage trading department at Salomon, he famously said, "Mortgages are about math." Home lending had an "actuarial foundation," just like auto loans, credit cards, or any other type of consumer debt. With enough historical information, bundles of any type of consumer debt could be analyzed statistically to anticipate how borrowers in aggregate would behave financially. Of course, accuracy in analyzing pools required that each member of the pool be well underwritten. Good underwriting lessened the risk of default by each individual. It couldn't predict behavior as accurately as statistical analysis of a group could, but without soundly underwriting each individual as a credit risk, analysis of a pool of individuals was meaningless. No one knew which individuals would prepay, but with a proper assessment of borrowers, an investor could predict what percentage of a pool of them would.[7]

The same thinking applies to the third risk of mortgage lending, that a borrower will default. Mortgages are relatively safe investments because people want to stay in their homes. But no matter how good one's underwriting is, divorce, illness, job loss, or any number of other changes can trigger default. The first line of defense is traditional underwriting, where a lender assesses the likelihood a person will repay a debt by verifying that person's job, salary, debt load, repayment history—all the items that help determine his or her creditworthiness. Despite the best underwriting, some borrowers will default, requiring the lender to recoup losses by repossessing the house and selling it. These properties are known as "real estate owned," or REO, and mortgage lenders know how to handle them. Wall Street investors, however, don't want REO. If a bond's underlying home loans go bad, they want someone else to take responsibility.

Enter Fannie and Freddie. They buy mortgages, package them into mortgage-backed securities, and then, for a fee paid by investors, guarantee the underlying mortgages against default. They assume the default risk. Their success also rests on the pooling of loans that can be scrutinized statistically. Fannie and Freddie cannot predict which mortgages will sour, but they can predict and price for their exposure by estimating with great accuracy what percentage of loans in a group will. As with prepayments, however, pooling to mitigate against default works only if the loans in a pool are well underwritten—if each borrower's ability to repay has been carefully assessed. If borrowers' prospects for repayment haven't been measured, statistical analysis is meaningless.

Creating a pool of poorly underwritten mortgages does nothing to lower risk. The whole purpose of securitization is defeated.

Mortgage-backed securities enabled Fannie and Freddie to discard their old model of making money solely on the spread between what they paid to borrow money and what they earned on the mortgages they bought with that money—a buy-to-hold model that had subjected them to interest-rate risk. They didn't abandon this model completely, but by the middle of the 1980s they had largely replaced it with a fee-for-service, buy-to-sell model—borrowing money to buy loans, packaging those loans as collateral for bonds, selling the bonds to repay the money they borrowed, then collecting a fee from investors to guarantee the underlying mortgages against default. The whole banking industry was increasingly relying less on the yield spread from loans and more on fees. Fannie and Freddie had simply followed suit.[8]

What did not change in the shifting focus to fee income was Fannie and Freddie's keen interest in good underwriting. Whether they held a mortgage or sold it through securitization, they were on the hook if a borrower defaulted, so they had a financial incentive to minimize defaults. If underwriting deteriorated, defaults would rise, and so would Fannie and Freddie's losses. To prevent this, they required every lender from whom they bought mortgages to follow prescribed underwriting standards. If a loan defaulted, Fannie or Freddie bought it back from the pool underpinning a bond, thus reimbursing investors. They then demanded proof that the original lender had properly underwritten the loan. If the lender provided it, Fannie or Freddie ate the loss. If not, the lender had to make Fannie or Freddie whole by buying back the loan. Under these arrangements, Fannie and Freddie established the housing market's best underwriting standards, giving all involved an incentive to enforce them. That in turn made (and makes) their collateralized bonds the gold standard in securitization.

For decades, critics of Fannie and Freddie have raised good questions about their historic arrogance, lack of transparency, and other shortcomings. But for all their faults and occasional failures in adhering to best practices, they are masters at managing the three pitfalls of mortgage lending: interest-rate risk, prepayment risk, and default risk.

Mortgage-backed securities are odd ducks. They are bonds, and the creation of private-sector bonds historically has been the purview of investment banks, not government entities or deposit-taking, federally insured banks or bank affiliates. But they are bonds backed by mortgage loans, a mainstay of federally insured banks and thrifts. Wall Street's denizens, starting with Ranieri's bond traders in the 1970s, longed to enter the securitization game. No law prevented Wall Street from competing directly with Fannie and Freddie in securitization. Economics did. First, because Fannie and Freddie guarantee mortgages against default and they themselves are viewed as guaranteed against bankruptcy by the federal government, investors treated their bonds—"agency MBS"—as if they were federally insured, a selling point that Wall Street couldn't match. Fannie and Freddie's perceived tie to the federal government also meant that they could borrow more cheaply than Wall Street firms, even those with the best ratings. For these reasons, Fannie and Freddie could always undercut potential competitors on price in the purchase and packaging of loans.

Thus began the investment banking industry's love-hate relationship with Fannie and Freddie. Wall Street made lots of money helping the two issue debt to buy home loans, yet it hated that it couldn't compete with them to repackage those loans. To get into mortgage securities, Wall Street had to turn to home loans that Fannie and Freddie found too big or too risky to buy: the "jumbo" market or the subprime market.

Congress created the jumbo mortgage market by capping the size of the mortgages it allows Fannie and Freddie to buy. The cap is meant to ensure the two companies work for the middle and lower classes, not the rich. In 1975 the limit was $55,000. Today, depending on the local market, it's between $417,000 and $729,750.[9] Mortgages above this "conforming loan limit," as it's called, are defined as jumbo. The subprime market has no official definition, but in practice it refers to loans for borrowers with impaired credit or no credit, or who can only afford a down payment below the prime market's standard of 20 percent.

In the late 1970s and early 1980s, Wall Street faced the twin obstacles of tax law and state law in trying to sell bonds backed by pools of subprime or jumbo mortgages. Tax laws were unfavorable toward investors buying mortgage-backed securities created by anyone other than Fannie, Freddie, or Ginnie. More troublesome, when Salomon Brothers, Bank of America, or any other Wall Street player created private-label bonds—meaning without Fannie, Freddie, or Ginnie—most states effectively barred the sale of them.[10]

In the early twentieth century, in the absence of federal securities laws, many states began to pass their own statutes to try to protect individual investors from problems in the growing sale of stocks and bonds. These are known as "Blue

Sky" laws because they were meant to curb, as Supreme Court Justice Joseph McKenna wrote in a 1917 ruling, "speculative schemes which have no more basis than so many feet of 'blue sky.'" In the 1920s, financiers created pools of home loans much like today's mortgage-backed securities, and sold them to the public with a guarantee that interest and principal would be paid. State insurance regulators purportedly policed this market. After the 1929 crash, however, an investigation by the governor of New York found that lax oversight, coupled with misleading and fraudulent sales pitches, had cost nearly 213,000 investors a total of $810 million. Most were "poor people and people of modest means" who had invested their life savings. By the 1970s all but a dozen states had restricted the sale of these securities by private industry. Congress explicitly exempted Ginnie, Fannie, and Freddie from these laws. Now, however, Wall Street looked longingly at the mortgage-backed bonds the government had rediscovered.[11] To create a robust market for mortgage-backed securities in the jumbo and subprime arenas, investment bankers would have to change the law. Enter Lew Ranieri.

First, Ranieri played an instrumental role in persuading Congress to pass the Secondary Mortgage Market Enhancement Act of 1984, which preempted state laws to allow Wall Street bankers to sell private-label mortgage-backed securities across the country. This cleared the way for state and local pension funds and other institutional investors to buy these securities. Typically, institutional investors must buy top-rated securities like those issued by or associated with the federal government. Wall Street's private-label bonds weren't associated with the federal government—in fact, that was their reason for being. But the new, 1984 law provided what its crafters, including Ranieri, thought was a good surrogate for a government guarantee: the law required that Wall Street's private-label bonds be rated by a "nationally recognized statistical rating organization," or NRSRO, better known as a credit-rating agency.[12]

The Securities and Exchange Commission bestows the designation NRSRO, but sparingly. Only ten firms have it now. During the mortgage boom and bust, only three companies did: Standard & Poor's, Moody's, and Fitch. Over the objections of competitors, Congress and the SEC gave these three firms a shared monopoly over the business of rating private-label mortgage-backed securities.[13] As Ranieri told the Financial Crisis Inquiry Commission, "Look at the language of the original bill. . . . It put them in the business forevermore. It became one of the biggest, if not the biggest, business[es]." As a former director at Moody's put it, "The rating agencies were given a blank check."[14]

Next, Ranieri persuaded Congress in 1986 to grant favorable tax treatment to a new type of trust—a real estate mortgage investment conduit, or REMIC—that would manage private-label mortgage-backed securities by slicing them into "tranches." These could, say, provide one investor with a stream of only principal payments from a pool and another with a stream of only interest payments, or sort mortgages within a pool from highest to lowest risk so investors could choose a target return.[15]

These two changes in the law gave birth to the market in private-label mortgage-backed securities, much of it backed by subprime mortgages. In 1995, Wall Street issued about $50 billion in PLMBS, but by 1997 this had doubled to $100 billion, or 25 percent of all newly issued mortgage-backed securities. In 2004, during the bubble, new issues of private-label mortgage-backed securities hit $1 trillion. In 2005 they peaked at $1.4 trillion, accounting for 55 percent of all new issues of bonds backed by mortgages. The figure declined to $1 trillion in 2006, before falling to zero in 2007. The implosion of the private-label market made Fannie and Freddie's mortgage-backed securities suffer too: as subprime defaults swelled and unemployment grew, defaults spread up the food chain into prime mortgages. By comparison, Fannie and Freddie's mortgage-backed securities performed relatively well during the crisis.[16]

The reason private-label mortgage bonds failed in such record numbers—and so many otherwise savvy investors foolishly funded them—is that the borrowers holding the underlying mortgages defaulted in record numbers. That's not as simple as it sounds. To know why this happened requires understanding how private-label mortgage-backed securities fundamentally differed from Fannie and Freddie's mortgage bonds, even though superficially they look similar. Those who understood the difference made money from the bubble and crash. Those who didn't lost their shirts. Risk managers at GE, AIG, Citigroup, and elsewhere who didn't grasp the distinction or simply ignored it lost money for themselves, their shareholders, taxpayers, and the public.

Subprime lending wasn't always suspect. Once, "subprime borrowers" simply meant consumers with dented credit or no credit. Possibly such borrowers could not afford a 20 percent down payment on the home they wanted to buy, or they had been late paying bills. Whatever the reason, they posed a higher risk of default than people with a top, or prime, credit profile, and for that reason paid a higher interest rate.

For most of the twentieth century, mainstream lenders—federally or state-chartered banks or thrifts—ignored subprime borrowers, leaving them to high-cost lenders on the fringe of the financial system. These so-called hard money, fringe lenders were independent state-chartered finance companies that had no depositors but instead raised money to lend by borrowing from banks or the debt markets. They were regulated by the states, which typically didn't pay them much attention. These were the original shadow bankers, companies that had no federal oversight or insurance but that interacted with lenders who did.

To decide whether to make a loan, hard-money lenders didn't consider whether a borrower could afford to repay it but only what they could recoup by selling the "hard" asset—a washing machine, a car, a refrigerator—that the borrower would buy with the loan. Mainstream lenders not only avoided this market; they too often arbitrarily pushed people into it by denying credit not based a borrower's financial track record but on skin color, gender, ethnicity, or zip code. Denying loans to people without regard to their credit history became known as "redlining" because bankers used to outline in red pen on maps those communities that were off-limits for lending. In the late 1970s and early 1980s this began to change.

In 1977 Congress passed the Community Reinvestment Act (CRA) to prevent banks from taking consumer deposits out of a community without also putting some of that money back into it to work as loans. This required banks to find creditworthy borrowers from among their depositors. To do so, bankers had to underwrite, and when they did, to their surprise they discovered many credit-worthy customers who weren't white, rich, male, married or even necessarily middle class. Later, after the subprime mortgage bubble burst, some bankers tried to blame the crisis on the Community Reinvestment Act, saying it had forced lenders to make the high-risk mortgages that caused the subprime bubble. That was false. The CRA had nothing to do with it: during the mortgage bubble, 94 percent of these subprime mortgage loans made by banks or bank affiliates had no connection to lenders' efforts to comply with the act. But the CRA, from its inception, did make mainstream lenders aware that markets they had once ignored were worth another look.[17]

One market their eyes fell on was subprime mortgage lending. By the 1990s, the high risks of making these loans had been mitigated by the fact that these loans could be sold to Wall Street. Whatever Fannie or Freddie wouldn't buy, Wall Street was eager to use to securitize private-label bonds.

Hard-money lenders also began to eye this market. Until securitization, hard-money lenders avoided what were known as "first-lien mortgages"—the lending of money to buy homes. The time horizon of thirty-year mortgages made holding them to maturity too risky for those focused on short-term lending to poorer, cash-strapped debtors with shakier credit. With securitization, they didn't have to.[18]

Securitization enabled fringe and mainstream lenders alike to switch from a lend-to-hold model to a lend-to-sell one. Just as it had revolutionized the government-sponsored, prime-mortgage market in the 1980s, securitization in the 1990s revolutionized the subprime-mortgage market by attracting lenders of many stripes: hard-money lenders; behemoth financial firms with federally insured banks somewhere in their holding companies; and state-chartered finance companies associated with firms like General Electric and General Motors, which had created lending arms to promote the sale of their products and then purchased thrifts or other specialty banks to expand further into finance.

It was a two-way street. Private-label securitization enabled subprime mortgage lending to flourish; subprime mortgage lending enabled private-label securitization to flourish. From "essentially zero" in 1993, subprime mortgage originations grew in three years to $70 billion, about 9.5 percent of all new mortgages, and to $160 billion in 1999, or 12.5 percent of the year's $1.3 trillion in mortgage originations. By the height of the bubble in 2005, subprime mortgage originations had grown to $625 billion, nearly 24 percent of all mortgages made that year. Most subprime mortgages featured adjustable rates and penalties for paying early. Less than half the subprime mortgages originated in 1996 were bundled into mortgage-backed securities. That ratio reached 75 percent in 2005, when subprime mortgage originations peaked.[19]

Changing technology and the federal government's preemption of state usury laws also fueled interest in subprime mortgage lending. Computers automated credit checks, standardizing the use of credit scores and providing quick, electronic access to consumers' financial histories and bank accounts. Profit margins became fatter in the 1980 federal law that lifted caps on what banks and thrifts could pay depositors, Congress also overrode states' caps on the interest that lenders could charge on home loans. In the prime market, transparency kept interest-rate hikes on mortgages in check. The subprime mortgage arena, where pricing was opaque, had no such brake.[20]

The line between mainstream and hard-money lenders quickly blurred. Major banks started subprime mortgage-lending subsidiaries, often by buying a

hard-money company. By the end of the 1990s, the process had shifted into top
gear. Citigroup bought subprime lender The Associates in 2000, for example,
while British bank HSBC bought Household International in 2002. These hard-
money lenders' approach to underwriting was very different from that of mainstream bankers. Wall Street greeted it with open arms.

As the subprime market grew, lenders and regulators tried to draw a clear distinction between predatory and subprime mortgage lending. Good subprime lenders
underwrote by assessing a person's ability to repay a loan, just as prime lenders
did. A good subprime mortgage benefited the customer financially. Predatory
mortgages, by contrast, were made without regard to whether a borrower could
repay and only with regard to whether the sale of the house collateralizing the
loan would make the lender whole in case of default. Predatory mortgages, like
all predatory loans, often saddled a borrower with high-cost debt that made him
or her worse off.[21] In reality, predatory and subprime lending quickly became
indistinguishable as bad practices, which made more profits in the short term,
chased out good ones.

Responsible subprime lenders did and do exist. They are the minority.
Because subprime lending is less transparent and competitive than prime
lending, it has always been rife with bad actors. "Unlike the conservative, staid
prime mortgage market . . . . the subprime market was the Wild West," Edward
M. Gramlich, a former member of the Federal Reserve System board of governors, told a gathering of central bankers in Jackson, Wyoming, in 2007.[22]

Very quickly in the decade leading up to the mortgage bubble, predatory
subprime mortgages—poorly underwritten by traditional standards and leaving
borrowers worse off—crowded out good subprime loans. Lenders practiced a
kind of reverse redlining: instead of shunning subprime borrowers, they eagerly
sought out customers with bruised credit, those who lived in communities once
shunned by lenders, or those who, lacking experience, could be easily steered
into a high-cost loan. Law professor Patricia McCoy called it the "crowd-out
effect." "The ability to bury risky product features in fine print allowed irresponsible lenders to out-compete safe lenders," she testified to U.S. senators in
2009. "Low initial monthly payments were the most visible feature" of these
loans, with many lenders qualifying borrowers on initial teaser rates rather than
on the much higher—and, for many buyers, unaffordable—rates that would
kick in after two or three years.[23]

L. William Seidman, *left*, was head of the Federal Deposit Insurance Corporation during the thrift crisis and bailout. Sheila Bair, *right*, headed the FDIC during the mortgage crisis and bailout. Photos used by permission from the FDIC.

"Nipping this in the bud in 2000 and 2001 with some strong consumer rules applying across the board that just simply said you've got to document a customer's income to make sure they can repay the loan, you've got to make sure the income is sufficient to pay the loans when the interest rate resets, just simple rules like that . . . could have done a lot to stop this," former FDIC chairman Bair later told the Financial Crisis Inquiry Commission.[24]

Bair had hit on the distinguishing trait of predatory lenders: they didn't (and don't) assess a borrower's ability to repay a debt. They didn't underwrite. This was counterintuitive: one would think lenders would underwrite because they would want to be repaid. That's why Greenspan assumed that lenders could police themselves: rational people, acting in their own best interests, would not push their business into bankruptcy—or so he thought. Predatory lenders do want to be repaid, but in their business model, instead of doing traditional underwriting, they rely on the asset-based underwriting that hard-money lenders use, looking only at the value of the item the loan is used to purchase and that can be sold if the borrower defaults.

Asset-based underwriting facilitates sky-high interest rates, another distinguishing feature of predatory lenders. When lenders don't use traditional underwriting, they have no idea what a borrower can afford. The less a lender knows, the higher the risk the borrower becomes and the higher the interest the lender charges. Subprime lenders charged high rates even to those whose good credit could have qualified them for a less expensive prime loan. No one knowingly pays more than they need to. These borrowers agreed to pay more out of igno-rance—subprime subsidiaries of banks didn't even offer the prime loans avail-able in other units of the company—or, too often, because mortgage brokers misled them into signing for loans with terms other than those originally presented. Mortgage brokers and loan officers had an incentive to push loans without regard to whether the borrower could afford it—or qualified for a less expensive one. These brokers and officers received a "yield-spread premium," a fancy name for a legal kickback, often hundreds or thousands of dollars, for each customer they steered into a higher-cost, subprime mortgage. During the bubble, roughly six of every ten people who received subprime loans likely qualified for a less-expensive mortgage. "One common assumption about the subprime mortgage crisis," a *Wall Street Journal* piece noted in 2007, "is that it revolves around borrowers with sketchy credit who couldn't have bought a home without paying punitively high interest rates. It turns out that plenty of people with seemingly good credit are also caught in the subprime trap."[25]

Predatory lenders turned interest rates—the price of money—upside down. With no underwriting, lenders were not using interest rates to protect them-selves against default. Instead, they charged as high a rate as possible, regard-less of whether a borrower could afford a loan at that price. The rates subprime lenders charged thus no longer reflected a borrower's credit risk but instead became a factor that increased his or her chance of default. Traditional underwriters, like hard-money lenders, also appraise the value of an asset, like a house, before making a loan, using the asset as collateral. But unlike tradi-tional underwriters, for whom collateral offers backup protection against default if underwriting fails, predatory lenders use collateral as their first line of defense.

A responsible lender charges an interest rate that reflects, among other things, the likelihood a borrower will default and will not make a loan that a customer stands little chance of repaying. But in the world of predatory lending, getting consumers on a treadmill of debt is the point. If a lender can keep a borrower paying unaffordably high rates for a while and then repossess and sell an under-lying asset, the lender profits not in spite of, but because of, the borrower's default. In the late 1990s, a legal-aid attorney from Atlanta described to U.S. senators an example of this unscrupulous practice common among subprime lenders: A cash-strapped client borrowed $54,000 on such onerous terms that even if she had made monthly payments for fifteen years, totaling $107,000, she would still have owed $47,000, or 87 percent of the loan.[26]

When such loans drive borrowers into default, the lender reaps the benefit. When the loan is a mortgage, the borrowers not only lose whatever equity they had in their house but also a place to live. With a house being the biggest asset most people buy in their lives and the one most use to build and pass on wealth, losing a home to foreclosure ranks among the top crises in personal finance. People take years to recover.[27]

When the housing boom became a bubble, around 2003, badly underwritten subprime mortgages carrying high interest rates appeared to be more profitable than properly underwritten ones. As they came to dominate the market, a linguistic version of Gresham's law set in, with a pejorative meaning of subprime chasing out any good connotation. By 2007, phrases like "toxic subprime" and "predatory mortgages" eventually became just "subprime," which had become a dirty word.

Hedge-fund manager John Paulson had a lackluster career by Wall Street standards.[28] A conservative in dress and politics, he was relatively unknown among readers of the financial pages, where names like George Soros and Warren Buffett popped up far more often. The mortgage meltdown changed that. Paulson shorted the housing market during the bubble, using over-the-counter derivatives to bet that the mortgage-backed bonds underpinning the mania would go bust. In 2007, when many Wall Street banks and other financial firms were teetering on the verge of collapse, he pocketed $4 billion.[29] He had become a member of a small but significant group of people—Buffett among them—who saw the bubble for what it was and in many cases profited from its collapse. What did they know? Mostly that housing prices had gone up too much, not just relative to historic trends but relative to mortgage holders' paychecks. And they had taken the time to understand how private-label bonds differed from those issued by Fannie and Freddie. When they examined how private-label MBS worked, these few investors realized that rising home prices were not part of a new era of increased demand, but a sign of danger.

21

The Subprime Prisoner's Dilemma

WHILE CUSTOMERS WITH THE BEST CREDIT CAN get an adjustable-rate mortgage, the thirty-year fixed-rate loans that Americans love still dominate the prime market. The exploding subprime mortgage machine, by contrast, consisted mainly of adjustable-rate loans. From 2001 to 2008, less than 12 percent of prime mortgage originations had adjustable rates, while 70 percent of subprime mortgages did.[1] And unlike prime mortgages, subprime adjustables typically carried baffling credit terms. By the bubble, they came with stiff penalties for prepaying, for example, yet were structured to force borrowers into doing just that, prepaying—and forking over those penalty fines, which were simply high fees by another name. So while private-label mortgage-backed securities looked like the mortgage-backed securities that Fannie and Freddie created, the mortgages underlying them handled the three basic risks of mortgage lending—interest-rate risk, prepayment risk, and default risk—very differently.

Subprime loans came in several varieties. Supposedly higher-end, lower-risk subprime loans, called "Alt-A" for "alternate prime," went to borrowers with higher credit scores, but with a gap in their credit profile that prevented them from being top grade. During the bubble, these mortgages—$475 billion in new loans in 2006—averaged $302,404, with down payments of 10 percent. The bulk of them, 63 percent, required borrowers to pay "interest only" for a time and then a balloon payment of the entire principal. These loans brought back mortgage features that had been standard in the 1920s.[2]

In many cases, interest-only loans were "negatively amortizing." In a self-amortizing mortgage, a monthly payment pays down part of the principal and all of the interest accrued that month so that by the end of its life the loan is entirely paid off. In a negatively amortizing loan, monthly payments didn't reduce a borrower's balance. They included nothing for principal and covered only some of each month's interest. The portion of interest not paid each month was then added to the principal, on which the next month interest would also be charged, and so on. Charging interest on interest and on principal swelled a borrower's indebtedness. Even if he or she made all monthly payments on time, the balloon payment due at the end of the loan would be more than the original amount borrowed.

Mortgage lenders had copied the idea of negative amortization from the credit-card industry, which had used it to get itself and its customers into trouble. At first, safety-and-soundness regulators allowed the practice because rising credit-card debt made the profits and balance sheets of federally insured banks appear stronger, making it seem less likely they would fail or have to draw upon the FDIC or taxpayers. Consumers also loved negative amortization at first, because it lowered monthly payments. But eventually, in 2001, regulators realized that constantly rising debt increased the chance borrowers would default. They banned negative amortization in credit-card lending, even as it emerged in subprime residential mortgages. The same banks that dominated the credit-card market also dominated mortgage lending. Why regulators banned the practice in one part of a bank's business and not another is a mystery.[3]

All told, subprime mortgages, including Alt-A loans, made up a third of the $3 trillion in home loans originated in 2006. Add in another $395 billion in adjustable-rate jumbo mortgages—those with principals above what Fannie and Freddie were allowed to buy—and half the mortgages in the United States originated that year were high-risk loans and most were extended on terms or using underwriting that Congress would later outlaw. Jumbo loans averaged $584,545. Alt-A and jumbo loans supported many borrowers who bought more home—often dubbed a McMansion—than they could afford. At least half of these loans—subprime, including Alt-A and jumbo—had low or no documentation, which meant that lenders had done little if anything to discern whether borrowers could afford to keep up their payments.[4] Deteriorating underwriting standards added to a burgeoning new lexicon: "NINJA loans" needed no income, no job, and no asset verification; "liar loans" let borrowers verify their

own incomes, which loan originators then often inflated to assure that the mortgage would be approved and they would get their commission.

Among the more than $600 billion in mortgages originated in 2006 that were
"subprime" but not "alt-A subprime," the average loan amount was $205,410,
with a down payment of 5 percent. At least 90 percent had adjustable rates, and
nearly all of these adjustables were of a pernicious variety known as 2/28s and
3/27s, structured to force customers into repeated, high-cost refinancings.[5]
These numerically named loans became the "workhorses of the subprime securitization market," dominating adjustable-rate, subprime mortgage lending
during the bubble. These mortgages were collateralized bonds that resembled
Fannie's and Freddie's mortgage-backed securities, but deceptively.[6]

The 2/28s and 3/27s also were called "hybrid adjustable-rate mortgages" or,
gruesomely but accurately, "exploding ARMs." Structured as thirty-year loans,
they started out with a fixed teaser rate for two or three years, but then adjusted
every six months, in theory for the next twenty-eight or twenty-seven years—
hence, "2/28" or "3/27."

Normally lenders peg adjustable-rate loans to a cost-of-funds index, or COFI,
created by the Federal Home Loan Bank of San Francisco. Lenders of 2/28s
and 3/27s, however, pegged rates to an index much less familiar to Americans,
the London Interbank Offered Rate, or LIBOR, which is the rate London banks
use to charge each other for short-term loans. Using LIBOR made it easier to
sell private-label mortgage-based securities abroad, to the unsuspecting. Major
banks that made subprime loans or securitized them or both would later be fined
more than $9 billion when investigators found they had manipulated the LIBOR
index upward during the bubble, making adjustable rates on subprime loans
higher.

Lenders structured these loans to create a dilemma for those who held them.
Borrowers would either have to pay an interest rate that had adjusted to a level
they couldn't afford, or refinance and pay the lender a high penalty for paying
off a loan early—a penalty they also couldn't afford. When borrowers protested
that they wouldn't be able to afford the loan after it adjusted, lenders told them
they could always refinance before the new rate kicked in. When the borrower
refinanced but couldn't afford to pay the penalty for doing so, the lender would
simply add it to the new principal—and then pay that amount to itself.

A prepayment penalty amounted to several percentage points of a mortgage.
For the average subprime loan of $205,000, it came to thousands of dollars.

Including the penalty fee in the refinanced loan meant that the new loan had to be bigger than the first. But that could only happen if the borrower's house increased in value, which obliging appraisers paid by the bank would say it had. In this way, home prices rose throughout the bubble not from demand but from the churning of loans through repeated refinancings.

Bankers justified this business model by saying that home prices would always go up. What many of them meant was that prices would go up long enough for them to find a chair to sit on when the music stopped. If a borrower defaulted, lenders reasoned they could foreclose and sell the mortgaged home in a rising market. But even as it (nominally) pushed up home prices, the assembly-line of mass-produced refinancings shrank each borrower's equity. In a prime loan, a borrower's equity grows with each monthly payment as principal is paid off. In a subprime loan, it fell as a proportion of debt each time the mortgage grew larger, with the lenders using the penalty fee to whittle away the mortgage holder's ownership stake. The industry's new lexicon called this process "equity stripping." Any appreciation in the home's value would belong to the lender if the borrower defaulted. Any depreciation, however, reduced the borrower's equity, making the homeowner, not the bank, the first to suffer when home prices fell. The result, to paraphrase analyst Joshua Rosner, was that millions of borrowers became homeowners without equity, just renters with debt.

The Kool-Aid that home prices would always rise or at least not decline spawned a speculative fever that caused many to regard their home not just as a place to live but also as an investment and a source of cash. Lenders used tempting but misleading math to make people feel comfortable amassing debt through home equity lines of credit. Yale economist Robert Shiller, a pioneer in behavioral finance, gives this example: A homeowner who paid $16,000 for a home in 1948 that sells for $190,000 in 2004 has gained $174,000, a seemingly terrific return. But when the gains are stated yearly and adjusted for inflation, the actual gain works out to "an increase of less than 1 percent a year," which is much less enthralling.[7]

Lenders and borrowers alike focused on the sexier numbers, those not adjusted for inflation. And though lenders often marketed refinancing as a way to lower monthly payments, they didn't include taxes or mortgage insurance costs in the stated calculation they dangled before borrowers. Many mortgage holders made bad choices, partly through ignorance but also because of aggressive, deceptive marketers.

This change in how subprime lenders and securitizers treated prepayment risk—that they *encouraged* prepayment—was key to understanding why subprime mortgages, and the bonds based on them, were doomed to failure. Unlike Fannie and Freddie, subprime securitizers did not use statistics to estimate what percentage would prepay. They wanted all of them to. So they designed their adjustable-rate loans to force borrowers to refinance, like clockwork, every few years.[8] Many states had banned prepayment penalties, but in 1996, regulators at the federal Office of Thrift Supervision—the same incompetents from the Federal Home Loan Bank System—came up with a new interpretation of the 1982 federal law that had allowed thrifts to diversify out of home loans to help them weather interest-rate risk. The law had already preempted states by allowing adjustable-rate mortgages and due-on-sale clauses and by gutting usury caps. Now thrift regulators again preempted state laws, this time those that banned prepayment penalties. Overnight, these penalties became a common feature of subprime home loans.

Bonds backed by pools of 2/28s and 3/27s also handled interest-rate risk differently from the way Fannie's and Freddie's mortgaged-backed securities did. Because subprime borrowers typically refinanced every few years, these purported thirty-year loans had such a short shelf-life that adverse swings in interest rates simply didn't worry investors.

With the aim of stripping out an owner's equity, subprime mortgage lenders from day one targeted customers who already had home loans. Opening doors for first-time homebuyers had never been their focus, despite what the subprime mortgage industry's lobbyists told Congress and regulators. By 1999 and through the bubble, six of every ten subprime mortgages were refinancings. Another three out of ten went to homeowners selling one house to buy another. Just one in ten went to a first-time homebuyer.[9]

To lure homeowners into refinancing, lenders promised lower monthly payments and the ability to take cash out to pay off credit-card debt or make home improvements. While prime borrowers also sometimes took cash out, they tended to use refinancing first and foremost to lower their interest rates. "In the subprime mortgage market, however, as much as 70 percent of loan proceeds are used for debt consolidation and other consumer credit needs," Treasury Undersecretary Gary Gensler told Congress in May 2000. "Subprime mortgage lending is therefore both part of the mortgage market and part of the consumer credit market." In the next few years, as rates came down and refinancings soared, prime borrowers made greater use of equity lines of credit and second liens. Subprime borrowers did so even more.[10]

Short-lived adjustable-rate mortgages with stiff, hard-to-avoid penalty fees became the centerpiece of private-label securitization and the essence of how subprime lenders dealt with interest-rate and prepayment risk. But what about the third mortgage-lending risk: default?

Because Fannie and Freddie insured against default the mortgages supporting their mortgage-backed securities, they kept underwriting standards high. Their profits sank when borrowers didn't repay. Subprime securitizers didn't want to insure mortgages against default. Instead they pushed that risk off to a third party by buying an over-the-counter derivative called a credit-default swap, which obligated the person on the other side of the contract to pay for any bad mortgages. Off the hook if a borrower couldn't repay, subprime lenders and securitizers became less and less concerned about underwriting. As long as they did their jobs, they received their commissions and fees whether or not borrowers defaulted: foreclosures were someone else's problem. Those who sold credit-default swaps bought into the narrative that home prices would always go up, so they thought there was little risk of losing money on a foreclosed home. On that basis they sold credit-default swaps to as many people as wanted them, not just to the holders of the bonds, as Fannie and Freddie did. Swap dealers happily accepted fees from any speculator who wanted to bet that the subprime mortgages backing a private-label bond would default. Selling massively to speculators, swaps dealers took on obligations bigger than they could honor if their assumptions proved wrong, that is, if home prices fell and borrowers failed en masse.

After the oil tanker *Exxon Valdez* ran aground off Alaska in 1989, spilling 11 million gallons of oil, a JPMorgan executive named Blythe Masters created the first major credit-default swap by selling Exxon a multibillion-dollar letter of credit—a promise to lend Exxon money if needed to fend off lawsuits and other costs stemming from the spill. To lessen any loss to JPMorgan should Exxon tap the loan but not repay it, the bank paid a fee to another bank, which agreed to cover some of JPMorgan's losses if that occurred. The second bank then paid a fee to a third bank to defray any cost of default it might face. On and on went the chain. Bank regulators applauded. They preferred that many banks suffer smaller losses than that a big bank suffer a big loss that could threaten its existence.[11]

Regulators required JPMorgan to hold less capital against the possibility of loss on the swaps than they required on loans, thus lowering JPMorgan's lending costs. Wall Street liked that.

Blythe started a revolution. Lenders everywhere bought these derivatives to hedge against default on all types of debt, including on the home loans backing private-label mortgage-backed securities. A credit-rating agency's stamp of approval did for private-label bonds what Fannie and Freddie's implicit federal backing did for their bonds—both reassured investors that the risks were low. Swaps and credit ratings went hand in hand: bonds with a guarantee against default—a swap—received a higher credit rating, and a bond with a better credit rating received a swap guarantee more easily. In this way, no one making the loans or securitizing the loans or selling the securitizations seemed to be on the hook if a borrower defaulted. Those working along this mortgage-backed security assembly line had no need for underwriting standards. With an eye on their quarterly and yearly bonuses, private-label workers figured "I'll be gone, you'll be gone" before any problems hit, a mindset they referred to as IBGYBG.[12]

As Wall Street bankers searched for more fees, they started to combine different slices of existing subprime mortgage-backed securities, stitching together new mortgage-backed securities out of existing ones and calling them collateralized debt obligations, or CDOs. These too could be sliced and glued back together in various combinations, called CDO-squared, and so on.[13] Credit-default swaps made it all possible.

Soon speculators vastly outnumbered those using the swaps as hedges against default. Wall Street now added a new creation, imaginary or "synthetic" bonds—indexes—based on the performance of real bonds. These "synthetic collateralized debt obligations" were the Wall Street equivalent of fantasy football teams, a way to make bets about real athletes without actually assembling them into a team.

That was how Long-Term Capital bet on exchange rates without having to buy actual currency. And this was what Ranieri meant about mortgages and math: If performance statistics existed about bonds as they did for athletes, which they did, an index could be created on paper and bets placed on whether the index would go up or down. Like real life versions of the fictional, betting-obsessed character Nathan Detroit in the musical *Guys and Dolls,* Wall Street gamblers lined up to roll the dice in this "floating craps game," as Ranieri called it. American International Group, or AIG, the biggest insurer in the world at the time, became the biggest gambler of all, selling credit-default swaps without limit or oversight, and thus without also setting aside capital needed to back up potential claims, as insurers typically are required to do. The swaps were in essence insurance, but because they didn't have insurance in their name, state regulators didn't oversee them. That job was left to federal bank regulators, who proceeded to exert little policing. In fact, the only federal bank regulators overseeing AIG were the Keystone cops from the Office of Thrift Supervision who had so bungled oversight of thrifts.

After the dot-com bust and the terrorist attacks of 2001, global investors poured "an ocean of money" into U.S. government and housing securities, including subprime securities.[14] Much of it was short-term money from the shadow banking industry, whose lobbyists had successfully persuaded Congress to leave them essentially without oversight—even though they posed enormous risks for taxpayers. This parallel financial world of short-term borrowers and lenders exploded in the 1980s and 1990s, creating a complex credit machine of money-market funds and hedge funds, commercial paper and repurchase agreements. Borrowings in the commercial paper market grew from $125 billion in 1980 to $1.6 trillion by 2000. Money-market funds—the lenders who often bought this paper—went from $200 billion in the early 1980s to nearly $2 trillion by 2000.[15] Securitization funneled this easy credit into a bubble.

From the start, subprime mortgages were plagued with problems. So, therefore, were the bonds for which they served as collateral in the private-label, mortgage-backed securities market. Bank of America, a pioneer in the field, encountered scandal as early as 1984. A *Wall Street Journal* headline from February 4, 1985, said it all: "Embarrassed Giant: How Bank of America Took $37 Million Bath in a Mortgage Scheme—It Was Escrow Agent in Deal Arranged by Two Felons; Some Directors in Dark."

By the mid-1990s, as subprime mortgage lending took off, some members of Congress were growing concerned about "reverse redlining . . . the practice of targeting residents of specific disadvantaged communities for credit on unfair terms, and in particular by second-mortgage lenders, home-improvement contractors and finance companies."[16] In 1994, Congress passed a law giving the Federal Reserve authority to set mortgage rules that all lenders, regardless of whether they were overseen by state or federal regulators, would have to follow. For once, a bill's name accurately described its purpose: the Home Ownership and Equity Protection Act was intended to prevent lenders from stripping homeowners of the equity they'd built up in their homes. Anticipating that lenders would evade the law, Congress gave the Federal Reserve broad authority to specify the rules. But the Fed, led by Greenspan and his extreme laissez-faire philosophy, didn't adjust the rules even when problems surfaced.

In 1998 Senator Chuck Grassley (R-Iowa), chair of the Senate Special Committee on Aging, held hearings entitled "Equity Predators: Stripping, Flipping and Packing their Way to Profits" to probe abusive subprime lending. " 'Equity predators' at first blush might sound like a new horror movie targeted to bring chills and thrills to teenagers across America," he said. "Unfortunately, the topic that we are talking about today is in fact a horror . . . [but] the target . . . is not teenagers, but anyone who has a good deal of equity in their home, especially unsuspecting senior citizens, especially females, who are equity-rich and cash-poor."[17]

Equity-rich, cash-poor customers would remain the preferred prey of subprime lenders and private-label securitizers over the next decade. Grassley said that 23 million American homeowners, with an average age of sixty-four, had no mortgage debt. "For many senior homeowners, the equity in their homes represents their lifetime savings and their largest asset," he noted, estimating these homeowners' collective equity as possibly more than $1 trillion. "It is no wonder that these folks have become the apple of many a lending company's eye."[18] Subprime lenders "purposely" structured loans with monthly payments that grew unaffordable so that the borrower, to avoid default, would have to "return to the lender to refinance," providing the lender "additional points and fees."[19] As the process repeated, the chance grew that the borrower would default, at which point the lender would take the house.

During the hearings, "Jim Dough," who had worked as an officer and manager at several predatory lenders, described their business model: "Finance companies try to do business with blue-collar workers, people who have not gone to college, older people who are on fixed incomes, non-English-speaking people, and people who have significant equity in their homes. In fact, my perfect customer would be an uneducated widow who is on a fixed income, hopefully from her deceased husband's pension and Social Security, who has her house paid off, is living off of credit cards, but having a difficult time keeping up with her payments and who must make a car payment in addition to her credit card payments."[20]

Most subprime mortgage customers used the loans to gain cash to consolidate debt or gain more credit. In 2000, a joint report from the U.S. Treasury and the Department of Housing and Urban Development summarized the experiences of several borrowers, including "Ms. J."

> Ms. J., who is 71 years old, testified . . . she received a phone call from a mortgage broker, who promised her that he would refinance her two existing mortgages, provide her with $5,000 in extra cash and lower her monthly payments. Ms. J. needed cash to repair her kitchen, so she agreed to meet. . . . [The broker] gained her trust by claiming that he liked her as a person and he wanted to help senior citizens because his own father had recently died of cancer. Later, the broker returned to Ms. J.'s house to have her sign the mortgage loan papers. Ms. J. said that she could not read the documents carefully because she suffers from vision problems and has a limited education. Ms. J. said she signed the mortgage loan documents based on the broker's promises and representations that the mortgage loan would provide her with cash to repair her kitchen and lower her monthly mortgage payments. Ms. J. received a $90,100 mortgage with an APR of 14.819%. The mortgage loan contained a 15-year balloon note that required a final payment of $79,722.61 (due when she was 86 years old). Ms. J. paid 10% of the loan amount, or $9,100, as a broker's fee. [Her] monthly payment increased to approximately 80% of her monthly income. Ms. J. did not receive any money from the proceeds of this transaction.[21]

The report described such " 'bait-and-switch' tactics to defraud the borrower" and "balloon payments that require refinancing" as common, concluding, as Grassley did, that these lenders structured loans with terms "the borrower cannot afford," and "frequently victimized . . . the elderly and minorities" with "excessive fees." Sales involved "aggressive solicitation of residents of low-income and minority neighborhoods, which may be underserved by conventional lenders."[22]

Clinton White House officials approved opening up credit to "lower-income borrowers and areas" that previously had been unavailable at any price, but warned that problems were growing, especially in refinancings that didn't benefit the borrower. Perhaps as many as half of those targeted by unscrupulous subprime lenders would have qualified for a better, less costly loan—a ratio that subsequent analysis would show persisted through the bubble.[23] Why would someone who could afford a cheaper loan accept a more expensive one? Mortgage brokers, compromised by the kickbacks they got for steering customers into high-cost loans, marketed these loans as having low monthly payments, though they often cited payments without including taxes or other costs. At the same time, they played down or hid features that would later make the loans significantly more expensive—sometimes within twenty-four hours. Mortgages of 1 percent interest were dangled in front of consumers in flyers that revealed only in the fine print that these were negative-amortizing loans. "It's all the art of distraction," Bruce D. Miller, chief executive of Dailey & Associates Advertising in West Hollywood, told the *Los Angeles Times*. "For some people, all they care about is the monthly payment. And that keeps them from digging in and concentrating on the hidden elements."[24]

In Senate hearings held by Senator Paul Sarbanes (D-Md.) in 2001, a widow from West Virginia testified that a lender foreclosed on her house after her mortgage had been refinanced seven times in sixteen months by four separate lenders. In two years, her home-equity loan went from $11,921 to over $64,000, but from all the transactions she received only $21.70 in cash. The rest of the debt, $52,000, went to fees for the financiers. "I signed a loan with Beneficial in May 1995. This was the beginning of my troubles," she said. "My monthly income . . . was $458 from Social Security and my payments were more than half of this. They took a loan on my house of about $11,921. The very next month, Beneficial talked me into refinancing the home loan for $16,256. I did not understand that every time I did a new loan, I was being charged a bunch of fees." Senator Sarbanes was incensed. "The whole process," he replied, "was geared to taking the equity out of that home."[25]

Iowa Attorney General Thomas Miller, in the same hearing, cautioned lawmakers not to believe the argument that industry lobbyists used to fight new rules: that curbing these practices would hamper lending and harm consumers. "Please keep this in mind when you hear the caution that legislative action will 'dry up credit,'" Miller said. "Drying up productive credit would be of grave concern; drying up destructive debt is sound economic and public policy." The "destructive" practices he went on to describe would characterize the housing bubble two years later: mortgages refinanced over and over with no benefit to the borrower, penalty fees rolled into ever bigger loans, marketers who promised enticing terms that in reality ruined the borrower financially. This "push marketing" was "misleading" and "fraudulent," intended "to push the loan to the very edge of the borrower's capacity to handle it," he said, "meaning these loans *create their own* risk."[26]

"The notion of consumers shopping for a refinance loan or a home improvement loan, comparing prices and terms, is out of place in a sizeable portion of this market," Miller added. "Frequently, these are loans in search of a borrower, not the other way around. Consumers who buy household goods with a relatively small installment sales contract are moved up the 'food chain' to a mortgage loan by the lender to whom the retailer assigned the contract; door-to-door contractors come by unsolicited with offers to arrange manageable financing for home improvements; telemarketers offer to 'lower monthly payments' and direct mail solicitations make false representations about savings on consolidation loans. Another aspect of push marketing is . . . to loan more money than the borrower needs, wants, or asked for."[27]

Miller said that although officials from thirty-one states had urged the Fed to exercise its authority under the 1994 law and write better mortgage lending rules, Greenspan and other federal officials had done nothing meaningful.[28] Officials from cities such as Cleveland had a similar experience. Home prices there climbed 66 percent from 1989 to 1999, with the median price going from $75,200 to $125,100, until the bottom fell out in 2000 and foreclosures shot up to seven thousand, twice what they had been five years earlier.[29] The county's treasurer, James Rokakis, went to federal officials to seek help, only to face inaction by Greenspan. Then several years later, as the bubble took hold nationwide in 2003, Cleveland suffered more devastation. By 2007, foreclosures had hit seventeen thousand. Row upon row of foreclosed houses devastated neighborhoods, with plummeting property values eroding the tax base that funded schools, police, and firefighters.[30] Communities across the country faced similar budget crises.

Five years before becoming head of the FDIC in 2006, Republican Sheila Bair served in the U.S. Treasury as an assistant secretary in 2001 and 2002, where she read, at Senator Sarbanes's request, the joint HUD-Treasury report on predatory lending. She became interested in working on legislation to address abuses, but the bill "faced significant resistance from the mortgage industry and within Congress." When she decided instead to enlist the Fed's help to craft voluntary "best practices," she was told that "Greenspan was not interested in increased regulation."[31]

In 2004, as the bubble inflated, the Federal Reserve did take one action. It fined CitiFinancial, a Citigroup subsidiary specializing in subprime mortgages,

$70 billion for making loans without regard to whether borrowers could repay.[32] Citigroup promised to base all future loans on traditional underwriting, not asset-based underwriting. But that didn't stop Citi from funding other lenders who made loans using only asset-based underwriting, or who bought or packaged such loans.

Subprime lenders trained their brokers in how to sell to unsuspecting consumers. One salesman described to congressional investigators how he "crisscrossed the nation" to teach staff from the country's largest subprime lenders—including two of the biggest, the thrift Countrywide and the finance company Ameriquest—how to "easily" earn millions of dollars by pushing bad products to "frankly unsophisticated and unsuspecting borrowers." He told trainees they needn't "be concerned about the quality of the loan, whether it was suitable for the borrower or whether the loan performed . . . . you were in a way encouraged not to worry about those macro issues. . . . I knew that the risk was being shunted off. I knew that we could be writing crap. But in the end it was like a game of musical chairs."[33]

Ranieri calls the deterioration of underwriting a "madness" and bemoans regulators' failure to do any policing. He told the financial crisis commission, "You had the breakdown of the standards, . . . [and in] the checks and balances that normally would have stopped them." The truth was, the standards hadn't broken down. They had never been very good.[34]

Feds Tell States: Shut Up, Sit Down

ANGELO MOZILO, HIS PERPETUAL TAN SET OFF by the stark white shirts he favored, founded Countrywide Financial Corporation in California in 1969. By the mid-2000s, it was the nation's largest mortgage and subprime mortgage lender. In both 2006 and 2007, Countrywide originated more than $400 billion in mortgages, a large chunk of them the poorly underwritten subprime loans that inflated the bubble.[1] Mozilo became the "face of the subprime mortgage scandal" just as Keating had been the face of the thrift scandal.[2] Like Keating, Mozilo showed how a failed regulatory system encouraged "charter shopping," in which federally insured institutions looked between commercial bank and thrift regulators—between the Office of the Comptroller of the Currency and the Office of Thrift Supervision—to see which was the more lenient. Because the regulators' funding depended on the number of institutions they supervised, they found themselves in a constant arms race to see who could let banks most easily bend the rules.

In the S&L crisis, this competition between state and federal thrift regulators culminated in California's lifting any restriction on investment by thrifts. In the lead-up to the mortgage bubble, the banks began playing federal regulators off against each other.

In 1996, for example, the Office of Thrift Supervision ruled that state consumer protection laws barring prepayment penalties and other onerous mortgage terms didn't apply to federally regulated thrifts or their holding companies. From 2001 to 2004, Comptroller of the Currency Jerry Hawke followed suit with a series of policy changes that similarly exempted all national

Angelo Mozilo, founder and former CEO of Countrywide Financial Corporation, testifies before the U.S. House Oversight and Government Reform Committee on March 7, 2008. The committee examined the compensation and retirement packages granted to CEOs of corporations involved in the mortgage crisis. Mozilo, according to a securities filing, earned about $144 million in pay and stock sales in 2007. AP Photo/Susan Walsh.

banks and, importantly, their subsidiaries, from state law.[3] This left state regulators helpless to stop abusive practices by federally regulated banks and thrifts.[4] With the states out of the way—having been effectively told to shut up and sit down—the two federal regulators embarked on an intense competition to see who could offer more laxity. Hawke, for example, extolled "national banks' immunity from many state laws . . . . [as] a significant benefit of the national charter."[5] JPMorgan Chase and HSBC, two of the biggest banks in the world and two of the top twelve subprime mortgage lenders in the United States, switched from state to national bank charters soon after Hawke's rule change, and "several large national banks moved their mortgage-lending operations into subsidiaries" to evade state laws and oversight by the Federal Reserve.[6]

At the Office of Thrift Supervision, staffer Darrel Dochow, who in the 1980s had allowed thrifts to set their own appraisal standards and had pushed for more lenient oversight of Charles Keating, persuaded Countrywide in March 2007 to switch from a national bank charter to a national thrift charter, promising to be less "antagonistic." Six months later, the director of the Office of Thrift Supervision, John Reich, promoted Dochow from a regional deputy director to director of the agency's western region.[7]

Even though they were both housed within Treasury, the Office of Thrift Supervision and the Office of the Comptroller of the Currency had started competing years earlier. With his 1989 thrift bailout bill, President George H. W. Bush dismantled much of Hoover's Federal Home Loan Bank system, and a key feature of his plan moved the chartering and oversight of federal thrifts into a new unit of the Treasury, the OTS. The change, he said, would prevent a recurrence of the reckless behavior that had cost taxpayers so much. Immediately, the two regulators began an unfettered race to the bottom. At the same time, Greenspan's Fed decided not to police subsidiaries or affiliates of federally insured banks or thrifts for compliance with consumer protection laws. As regulators both looked the other way and tied the states' hands, lenders began to house their subprime mortgage operations outside their federally insured banks and thrifts, putting them instead "in largely unsupervised nonbank affiliates on the wild frontier of the mortgage markets," as former New York Fed president Geithner put it.[8] And a wild frontier it was.

By preempting the states' laws, federal regulators sabotaged states' ability to enforce any consumer protections. As state-chartered banks and thrifts switched to federal charters to avoid compliance, state-regulated finance companies complained to local legislators that they were now at a competitive disadvantage to federally charted lenders. Legislators obliged by modifying laws or abandoning attempts to impose or enforce new rules.

Congress too slapped state regulators out of the way. In 1980, 1982, 1984, 1986, 1987, 1989, 1994, and 1999, federal lawmakers passed laws preempting state consumer protection laws and weakening oversight, even as they expanded deposit insurance. At each step, Congress disregarded the pact it had struck in the 1930s to provide oversight in exchange for the benefits of a taxpayer-funded safety net.

In 1980, in addition to uncapping the interest that banks could pay on deposits, Congress preempted state usury laws that had capped the interest lenders could charge on home loans. In 1982, legislation that deregulated thrifts also preempted state laws that had limited or banned adjustable-rate mortgages, large balloon payments of principal at the end of a loan, prepayment penalties, and "due-on-sale" clauses.[9] In 1984 and 1986, Congress overrode state laws on private-label securities and adopted favorable tax treatment for investors in these bonds. The 1987 law funding a mini-bailout for thrifts further eroded bank regulations.

The thrift bailout bill of 1989 also handed the still relatively small market in private-label mortgage-backed securities an unintended boost: it created the Resolution Trust Corporation to sell the real estate and other assets the federal government would inherit from those thrifts that regulators now had the money to close. The Resolution Trust had a twofold mandate: it had to sell this property at the highest price possible and as quickly as possible, but, at the same time, without having an impact on market prices.[10] It wasn't supposed to lower prices by flooding the market, or to inflate prices by artificially withholding properties from sale. But the agency held so many mortgages, many of them too risky to meet the underwriting standards of Fannie and Freddie, and so many commercial properties and other assets with questionable values, that it could not sell them quickly without affecting the market. Officials hit on the idea of creating bonds collateralized by a medley of these lower-grade properties, some $25 billion worth. It was a huge success that enabled the agency to sell its huge inventory faster than otherwise would have been possible. The unanticipated benefit for Ranieri and Wall Street was that, for investors, the Resolution Trust's bonds legitimized the securitization of subprime mortgages.[11]

Then, in 1994, Congress turbocharged its preemption of state consumer protection laws by tearing down barriers to branching across state lines.[12] Community banks weren't annihilated, as some feared, but any restraint on the size of big banks dissolved. The Gramm-Leach-Bliley Act of 1999 became the capstone in this ongoing march toward bigness: the law, which formally blessed the deregulation that had already occurred and purportedly tried to impose rational oversight of those activities, ushered in the creation of financial conglomerates of unprecedented size, scope, and complexity.

In varying degrees, regulators and lawmakers from both sides of the aisle intended all these laws to help the thrift industry, smooth out regional economic ups and downs, and fulfill Greenspan's plan to create U.S. financial giants big enough to compete internationally.[13] A striking omission from these efforts to preempt so many state regulations and to deregulate financial services, however, was sufficient concern that lenders might abuse their new powers.[14] In the end, deregulation could not save the thrift industry, but it did create two new industries: subprime mortgage lending and private-label securitization. Bankers and regulators alike heralded them as innovations.

Free-standing finance companies with no federal supervision and only modest state oversight originated 50 percent of the high-risk mortgages that fueled the mortgage bubble. The other 50 percent came from affiliates and subsidiaries of federally insured banks and thrifts. But in many ways federally insured institutions also funded the loans the finance companies made by oiling the subprime securitization machine with lines of credit and insurance—swaps—against mortgage defaults.[15] Although firms unaffiliated with federally insured banks or their holding companies made half the toxic loans, Wall Street bankers tied to federally insured deposits gave them the money and means to do it.

Take Goldman Sachs. Under Hank Paulson as CEO, before he became Treasury secretary in 2006, Goldman "provided billions of dollars in loans" to subprime mortgage lenders such as the thrifts Countrywide and Washington Mutual and independent companies like Ameriquest and New Century. It extended lines of credit and bought billions of dollars' worth of loans from them that it then securitized and sold. From 2004 to 2006, it issued subprime mortgage-backed securities or variations of them—collateralized debt obligations and synthetic collateralized debt obligations—totaling an estimated $112 billion.[16] All the major Wall Street players operated similarly, with tentacles in every facet of the subprime world.[17] Citigroup, JPMorgan, HSBC, Wells Fargo, National City, Lehman, Bear Stearns, Merrill Lynch, Morgan Stanley, and Goldman originated loans to create their own pipelines, buying up freestanding finance companies or creating new subsidiaries to do it. "Almost always, these operations were sequestered in nonbank subsidiaries, leaving them in a regulatory no-man's land" where they operated without rules or oversight.[18]

At the end of the 1990s, the top twenty-five subprime lenders accounted for almost 50 percent of subprime mortgage originations. By 2003, after an industry shakeout, the top twenty-five subprime mortgage lenders accounted for 93 percent.[19] Two categories of company dominated.

On one hand were those free-standing, independent mortgage originators that didn't take deposits but instead raised money through Wall Street. These firms went bankrupt when the bubble burst in 2007 or, if owned by a Wall Street firm, were wound down.[20] No one talked about bailing them out. Even in the mortgage industry, few today remember their names. On the other hand were bank, thrift, and investment-bank holding companies. All had federally insured institutions within their corporate structure, and policymakers cared very much what effect their collapse would have on the broader financial system.

The big thrifts dominating subprime mortgage lending—Washington Mutual, Countrywide, Fremont, and Indymac—all had to be closed or sold. Washington Mutual, known as WAMU, had assets of over $300 billion and was the third-largest federally insured institution to fail (as of this writing). The two ahead of it, Bank of America and Citigroup, were deemed too big to fail and were rescued with a taxpayer bailout. IndyMac—an offshoot of Countrywide, which itself had to be sold to Bank of America in early 2008 to avert collapse—ranks as of this writing as the costliest failure ever to the federal deposit insurance fund, at over $13 billion, even though it was the sixth-largest federally insured institution to collapse.[21] Steven Mnuchin, who was a Goldman Sachs partner before becoming Donald Trump's Treasury secretary, bought Indymac in 2009 and made a fortune in part foreclosing on homeowners whose loans came with the acquisition. His partners in the deal included John Paulson and George Soros, which shows that humble, simple folk can put politics aside to make money.[22]

Big commercial banks, including Citibank, JPMorgan, Bank of America, and Wells Fargo, were each part of holding companies that owned many subsidiaries engaged in a full range of subprime financial activities and that had to be bailed out by taxpayers. The country's five major U.S. investment banks at the time—Goldman Sachs, Morgan Stanley, Lehman, Merrill Lynch, and Bear Stearns—also had assembly lines that originated, bought, funded, and securitized subprime mortgages.

But commercial-bank holding companies and investment-bank holding companies, even though both owned federally insured banks and operated identically, were not regulated equally. They differed in name only but, thanks to a loophole in Gramm-Leach-Bliley, were treated far differently.

The "functional regulation" framework embedded in the Gramm-Leach-Bliley law required the Fed to supervise financial holding companies, but the law relegated supervision of specific holding companies' subsidiaries to others according to their expertise—the federal bank regulators, the SEC, and more than a hundred state banking and insurance regulators.

Curiously, the law required the Fed to supervise the holding companies of the big commercial banks but not those of the investment banks, even though these financial holding companies were identical. Thanks to Wall Street lobbyists, investment firms were to be supervised by the Fed only if they volunteered to be. None did. Even Greenspan's laissez-faire Fed would have required investment bank holding companies to keep more capital as a cushion against loss on investments, and the big five didn't want to do that. Holding more capital made borrowing more expensive.[23]

This exemption for investment banks was a big win for their lobbyists, but not for taxpayers. It gave these firms access to federally guaranteed deposits without oversight by the Fed, undercutting the foundational philosophy behind the legislation—that in exchange for allowing a holding company to own both investment and commercial banks, the Fed would look across the treetops of such empires and police the holding company and subsidiaries for risky behavior that might require its federally insured banks to draw on the FDIC or, eventually, taxpayers. The difference between commercial bank holding companies and investment bank holding companies was for practical purposes zero. Only quirks in the law gave each an advantage over the other: holding companies that emphasized commercial banking "enjoyed greater access to insured deposits" while those emphasizing investment banking enjoyed less oversight.[24]

"We have learned that voluntary regulation does not work," George W. Bush's SEC chair, Christopher Cox, testified to Congress in October 2008 just weeks after Lehman's collapse. Cox, a seventeen-year Republican House member before going to the SEC, had been—prior to the mortgage crisis—as extreme a proponent of laissez-faire capitalism as Greenspan. Now he told lawmakers that "experience has taught that regulation must be mandatory, and it must be backed by statutory authority. It was a fateful mistake in the Gramm-Leach-Bliley Act that neither the SEC nor any regulator was given the statutory authority to regulate investment bank holding companies other than on a voluntary basis."[25]

The volunteer system had effectively ended a month earlier, in September, because all five of the nation's big five investment banks had either collapsed (Lehman), or had been merged with commercial banks to avert collapse (Bear Stearns to JPMorgan; Merrill Lynch to Bank of America), or had been converted to bank holding companies to reassure markets that the Fed stood behind them (Goldman Sachs and Morgan Stanley). Drawing on the examples of Drexel Burnham Lambert and Salomon Brothers, Cox noted that federal regulators historically did not rescue investment banks, leaving them to either fail or arrange their own sale to avert bankruptcy. The Fed changed that policy in March 2008 when it funded JPMorgan's purchase of Bear Stearns, officially stretching to investment banks the safety net that prevented runs at commercial banks.[26]

The government's decision to let Lehman go down was the exception that proved the rule. Lehman's bankruptcy in mid-September 2008 set off runs at the remaining three big investment banks, further froze the credit markets, and rattled depositor confidence in commercial banks. It forced the federal government to pledge tens of trillions of dollars to stand behind money-market funds, the commercial paper market, and all newly issued debt of bank holding companies. At the same time, Paulson, Bernanke, Geithner, and Bair worked tirelessly to ensure that the remaining three investment banks didn't collapse but were either sold or converted to Fed-supervised holding companies. Two weeks later, Congress increased the limit on federal deposit insurance 2.5 times, to $250,000 from $100,000—the same proportional increase it had made in 1980 when it raised the amount to $100,000 from $40,000 to entice depositors to keep their money in troubled thrifts.

The bubble and crash highlighted another flaw in Gramm-Leach-Bliley. Although the law required the Fed to oversee the holding companies of the biggest commercial banks, it simultaneously told the Fed to rely as much as possible on other regulators to do so. The Fed interpreted this mandate, known as "Fed-lite," to mean it couldn't itself look into the inner workings of a bank company's subsidiaries but instead had to rely on other regulators to relay what they saw. As a result, the Fed didn't see the big picture of the holding companies it supervised, nor did any other regulator.[27]

Functional oversight failed because it put or was interpreted to put regulators in silos, limiting what each could see of what the other was doing. The law thus made financial companies less supervised even as it enabled them to become bigger and more complex. Meanwhile, Congress time and again carved out exceptions that allowed commercial banks and investment banks, as well as nonbank giants, to benefit from owning federally insured—and taxpayer backed—entities without sufficient oversight. By sprinkling legislation with new loopholes even as it plugged others, Congress undercut its own efforts to rationalize oversight and to rein in the mixing of commerce and banking.[28]

The mini-bailout bill of 1987 and the Gramm-Leach-Bliley Act purportedly clamped down on loopholes that enabled nonfinancial companies to own banks while escaping Fed oversight. Yet Congress allowed AIG, General Electric, Lehman Brothers, Goldman Sachs, Merrill Lynch, General Motors, Volkswagen, BMW, Target, and Morgan Stanley, among others, to bypass these restrictions by obtaining a thrift or a special type of federally insured, state-chartered bank called an industrial loan corporation. Many owned both industrial loan corporations and thrifts. Almost all became key players in the mortgage bubble and would need taxpayer bailouts or other help.[29] So when Paulson, as Treasury secretary, heroically worked to save the country's financial and economic system, he was cleaning up a mess he had helped make when he sat on the investment banking industry's side of the table as head of Goldman Sachs and successfully waved off federal oversight.

Regulators, too, with their lax interpretations of the law, contributed to this "balkanized regulatory system . . . riddled with gaps and turf battles" with no one "accountable for the stability of the entire system."[30] When the crisis hit, Treasury and the Fed coordinated in the Herculean task of saving the system. It was an ad hoc, chaotic effort that easily could have failed, but it showed that, despite Gramm-Leach-Bliley's flaws, regulators had tools they could have used much earlier to push back against a silo mentality—if they had wanted.

By 2012, the ten biggest bank-holding companies owned twice the number of subsidiaries that they had twenty years earlier. In 1991, only one U.S. holding company had more than five hundred subsidiaries. By 2012, Goldman and JPMorgan each had more than three thousand, and Morgan Stanley had nearly that many. Bank of America had more than two thousand.[31]

The growth in complexity daunted regulators. Lehman Brothers' holding company, for example, had "over 200 significant subsidiaries," but the SEC had no jurisdiction over 193 of them, including "over-the-counter derivatives businesses, trust companies, mortgage companies, and off-shore banks."[32] Over-the-counter credit-default swaps had grown to a $55 trillion market that federal regulators were unable to patrol for safety and soundness.[33] Among the biggest players was insurance giant AIG, whose $440 billion in credit-default swaps nearly killed the company and the economy. Because Gramm-Leach-Bliley allowed AIG to own a thrift but exempted it from Fed oversight, the only federal officials monitoring AIG's operations were those in the Office of Thrift Supervision. John Reich, director of OTS, told congressional investigators "that as late as September 2008, he had 'no clue—no idea—what [AIG's credit-default swap] liability was.'" Mike Finn, former director for the Office of Thrift Supervision's northeast region, revealed the fundamental incompetence of agency officials when he said that the agency's duty in overseeing AIG's holding company was to ensure the safety and soundness of its FDIC-insured banks and not to focus on the impact other subsidiaries might have. The opposite was true. At a very basic level he simply didn't understand his job.[34]

Taxpayers bailed out AIG three times in 2008, for a total of $185 billion, giving the U.S. government an ownership stake in the company. AIG eventually repaid the money, earning the Treasury a profit, but events could certainly have turned out differently. AIG's shareholders thanked taxpayers for saving the company from bankruptcy by suing the government for $40 billion, claiming that the terms of the bailout had been too onerous. They scored a pyrrhic victory—and scorn for their ingratitude—by winning the suit but no money. The judge ruled that the Fed overstepped by taking ownership in the company but that it didn't have to pay damages because shareholders had suffered none.[35]

Wall Street loved functional regulation. It not only prevented the Fed from overseeing America's five big investment banks, but also stymied its oversight of commercial banks by making Fed officials rely as much as possible on the SEC to police these firms' securitization operations. And oversight by the SEC amounted to next to no oversight, largely because of the way the SEC is funded.

The Fed and other banking agencies are self-funded, which means their budgets come from operations or from fees they charge the banks they oversee. Even though self-funding poses its own conflicts of interest and, as the record shows, hardly ensures good oversight, it's still better than what the SEC must endure. Bank regulators don't have to go hat in hand to Congress each year to have their budgets approved. The SEC does, and its funding can be cut or held up by any firm that makes a campaign donation to enlist the help of any of Congress's 535 members.[36] "Once word of a proposed SEC regulation got out, industry lobbyists would rush to complain to members of the congressional committee with jurisdiction over the financial activity at issue," former SEC chair Arthur Levitt told crisis investigators. These lawmakers "would then 'harass' the SEC with frequent letters demanding answers to complex questions and appearances of officials before Congress. These requests consumed much of the agency's time and discouraged it from making regulations." It became, in Levitt's words, "a blood sport to make the particular agency look stupid or inept or venal." Industry also tries to harass and make life miserable for the self-funded financial regulators, but because their budgets aren't up for grabs each year, they feel such efforts less keenly.[37]

Having to beg for money during annual appropriations politicizes the SEC's budget and keeps the agency on a short leash that industry can yank any time. The same system holds the Commodity Futures Trading Commission hostage. It leaves both agencies chronically underfunded and overly subject to political pressure from the companies whose activities they are supposed to police on behalf of the public. (Of note is that the big five investment banks, which chose not to have Fed oversight under Gramm-Leach-Bliley, did persuade Congress eight years earlier to allow the Federal Reserve to act as their lender of last resort, and when the crisis hit in 2007 they eagerly borrowed under that provision. Ironically, the provision was part of the 1991 legislation that Congress passed after the thrift bailout with the aim of preventing regulators from ever again keeping federally insured zombie institutions open at a mounting cost to taxpayers. Until the mortgage crisis hit, however, no regulator seemed concerned that the safety net for commercial banks had been enlarged to cover investment banks but with no commensurate safeguards.)[38]

Even after the mortgage crisis, the SEC continued to coddle the industry. Not until 2012, and only after being publicly embarrassed, did the SEC change its policy of allowing defendants to say they neither admitted nor denied charges when they settled civil fraud or insider trading cases with the agency—even if the defendants already had been convicted criminally on the same charges.[39] And it infamously failed for years—despite being tipped off—to catch Bernie Madoff, who stole billions of dollars from thousands of investors in one of the biggest Ponzi schemes of all time. He was arrested by FBI agents a few weeks after Cox testified about the failure of voluntary oversight.[40]

Shadow bankers such as money-market funds, GE Capital, and General Motors Acceptance Corporation posed gargantuan problems during the crisis. Although they too were free of oversight by the Fed or Treasury, many turned to officials at these agencies—and to taxpayers—for help. General Motors and Chrysler together got more than $61 billion in bailout money, of which $12 billion as of this writing hasn't been repaid. GE, whose subsidiary made nearly $50 billion in subprime loans, received no bailout money directly, but, as the biggest borrower in the then $1.8 trillion commercial paper market, it benefited greatly when the government helped to unfreeze that market by stepping in to guarantee it. Treasury Secretary Paulson and Fed Chair Bernanke felt they had no choice but to extend the safety net to commercial paper. General Electric CEO Jeff Immelt contacted Paulson at least twice during the fall of 2008 as GE, like hundreds of American companies during the crash, struggled to stay liquid. Allowing the crisis to destroy iconic American companies was unthinkable.[41]

Many executives who practiced bad underwriting and risk management still describe themselves as victims of the crisis rather than its cause. Former

Countrywide head Mozilo, who has escaped criminal and civil prosecution, denies that Countrywide or its lending practices played any role. "Countrywide or Mozilo didn't cause any of that," he said in 2014, shortly after learning that the U.S. Department of Justice would not pursue a civil case against him. He agreed to forgo at least $37.5 million in severance pay triggered when Bank of America bought Countrywide in 2008 to save it from collapse, yet he has a pension and retirement package worth tens of millions.[42] His reputation is in tatters, but he has the means and time to write a book so that, he says, his grand-children will "know the truth" about his role in the Great Recession.[43]

Lehman CEO Richard Fuld told Congress that his bank was a "casualty of the crisis of confidence" in the banking system.[44] John Mack, head of Morgan Stanley during the crisis, said after he stepped down that the public should "stop beating up" on JPMorgan CEO Jamie Dimon and Goldman Sachs CEO Lloyd Blankfein for remaining at the helm of their firms and commanding multimillion-dollar pay packages despite the tens of billions of dollars in fines the companies have had to pay for wrongdoing.[45]

In fact, the subprime mortgage industry's problems were, as the crisis commission put it, "before our very eyes." Yet the heads of the giant financial companies that caused the crisis evaded jail time, causing an angry public to coin the phrase "too-big-to-fail." That stood in contrast to the thrift crisis, when the government prosecuted hundreds of savings-and-loan executives.[46] Regulators fined the big companies involved in the mortgage crisis hundreds of billions of dollars, but they didn't pursue individuals. An email from a longtime SEC official, Reid Muoio, who headed the agency's investigation of mortgage securities, suggests why: Muoio "told colleagues that he had seen the 'devasting [sic] impact our little ol' civil actions reap on real people more often than I care to remember. It is the least favorite part of the job. Most of our civil defendants are good people who have done one bad thing.' "[47] A counterargument is that charging a company hurts shareholders and others who had nothing to do with the wrongdoing, whereas charging individuals not only holds the culprits accountable but also sends a message to others. Regulators didn't see it that way.

A Number Out of the Air

AS THE RISE IN HOUSING PRICES SLOWED by the end of 2006, borrowers "in droves" suddenly found they could not refinance their high-cost adjustable-rate loans and defaulted.[1]

In April 2007, New Century Financial, one of the top three subprime mortgage lenders, filed for bankruptcy. In June, Standard & Poor's downgraded one hundred subprime mortgage bonds. In July, as Bear Stearns CEO James E. Cayne played golf (he was known to love smoking pot, playing bridge, and being out of the office), two of his investment bank's hedge funds collapsed from subprime losses, and Countrywide Financial warned in an SEC filing of "difficult conditions." By August, all of the independent finance companies that made toxic subprime loans were out of business or on the brink of becoming so, and bank holding companies scrambled to wind down or sell their subprime subsidiaries.[2]

By late summer, the Fed, worried about market turmoil and deflation, began reducing interest rates to try to spark borrowing and spending, becoming more frantic as the crisis unfolded. It lowered the discount rate—the cost for banks to borrow from the Federal Reserve's discount window—eleven times from August 2007 through December 2008, taking it from 5.75 percent to 0.5 percent.[3] The discount window is intended for short-term borrowing to alleviate temporary cash crunches. The Fed also reduced the federal funds rate—what banks charge each other to borrow funds overnight—nearly a dozen times, from 5.25 percent in September 2007 to zero by the end of 2008. The nearly two dozen rate cuts in sixteen months slashed borrowing costs, but consumers, already carrying too much debt, responded slowly, hobbling any recovery.[4]

Bad news kept coming. In March 2008, federal banking officials bought $30 billion of Bear Stearns' bad assets to orchestrate the firm's sale to JPMorgan, averting a collapse but humiliating the once arrogant investment bank and prompting some to wonder if this was in any way payback for the firm's refusal to contribute money to salvage Long-Term during that crisis.[5]

In mid-July, as subprime lender IndyMac became the FDIC's costliest failure ever (as of this writing), Bernanke and Paulson faced trouble at Fannie and Freddie and, to a lesser and certainly less publicized extent, at the twelve Federal Home Loan Banks. Confusion over the difference between Fannie and Freddie's mortgage-backed securities and Wall Street's continued to unnerve the economy. Fed and Treasury officials started to see the enormity of the problem.

Paulson asked Congress for authority to use tax dollars to take over Fannie and Freddie, commenting, "If you've got a bazooka, and people know you've got it, you may not have to take it out."[6] Congress came through: on July 30, President Bush signed the Housing and Economic Recovery Act of 2008, which, in addition to providing Paulson with money to bail out the housing twins, also set up a new, tougher regulator for Fannie and Freddie and the home loan banks—the Federal Housing Finance Agency. On September 7, eroding market trust forced Paulson to fire his bazooka and take control of Fannie and Freddie at a cost of nearly $200 billion, prompting fellow Republicans to deride him as "Comrade Paulson."[7]

Paulson, Bernanke, Geithner, and Bair from then on faced one enormous problem after another. In March, the Fed had created a discount window for investment banks, where they could borrow short term to meet liquidity needs.[8] The decision by the Fed to do this, to lend to institutions it didn't regulate, was notable. By the end of September, that decision was moot because the investment banks had disappeared, merged, or changed themselves into bank holding companies, which the Fed did oversee. Lehman filed for bankruptcy on September 15. Merrill Lynch averted the same fate by agreeing to be purchased by Bank of America. On September 21, Morgan Stanley and Goldman Sachs converted to bank holding companies, signaling to the market that they had the Fed and its lending resources behind them and that henceforth they would rely more on cheap, federally insured deposits as a source of funding.

Then subprime mortgage giant Washington Mutual failed, in the third largest bank collapse in U.S. history, with its banking operations sold to JPMorgan. AIG, the world's biggest insurer, faced a liquidity crisis created by customers demanding to be paid, under the terms of their credit-default swaps, for all the mortgages and bonds that had gone bust. To avert its collapse, the government injected tens of billions of dollars in exchange for an ownership stake.[9]

But Lehman's bankruptcy caused the biggest problem, opening everyone's eyes fully to the reality that this was an economic crisis rivaling the Great Depression. In part because of the sloppy way the government handled the bankruptcy, it set off panic in the shadow banking world, forcing the Fed and the Treasury to prop up two multitrillion-dollar industries. Treasury guaranteed money-market funds to stop runs by customers worried because the funds in these institutions, unlike deposits at commercial banks, lacked federal deposit insurance. Bair insisted that Treasury coordinate this step with the FDIC to ensure that a guarantee of money market funds wouldn't be unlimited. That, she knew, could have the unintended effect of causing runs at commercial banks, whose customers might withdraw deposits above FDIC insurance limits of $100,000 (soon to be $250,000) to move them into newly guaranteed money-market accounts. As Treasury unveiled its program, the Fed, to try to unfreeze credit, unveiled its own, promising in effect to insure the commercial paper market by becoming its buyer of last resort.[10]

The banking system also needed help. Losses from residential mortgage defaults left gigantic bank holding companies undercapitalized and unable to borrow—a problem that had to be resolved, if only to ensure that most of the federally insured banks survived. Bair agreed that the FDIC would insure new debt issued by bank holding companies, an extraordinary expansion of insurance but one without which, in Geithner's words, "the broader institutions and their nonbank affiliates would have come crashing down."[11]

Together, these extraordinary measures by the regulators addressed liquidity concerns by assuring creditors, including depositors, that they could get their money.

Bernanke, Paulson, Geithner, and Bair now turned to a deeper issue: mortgage defaults were eroding balance sheets and quickly pushing the nation's biggest banks toward insolvency. A liquidity crunch can cause insolvency by forcing an institution to sell assets at fire-sale prices to raise cash; in turn, "solvency problems could sap confidence" and ignite runs, causing a liquidity crunch. Bank regulators knew they had to get money into banks. The makeshift IOUs the government had used to make thrifts appear solvent wouldn't do. They needed cash, not a promise of cash.[12]

Paulson had to ask Congress at the worst possible time, an election year, but the system was too fragile for him to wait any longer. He asked for $700 billion in taxpayer money to bail out the nation's insolvent banks, arguing that their failure would bring down the entire financial system. The figure came from a seat-of-the-pants calculation by Neel Kashkari, Paulson's assistant at Treasury, who effectively became the "federal bailout chief." Paulson agreed to the sum because he and his staff thought Congress wouldn't approve the $1 trillion they thought was actually needed. In a shack in the back woods of Nevada County, California, in December 2009, wearing a Cleveland Browns t-shirt and unwinding from the exhaustion of the crisis, Kashkari recalled how he had made the calculation on his BlackBerry: "We have $11 trillion residential mortgages, $3 trillion commercial mortgages. Total $14 trillion. Five percent of that is $700 billion. A nice round number." It was also, he said, "a number out of the air."[13]

The three-page document Treasury officials handed to lawmakers asked for powers to handle failing banks that "could not be reviewed by any court of law or any administrative agency." It was a request to be free of checks or balances, and it contained nothing to help homeowners. Congress voted it down. But the election was around the corner and events were spiraling out of control, so Paulson went back to Congress, where elected officials also had no choice but to act. Fear of an economic Armageddon, of financial and civil unrest, motivated everyone.

On October 3, President Bush signed the Emergency Economic Stabilization Act of 2008, giving Paulson the requested $700 billion under the Troubled Asset Relief Program, or TARP. The legislation also temporarily raised federal deposit insurance to $250,000 from $100,000 to assure depositors and guard against runs, and gave regulators the authority to suspend mark-to-market accounting rules that, some on Wall Street argued, had made the meltdown worse by requiring holders of mortgage-backed securities to write down the assets in real time, further depressing prices. But others, including Paulson and other regulators, disagreed, believing, correctly, this accounting treatment was not to blame.[14]

Mark-to-market accounting, also called fair-value accounting, is distinct from historical-cost accounting, in which assets are listed at the price paid for them. Generally, assets held at the price originally paid—the historic cost—are those that an organization intends to hold long term and therefore doesn't need to mark up or down as prices for similar items fluctuate. An asset valued at its historical cost, however, must be written down if it's clear it has lost significant value and is unlikely to regain it any time soon. Accountants call such assets "impaired."

Once written down these assets cannot, as a general rule, be written "up" if values recover. By contrast, generally accepted accounting rules call for some assets—derivatives—to be valued using fair-value accounting. That requires marking these assets to market prices regularly, usually quarterly, to reflect their rise or fall in value in real time. A company must include these changes on its balance sheet. If it uses a derivative as a pure financial bet—rather than as a hedge, to manage risk—it also must include the changes on income statements. More complicated is when derivatives used as hedges must be included on an income statement. In any case, derivatives can make earnings volatile.

During the meltdown, industry executives bemoaned mark-to-market accounting. Among the critics were officials at the Federal Home Loan Banks, whose executives had helped fuel the bubble by extending too much credit to thrifts and banks to make crazy loans and mortgage-backed securities. The critics argued that marking to market made the crisis worse unfairly. The plunge in prices of mortgage assets was not normal, they argued, but, rather, reflected investor hysteria. Pegging securities to the market under such conditions over-stated how much value they had lost. Others, however, argued that the crisis revealed the true value, or lack thereof, of these assets—that they were impaired and a substantial markdown was inevitable. This group included investors and also regulators such as Paulson. Notably, it also included Charles Bowsher, former comptroller general of the United States, who was chairman of the Federal Home Loan Bank System's Office of Finance from April 2007 until March 2009, when he resigned as a lone voice of protest against the Federal Home Loan Banks' accounting practices on this issue.[15]

The investors, Paulson and Bowsher, proved correct, but elected officials bought the largely self-serving argument of lenders that mark-to-market write-downs were further depressing the going price for assets, helping to propel a downward spiral much like what foreclosures were doing to housing prices. Policymakers in their minds faced a dilemma: if mark-to-market accounting was suspended, the books of the nation's largest financial companies would mislead investors by carrying assets at inflated values, but allowing it to continue could made the recession worse by possibly deflating values too much. Regulators felt they had no choice but to go along to get the larger bill passed with the $700 billion they needed.[16] Even with this accounting relief, however, the nation's major banks edged toward insolvency, because bad loans—loans that consumers couldn't repay—were the problem, not accounting.[17] In the thrift crisis, the government couldn't close insolvent institutions without bankrupting the thrift insurance fund and thus tapping tax dollars, which would have been political death before an election. In the mortgage meltdown, the government couldn't close all the troubled banks without bankrupting the FDIC and requiring a taxpayer bailout so large it was unthinkable.

Paulson and other officials got the bill passed, but soon realized that their initial vision for how to use TARP wouldn't work. Using the money to buy bad assets from troubled banks would help repair balance sheets, but it would exhaust the fund almost overnight. Using it to buy a stake in banks—an ownership position that boosted capital—was more efficient. In his recounting of the crisis, Geithner gives a good explanation of why boosting the denominator of a leverage ratio was more efficient than reducing the numerator: "Imagine a bank with $1 trillion in mortgage assets and $25 billion in capital, a 40:1 leverage ratio. To get it to a much safer 20:1 . . . the government could buy $500 billion of its assets, which would drain most of TARP on one institution. Or it could inject $25 billion in additional capital, achieving the same ratio with one-twentieth of the cash."[18] The Reconstruction Finance Corporation had reached the same conclusion in the 1930s, when it found that lending money to overly extended banks in exchange for assets just made them more indebted. Instead, the RFC injected capital. One of the RFC's beneficiaries was National City, precursor to Citibank, which now would receive a much larger infusion under TARP.[19]

The money dulled the crisis, but the stock market continued to fall, and with it the retirement savings of tens of millions of Americans. On top of that were the sheer number of Americans losing their homes—mortgage delinquencies rose to more than five million by 2009, five times normal—and, as the recession grew, losing their jobs. It was not a good way for an incumbent party to enter fall elections. At one point, GOP presidential candidate John McCain (of "Keating Five" fame during the thrift crisis) suspended his campaign to return to Washington to be briefed on the crisis. Regulators, trying to remain politically neutral, called a meeting with President Bush and McCain that also included Democratic candidate Barack Obama, and congressional leaders. Obama, it turned out, was in daily contact with people like Warren Buffet and Paul Volcker and was on top of the situation. When eyes around the table turned to McCain to speak first, because he initially requested the meeting, he showed little grasp of what was going on. Obama's knowledge of the situation, by contrast, impressed even the aides to McCain. Author Jonathan Alter describes how one "Republican at the table joked to the person sitting next to him, 'after this, even we're going to vote for Obama.' That was the level of Obama's dominance in this meeting."[20]

To stabilize banks and encourage them to lend again, regulators forced the biggest federally insured institutions to take billions in TARP money. Even banks that thought they didn't need the money had to take bailout funds, as camouflage, so the market couldn't selectively punish those that really needed it.

Reviving lending was necessary to restart economic activity, but it was not a cure-all. Consumers, the drivers of growth, remained over their heads in debt. Still, unsticking credit was an all-consuming aim for Paulson and Bernanke— and an all-consuming hope for businesses around the country that now worried every day that they wouldn't have enough cash on hand to make payroll. The Fed eventually revealed that during the worst days it extended trillions of dollars in emergency credit not just to U.S. banks "but also to motorcycle makers, telecom and foreign-owned banks."[21] To meet liquidity needs during the crisis, General Electric, Caterpillar, Verizon, Harley-Davidson, and Toyota all received credit from America's central bank.

Consumers, however, didn't need more credit; they needed less debt. Many economists across the political spectrum favored short-circuiting defaults by reducing interest or principal, or both, to make mortgages affordable.

When a commercial real estate borrower gets into trouble, lender and creditor sit down and work out a way to reduce debt. Such "work-outs" benefit everyone. The bank recovers more money than it would by foreclosing and selling a property at a fire-sale price, and the borrower avoids bankruptcy. With consumer mortgages, however, common sense evaded these same bankers. In the past, courts had allowed homeowners who owed more on their mortgage than their house was worth—that is, those who were "underwater"—to restructure the loan through the bankruptcy process. A 1993 Supreme Court ruling ended that.[22] Now, in the mortgage meltdown of 2007, as foreclosures escalated and worsened the downturn, consumer groups, many investors, members of Congress, and economists favored changing the bankruptcy code to allow such work-outs again. Bankruptcy courts were adept at holding financially troubled consumers accountable to repay as much of their debt as possible.[23] And allowing bankruptcy judges to reduce mortgage principal paradoxically might mean they wouldn't have to: knowing that borrowers could file for bankruptcy would make banks more willing to negotiate to avoid that. But bankers, backed by Larry Summers and others in the Obama administration, fought any suggestion of reducing mortgages. They argued that the moral hazard created by bailing out banks was unavoidable for the greater good, but that the same didn't apply for consumers.

Banks opposed any restructuring of mortgage principal, but they were slightly less hostile to cutting interest rates. Reducing interest requires no write down on a balance sheet because interest is booked only as it comes due each month. Reducing it only reduces what gets booked later. But reducing principal, which is booked as an asset when a loan is made, does require a balance sheet write-down. Banks didn't mind reducing what customers *would* owe them in the future as much as they minded reducing what customers *did* owe them now. In addition, while banks recognized that they were better off agreeing to cut principal in such unusual times, they didn't want to set a precedent for normal times. And they had another reason for opposing principal reductions: they feared that if consumers could save a home through bankruptcy, many more would file, and they would throw their credit-card debt into the mix as well for reduction by the court. The banks that dominated mortgage lending also dominated the credit-card market. They didn't want a double hit.

Many in the public also objected to renegotiating mortgages. CNBC reporter Rick Santelli ignited populist opposition with a famous televised rant just after Obama took office and principal reductions were discussed. "How many people want to pay for your neighbor's mortgage that has an extra bathroom and can't pay their bills? Raise their hand," he said, calling it a plan to "subsidize the loser's mortgages."[24] Some say his tirade sparked creation of the Tea Party. Americans for Prosperity, a group created and funded by the billionaire Koch brothers, certainly did, becoming a platform for the Tea Party as it whipped up anger against bailouts, for either mortgage holders or Wall Street bankers. On the Left, equally angry protestors created the Occupy Wall Street movement, though they tended to favor efforts to help homeowners.[25]

Instead of calling for bankruptcy reforms to reduce mortgages, however, the Obama White House asked banks to voluntarily renegotiate them, promising the plan would cut foreclosures. It didn't work well. Bloomberg wrote in mid-2012: "Obama didn't deliver on his vow . . . to avert as many as 9 million foreclosures. While his plan was undermined in part by the weak U.S. economic recovery, it also lacked broad and aggressive measures. Relief programs have tinkered around the edges of the housing finance system because Obama's advisers chose early on not to expend political capital forcing banks to forgive mortgage debt. Instead, they created homeowner aid programs with voluntary participation by lenders and strict rules to avoid rewarding speculators or irresponsible borrowers."[26]

In 2012, Summers admitted that the Obama White House had made a serious mistake "around questions about housing," saying he now agreed that "household debt" and not a breakdown in bank lending "was the driving force behind the dramatic collapse in household spending." The driving mission of the Bush and Obama administrations to deal with the downturn had been to try to thaw credit to spark borrowing and spending. But consumers needed less debt. A better way to save the banks, he now agreed, would have been to "to attack the household-leverage problem directly," including by lowering many homeowners' mortgage principal.[27] Helping banks, which had hurt themselves by providing too much mortgage credit and would have collapsed without taxpayer help, was necessary but ineffective without a commensurate focus on cutting consumer debt. Summer's enlightenment came too late to help consumers or the economy.

Popular sentiment against mortgage write-downs wasn't the only obstacle. Securitization itself "impeded the ability of home owners to renegotiate their mortgages" by making it nearly impossible to figure out who actually owned a mortgage.[28] The national banks lobbying against reducing subprime mortgages' principal were the same banks that serviced that debt, earning a fee for collecting monthly payments and passing them on to investors.[29] They performed well as servicers. When it came to handling foreclosures, especially in such epic numbers, they failed: they repeatedly lost the documents that courts require before a home can be repossessed, and because banks provided consumers with no consistent contact person, those facing foreclosure had to repeatedly reexplain wrongful actions or other problems. The most infamous scandal involved "robo-signing," where bank employees signed "hundreds of affidavits per week attesting that they had reviewed and verified all the business records associated with a foreclosure, when in fact they never read through the material and just blindly signed off." Those records were often improperly prepared by bank servicers who couldn't figure out which lender owned a loan because it had been sold and resold to securitizers, who kept bad records. Mortgage bankers' recordkeeping was so sloppy, in fact, that it became a scandal in its own right: a company created and owned by the industry, known as MERS, for Mortgage Electronic Registration Systems, in theory provided a centralized record of mortgage transactions so at any moment one could find what institution owned a particular home loan. In practice, the disarray of MERS records often made identifying loan holders nearly impossible, at least in the short term as the housing market collapsed. The ineptitude raised questions about whether such a private registry could or should replace public land records.[30] Technically, only the owner of a loan can foreclose. Lacking this and other information, "foreclosures went ahead anyway because of the fraudulent affidavits."[31]

Mortgage servicers—who were also the major mortgage lenders—had built a system—MERS was just one part—to service massive numbers of new loans, not massive numbers of foreclosures. Even in the best of times, foreclosures happen, and servicers have contracts in place to handle them and to be paid quickly for doing so. As defaults came in record waves, getting paid quickly for handling a foreclosure discouraged servicers from doing what would have been in everyone's best interest—working with lenders to modify loans. Servicers didn't get paid immediately for working on modifications.

In 2013, federal regulators reached a $9.3 billion settlement with a dozen banks—including Bank of America, Wells Fargo, JPMorgan Chase, Citigroup, Morgan Stanley, and Goldman Sachs—over robo-signings that had affected nearly four million borrowers.[32] That was on top of a $25 billion settlement over the same issue a year earlier that the five largest servicers—Bank of America, Wells Fargo, JPMorgan Chase, Citigroup, and Ally Financial—reached with the Justice Department and forty-nine state attorneys general. (Ally was the new name with which General Motors rebranded its tarnished GMAC Bank.)[33]

With the mortgage meltdown, policymakers returned to a full-scale bailout that put more taxpayer money at risk than ever, far eclipsing the bailout of the thrift crisis, though by luck many of the guarantees never had to be paid out. From the 968 companies receiving $623 billion in actual taxpayer dollars, $390 billion was returned, leaving $233 billion not yet repaid as of this writing. Taxpayers have still made a profit, however, because of $308 billion the government earned from dividends, interest, and other fees. The net profit for taxpayers overall, as of January 2017, was $75.8 billion, the bulk of it from Fannie and Freddie, whose profits now go directly to the U.S. Treasury.[34] (This is why, even though the Great Recession holds the title as the biggest bailout, the thrift crisis, as second largest, remains the costliest.)

But there were larger, less quantifiable costs. Three researchers at the Fed, in a paper titled *How Bad Was It?*, assessed the toll of the mortgage crisis on the country as a democracy:

> The financial crisis resulted in a significant loss of trust in government institutions and the capitalist economic system. Many households' confidence in the financial system was shaken when roughly one-fourth of their accumulated household wealth evaporated in a matter of months. Further, the officials they entrusted to govern and to impartially regulate the financial services industry offered massive support and preference to a handful of the largest institutions. Deemed "too big to fail," these financial intermediaries lacked discipline and accountability leading up to the crisis and proved to be largely immune from the downside of the excessive risks they took. . . . Subsequent losses when the boom turned bust were disproportionately borne by taxpayers. Privatized gains, socialized losses was the banking model.[35]

This massive instance of moral hazard could have been avoided if the Fed had required lenders to underwrite mortgages by assessing borrowers' ability to repay them. Such a policy would have spared the country the bubble and its fallout. Many factors contributed to the mortgage crisis, but the root causes were simple: easy credit, lack of underwriting, and lack of oversight. And when the bust came, regulators and policymakers compounded it by bailing out lenders without also helping borrowers.

Alan Greenspan made front-page news in the fall of 2008 when he publicly renounced his belief that markets can police themselves. "I made a mistake in presuming that the self-interest of organizations, specifically banks and others, was such that they were best capable of protecting their own shareholders and their equity in the firms," he told Representative Henry Waxman (D-Calif.).

> WAXMAN: "You have been a staunch advocate for letting markets regulate themselves. And my question for you is simple. Were you wrong?"
> GREENSPAN: "Yes. I found a flaw, but I've been very distressed by that fact."

Many people contributed to the crisis, but no one more than Greenspan, whose laissez-faire ideology, inspired by Ayn Rand, guided the Fed to adopt a see-nothing, do-nothing policy in the decade leading to the bubble. When he stepped down in early 2006, just before the crisis hit, he insisted that the "froth" in the mortgage market posed no threat. He acknowledged "particular concern" over a rise in high-risk mortgages, but said that housing was regional. Given the expense of closing costs, a quick nationwide run-up or run-down in prices was unlikely.[36]

He had articulated this view three years earlier in a talk to community bankers: "It is, of course, possible for home prices to fall as they did in a couple of quarters in 1990. But any analogy to stock market pricing behavior and bubbles is a rather large stretch. First, to sell a home, one almost invariably must move out and in the process confront substantial transaction costs in the form of brokerage fees and taxes. These transaction costs greatly discourage the type of buying and selling frenzy that often characterizes bubbles in financial markets. Second, there is no national housing market in the United States. Local conditions dominate, even though mortgage interest rates are similar throughout the country. Home prices in Portland, Maine, do not arbitrage those in Portland, Oregon."[37]

In 2005, with the bubble in full swing, he told Congress that securitization was an innovation that would minimize any harm that an increase in foreclosures posed to financial institutions. "Nationwide banking and widespread securitization of mortgages," he pronounced, "makes it less likely . . . [lenders] would be impaired than was the case in prior episodes of regional house price corrections." Ben Bernanke, a Federal Reserve Board governor at the time, echoed Greenspan, saying on CNBC: "We've never had a decline in house prices on a nationwide basis."[38]

They were wrong on all counts. Closing costs didn't protect against a bubble: in the subprime market, where lenders deliberately churned refinancings, they drove it. Subprime securitization made the market national: the big commercial and investment banks, operating from coast to coast, used badly underwritten subprime securitizations to spread undue risk nationwide, magnifying its effect rather than diluting it.[39]

In May 2007, almost eighteen months after succeeding Greenspan as Fed chairman, Bernanke downplayed the growing problems. He failed to grasp, for example, the implosion of two Bear Stearns hedge funds as a bellwether event. "The effect of the troubles in the subprime sector on the broader housing market will likely be limited," he said, "and we do not expect significant spillovers from the subprime market to the rest of the economy or to the financial system."[40] Within weeks, the financial firestorm would overwhelm him.

Federal Reserve Board Chair Ben Bernanke, *right*, talks with former chairs Paul Volcker, *left*, and Alan Greenspan, *center*, after participating in the ceremonial signing on December 16, 2013, of a certificate commemorating the hundredth anniversary of the signing of the Federal Reserve Act. AP Photo/Pablo Martinez Monsivais.

Greenspan and Bernanke often talk about how hard it is to spot an asset bubble like the one behind the Great Recession, which involved homes, the biggest assets most people ever own, and tell us it's just as hard to know how to prevent one. Bernanke points out that raising the cost of borrowing to quell speculation often is not the best approach. In early 2002, a year before its boom became a bubble, the housing market was doing well even as much of the rest of the economy still lagged from the 2001 recession.

How to tame a bubble in one sector while the rest of the economy is in a slump was the dilemma the Federal Reserve faced in the 1920s, when stock market speculation soared as manufacturing, farming, and other consumer spending sagged. Tightening credit might cool speculation in stocks or housing, but it would hurt other sectors, where deflation called for more credit.

"Those who argue that you can incrementally increase interest rates to defuse bubbles ought to try it sometime," quipped Greenspan in reply to those who said he caused the mortgage mess by making money too cheap for too long. These critics, which included Stanford economist John Taylor, make the argument that bubbles can't happen without easy credit. That's true, but it's easy to imagine and understand why most people might react just as Greenspan did in the face of a faltering economy after a national terrorist crisis. It's also true that easy credit doesn't guarantee a bubble if other forces—like oversight—are at work, and that's where Greenspan fell short. Bernanke says a more targeted way to curb financial bubbles is for bank and securities regulators to set rules and enforce them before a crisis develops. Greenspan's flaw was that he opposed such prophylactic intervention, even though he readily intervened after problems hit. Wall Street could rely on him to don his lifeguard outfit and lower rates to soften the blow any time markets fell—a policy if ever there was one that encouraged moral hazard among investors, who could keep their gains but count on Greenspan to dull their losses. His failure to write effective national mortgage rules when Congress told him to do it in 1994 was part of his larger failure to use the tools available to him as a bank regulator to patrol bank holding companies, particularly nonbank affiliates, to prevent misuse of the easy credit he had created.[41]

During the crafting of Gramm-Leach-Bliley, Greenspan wrestled with Treasury over which agency would oversee holding companies. He argued that governments around the world were more familiar with the Fed and thus would feel more confident letting U.S. firms do business within their borders if the central bank of the United States was the overarching regulator. After winning that battle, the Fed proceeded to do little to exercise its hard-won authority, even though Gramm-Leach-Bliley authorized it to examine "to the fullest extent possible . . . any subsidiary that could have a materially adverse effect on the safety and soundness of a depository institution."[42] Flaws in the law itself encouraged the Fed's inclination to regulate as little as possible. In addition to preventing the Fed from overseeing the five biggest investment banks, the law required financial regulators to do their jobs by relying as much as possible on each other's expertise. Regulators interpreted this stipulation as narrowly as possible, concluding it meant they should stay out of each other's way. This created a culture in which each regulator focused on a narrow patch rather than on the big picture, and it occurred despite the fact that, well before and even with Gramm-Leach-Bliley, bank regulators have broad authority to talk to each other, to coordinate, and to throw out bad actors who threaten the safety and soundness of federally insured institutions. They could have put their heads together and worked collaboratively, as they eventually did during the crisis.[43] Instead, Greenspan and his staff repeatedly heard consumer groups and state attorneys general complain about subprime problems, yet did little, assuming the market would fix itself. Evidence that the Fed could have acted much sooner came September 15, 2009, when it reversed its policy of not policing affiliates of bank holding companies for compliance with consumer protections. "The Federal Reserve," read the statement, "will implement a consumer compliance supervision program in nonbank subsidiaries of bank holding companies . . . with activities covered by the consumer protection laws and regulations the Federal Reserve has the authority to enforce. The policy, which will take effect immediately, also provides for the investigation of consumer complaints against these nonbank entities. . . . The policy . . . is designed to improve the Federal Reserve's understanding of the consumer compliance risk that certain products and services may pose to the holding companies and consumers and to guide supervisory activity for these entities."[44] Translation: The Fed had dropped the ball.

The change reversed a policy the Fed had embraced in January 1998, when it formally adopted a long-standing policy of "not routinely conducting consumer compliance examinations of nonbank subsidiaries of bank holding companies." The General Accounting Office, the investigative arm of Congress, questioned this policy in a report in November 1999, but the Federal Reserve took no action. These were profound mistakes that failed the American public, Rich Spillenkothen, the Federal Reserve's top bank regulator from 1991 to 2006, told financial crisis investigators in 2010:

> Senior supervisors and regulatory agency leaders in the 5–7 years preceding August 2007, myself included, bear responsibility for the performance of the supervisory process during this period. Decisions made and actions taken—or not taken—had consequences. Flawed policies and rules, regulatory gaps, and shortcomings in the execution of supervisory programs all played a role. But a number of more fundamental factors—such as a general acceptance of specious conventional wisdom, a philosophical skepticism and ambivalence toward regulation, insufficient attention to the lessons of history, and organizational, cultural, and structural impediments—affected the ability of the Federal Reserve and other regulatory agencies to recognize the severity of emerging problems in a timely manner and address them before they triggered a broader crisis.[45]

To their credit, Bernanke, Greenspan, and Cox all eventually recognized that regulators had failed.[46] Financial executives, they realized, are terrible at policing themselves.

Treasury Department officials also contributed to the failures by making it harder for states to enact and enforce better rules and by too often acting as cheerleaders for the industry rather than as responsible overseers. The Treasury's Office of Thrift Supervision, for example, hosted a housing conference after the crash began, on December 3, 2007, featuring industry executives and regulators from the Fed and from the Office of the Comptroller of the Currency to discuss a "housing slump" and rise in "foreclosures." Watching a recording of the conference is painful, given what we know was happening. Tanned, silver-haired Countrywide chairman and chief executive Mozilo, on a panel moderated by CNBC anchor Maria Bartiromo, summed up the prevailing attitude: Efforts to stop rising foreclosures were "dealing clearly with the results and not with the cause. Nobody's addressing the cause and that's what has to be addressed ultimately and that's the fact that values of homes continue to go down." The reason values were falling, he said, was a lack of "liquidity," of consumers not being able to borrow to buy a house. What was needed? More credit. He sounded just like Charlie Mitchell at National City in 1929 as the stock market got shaky before the big crash—if only stock prices hadn't gone down, if only consumers could borrow more money to buy more stock, there wouldn't have been a crash.[47]

Many elected officials knew what was happening and should have done more to stop it. Government hearings—in 1998, 2000, and 2001, for example—documented abuses in subprime mortgage lending. FBI investigators in 2004 warned of an "epidemic" of false documentation and other fraud in subprime lending in an effort to head off the "next S&L crisis." Many states begged their federal counterparts for help in curbing the abuses.[48]

Why didn't Congress take the Fed to task for failing to write mortgage lending rules to snuff out the worst practices? Government and industry officials argued that such rules would stifle innovation and reduce first-time home buying, even though evidence showed that subprime lending wasn't an innovation and wasn't focused on first-time buyers.[49] The predatory features in many of those loans meant that many more people lost a home to foreclosure than were put into one for the first time.

The Federal Reserve finally, in 2008, did write rules requiring underwriting and banning kickbacks for steering borrowers into expensive loans, but it was too late to avert the crisis.[50] "It's clear the Fed should have acted earlier," said former FDIC chair Bair. "Financial innovation is great, but you have to have some basic rules. One of the most basic rules is that a borrower should have the ability to repay."[51]

Acknowledging securitization as a "brilliant" innovation of the twentieth century, Cleveland's Rokakis bemoaned its misuse. "It freed up a lot of capital. If it had been done responsibly, it would have been a wondrous thing because nothing is more stable, there's nothing safer, than the American mortgage market. . . . It worked for years. But then people realized they could scam it."[52] In 2010, Bernanke told crisis investigators, "One of the lessons of the crisis is that innovation is not always a good thing. . . . There are innovations that have unpredictable consequences. There are innovations whose primary purpose is to take unfair advantage, rather than to create a more efficient market. And there are innovations that can create systemic risks even if from the perspective of the individual firm . . . that risk is not evident."[53]

Avid proponents of home lending, especially to low-income borrowers, drowned out the naysayers. Cheerleaders included Presidents Bill Clinton and George W. Bush, whose administration paid little attention to the developing crisis and even took steps that made it worse. In 2001, for example, Bush's Department of Housing and Urban Development undercut consumers' ability to fight unfair practices in the subprime arena: it said that consumers could not bring class-action suits under the Real Estate Settlement Procedures Act of 1974, which requires mortgage lenders and brokers to disclose the costs involved in the process of residential home buying and specifically prohibits kickbacks. Barring class-action suits on complaints that "yield-spread premiums"—extra money lenders paid mortgage brokers to steer borrowers into more expensive, subprime loans—were kickbacks effectively quashed all lawsuits on the issue. Most individuals simply couldn't afford to bring one on their own. These kickbacks flourished as a result.[54]

Bush praised the subprime market for opening doors to home ownership and said it didn't need more rules. "America is a stronger country every single time a family moves into a house of their own," he told a gathering of the National Association of Homebuilders in October 2004. That evening he announced new initiatives to help low-income families become homeowners, including a zero-down payment plan for first-time homebuyers using mortgages federally insured through the Federal Housing Administration.[55]

The higher a down payment, the lower the risk of default. But the golden rule of putting down 20 percent of the purchase price for a new home gave way well before the boom, with the costs of buying a home soaring, particularly in the subprime area, once Congress overrode state usury laws and permitted lenders to charge as much as they wanted. Evidence shows that 3 to 5 percent down can, with good underwriting that includes a second layer of credit analysis through private mortgage insurance, bring default rates pretty close to those for loans with down payments four times higher.[56] The key is "good underwriting," and that had disappeared.

The increase in home ownership, especially among minorities, that Bush touted as one of his presidency's goals turned out to be a bust. The Financial Crisis Inquiry Commission described the "talk of opportunity [as] tragically at odds with the reality of a financial disaster in the making." Most of the people targeted for a subprime loan who then lost a home to foreclosure had started out with a good home loan on a house in which they had built up equity.[57] Though white non-Hispanic families numerically made up a majority of victims, Hispanic and black families bore a disproportionate share of the losses because they received a disproportionate share of subprime refinancings, even when individuals had good credit profiles.[58]

Mortgage originations and prices peaked in 2005 before plummeting. By mid-2008, as foreclosures mounted, home prices had returned to pre-bubble levels.[59] By 2009, for the first time in eighty years, home prices had fallen nationwide, by an estimated $5.5 trillion, or 30 percent, from three years earlier. They didn't begin to recover until 2012. Bonds backed by home loans that Greenspan said would spread risk away from federally insured banks in fact damaged the entire economy on a scale not seen since the 1930s.[60]

Seriously delinquent mortgages rose from 1 percent of those outstanding at the start of the decade to nearly 10 percent at the height of the crisis, and states with high concentrations of subprime loans approached 14 percent. Early estimates predicted that one in every five subprime mortgages made during the bubble would default. The actual default rate turned out to be more than twice that.[61]

The biggest clue that housing markets were askew was that average home prices shot up much faster than average income, with some economists estimating that prices were as much as 20 percent too high. From the 1960s until the 1990s, home prices and income mostly moved in tandem.[62] Then, as housing prices skyrocketed in the 1990s and early 2000s, consumers spent faster than their income rose. Personal savings fell sharply and household debt soared, with mortgage debt at the heart of the increase.[63] A *New York Times* reporter surmised that Greenspan, Bernanke, and others missed such clear signals for reasons "more psychological than economic. They got trapped in an echo chamber of conventional wisdom. Real estate agents, home builders, Wall Street executives, many economists, and millions of homeowners all said home prices would not drop."[64] They had consumed the Kool-Aid.

Columbia University economist David Beim estimates that the increase in household debt in the run-up to the Great Recession was matched in America's history only once, in the run-up to the economy's other near-death experience, the Great Depression.[65] "For the past 25 years we have been over-consuming and over-borrowing to do it," Beim wrote in 2009. "That problem can only be solved by debt reductions. How do you reduce debt? . . . Repay it or default on it."

While many have studied the 1920s, the crash of 1929, and the Depression, economists Atif Mian and Amir Sufi point to the particular wisdom of Charles Persons, who published a November 1930 paper in the *Quarterly Journal of Economics* titled "Credit Expansion, 1920 to 1929, and Its Lessons." He reached conclusions, say Mian and Sufi, "eerily" predictive of what happened in the Great Recession: "The existing depression was due essentially to the great wave of credit expansion in the past decade. . . . Our period of prosperity was based on nothing more substantial than debt expansion."[66]

In the late 1970s and through the 1990s, as financial deregulation became popular, some favored a loosening of rules, some of oversight, some of both. Economist Hyman P. Minsky, to the contrary, developed the view that, whatever the rules, government oversight is needed to keep borrowed money that starts out financing well-thought-out investments from becoming a form of gambling that destabilizes the system. He did not subscribe to the notion that severe downturns are a natural part of the credit cycle, as some on Wall Street argue, but, rather, believed that they are the consequence of an inadequate response to such cycles, that is, they are what happen when we let credit run amok.

Minsky thought that financial markets in particular need oversight because they are inherently unstable, being prone to boom-and-bust cycles of debt that affect the entire economy. His ideas hadn't had much influence but came into vogue starting in 2006, with the collapse of the housing market. Wall Street executives began referring to the seemingly sudden collapse of home prices as a "Minsky moment," that is, a financial crisis sparked by excessive borrowing, specifically by home buyers who increasingly defaulted under the weight of excessive debt.

Minsky viewed borrowers as investors who fall somewhere on a scale of risk that ranges from being reasonably prudent to being doomed to fail. Those who can pay principal and interest on debt he considered to be borrowers taking reasonable risk. He viewed as "speculators" those who can pay only interest but no principal. Investors who cannot even pay interest fully, let alone any principal, he deemed as having fallen into unsustainable territory. He even referred to this latter group as "Ponzi" investors in the sense that their financial demise is almost inevitable, even if their activities are not necessarily fraudulent (though they often are). As the "Ponzi" investor group becomes more and more prevalent and enough money isn't repaid, the bubble turns to bust.

Minsky has critics, most notably those who argue that price bubbles don't even exist because prices reflect the market's collective information at any moment. That prices for a particular asset stay high for a time—say on a house—and then plummet merely reflects changing market views. Such criticism, however, is in the end uninteresting. It's like saying that everyone dies from heart failure, which is true but unenlightening. Far more interesting is the disease that causes the heart failure, and when it comes to finance, for many economists—Persons in the 1930s; Minsky in the 1980s; and Beim, Mian, and Sufi today—it's too much debt, too much easy credit.

Yet even Wall Street executives who embrace Minsky's theory misuse the phrase "Minsky moment" because for too many a sudden downturn seems to have been unpredictable. Usually, however, that's not the case. Plenty of people, though they might be in a minority, have predicted severe downturns caused by the bursting of an asset bubble. Often, they are the ones who make money at such times, at everyone else's expense. They make hay with the Minsky moment, which, at its essence, reflects a lack of sound underwriting, which raises default risk, which provides opportunity for the clear-sighted.[67]

Fannie and Freddie didn't cause the housing bubble. They didn't create subprime securitization, and they didn't buy most of the toxic mortgages and bonds it produced. They did, however, contribute to the catastrophe.

As investors worldwide clamored for higher yielding, private-label mortgage-backed securities, Fannie and Freddie couldn't resist the temptation to enter the subprime mortgage market so as not to lose out on the mortgage market's fastest-growing segment.[68] By the height of the bubble, in 2005 and 2006, Wall Street was securitizing more loans than Fannie and Freddie did.[69] To regain market share—and trigger multimillion-dollar paychecks for meeting overly ambitious earnings targets they had promised shareholders—the two companies bought the triple-A slices of private-label subprime mortgage-backed securities, supposedly the safest parts. The Bush White House encouraged this by allowing Fannie and Freddie to count these purchases toward their obligation to buy home loans held by people across the income spectrum.

Depending on how one counts, Fannie and Freddie bought—they funded—between 25 and 40 percent of the more than $2 trillion in private-label subprime mortgage-backed securities issued from 2004 through 2006. Like Hoover's Federal Home Loan Banks, they helped make cheap credit available for the bad lending fueling the bubble. That Fannie and Freddie bought these securities also helped to legitimize subprime securitizations: It gave pension funds and foreign governments false comfort that private-label securities, which on the surface looked similar to the mortgage-backed securities they for years had bought from Fannie and Freddie, were the same as agency mortgage-backed securities and just as safe.[70]

Regulators in the Clinton and Bush administrations also encouraged Fannie and Freddie's foray into high-risk mortgages by allowing the companies' executives to promise shareholders double-digit earnings growth year after year. Fannie and Freddie's business of guaranteeing mortgages produced reliable profits but, because their mutual competition had made the market so efficient, not double-digit ones. To meet targets—and trigger higher compensation—the companies chased higher yields with a ferocity that became a driving force at both firms.[71]

When the government seized control of Fannie and Freddie, subprime loans accounted for 10 percent of their assets but 50 percent of their $3.1 billion in losses between April and June 2008. Their holdings in subprime and other questionable mortgages amounted to 20 percent of their assets, but 80 percent of Fannie's losses and 100 percent of Freddie's.[72] In normal times, they could have weathered the losses. But they couldn't weather a loss of trust. Investors, not understanding the difference between private-label and agency bonds, and even more uncertain of how much of the subprime securities the two companies owned, became nervous about lending to them. Liquidity threatened to dry up, which would have frozen their ability to roll over billions of dollars in debt, plunging them into bankruptcy and, as presidential candidate Barack Obama put it, dealing "a body blow" to the financial system.[73]

Of approximately $5 trillion in outstanding Fannie and Freddie mortgage-backed securities and corporate debt in mid-2008, more than half was held by federally insured banks ($1 trillion), pension and mutual funds ($1 trillion), and foreign investors, especially the Chinese and the Russians, who owned $500 billion between them.[74] As mainstays of America's $10 trillion housing market and of the national and world economies, not to mention of the balance sheets of federally insured banks, failure of the two companies would have threatened it all.[75]

Paulson's takeover of Fannie and Freddie caused their stock to plummet to pennies per share, but it restored confidence and preserved the value of their mortgage bonds and corporate debt, thus sparing already troubled U.S. banks from having to write those down. Still, more than six hundred banks suffered $8 billion in losses on preferred shares in the housing twins, leading to two distressed mergers and fifteen outright failures.[76]

Even so, as the nation's largest mortgage financiers, both firms helped stabilize housing during the crisis. Their relatively strong underwriting standards, the Financial Crisis Inquiry Commission concluded, produced "substantially lower" delinquency rates, which meant their mortgage-backed securities "essentially maintained their value throughout the crisis."[77]

Though the takeover averted a larger crisis, it did nothing to resolve the debate over whether Fannie and Freddie are needed and whether they should continue with full, partial, or no government backing. In putting them into conservatorship rather than receivership, the government promised to restore stability and then return them to the private sector. A decade later, in 2018, they were still held in conservatorship. Both returned to profitability in 2012, repaid the $187 billion in taxpayer funds that bailed them out, and now funnel their profits into the U.S. Treasury, for a total net return to the public, at the end of 2016, of $70 billion and counting.[78]

Also to blame for the bubble are the enablers, that is, the accountants, lawyers, and other third-party consultants whose approval of questionable practices and securities made it possible. One group among these stands out: credit-rating agencies.

For years, Standard & Poor's, Moody's, and Fitch have dominated the business of assessing the riskiness of companies and securities. Yet these companies have a conflict of interest because they are paid to rate securities by the firms issuing the securities, not by the investors relying on the opinions. Traditionally investors have had no recourse when those ratings prove worthless: the credit agencies have avoided legal liability, even for ratings done without sound underwriting, by successfully arguing in court that ratings are opinions protected by the First Amendment of the U.S. Constitution.[79]

During the crisis, Merrill Lynch discovered that $55 billion in mortgage securities carrying a "super-safe" rating cost it billions of dollars in losses.[80] Of the 7,500 mortgage securities to which Moody's gave its top rating in 2006, more than 80 percent had to be downgraded, 73 percent of them all the way down to "junk" status.[81] Ratings of mortgage-backed securities made up nearly half of Moody's revenues during the years of the bubble.[82]

The stress tests these credit-rating agencies used to assess risk had severe shortcomings. Moody's and Standard and Poor's, for example, assumed that no major downturn in housing would occur, leading them to assume, wrongly, that (1) mortgage defaults would fall within historic rates, and (2) each foreclosure would be a discrete, uncorrelated event. But in the crisis foreclosures were not uncorrelated: they were connected in a vicious cycle. As they engulfed neighborhoods around the nation, home prices fell in wide geographic swaths, which further reduced values, causing more defaults that, in a highly correlated market catastrophe, accelerated the price declines.[83]

In 2015, Standard and Poor's paid $1.37 billion to the U.S. Justice Department and twenty state attorneys general to settle civil fraud charges over its ratings. The settlement ended an unusual feud between the agency and the U.S. government over whether each had taken actions to retaliate against the other.[84] After the White House successfully pushed Congress to pass reform legislation in 2010 to make credit agencies liable for their ratings—that is, to say the First Amendment no longer protected them against sloppy work—Standard and Poor's cut the AAA credit rating of U.S. Treasury bonds. When the Justice Department filed suit in 2011 over Standard and Poor's misleading rating practices, the agency accused the government of filing the suit to retaliate for its downgrade of the government's rating. The government allowed Standard and Poor's to reach the settlement without admitting or denying fraud, but insisted that the agency declare it had no evidence the government had acted maliciously.[85] Embarrassingly, as part of its defense, Standard and Poor's argued that its routine claims of objectivity in its ratings were no more than "classic puffery," marketing hyperbole that investors knew not to believe.

How could Standard and Poor's and the other credit-rating agencies charge millions of dollars for puffery? The 1984 law that Ranieri helped craft required a credit rating on all private-label mortgage-backed securities—which gave the ratings agencies a captive market. And each credit-rating agency knew that if it didn't deliver the rating a client sought, the client would simply go to one of its two competitors.

In 2005, one hedge-fund manager was laughed at when he told an audience of securitizers that he saw a lot of "irrationality" in the market.[86] Even as late as the fall of 2008, some continued to deny that the subprime market had become almost entirely predatory. One industry paper absurdly advocated that people differentiate among three types of loans: abusive, predatory, and fraudulent.[87] But some saw the end was near.

Goldman Sachs, which created and sold $100 billion in subprime mortgage securities during the bubble, was among the first to figure out the gig would soon be up. In December 2006, when Goldman executives noticed delinquencies in subprime mortgages rising, they "quietly and abruptly reversed course," betting against the subprime mortgage-backed securities market for an eventual profit of $3.7 billion.[88] Senate investigators unearthed emails from Goldman's executives disparaging products they sold clients during this period, calling securities "pigs" and "crap" and talking of how "to dupe" someone into a sale.[89]

A frequent narrative that executives at the heart of the catastrophe tell is that no one could have predicted what happened, no one could have seen it coming. Yet many economists, including Robert Shiller at Yale and Nouriel Roubini at New York University, did, as did the *Economist,* which on the cover of its June 2005 issue proclaimed, "House Prices: After the Fall." So did Goldman and state attorneys general and many consumer groups. "Everybody in the whole world knew that the mortgage bubble was there," Richard Breeden, former SEC chairman under President George H. W. Bush, told the crisis commission. "It wasn't hidden. . . . You cannot look at any of this and say that the regulators did their job. This was not some hidden problem. It wasn't out on Mars or Pluto or somewhere. It was right here. . . . You can't make trillions of dollars' worth of mortgages and not have people notice."[90]

At an August 2005 annual meeting of "prominent central bankers, finance ministers, academics, and financial market participants from around the world" in Jackson Hole, Wyoming, Larry Summers branded economist Raghuram Rajan a "luddite" for suggesting that compensating financial executives for short-term gains without holding them responsible for long-term losses made financial markets riskier. "I felt like an early Christian who had wandered into a convention of half-starved lions," Rajan wrote later.[91]

The crisis commission asked Michael A. Neal, then chairman and CEO of GE Capital, to testify about shadow banking. GE, through a division it bought in 2004, made about $50 billion in subprime loans from 2005 to 2007.[92] "I am proud to lead a company that is focused on lending to Main Street businesses and consumer activity," Neal said. "Still, the turmoil in the markets over the past two and a half years has been unlike anything I had seen or experienced during my more than 30 years at GE." It was the "we never saw it coming" routine. He did not explain why those in charge of risk management at the company didn't know that the mortgages GE was selling—mortgages structured to force borrowers to refinance repeatedly—were unlike any made in the previous thirty years. As risk managers, their job was to know such things.[93]

By 2015, GE had largely exited the finance business to return to its industrial roots.[94] Why? Tougher regulations passed in the wake of the crisis. "It was more fun being a free spirit than being bound by Scripture," Ben Heineman, a former GE general counsel and GE Capital director, told a reporter. Heineman retired from GE. So did Neal, who despite his innocence about risk at GE is now on the risk-policy committee of the board at JPMorgan.[95]

Underwriting, transparency, oversight, and accountability are the essence of the Dodd-Frank Act that Congress passed in 2010 in response to the crisis. It adopted many consumer safeguards and attempted to fix the many problems that functional regulation created under Gramm-Leach-Bliley.

It said mortgage lenders could no longer pay brokers or loan officers to steer customers into higher-priced loans, and prepayment charges must expire early enough to give consumers time to shop without penalty for a cheaper mortgage before a rate adjustment. It required lenders to assess a borrower's ability to repay a loan, including, if a loan adjusts, at the higher rate. And it said they must use traditional underwriting, verifying income, job, and credit—no more asset-based underwriting. It made it harder to foreclose on a home in case of default if the lender failed to do proper underwriting. The easiest way lenders could prove in court that they properly underwrote was to show that a mortgage either was or could have been sold to Fannie or Freddie, underscoring that, despite the criticism of the twin mortgage giants, people on many sides of the debate agree that those agencies' mortgage underwriting is very good.

The act created the Consumer Financial Protection Bureau, a new agency within the Federal Reserve focused exclusively on upholding rules to safeguard retail customers when they buy financial products, no matter what type of company sells them. While other regulators still retain some responsibility to enforce consumer protections, Congress focused this authority in one place, the CFPB, to try to prevent regulators from ever again favoring profits over consumer protection, as they did during the bubble.

The law restored the ability of states to help enforce consumer protection laws alongside federal regulators. It did away with the Office of Thrift Supervision by folding it into the Office of the Comptroller of the Currency and by giving the Federal Reserve oversight of thrift holding companies. These changes should make it harder for banks to shop around for the most lenient federal regulator, but they didn't go as far as those who favor streamlining bank regulators into one or two agencies would have liked.

Dodd-Frank retained the concept of functional regulation but fixed some of its flaws. One of the biggest was that Gramm-Leach-Bliley either blocked or regulators thought it blocked the Federal Reserve from robustly peering into a bank holding company's non-bank subsidiaries. Dodd-Frank rolled back the silo mentality of "Fed-Lite," for example, by giving the Fed greater authority to review operations of subsidiaries that are overseen by other regulators, such as the Securities and Exchange Commission. This reinforces the idea that the Fed's job is to police non-bank subsidiaries to detect and curtail risks that could damage a federally insured banking affiliate and, ultimately, taxpayers. Dodd-Frank also requires Fed officials to review any activity that a bank could engage in that, for whatever reason, is being conducted in a subsidiary that does not carry federal deposit insurance. The idea is to ensure that bank regulators never again turn a blind eye to bad products such as toxic mortgages just because a holding company makes them outside of its FDIC-insured banks. This should curtail regulatory arbitrage among a holding company's subsidiaries.

To curtail the too-big-to-fail doctrine, the law also created the Financial Stability Oversight Council, whose members are the major regulators, to look at the big picture and identify financial companies, not just banks, that pose a risk to the economy. The council identifies such companies as "systemically important financial institutions," or SIFIs, a designation that requires a company to hold higher levels of capital than other firms must hold against liabilities. The act requires the Fed to oversee systemically important "nonbank financial companies" as a prudential regulator, as well as impose stricter prudential oversight on bank holding companies with assets of more than $50 billion. It requires the largest bank companies and other SIFI-designated firms to have the corporate version of a living will, a plan for an orderly winding down in case of insolvency, through bankruptcy court for the parent firm and its nonbank subsidiaries and through the FDIC for its federally insured banks.

The SIFI designation is the provision in Dodd-Frank that could prevent a situation like the one in the run-up to the mortgage bubble, where the five largest independent investment banking companies eluded Fed oversight. The five are now either gone or converted to bank holding companies, so the question is moot for the moment. Still, this provision would make it easier for bank regulators to ride herd on any behemoth financial company that, like the former Big Five, tried to evade oversight by arguing their investment banking operations outweigh their commercial banking activities. This provision essentially acknowledges that the distinction that Gramm-Leach-Bliley made between investment bank holding companies and commercial bank holding companies was ridiculous. It too should help curb charter shopping.

Additionally, Dodd-Frank said that if an orderly failure of a systemically key company isn't possible through that procedure, the Federal Deposit Insurance Fund can, in consultation with the other federal regulators and the president, seize an entire financial holding company, not just its federally insured banks, and manage that entire company through an "orderly liquidation." Democrats and Republicans overwhelmingly supported this expanded FDIC authority, which under certain circumstances would give the agency oversight not just of federally insured institutions but also of investment banks, insurance firms, and other financial players. Giving the FDIC such expanded authority underscores the extent to which the financial activity of nonbanks can threaten the entire financial system and, through deposit insurance, taxpayers. Dodd-Frank's liquidation procedures attempt to ensure that no company is too big to fail. Just as important, as then–FDIC Chair Martin J. Gruenberg put it, such authority helps ensure a failed firm's "shareholders, creditors and culpable management . . .

[will] be held accountable without cost to taxpayers." As evidence that these Dodd-Frank provisions have muted the moral hazard of taxpayer-funded bailouts, he cites "the fact that the credit rating agencies have lowered the credit ratings of the eight U.S. globally systemic banking organizations . . . because of a reduced expectation of taxpayer support in the event of failure."[96]

Under Dodd-Frank hedge funds must now register with the SEC and are subject to stricter record-keeping and filing rules and to periodic examinations. The SEC and Commodity Futures Trading Commission now share oversight of over-the-counter derivatives, which with some exceptions must now be traded on exchanges so that pricing and concentrations of risk are transparent. Over-the-counter derivatives traders must comply with record-keeping rules, prohibitions against fraud, and the vetting of counterparties—all the templates adopted for securities markets after the 1929 crash.[97]

The law made rating agencies liable for the ratings they issue by allowing investors who relied on them to successfully sue if the ratings are defective. Credit raters are allowed to be wrong, but they can be shielded from liability for being wrong only if they demonstrate that they did the homework necessary—that they underwrote—to make a reasonable determination of a security's risks.[98]

The law strengthened whistleblower protections and created a "bounty" program in which the SEC pays whistleblowers—and keeps their names anonymous—for tips that lead to sanctions of at least $1 million. Awards can be up to 30 percent of the money the SEC collects. In 2017, for example, a financial executive at agricultural giant Monsanto received $22 million for tips that led to an $80 million enforcement action against the company for accounting violations and misstated earnings for its weed killer Roundup. The whistleblower's identity is not public.

Last but hardly least, the law imposed the "Volcker Rule," which bars banks and their holding companies from trading for their own proprietary accounts—that is, from speculating with federally insured deposits or money subsidized by such accounts.

Homeownership grew from 67 percent of households in 1999 to a peak of 69.1 percent in 2005, but by 2016 stood at just 63.5 percent—what it was in 1966. Given that increasing home ownership was always promoted as the mortgage frenzy's great benefit, the bubble, crash, and drawn-out recovery were a giant step backward.[99] It was much ado about nothing.

At the end of 2017, household debt reached a record $13.15 trillion, surpassing by $473 billion the previous record, in mid-2008, just after the collapse of the housing bubble.[100] The rise was driven by increases in mortgage, car, and credit-card debt. Credit-card borrowing reached a record—somewhere between $931 billion and $1.021 trillion, depending on how you count—an increase of 7 percent from a year earlier and pushing average household credit-card debt to $15,983. The 2017 numbers reflected in part that Americans continue to finance many healthcare expenses with plastic. Consumers borrowed slightly less using their homes as collateral, but delinquencies in auto and credit-card borrowing rose. The trend wasn't dire, but it concerned many economists, especially in the context of a new, all-out push under the Trump administration to roll back Dodd-Frank and deregulate financial services, to raise taxes on the middle class, and to swell the national debt.[101] Going into 2018, Wall Street and politicians alike appeared addicted once again to providing retail consumers with easy credit, a phenomenon that began full force in the 1920s and, except for a few momentary pauses, has never stopped gathering steam.

PART FOUR

COCKROACHES IN THE KITCHEN

24

Fake Accounts

WHEN JOHN STUMPF, CHAIR AND CEO OF Wells Fargo, testified before both the House Financial Services Committee and the Senate Banking Committee in the fall of 2016, he answered legislators' angry questions without becoming visibly rattled.[1] His impassive demeanor won him few friends. Members of both committees grilled him about a newly revealed scandal that had taken place over several years: 5,300 Wells employees had opened 2 million checking and credit-card accounts without customers' approval, then imposed late fees and other charges to bilk them of millions of dollars. The bank fired the employees, and the Consumer Financial Protection Bureau fined the bank $185 million. Justice Department lawyers launched a criminal probe.[2] Now the question was whether the bank's top executives would be held accountable. Creating fake accounts so abused consumers that Stumpf likely could not have saved his job. Yet his flat responses conveyed an indifference that cemented his fate even as investors filed suits against the Wells board and key executives. He was fired a month after the hearings.

The creation of fake accounts started around 2006 and was common practice by 2011 at the bank—though not yet public—when Wells signed a consent decree with federal regulators and paid $85 million in civil penalties in another matter, for paying employees extra to falsify customers' incomes on mortgage applications during the bubble.[3] At the 2016 hearings, Stumpf told lawmakers that even as Wells spent shareholder money to pay millions of dollars in fines for mortgage misdeeds, its executives didn't review its other retail operations to look for instances of similar fraud. Then, when the fake account scandal did surface internally, the bank responded by punishing employees who protested the practices or reported them on the company's ethics hotline. At least a few were fired.[4] The bank's board of directors rewarded Carrie Tolstedt, head of the Wells group responsible for the fake accounts, more than $124 million when she retired in summer 2016, as news of the scandal became public. (Eventually she had to return $67 million of that, having to make do with $57 million.)[5]

"Millions of Americans were ripped off by their banks and seemingly let down by their government [bank regulators,]" House Financial Services Committee Chair Jeb Hensarling (R-Tex.) said at the hearing. "Fraud is fraud. Theft is theft, and what happened at Wells Fargo . . . cannot be described in any other way."[6] Hensarling even connected rules and enforcement of the rules: "True consumer protection is the preservation of competitive, innovative free markets that are vigorously policed for . . . fraud and deception." He and other lawmakers criticized regulators at the Office of the Comptroller of the Currency and the consumer bureau for failing to detect the scheme. They had learned about it from stories in the *Los Angeles Times*.[7]

A year later, in August 2017, Wells disclosed it had discovered an additional 1.4 million fake accounts, bringing the total to some 3.5 million.[8] In addition, just a few weeks earlier, Wells admitted to charging thousands of customers for auto insurance they didn't ask for and, in many cases, could not afford.[9] Warren Buffet, a major shareholder via his company, Berkshire Hathaway Inc., predicted that more problems could well surface, quipping, "There's never just one cockroach in the kitchen."[10]

The unfolding Wells Fargo scandal demonstrated that despite Wall Street's well-publicized culpability in the subprime meltdown, the temptation to use illicit means to pursue big profits never ends. The question is how to keep that temptation in check.

A test case arose soon afterward, in early 2017, when a newly inaugurated President Trump did his best to halt a new rule from the Department of Labor, slated to take effect in April of that year after years of debate within industry and Congress, that required financial advisers to act as fiduciaries—that is, in the best interest of their customers—when advising retirees on how to manage money in a company 401(k) plan or other savings account. Wall Street bankers wanted to derail the rule and preserve the conflict of interest it seeks to eliminate. They favored a laxer requirement known as a suitability standard, which permits conflicts of interest, and requires only that advisers recommend investments that match a client's tolerance for risk, not necessarily those that also will make the client the most money. This standard, unlike the fiduciary rule, allows advisers to profit at a customer's expense.[11] The fiduciary standard aims to mitigate the conflict-of-interest that investment advisers have when they give advice but also sell products that might be more expensive than a competitor's products. A suitability test lets advisers benefit from that conflict and frees them to charge customers more than necessary without fear of legal consequences.

White House National Economic Council Director Gary Cohn, who left his job as the second highest executive at Goldman Sachs to join the Trump administration, told the *Wall Street Journal* that the Labor Department's fiduciary rule is "bad" because it's like "putting only healthy food on the menu, because unhealthy food tastes good but you still shouldn't eat it because you might die younger."[12] Dale Brown, CEO of the Financial Services Institute, a lobby group fighting the fiduciary rule, told a reporter that "retirement savers need access to advice to plan for a dignified retirement—and that's what our adviser members provide."[13] His argument—Wall Street's argument—boils down to this: a financial adviser can offer retirees more choices if some of the choices aren't in the retiree's best interest.

The claim that the rule ties advisers' hands is nonsense, of course. Advisers can always give a consumer choices under a fiduciary standard, as long as they spell out which choice is likely to best benefit the client financially. In a court case that Brown and Wall Street firms filed in 2016 to block the Labor Department rule, they argued, contrary to what Brown tells reporters, that what they provide to retirees is not advice but a sales pitch: "a short-term relationship whose essence [is] sales rather than significant investment advice provided on a regular basis and through an established relationship."[14] A sales pitch doesn't have to be in a customer's best interest, but, under the fiduciary rule, advice does. That Brown described Wall Street firms to reporters as advisers but to judges as marketers prompted the Consumer Federation of America to tweet, "Which is it, Mr. Brown?"

Those favoring the rule found the lawsuit especially irritating because the Labor Department had listened carefully to industry's critique and adopted several key changes that Wall Street wanted. In the end, Wall Street moved the goal posts, making it clear that no rule would satisfy it because its members didn't want to be bound as fiduciaries. Within days of taking office under his pledge to "drain the swamp" of special interests, Trump took steps to thwart the rule's implementation, ordering his administration to delay implementation. Then in early February, a federal judge in Texas, Barbara Lynn, ruled against Brown and in favor of the Labor Department's rule, saying "Congress gave the [Labor Department] broad discretion to use its expertise and to weigh policy concerns when deciding how best to protect retirement investors from conflicted transactions." She found it "reasonable" for the department to encourage compensation models that "protect plan participants and beneficiaries" of retirement plans.[15] The plaintiffs claimed that the rule trampled their free-speech rights because "salespersons now may speak as a fiduciary, or not at all." Judge Lynn "didn't buy" that argument, as *Forbes* magazine put it. "At worst," she said, "the only speech the rules even arguably regulate is misleading advice."[16] A year later, in March 2018, a U.S. circuit court struck down that ruling, saying the rule was "unreasonable" in having broadened the definition of financial advice.[17] The court decision effectively kills the rule unless Trump's administration appeals it, which proponents don't expect.

The stakes for retirees are enormous. A company offering a 401(k) plan has a fiduciary duty to run it in the best interest of beneficiaries. But the banks those companies hire to set up and run the plans and inform employees about them don't have the same obligation, or at least they didn't before the new rule. As retail brokers, these bankers sell financial advice on scores of mutual funds, IRAs, and other investments, including many that appear in 401(k) offerings. Labor Department officials found that these firms have an incentive to steer employees to higher-cost investments, especially those they themselves offer or from which they receive a fee. By the twenty-first century, these activities fell outside the Labor Department's out-of-date definition of a fiduciary. President Obama's Department of Labor fixed that with the new rule that Wall Street— and then Trump—fought hard to undo.

The issue affects millions of employees who, as they prepare to retire, receive a barrage of marketing material on what to do with their money. These pitches are invariably weighted in favor of moving it from the company's plan to an Individual Retirement Account, even if costs are higher than an alternative.[18] Small differences in fees add up. Take an employee with thirty-five years until retirement and $25,000 in a 401(k): If yearly returns average 7 percent and expenses 0.5 percent, assuming no additional contributions, the balance will be $227,000 at retirement. Raise fees to 1.5 percent and the balance is $163,000, a reduction of 28 percent. This employee might not even notice the fees because, after all, his investment made money. But he's out $64,000.[19]

Public pressure made Trump—and many Republicans in Congress—back down for a time, at least somewhat. The rule was pushed to be fully implemented until July 2019, even as the White House busily appointed staff to the Labor Department who don't like it and presumably will work to thwart it. Through the legal battles the Labor Department continued to collect comments, which regulators consider when writing rules, though many of the thousands of postings opposing the rule are suspect: A *Wall Street Journal* analysis found that a "significant number" of the comments against it—as many as 40 percent— are fake. They were not submitted by the person named on the comment.[20] One man, for example, Robert Schubert, told the *Journal* that the comment he allegedly posted, "I do not need, do not want and object to any federal interference in my retirement planning," is a fraud and does not reflect his views. The Labor Department is the fifth agency—the Consumer Financial Protection Bureau and the Federal Communications Commission among them—where the *Journal* found fake comments posted. The *Journal* notes that "submitting fraudulent statements or representations to the federal government is a felony." Whether the Trump administration will pursue the matter remains to be seen.

As the circuit ruling came down, Wall Street executives had been lobbying the SEC for months to lift the fiduciary standard in all areas, and Trump has filled the SEC's five-member commission with people amenable to such a change, including Hester Peirce, from the Koch-affiliated Mercatus Center, who has publicly stated her opposition to the Department of Labor rule.[21] The costly debate, which should have been simple to resolve, illustrates the first, most important problem in developing sensible rules governing financial services: money. The only way Congress will focus on fact-based policy rather than on carrying water for various industries is to limit the way campaign contributions affect the creation of policy.

One costly example was lawmakers' decision in Gramm-Leach-Bliley to allow specialty banks to operate without the same federal oversight as other federally insured banks, even though taxpayers are equally on the hook. As the fiduciary rule shows, many politicians are willing to go to bat for Wall Street against consumers' interests. As long as they receive money from corporations, including those in the well-heeled financial services industry, they too often favor what lobbyists want over what's best for the public. Limit the role of money in the equation and lawmakers would have to discuss financial issues squarely, more comprehensively, with an eye on sound policy.

The questions surrounding banking and its shadow industries raise again the issues that emerged at the country's founding: When is a bank too big or too powerful? What are its proper activities? Should a bank be allowed to own a company that's not a bank? Should banks be free to speculate with federally guaranteed deposits? What is the government's role in overseeing the corporations and banks it grants charters to on the public's behalf?

Today, we think of combining commerce and banking as taboo, but Congress long has let the two mingle. At the country's start, banks were often chartered for a specific commercial project such as building a canal or a water system, and this mixing of commerce and banking was enabled by an incorporation that granted limited liability to shareholders but also restricted the company's activities and had a fixed expiration date. Proprietary trading, a fancy term for speculation, is among the most controversial activities an incorporated bank can engage in. The Volcker rule banned it, but Wall Street has successfully pushed to undo that and has sympathy among Republicans in Congress and the White House.

And how should banks be policed? Should we do away with deposit insurance and the enhanced oversight that accompanies it, as some suggest, and let the markets keep bankers accountable? That was the system before the 1929 crash. Or should we keep deposit insurance and find a more effective way to oversee banks on behalf of taxpayers?

Touching on these issues is a more immediate one: Republicans now in control of the White House and Congress are working to undo much of the Dodd-Frank Act and return the financial system to one that relies much more on self-regulation. Yet in the rush to dismantle Dodd-Frank, they have not mentioned returning deposit-insurance limits to $100,000. The result is that bankers will keep all the benefits of having deposits insured up to $250,000 but without the added oversight that was supposed to go with it to protect taxpayers.

Credit-rating agencies hope that Congress will once again shield them from being sued by investors who rely on their assessments. Mortgage lenders have succeeded in weakening underwriting rules that require them to assess a borrower's ability to repay a loan. Wall Street wants to do away with the Consumer Financial Protection Bureau or make its budget subject to annual appropriation, the same leash it uses to make the SEC and the CFTC obey. The consumer agency particularly rankled Wall Street in July 2017 when it issued a new rule restoring the ability of consumers to join together to take companies to court in class-action suits, overriding a clause that most financial firms put in every consumer contract mandating that complaints be settled through binding arbitration. Mandatory arbitration typically works to the disadvantage of consumers bringing a complaint. Wall Street lobbyists, often using the Chamber of Commerce as a front, nonetheless push arbitration and deride class-action suits, using ad hominem attacks to vilify class-action attorneys by pointing out that the lawyers typically make the bulk of the money when they win such suits compared with the consumers they represent, who often gain little and must wait years to win even that.[22] But the degree to which lobbyists for Wall Street and other industries fight to kill class actions—and pay an army of lawyers big bucks to help them—attests that such suits are costly for business. That means that, even if current victims don't win much, class-action victories can deter criminal behavior and thus benefit future consumers. Class actions, consumers groups argue, are the only way to hold businesses accountable. On November 1, 2017, Donald Trump signed a joint resolution from Congress gutting the Consumer Financial Protection Bureau's rule. As long as Wall Street keeps funneling money to politicians, lawmakers can't think clearly about these issues.[23]

Another area under attack, from Wall Street and from archly conservative groups such as the Mercatus Center, are provisions in Dodd-Frank to replace the ad hoc system that regulators had to rely on during the financial crisis to handle the failure of Lehman and other major financial institutions with complex holding companies. Critics are paying particular attention to what's known as "single point of entry," a policy the FDIC and the Federal Reserve adopted under authority from Dodd-Frank to enable the agencies to better handle, protect the health of, and contain damage to subsidiaries of a large bank or other troubled financial holding company. Allowing the FDIC to seize a corporate holding company in certain circumstances in theory will enable regulators to wall off a financial corporation's problem companies from its healthier ones while still holding shareholders of the parent corporation accountable. It would replace a system where holding companies file for bankruptcy and the FDIC seizes federally insured subsidiaries. It is a blueprint for a rational process—in contrast to the seat-of-the-pants one regulators had in the crisis—to prevent the problems of one subsidiary or affiliate from spreading uncertainty and risk through the corporation's entire system and thus to the larger financial system, particularly when federally insured institutions would be hurt.[24] It's one way that Dodd-Frank tries to ensure no company is too big—or unwieldy—to fail.

Also under attack as part of Dodd-Frank's provisions to end too-big-to-fail scenarios are those enabling the government to designate large banks and other financial companies, particularly insurance companies, as systemically important financial institutions, or SIFIs. Companies with the designation must take more precautions against risk, which raises the companies' costs, and, as described in the previous paragraph, it gives the FDIC greater power to manage giant financial companies that cannot manage an orderly failure on their own. To those who lived through the crisis, these expanded powers are a small price to pay to guard against reckless behavior that in the end proves even costlier, usually for taxpayers. Such a provision, for example, might have given the federal regulators insight into and tools to prevent AIG's risky sale of credit-default swaps before those derivatives nearly took down the U.S. economy. Now, with a sympathetic ear in Trump, financial giants like Prudential and MetLife have successfully sued to evade the designation, arguing in part that they don't have the short-term funding and therefore exposure to runs that commercial and investment banks do. And nine months into the Trump administration, a group of regulators led by Treasury Secretary Steve Mnuchin lifted the systemically important designation from AIG, saying the company that required a $185 billion bailout to prevent its collapse no longer posed a potential threat to the system.[25]

Hester Peirce, commissioner of the SEC, compares portions of Dodd-Frank's too-big-to-fail remedy to an "automatic flush toilet" that she argues creates both uncertainty about whether the government will step in and certainty, in the guise of moral hazard among creditors, who assume the government will step in and they will be repaid in the event of an FDIC takeover of the holding company.[26]

About the same time that Mnuchin acted on AIG, the Commodities Futures Trading Commission, whose role in policing derivatives markets Dodd-Frank greatly strengthened, announced that it wanted to encourage firms to self-report wrongdoing in exchange for lighter penalties.[27] The new policy emphasizes that it's intended as a carrot to encourage firms to come clean well before regulators are about to step in. How the policy will play out, however, under Trump's announced intention to push regulations back to 1960s levels, when seat belts weren't required in cars (at least not until 1966) and toxic dumps proliferated, remains to be seen.[28]

Trump named a former bank executive, former OneWest Bank CEO Joseph Otting, to be comptroller of the currency. Trump's interim comptroller, Keith A. Noreika, already had made it easier for banks to make harmful, payday-style loans, which use asset-based underwriting rather than assessing if people receiving the loans can afford to repay them. Noreika also "softened a policy for punishing banks suspected of discriminatory lending."[29] All these changes to policy are easily done internally or under an obscure law, the Congressional Review Act, passed in 1996 at the request of then speaker of the House Newt Gingrich. The law gives Congress sixty days to override "major regulations" enacted by federal agencies. With one party controlling both Congress and the White House, a presidential veto is unlikely. And the act comes, in the *New York Times*' words, "with a scorched-earth kicker: If the law is used to strike down a rule, the federal agency that issued it is barred from enacting similar regulation again."[30] That was the means used to squash the CFTC's rule allowing class-action suits instead of mandatory arbitration.

Money has always played a role in the development of public policy, but never more so than now. Boards of directors and managers in theory work for shareholders, the people who own publicly traded companies and represent the "capital" in "capitalism." But those who purportedly work for shareholders too often work to hamstring them: Wall Street executives use outsized salaries to make campaign donations to lobby Congress and the SEC to restrict the say that shareholders have in electing directors or in setting executive compensation. Shareholders can't keep management focused on a company's long-term value when executives use the company's assets—shareholder money—to persuade lawmakers and regulators to limit shareholder power.[31]

For decades after World War II, executive pay rose less than 1 percent a year. Once investment banks went public, however, financial service executives steeply accelerated what they paid themselves, far outstripping other industries in a divergence not seen since the 1920s.[32] Today, financial industry lobbyists lead lobbyists for other industries not only in pay but also in political largesse and influence. From 1998 to 2005, financial services spent more than any other economic sector to lobby Congress, the White House, and federal agencies. In 2006, its federal lobbying expenditures fell to number two, after healthcare, but they have stayed among the top three ever since.[33] Financial executives made $1.1 billion in federal campaign contributions for the two-year election cycle ending in 2016, for example, more than the combined total contributed by their counterparts in communications/electronics ($293 million), healthcare ($264 million), energy ($167 million), agribusiness ($106 million), transportation ($86 million), and defense ($29 million.)[34]

Just as finance dominates lobbying, a club of four hundred families in the United States dominates political donations, and many of their fortunes come from finance. Campaign contributions went into hyperdrive in 2010 after the *Citizens United* decision, in which the Supreme Court ruled that the First Amendment protects corporate political spending as free speech. At issue was what power corporations have and what power the government, which creates them in the first place, has to rein them in. The decision freed corporations and other organizations and individuals to make political contributions virtually without limit, a decision that surely would have astonished the founding fathers. *Citizens United* unleashed a "fundraising arms race" of political action committees—PACs—and nonprofit organizations, ostensibly with an arm's-length relationship to a candidate or party, that create a network of "dark money" and "dead-end disclosures" to mask who is giving what.[35] A *New York Times* review of Internal Revenue Service records in 2015 found that the ruling "has made most of the presidential hopefuls deeply dependent on a small pool of the richest Americans."[36]

Overall, "just 158 families have provided nearly half of the early money for efforts to capture the White House. They are overwhelmingly white, rich, older and male, in a nation that is being remade by the young, by women, and by black and brown voters. . . . And in an economy that has minted billionaires in a dizzying array of industries, most made their fortunes in just two: finance and energy."[37] Finance literally plays an outsized role in shaping U.S. democracy—and in undermining it, as financial crises show. It is no longer the lubricant of the economy but more and more the economy itself, the very outcome that made Jefferson and other early Americans—including Hamilton—fear corporations and banks.

The 158 families tilt towards the GOP, with 130 of them top donors to Republicans, their "families and their businesses [providing], for instance, more than half the money raised" by mid-2015 by GOP candidates and PACs for the 2016 presidential race.[38] Atop the list of Republican donors in this group was hedge-fund billionaire Robert Mercer, who had given $11.3 million, mostly to Texas Senator Ted Cruz by August 2015, but who, with his daughter, then switched allegiance to Donald Trump.

Mercer, a co-CEO of the Wall Street hedge fund Renaissance Technologies until forced to step aside in late 2017 because of investors' backlash against his divisive politics, made contributions that topped $18.5 million by mid-2016. The hedge fund's chairman, James Simons, provided some counterweight, donating $11.5 million to Democrats.[39] And there are other billionaires in the Democrats' camp, including financier George Soros. But the top donors are, as a group, overwhelmingly Republican. Their influence in the political process threatens to unbalance policy debates and favor Wall Street in ways that do not benefit voters or taxpayers. The Mercers, for example, gave $10 million to help Steve Bannon fund the far-right publication Breitbart—which often publishes conspiracy theories full of false claims and Russian propaganda and is frequently cited by white supremacists and other Trump supporters—and pushed Bannon's influence on Trump, for whom he became a chief strategist before being fired. The Mercers and Bannon founded Cambridge Analytica, a voter-profiling firm used by the Trump campaign that "improperly acquired the private Facebook data of [tens of] millions of users," setting off "government inquiries in Washington and London, and plunging Facebook into crisis," including over questions about whether the firm broke election laws and coordinated with the Russian government to sway the election.[40]

The question of money and politics is part of a larger debate over the growing concentration of wealth.

"To peruse the top donors in presidential politics is to take a cross section of the wealthiest 1 percent of Americans," the *New York Times* reported in August 2015. "The intensifying reliance on big money in politics mirrors the concentration of American wealth more broadly . . . in an era when a tiny fraction of the country's population has accumulated a huge proportion of its wealth."[41] Michael J. Malbin of the Campaign Finance Institute, a nonprofit that examines federal and state campaign spending, writes that "the question is whether we are in a new Gilded Age or well beyond it—to a Platinum Age."

In 2005 and 2006, at the height of the mortgage bubble and shortly before the taxpayers' bailout of Wall Street, Citigroup produced three memos analyzing rich people. "The world is divided into two blocs—the plutonomy and the rest," its analysts write in one dated October 16, 2005. "The U.S., U.K. and Canada are the key Plutonomies, economies powered by the wealthy." The report concludes that "the rich are getting richer, they dominate spending" and that "their trend of getting richer looks unlikely to end anytime soon," except for one pesky problem: voters. "Whilst the rich are getting a greater share of the wealth, and the poor a lesser share, political enfrachisement (*sic*) remains as was—one person, one vote." This could empower a "backlash" by labor or society at large.[42]

French economist Thomas Piketty helped turn wealth inequality into an international conversation with his book *Capital in the 21st Century,* published in America in 2014. The book, based on years of work, including with French economist Emmanuel Saez, examines a trend in capitalist economies: the growing economic disparity—in income and wealth—between the top 1 percent of the population and the other 99 percent. Even the Pope weighed in, decrying an "idolatry of money" in secular culture and warning that economic inequities would lead to "a new tyranny."[43] Piketty helped propel the conversation in part because he's avowedly non-Marxist, saying a "vaccination" early on made him immune to it.[44] That shielded his observations against knee-jerk efforts to tag him as a socialist or communist.

For Piketty, who says he is working in the tradition of both Karl Marx and Adam Smith, the ability of a few to amass assets faster than most people's wages increase creates an imbalance that, ethical considerations aside, hurts the economy. This, he argues, is capitalism's Achilles' heel. The rich have been getting richer at a pace that far exceeds everyone else's gains, and this is an unhealthy develop- ment not only for the economy but ultimately also for democracy.

The *New York Times* provides a good summary of Piketty's finding: "In 2012 the top 1 percent of American households collected 22.5 percent of the nation's income, the highest total since 1928. The richest 10 percent of Americans now take a larger slice of the pie than in 1913, at the close of the Gilded Age, owning more than 70 percent of the nation's wealth. And half of that is owned by the top 1 percent."[45] Similar concentrations of wealth prompted the Pujo hearings at the beginning of the twentieth century.

The real income of the bottom 99 percent of households, according to Emmanuel Saez, fell 11.6 percent during the Great Recession, from 2007 through 2009.[46] It then grew "a negligible 1.1 percent from 2009 to 2013" before finally gaining some traction from 2013 to 2015, when it grew by 6 percent. "Hence a full recovery in income growth for the bottom 99 percent remains elusive," Saez wrote in mid-2016.[47] "Six years after the end of the Great Recession, those families have recovered only about 60 percent of their income losses due to that severe economic downturn." By contrast, Saez found that the average income of the top 1 percent of American households grew 37 percent from 2009 to 2015, from \$990,000 to \$1.36 million, while the average income of the other 99 percent grew by about 7.6 percent in the same period, from \$45,300 to \$48,800. No doubt the 99 percent welcomed their extra \$3,500 a year, but perhaps less enthusiastically when they considered that the top earners gained almost a hundred times more. Even those numbers hid much greater gains for the top of the top and far less progress for the lower half of the 99 percent. From 1980 to 2014, the average income gain for adults grew 61 percent, but the average for the bottom half of earners "stagnated at about \$16,000."[48] "In contrast," Piketty, Saez, and a colleague wrote at the end of 2016, "income skyrocketed at the top of the income distribution, rising 121 percent for the top 10 percent, 205 percent for the top 1 percent, and 636 percent for the top 0.001 percent."[49] The numbers are similar when it comes to wealth, which is a person's balance sheet: what's left when all obligations are paid. In 2016 Saez estimated that "the top 1 percent controls 42 percent of the nation's wealth, up from less than 30 percent two decades ago. The top 0.1 percent accounts for 22 percent, nearly double the 1995 proportion."[50]

Some economists argue that Piketty and colleagues exaggerate the rate at which the economic gap is growing. A group of Fed economists, for example, say the top 1 percent really controls 34 percent of wealth, not 42 percent, and that its share of income grew by 18 percent, not by the low 20s. For those on the losing end of these numbers, such arguments do nothing to mitigate their sense of having been left out of gains. That can't be good economically or politically.

While economists argue over how to fix the problem, no one disputes that the rich get richer while the poorer rise far less, if at all, resulting in a financial skewing that has not been seen for ninety years.[51] "One specific concern," the Fed economists conclude, "is that wealth concentration may feed on itself, if undue political influence is being exercised by those who can . . . finance election campaigns and generate an even more favorable tax or regulatory environment for themselves in subsequent periods. The primary concerns about the effects of rising wealth inequality involve investment and economic growth. Rising wealth concentration may intensify financing constraints for the non-wealthy, affecting investment in education, entrepreneurship, and other risk-taking for those with diminished resources."[52]

In short, the wealth gap is troubling, and at its center, with its outsized influence over politics and the allocation of resources, is the financial services world. Wall Street is not the only industry funding this chasm, but it's second to none.

Not surprisingly, as the gulf between the haves and have-nots grows, America's middle class is shrinking. A study by the Pew Charitable Trusts revealed that from 2000 to 2014, the number of people identified as middle class fell in nearly nine-tenths of the 229 metropolitan areas it studied. The authors warned that the middle class "may no longer be the economic majority" and repeated previous findings that "after more than four decades of serving as the nation's economic majority, the American middle class is now matched in number by those in the [combined] economic tiers above and below it."[53]

The report defined "middle-income" Americans as adults with an annual household income two-thirds to double the national median, adjusted for household size. For a three-person household in 2014, for example, the national middle-income range was defined as $42,000 to $125,000 annually. For a one-person household, it was $24,000 to $72,000, and for a five-person household $54,000 to $161,000. The report defined lower-income households as those with incomes less than 67 percent of the median and upper-income households as those with more than double the median.

As the middle dwindles, communities become at once poorer and richer. For example, in Goldboro, North Carolina, the study showed that middle-income adults fell from 60 percent of the population in 2000 to 48 percent in 2014. This signaled "an unambiguous" economic loss as adults in lower-income households increased from 27 percent to 41 percent in the same period. In Midland, Texas, middle-class adults fell from 53 percent to 43 percent of the population, but upper-income households rose from 17 percent of the population to 20 percent.[54] According to the report, "new economic research suggests that a struggling middle class could be holding back the potential for future economic growth."[55]

A Federal Reserve report on America's "economic well-being" for 2015 found similar trends. Based on a survey of nearly 5,700 people, the study concluded that 69 percent of adults were "living comfortably" or "doing okay," up from 65 percent in 2014. That bare number, however, conceals what may be wide differences. A category that includes both "comfortable" and "okay" might capture people who are worlds apart financially.[56] The report found that 22 percent of working adults had to work two or more jobs to make ends meet and that nearly half of adults said they did not have the money to handle a financial emergency of four hundred dollars without "selling something or borrowing money." At the same time, 40 percent of those who desired credit "faced a real or perceived" difficulty obtaining it. A third of respondents said they found it "difficult to get by" or were "just getting by," which the report says translates into 76 million adults struggling financially.

The Urban Institute, a nonprofit research and policy group, hosted a conference in 2017 on families who "live paycheck to paycheck—often while coping with volatile income and expenses. With little to no savings and a limited social safety net, [these] families are vulnerable to inevitable financial shocks." For many, finding affordable access to the banking, payment, and credit system is a constant, sometimes insurmountable, hurdle. A study by the Pew Charitable Trusts showed that "substantial fluctuations in family income are the norm," with nearly half of U.S. households experiencing a gain or drop of more than 25 percent in a given two-year period, "a rate of volatility that has been relatively constant since 1979." Pew concluded that "substantial fluctuations in family income are the norm."[57]

More than half of all households cannot replace even a month of income through easily accessible savings, and the poorest households can replace less than two weeks' income. Although by 2015 unemployment had fallen to 5 percent, 70 percent of families faced some financial strain due to income, spending, or debt, and often all three.[58] In 2015, "When asked whether they would prefer to have financial stability or to move up the income ladder, 92 percent of Americans chose security, an increase of 7 percentage points since 2011."[59]

These organizations—the Fed, Pew, the Urban Institute—are among many that have grappled for years with how banking and credit can be provided in ways that benefit customers from the middle class on down and don't just make households poorer by locking them into expensive products that help only a bank's bottom line. Savings are already scarce; they become scarcer when whittled away by high fees.

No wonder voters are angry, particularly those in America's Rust Belt with no college degree who have watched jobs disappear to automation and to cheaper labor around the world. A *Times* reporter in November 2016 wrote that in Indiana, "a state with a lower rate of unemployment than the national average, and a strong rebound from the recession in many ways, the economic and political frustration [was] palpable."[60] It hardly cooled people's anger that none of the key players in the financial crisis went to jail. A *Times* headline on a story about voter anger over the recession and bailout of banks pointed to "The Impunity That Main St. Didn't Forget," the too-big-to-jail syndrome.

Since the country's inception, in its many debates over money, banking, and credit, American leaders have acknowledged the social corrosiveness of financial disparity. The founding fathers believed that severe inequity undermines democracy. "The founders worried a good deal about people getting too rich," writes Princeton economist Angus Deaton. "Jefferson was proud of his achievement in abolishing the entail and primogeniture in Virginia, writing the laws that 'laid the ax to the root of Pseudoaristocracy.' He called for progressive taxation and, like the other founders, feared that the inheritance of wealth would lead to the establishment of an aristocracy."[61]

Rutgers economist Joseph Blasi and Harvard economist Richard Freeman, two coauthors of the book *The Citizen's Share,* write that "Citizen ownership—often stigmatized as 'socialist' or pie in the sky—has a pedigree stretching back to the American Revolution. . . . Current levels and trends in inequality would almost certainly have terrified the founders, who believed that broad-based property ownership was essential to the sustenance of a republic."[62]

George Washington took it as a given "that America, under an efficient government, will be the most favorable Country of any in the world for persons of industry and frugality, possessed of a moderate capital, to inhabit. It is also believed that it will not be less advantageous to the happiness of the lowest class of people because of the equal distribution of property, the great plenty of unoccupied lands, and the facility of procuring the means of subsistance."[63] The authors note that James Madison, who worried about angry mobs wanting to confiscate property, was equally concerned that "inequality in property ownership would subvert liberty, either through opposition to wealth (a war of labor against capital) or 'by an oligarchy founded on corruption' through which the wealthy dominate political decision-making (a war of capital against labor)," and that "John Adams favored distribution of public lands to the landless to create broad-based ownership of property, then the critical component of business capital in the largely agricultural U.S."[64]

The Citizen's Share cites an event that to the authors captures the founders' vision: "On February 16, 1792, Washington signed into law a bill from the U.S. Congress that cut taxes for ship owners and sailors in the American cod fishery, in an effort to revive the failing industry. However, the tax cut was conditioned on a broad-based profit-sharing arrangement between ship owners and the crews—a centuries-long custom of sharing the profits made from every catch. The legislation was supported by two politicians who typically agreed on very little: Secretary of the Treasury Alexander Hamilton and Secretary of State Thomas Jefferson."[65] Though they fought bitterly over currency and debt, Hamilton and Jefferson agreed on the need for economic fairness. This common commitment to fairness, in fact, bred their arguments over the power of banks and corporations.

Blasi and his coauthors point out that solutions to this problem from the Right and Left typically raise taxes on the rich, lower taxes on business, impose more or fewer regulations on business, or increase or decrease "social welfare" programs for investment in education, training, and infrastructure. "But none . . . addresses the essence of the problem: the huge concentration of capital ownership and capital income."[66] They argue that stock ownership plans are the way to go, though the example of Enron, which had a rich stock-ownership plan but poor management, shows the necessity of good corporate governance as well.

The wealth gap was an issue during the 2016 presidential campaign. People from both ends of the political spectrum agreed that differences are okay, but extreme differences are not. Economist Joseph Stiglitz wrote that extreme inequality "threatens our democratic institutions."[67] Michael Strain at the American Enterprise Institute commented that "the political moment we are in now—represented by Trump on the right and Sanders on the left is in large part the result of slow growth," which hurts the population unequally. The "effect on our pocketbooks," he writes, "gives space for the lesser angels of our nature to come to the fore. On the individual level, this is understandable and unfortunate. On the social level, it hurts the functioning of our democracy."[68]

25

Who Should Own a Bank

IN THE WAKE OF THE MORTGAGE CRISIS and recession, one large financial company, Nationwide Insurance, ran TV ads touting the advantage of not being publicly traded. "We put members first because we don't have shareholders," the ad's voiceover says.[1]

The message played to the public's anger at Wall Street, but it hit on a persistent problem underscored by the Wells Fargo scandal and the fight over the fiduciary rule: the inherent conflict of interest that's unique to publicly traded financial companies, which must choose between maximizing profits for their shareholders and maximizing profits for customers. This problem emerged when investment banks converted from partnerships—where each partner's money and reputation was at risk—to shareholder-owned companies, where executives are paid based on how much profit they make using other people's money. As Wells Fargo shows, publicly traded financial firms face constant pressure to cut corners to meet earnings targets, often ones they have unrealistically set for themselves. The goals of maximizing shareholder value and giving customers the best financial advice often collide. Can stockholder-owned financial institutions ever be a safe place for financial consumers?

Similar questions about conflicts of interest surround Fannie Mae and Freddie Mac, particularly now that they are operated by the government. Did their shareholder structure cause executives to take undue risk, with an eye to their own bonuses? With the two wildly profitable again, the legal tug of war has escalated between the federal government, which likes to fill the Treasury from their profits, and shareholders who hope to restore the value of their stock by forcing the government to return the firms to the private sector. Many of these shareholders are speculators in the hedge-fund industry who bought their shares for pennies on the dollar in the hope of a gigantic windfall should that ever happen. In legal battles the hedge-fund shareholders have raised good questions about what property the government can and cannot take and under what circumstances, but that these Wall Street speculators might land a gargantuan profit from taxpayer subsidized entities disquiets members of Congress on both sides of the aisle—just as the speculators on Continentals disgusted Jefferson. Many in the GOP have long said the two companies' ties to government should be severed completely, only to find that, like Democrats before them, once they attained power they did not want to forgo the money the two generate for the federal budget.

The conflict of interest inherent in shareholder-owned financial firms has bedeviled policymakers since Hamilton and Jefferson. The United States has tried several tactics, from having the firms overseen by a central bank to letting the states determine the best remedy. From the mid-1800s until the 1930s, bank shareholders often faced a double liability: they could lose their equity investment plus that much again if the bank failed. The idea was to give shareholders a financial incentive to make sure that the bank's management wasn't tempted by practices that promised short-term profits but were harmful to the bank's long-term health. Double liability was abandoned in the 1930s, once banks received deposit insurance and more government oversight, so that they could more easily attract investors during the downturn.

Today, mutuals like Nationwide, which are owned by policyholders, or cooperatives like credit unions, try to avoid conflicts of interest by making customers owners. This governance structure doesn't eliminate all problems or guarantee against bad actors, but it avoids some of the pressure that executives at publicly traded banks face to meet profit targets at their customers' expense. Another way to address conflicts of interest at publicly traded banks and the high risk-taking that often engenders would be to regulate them like utilities, recognizing the public's need for a payment and credit system and the system's underlying importance to—and potential to harm—the economy. Advocates of this approach include Thomas M. Hoenig, former vice chair of the Federal Deposit Insurance Corporation and president of the International Association of Deposit Insurers, who says it would narrow the "safety net" of deposit insurance "to what it was originally intended to cover": commercial banking, "narrowly

defined" as institutions that are part of the payments system and that act as intermediaries matching deposits to borrowers. Regulating banks as utilities would
allow them to be publicly traded, but boringly so: regulators would control the
rates they charge and profits they make. Taking large risks would be forbidden.[2]
A utility model also has been suggested for Fannie and Freddie. It would enable
them to continue as publicly traded corporations and thus to retain access to the
capital markets, but the privilege would come with an explicit government
mandate to keep revenues—and promises to investors—realistic.[3]

Others would get rid of deposit insurance and treat banks as well as Fannie
and Freddie just like any other companies, letting them fail when they get in
trouble. John A. Allison, a long-time banker and former head of the Cato
Institute, a Koch-founded and funded think tank, falls in this camp.[4] He has a
point and is at least consistent, unlike much of the banking industry that advocates simultaneously for government subsidies and against government oversight. Allison's vision of returning to the system the United States had before the
1930s probably would not go over well with voters, however. Given that reality,
the issue policymakers should focus on is how to make regulators do their jobs
and not lose sight of the fact that, for better or worse, they work for taxpayers.

For banks, the Republican platform in 2016 included a provision to reinstate
the separation between investment and commercial banking. Yet as Hensarling
and Trump talk of gutting regulations, separating commercial and investment
banking is no longer discussed and bolstering oversight has never been central
to these conversations. Though Hensarling beat up regulators for missing the
problems at Wells Fargo, he failed to ask the bigger question: why did they miss
it, and in what ways did he, as head of the U.S. House Financial Services
Committee, fail to oversee the overseers?

Bank and securities regulators did engage in some self-reflection after the
housing crash. The Fed was concerned enough about its own shortcomings that,
in 2009, it commissioned Columbia Business School professor David Beim to
delve into the agency's banking oversight division. Beim found that the problem
was no single policy or practice but rather a culture at the Fed that made its officials too deferential to the banks they policed, creating a kind of "regulatory
capture" that had Fed executives fearful of rocking the boat.[5]

Since then, a whistleblower at the Federal Reserve Bank of New York
released forty-six hours of taped conversations about the agency's oversight of
Goldman Sachs that suggests little has changed.[6] The Fed had hired the person,

a lawyer with a specialty in compliance, Carmen Segarra, in late 2011, to determine whether Goldman had a plan to reduce conflicts of interest, as regulations
require. After she found the firm did not, her superiors pressured her to soften
her conclusion. She refused and was fired seven months after she started.
During that time, she began making the tapes as a way to verify the problems
she found not only at Goldman but also among Fed regulators.[7] Conflicts of
interest had been a vexing problem at Goldman—and for regulators—as a list
compiled by the news organization Propublica shows:

- In 2014 the bank "was among 10 Wall Street firms that were fined a total of
  $43.5 million for allegedly using the promise of favorable research, which
  was supposed to be impartial, to win business for their investment-banking
  divisions. The firms paid small fines without admitting wrongdoing."
- Also in 2014, U.S. senators "accused Goldman of deliberately pushing
  up the price of aluminum and giving confidential information to traders
  in the metal, providing them an unfair advantage. Goldman denied the
  allegation; two other firms also were criticized at the hearing."
- In 2010, the SEC fined Goldman a record $550 million in relation to conflicts
  in structuring mortgage bonds. The next year, the firm faced a shareholder
  lawsuit over a deal involving its advisory role to energy company El Paso in
  its sale to Kinder Morgan. Goldman held a $4 billion stake in Kinder
  Morgan. A judge harshly chastised the bank for its handling of the conflict.
- In 2009, the SEC investigated executives at Goldman and at the hedge
  fund run by John Paulson over a complex mortgage-securities deal called
  Abacus. Paulson had hand-picked securities that he wanted Goldman to
  put into an index that he could bet would fall in value and to find investors who would bet it would go up. Goldman failed to disclose to investors on the opposite side of Paulson that Paulson had crafted the index, a
  fact the agency said a reasonable investor would want to know. "Each of
  them knowingly participated . . . in a scheme to sell a product which, in
  blunt but accurate terms, was designed to fail," an SEC lawyer wrote in
  a memo in October 2009. "They should be sued for securities fraud
  because they are liable for securities fraud."[8]

Internal emails, memos, and other documents obtained by Propublica and
Senate investigators show that regulators were reluctant to aggressively probe

either Goldman or Paulson. In the end, in July 2010, Goldman paid $550 million to settle charges it had withheld material information from investors, but it did so without admitting or denying guilt. A spokesman for Paulson's hedge fund denied the deal was fraudulent, saying that "there was no 'scheme' nor was Abacus 'designed to fail.'" An SEC lawyer who retired in 2014 after years of frustration over what he perceived as the agency's regulatory capture says it "polices the broken windows on the street level and rarely goes to the penthouse floors."[9]

Ending federal deposit insurance is likely a nonstarter. Therefore, in exchange for providing it and for granting banks incorporations on the public's behalf, Congress should ask itself how it can ensure that regulators do their job of making sure financial institutions are properly and safely run.[10] Key to good oversight is ensuring that no bank or bank holding company is too big to fail. Pundits on the Left and the Right agree on the need to end the too-big-to-fail doctrine, especially given the advantage—and the moral hazard—it gives to the largest banking firms over smaller rivals.[11] And those who break the law should go to jail. Resolving these issues will depend on whether we can curtail the lobbying that rests on campaign donations rather than on formulating sound policy.

In the fall of 2014, just five years after the official end of the Great Recession, a bipartisan Senate committee completed a two-year probe into how three Wall Street titans—Goldman Sachs, JPMorgan Chase, and Morgan Stanley—had aggressively entered commodities markets in the previous decade to become "major players" in the buying and selling of aluminum, uranium, coal, copper, natural gas, and jet fuel. The three banks had grown so powerful, the committee's report said, that they were able to manipulate consumer prices and gain "inside information" for their traders.[12]

The activities they engaged in included trading and stockpiling materials as well as "operating coal mines, running warehouses that store metals, operating oil and gas pipelines, planning to build a compressed natural gas facility, acquiring a natural gas pipeline company and operating power plants."[13]

"The United States has a long tradition of separating banks from commerce," the report noted, but "that tradition is eroding, and along with it, protections from a long list of risks and potentially abusive conduct, including significant financial loss, catastrophic event risks, unfair trading, market manipulation, credit distortions, unfair business competition, and conflicts of interest." The senators pointed to a key bank regulator—the Federal Reserve—who they said had "identified" these activities as "a significant risk" but had taken insufficient "steps to address it." They noted that "more is needed to safeguard the U.S. financial system and protect U.S. taxpayers from being forced to bail out large financial institutions."[14]

A year earlier, analyst Joshua Rosner raised the commerce-and-banking issue at a House Financial Services Committee hearing, saying that prices for electricity and aluminum—and the planes and soda cans made of aluminum—as well as possibly gasoline prices were higher as a result. "Since 2003," Rosner testified, "our government and central bank have allowed an unprecedented mixing of banking and commerce. So far that grand experiment has gone better for the banks than it has for consumers. Our largest bank holding companies now seek further control over other nonfinancial infrastructure assets. . . . We're on the threshold of a new Gilded Age, where the fruits of all are enjoyed by a few."[15]

Accusations that Wall Street has used derivatives to manipulate energy and even food prices are not new. Paul Cicio, president of the Industrial Energy Consumers of America, a consortium of companies that are heavy users of oil, coal, and natural gas, testified in Senate hearings in 2007 seeking transparency in the trading of energy derivatives. That trading, he noted, dwarfs the actual physical trading in those commodities and was caused by a glut of speculators from "hedge funds [and] Wall Street trading companies," who engaged in "excessive financial speculation, market power, market manipulation . . . to the benefit of investors and to the detriment of every consumer in the country."[16] "Transparency," he said, is the only way to ensure prices aren't manipulated. Dodd-Frank's requirement that most over-the-counter derivatives be traded on exchanges has made trading and pricing more transparent, but the legislation is now under threat from Congress and the Trump administration.[17]

It's not just banks moving into commerce, but also commercial enterprises taking up banking. Rana Foroohar, in her 2016 book *Makers and Takers: The Rise of Finance and the Fall of American Business,* chronicles how nonfinancial businesses from Apple to GE have long mixed banking and commerce. "The business of corporate America is no longer business—it is finance," Foroohar wrote in the *Financial Times.* "American firms today make more money than ever before by simply moving money around . . . . from purely financial activities, such as trading, hedging, tax optimization and selling financial services." Airlines, she notes, often "make more money from hedging on oil prices than on selling seats—even though it undermines their core business by increasing commodities volatility." Car companies often make more profit from financing a car sale than they do on the actual car sale.[18]

Over the long term, she says, this is bad for the economy. "A wealth of academic research [shows] that not only has finance become an obstacle to growth, but also that financial engineering is destroying long-term value within companies." She points out that GE, "America's original innovator, only recently stopped being a 'too-big-to-fail' bank" by shedding much of its finance business to avoid oversight under Dodd-Frank.[19]

Michael Masters is a hedge-fund manager who made a name for himself outside Wall Street in 2008 when he testified before Congress in favor of regulating derivative speculators—those who buy derivatives on various commodities as a pure bet rather than as a way to hedge against adverse changes in price. He published a research report that year entitled *The Accidental Hunt Brothers: How Institutional Investors Are Driving up Food and Energy Prices,* a reference to the billionaire Texas siblings who scandalously tried to corner the silver market in 1980.[20]

Masters understands that speculators provide much needed and beneficial liquidity in the derivatives markets, taking the other side of securities contracts with those who need it as a true hedge. He estimates that before 2000—when Congress completely deregulated the over-the-counter derivatives markets—speculators made up 20 to 25 percent of those trading in derivatives for commodities such as gas, wheat, and corn. After the Commodities Futures Modernization Act of 2000, he says, that ratio flipped, with speculators making up as much as 75 percent of the demand for the derivatives. Institutional investors saw these contracts as profitable assets that could be bought and sold easily. Even without any price manipulation, speculative demand grew so dramatically that it raised the cost that the commodities' end users had to pay for derivatives, an increase they had to pass along to consumers in higher prices for bread at the grocery or gas at the pump. Hedgers in effect were competing with speculators for the same commodity: an over-the-counter derivatives contract. Rather than provide liquidity, which lowers prices, an oversupply of speculators helped drive prices up, making it more expensive for true hedgers to hedge.[21] Masters favors limiting the positions that speculators can hold and supports the price transparency that the Dodd-Frank Act brought to the industry.

"Markets need to be more transparent, they need more regulation, they need more accountability and oversight," he says.[22] He likens the complexities of commodity trading and how Wall Street talks about them to the use of Latin for religious services in the Middle Ages, as a way to prevent most people from understanding what's happening. "Markets are just human creations, they are not a god," he says, and the public needs to understand them.[23]

In 2008, Masters founded Better Markets, a nonprofit research and policy group that pushes for financial reform and has supported the Dodd-Frank Act. He was accused one time in one story—in the *National Review*—of having a potential conflict of interest because Better Markets pushes for reforms that industry critics—who, not incidentally, don't like his pushing for more oversight of their activities—say could benefit Masters' hedge-fund trades.[24] He's undeterred, and the group has become a respected and influential, if not always liked, voice against efforts to roll back regulatory changes made after the financial crisis.

Another influential group is the Volcker Alliance, founded in 2013 by the widely revered former Federal Reserve Board chair to help "rebuild public trust in government." Its board is a bipartisan group that includes many former financial regulators, such as Sheila Bair, William H. Donaldson, and Alice Rivlin. The group focuses especially on financial service issues, but its concern is broader. Volcker fears that the knee-jerk disrespect many now have for government will discourage talented people across the political spectrum from entering public office and public policy positions, at great loss to the country in many areas, not just finance.[25] Still, banks, money, and credit are so key to the economy and to society that they deserve special consideration and the government must play a role. That doesn't mean bigger government, according to Volcker, but rather better government. Using the lapses in oversight that contributed to the mortgage crisis as a case study in inefficiency, he points to the alliance's goal of encouraging "more effective and economical means of carrying out agreed public policies." That's easier said than done. In December 2016, at a conference in Washington, D.C., hosted by the Volcker Alliance and the Institute for New Economic Thinking, the glitterati of the relatively dull world of finance, along with the requisite reporters and think tank denizens, discussed regulatory gaps and whether banks are special or just like any other type of company and therefore undeserving of special treatment, either in government assistance or oversight. But a headwind named Donald Trump soon drowned out the debate, as the nation became spellbound with questions of treason, espionage, and Russia's attempt to rig the U.S. election.

As Republicans in Congress push to undo regulation, it is unlikely they will consider tightening oversight of the shadow banking system. They are also probably not going to try to curb abuses in the world of dark pool traders (who "buy and sell large blocks of shares anonymously, with prices posted publicly after the deals are done") and high-frequency traders (who "profit by anticipating and exploiting" large, market-moving orders before they become public)—even though the secrecy surrounding these traders and their methods undermines trust and efficiency in the market.[26]

Nor is Congress likely to ponder the efficacy of a practice that dates from the 1930s, that of allowing stock exchanges and other key Wall Street institutions to "self-regulate." The SEC is supposed to oversee these self-regulatory organizations, but neither those organizations nor the SEC are known for their vigilance, much less their effectiveness. Of all executives in all industries, the money men (and some women) of Wall Street banking might seem least qualified to police themselves, given that their product—money—by its very nature tempts people to cheat. Their lobbyists, however, have convinced Congress otherwise. Industry groups write the nation's accounting rules, oversee its exchanges, and implement consumer protections among dealers. One industry group, the Financial Industry Regulatory Authority, or FINRA, is charged with protecting "America's investors by making sure the broker-dealer industry operates fairly and honestly." Of the twenty-one members of its governing board, half are affiliated with financial companies such as Vanguard, JPMorgan Chase, Merrill Lynch, and Bridgewater.

The current leadership in the White House and Congress has the country contemplating a return to the days of Wild West banking. They target Dodd-Frank reforms, blaming these regulations for accelerating the steady decline in state-chartered banks, which since 1985 have dropped from 13,000 to 1,900. They say that the law thwarts home lending, curbs credit for small businesses, and has slowed recovery from the Great Recession. Central to the assault is a frontal attack on the Consumer Financial Protection Bureau, whose staff have irked industry—including commercial bankers who enjoy federal deposit insurance— with their insistence that lenders underwrite based on whether borrowers can afford to repay loans. When the agency's departing director, Richard Cordray, stepped down, a fight erupted over whether Cordray's chief of staff could step in as acting director or whether Trump's interim pick, Mick Mulvaney, would assume that role. Both showed up for work in November 2017, with Mulvaney "carrying a bag of donuts" and Cordray's pick "having just filed for an injunction." By the end of the month, a Trump-appointed judge ruled for Mulvaney.[27] Mulvaney, a former Republican congressman from South Carolina who in addition to running the CFPB is Trump's budget director, has dropped the CFPB's suit against a payday lender that under the Obama administration the agency accused of unfairly taking millions of dollars from financially strapped customers. And he created a controversy when he suggested to a gathering of bankers in April 2018 that they needed to make campaign contributions if they want to be heard, an arrangement politicians call "pay to play." "We had a hierarchy in my office in Congress," Mulvaney said. "If you're a lobbyist who never gave us money, I didn't talk to you. If you're a lobbyist who gave us money, I might talk to you." According to *Forbes,* he then urged them "to keep up their campaign contributions if they wanted to push through changes" to hobble the watchdog agency.[28]

Critics of Dodd-Frank also say they would let badly run institutions fail, no matter how large, but that's easy to say until one's in the middle of a crisis. The presidents Bush, father and son and both avowedly free market, likely could never have predicted they would preside over the nation's biggest bailouts. Before becoming Treasury secretary, Paulson probably wouldn't have predicted he would become Mr. Bailout.

Hensarling and former Federal Reserve Board governor Kevin Warsh, now a fellow at the Hoover Institution, are among a rising chorus of critics of the Federal Reserve, suggesting that it is misguided and too powerful, and that it often hampers rather than helps the economy. Calling the Fed "poorly positioned to respond with force, efficacy and credibility" to a downturn, Warsh recently cautioned that "the Fed is vulnerable. Its recent centennial as our nation's central bank should not be confused with its permanent acceptance in the American political system."[29]

Others favor putting the United States back on the gold standard as a way to curb inflation and further restrict the Federal Reserve's power, even though many Trump supporters are in farm country, a traditional foe of the gold standard in American politics. Trump told a reporter in 2016, "Bringing back the gold standard would be very hard to do, but, boy, would it be wonderful. We'd have a standard on which to base our money."[30]

As president, having placed a portrait of Andrew Jackson on the wall of the Oval Office, Trump has continued to remark on how wonderful a return to the gold standard would be. Jackson, of course, was the man who killed Alexander Hamilton's central bank, encouraged an unhealthy proliferation of poorly regulated state-chartered banks, and required citizens to use gold or silver to repay federal debt, including for purchases of federal land. His policies created a five-year recession that left U.S. currency and finances in turmoil, until Lincoln and Chase created the national bank system during the Civil War.[31]

Then–FDIC chairman Marty Gruenberg recalled in November, 2017, at a gathering of financial experts to discuss repeal of Dodd-Frank, that when he first joined the agency in 2005 the banking industry seemed to be healthy and humming along, so much so that friends asked him if he would be "bored" working there.[32] The FDIC had had two-and-a-half years without a failure, the longest stretch in the agency's history, and "the number of problem banks was approaching historic lows." Then, of course, all hell broke loose, with one of the two most cataclysmic banking crises in U.S. history. "The key lesson that we should learn from the crisis," he said, "is that we should guard against the temptation to become complacent about the risks facing the financial system."[33]

At a briefing at the London School of Economics in the fall of 2008, the Queen of England, whose own fortune the financial crisis eroded by some $40 million, asked why no one saw it coming. "Why did nobody notice it?" Eight months later, economists wrote her an answer: "Your Majesty, the failure to foresee the timing, extent and severity of the crisis and to head it off, while it had many causes, was principally a failure of the collective imagination of many bright people, both in this country and internationally, to understand the risks to the system as a whole." In other words, the experts failed.[34] Given the political landscape, they will again.

By summer 2017, a financial product returned to the market, but with a new name, "nonprime," meant to connote it was not the same-old subprime mortgage of yore. It would, its purveyors promised, be "properly underwritten" this time.[35]

In February 2018, Wells Fargo ousted four of its directors amid pressure from the Federal Reserve, which had just told the bank it could not grow any larger until it demonstrated better leadership and a grasp of legal and reputational risks.[36] In April, regulators at the Consumer Financial Protection Bureau and the Office of the Comptroller of the Currency fined Well Fargo $1 billion for forcing consumers to buy auto insurance they didn't need.[37]

That same month, even as his office negotiated with Wells, Joseph Otting, a former banker and Trump's new comptroller of the currency, told a gathering of financial executives, "I like bankers." They are, he said, "our customers."[38] Once again, bank regulators forgot who the real customers are: U.S. taxpayers.

In May 2018, Congress watered down Dodd-Frank, leaving "fewer than 10 big banks . . . subject to stricter oversight" on rules requiring stress tests and determinations of "systemic" importance and on disclosures under the Home Mortgage Disclosure Act.[39] In June, the Fed and other federal bank regulators proposed giving banks more "wiggle room" under the Dodd-Frank ban on proprietary trading—the so-called Volcker Rule, intended to curb high-risk trading using federally insured deposits.[40]

NOTES

Preface

1. Shiller, *Finance and the Good Society,* preface.

Introduction

1. Paulson, *On the Brink,* p. 69; Nakamoto, "Citigroup Chief Bullish on Buy-Outs."
2. Galbraith, *Great Crash;* Bordo, Goldin, and White, *Defining Moment.*
3. Bordo, Goldin, and White, *Defining Moment.*
4. Financial Crisis Inquiry Commission, *Financial Crisis Inquiry Report*, p. 171.

Chapter 1. The Danger and Necessity of Banks

1. Peirce, *Meteorological Account of the Weather in Philadelphia.*
2. Federal Reserve Bank of Philadelphia, *First Bank of the United States;* MeasuringWorth. com, "What Was the U.S. GDP Then?"; Phillips, "Long Story of U.S. Debt"; Congressional Research Service, *Costs of Major U.S. Wars,* p. 1.
3. Jefferson, *Jefferson's Account.*
4. Hammond, *Banks and Politics,* pp. 104–107.
5. "Report on a National Bank" and Alexander Hamilton to George Washington, Feb. 23, 1791, both in Hamilton, *Alexander Hamilton's Papers on Public Credit, Commerce, and Finance.*
6. Hamilton, *Working Papers,* vol. 8, pp. 110–111 footnotes.
7. Jefferson to Madison, Oct. 1, 1792; Madison, *Debates*, vol. 5.
8. Sylla, "Early American Banking," p. 110; Bodenhorn, *State Banking in Early America,* p. 240.
9. Jefferson, *Writings of Thomas Jefferson* (on banks, see vol. 10; for "standing armies" quotation, see vol. 10, p. 31).

10. Hamilton, *Alexander Hamilton's Papers on Public Credit, Commerce, and Finance*, p. 83.
11. Ibid. p. 55.
12. Ibid. p. 83.
13. Ibid. pp. 11, 85–86, 102, 105, 111, 113–114, 125; Federal Reserve Bank of Philadelphia, *First Bank of the United States*, pp. 161–163.
14. Hamilton, *Alexander Hamilton's Papers on Public Credit, Commerce, and Finance*, p. 76.

Chapter 2. A Cheat on Somebody

1. Hamilton, *Alexander Hamilton's Papers on Public Credit, Commerce, and Finance*, p. 122.
2. Ibid., p. 55.
3. Felsenfeld and Glass, *Banking Regulation in the United States*, pp. 28–29.
4. Gallatin, *Writings of Albert Gallatin*, p. 563.
5. Hammond, *Banks and Politics*, p.146.
6. Ibid., p. 35.
7. John Adams to François Adriaan Van der Kemp, Feb. 16, 1809.
8. Hamilton, *Alexander Hamilton's Papers on Public Credit, Commerce, and Finance*, p. 233 ("Report on Manufactures").
9. Wright and Cowen, *Financial Founding Fathers*, pp. 25, 27.
10. Ibid. p. 65.
11. Federal Reserve Bank of Philadelphia, *First Bank of the United States*, pp. 4–7; Fraser, *Every Man a Speculator*, pp. 15–23; Chernow, *Alexander Hamilton*, pp. 357–359, 379.
12. Thomas Jefferson to Edmund Pendleton, July 24, 1791.
13. Hamilton, *Working Papers*, vol. 7, pp. 247, 267; Hamilton, *Works of Alexander Hamilton*, vol. 4, pp. 266–267.
14. Wright and Cowen, *Financial Founding Fathers*, p. 23.
15. Fraser, *Every Man a Speculator*, p. 19.
16. Hattem, *Newburgh Conspiracy.*
17. Thomas Jefferson to John Adams, Aug. 22, 1813.
18. Thomas Jefferson to Charles Pinckney, Sept. 30, 1820.
19. Hamilton, "Second Report on the Public Credit," in *Alexander Hamilton's Papers on Public Credit, Commerce, and Finance*, p. 173.
20. Hammond, *Banks and Politics*, pp. 9–10.
21. Ellis, *Quartet*; Sylla, "Early American Banking"; ibid., p. 99.
22. Bernanke, *Courage to Act*, pp. 33–40; Hammond, *Banks and Politics*, pp. 96–98.

Chapter 3. Inc.

1. "East India Company."
2. Alexander Hamilton to George Washington, Feb. 23, 1791, in Hamilton, *Alexander Hamilton's Papers on Public Credit, Commerce, and Finance*, p. 125.
3. Hammond, *Banks and Politics*, pp. 66, 128.
4. Ibid. p. 72.

5. Ibid., pp. 72, 146; Sylla, "U.S. Banking System," p. 2; Federal Reserve Bank of Philadelphia, *First Bank of the United States.* p. 10, footnote. In ibid., p. 66, Hammond writes that four banks existed; the Federal Reserve Bank of Philadelphia claims there were three.
6. Sylla, "Forgotten Men of Money," pp. 173–188, quotation on p. 175.
7. Ibid.
8. Wilson, "Bank of North America," pp. 3–28, quotation on p. 3; Bodenhorn, *State Banking in Early America,* p. 8.
9. Sylla, "U.S. Banking System," p. 2.
10. Hammond, *Banks and Politics,* p. 40.
11. Ibid., p. 40; Wilson, "Bank of North America."
12. Wilson, "Bank of North America," pp. 6–7, 15, 28; Fraser, *Every Man a Speculator,* pp. 15, 19.
13. Hammond, *Banks and Politics,* pp. 96–97.
14. Chernow, *Alexander Hamilton,* p. 225; ibid., 95.
15. Hammond, *Banks and Politics,* 96.
16. Ibid., pp. 92–93.
17. James Madison to Thomas Jefferson, Oct. 17, 1788: Madison, *Debates on the Adoption of the Constitution,* vol. 5.
18. Hammond, *Banks and Politics,* pp. 103–107, footnotes; Hamilton, *Working Papers,* vol. 8, pp. 110–113, footnotes; Jefferson, *Complete Anas,* p. 192; Madison, *Debates;* Bodenhorn, *State Banking in Early America,* pp. 126–127.
19. Hammond, *Banks and Politics,* pp. 108–110; Hamilton, *Alexander Hamilton's Papers on Public Credit, Commerce, and Finance;* Alexander Hamilton to George Washington, Feb. 23, 1791, pp. 72, 113–114, 122–123.
20. Hammond, *Banks and Politics,* pp. 104–107.
21. Hamilton, *Working Papers,* vol. 8, p. 112, footnotes; Madison, *Debates.*
22. Federal Reserve Bank of Philadelphia, *First Bank of the United States,* p. 9.
23. Ibid., p. 6.
24. Felsenfeld and Glass, *Banking Regulation in the United States,* p. 15; Chernow, *Alexander Hamilton,* p. 355; "Supreme Court History."
25. Shalhope, *Baltimore Bank Riot,* p. 2.
26. Kumpa, "Bank of Maryland Fiasco."
27. Shalhope, *Baltimore Bank Riot,* p. 1; Scharf, *History of Baltimore,* pp. 784–786; Rice, *Maryland History in Prints,* p. 94; ibid.
28. Scharf, *History of Baltimore,* pp. 784–786.
29. De Tocqueville, *Democracy in America,* vol. 2, pp. 619–620.
30. Ibid.
31. Benton, *Thirty Years' View,* pp. 187, 191.
32. Unger, *Greenback Era,* p. 33.
33. Hammond et al., *Campaigning for President,* p. 434; Hammond, *Banks and Politics,* p. 444; Bodenhorn, *State Banking in Early America,* p. 190.
34. Sylla, *U.S. Banking System;* Federal Reserve Bank of Philadelphia, *First Bank of the United States.*
35. Jalil, *New History of Banking Panics.*

36. Sylla, *Early American Banking,* p. 110; Bodenhorn, *State Banking in Early America,* pp. 190–193, 289; Hammond, *Banks and Politics,* pp. 573–580, 600–603.

37. Hamilton, *Working Papers,* vol. 8, p. 102.

38. Ellis, *Quartet,* p. xviii.

39. Ibid.; Bromwich, "Wild Inauguration."

40. Ellis, *Quartet,* p. xviii; Sylla, *Early American Banking,* p. 107; Bodenhorn, *State Banking in Early America,* p. 190.

41. Sylla, *Early American Banking*, p. 106.

42. Ibid., p. 107; Bodenhorn, *State Banking in Early America,* pp. 192, 210.

43. Bodenhorn, *State Banking in Early America*, pp. 192, 210.

44. Federal Reserve Bank of Philadelphia, *First Bank of the United States*; ibid., p. 192; Hammond, *Banks and Politics,* p. 572.

45. Bodenhorn, *State Banking in Early America,* pp. 8, 158–160; Bodenhorn, "Zombie Banks"; Macey and Miller, *Double Liability.*

46. Hammond, *Banks and Politics,* p. 601.

47. Ibid.; Federal Reserve Bank of Philadelphia, *State and National Banking Eras,* p. 5.

48. Davis, *Origin,* pp. 20–21.

49. Ibid. p. 22.

50. Federal Reserve Bank of Philadelphia, *State and National Banking Eras.*

51. Davis, *Origin,* p. 13.

52. Ibid., pp. 13–14.

53. Hammond, *Banks and Politics.* The discussion through the next paragraph relies on pp. 107, 349–350, 435, 491, and 601–615.

54. Preston, *History of Banking in Iowa,* p. 8.

55. Knox, *History of Banking in the United States,* p. 777.

56. Sylla, "Forgotten Men of Money," p. 176; Federal Reserve Bank of Philadelphia, *State and National Banking Eras,* pp. 3–4.

57. Preston, *History of Banking in the United States,* p. 4.

58. Hammond, *Banks and Politics,* p. 146.

59. Davis, *Origin,* p. 25.

60. Sylla, *U.S. Banking System*; Federal Deposit Insurance Corporation, *Timeline of Banking;* ibid., p. 23.

61. Sylla, *U.S. Banking System.*

62. Wright and Cowen, *Financial Founding Fathers,* p. 25.

Chapter 4. The Civil War Tames Currency

1. Congressional Research Service, *Costs of Major U.S. Wars*; MeasuringWorth.org., "What Was the U.S. GDP Then?"; Chase, *Report of the Secretary of the Treasury,* pp. 4–5.

2. Hammond, *Banks and Politics,* p. 721.

3. Unger, *Greenback Era,* p. 14; Wright and Cowen, *Financial Founding Fathers,* p. 44.

4. Wright and Cowen, *Financial Founding Fathers,* pp. 44–45.

5. Friedman and Schwartz, *Monetary History,* pp. 21–23.

6. Ibid. p. 21.
7. Davis, *Origin,* p. 15.
8. See Letter to Hon. Benjamin Eggleston in ibid., p. 89.
9. Ibid., p. 111.
10. Wright and Cowen, *Financial Founding Fathers*, p. 44.
11. Davis, *Origin,* p. 84.
12. Friedman and Schwartz, *Monetary History,* p. 46.
13. Jaremski, *State Banks,* p. 1.
14. Davis, *Origin*, p. 25; Federal Deposit Insurance Corporation, *Timeline of Banking,* p. 2.
15. Federal Reserve System, *Changes,* p. 6.
16. Wright and Cowen, *Financial Founding Fathers*, p. 45.
17. Bernanke, *Federal Reserve,* pp. 9–10.
18. Dewey and Shugrue, *Banking and Credit,* p. 301.
19. Noyes, *History of the National Bank Currency.*
20. Bernanke, *Federal Reserve,* p. 13.
21. Lowenstein, *America's Bank,* p. 18.
22. Bernanke, *Federal Reserve*, p. 10.
23. Sprague, *History of Crises.*
24. Federal Deposit Insurance Corporation, *Timeline of Banking*; Moen and Tallman, "Panic of 1907"; Sylla, "U.S. Banking System," p. 4; Sprague, *History of Crises.*
25. Bernanke, *Federal Reserve,* pp. 9–10.
26. Federal Reserve Board, "Who Owns the Federal Reserve?"
27. Bernanke, *Federal Reserve,* p. 10.
28. Federal Reserve Act.
29. Bernanke, *Federal Reserve,* pp. 3, 107.
30. Ibid., p. 7.
31. Federal Reserve System, *Changes,* pp. 1–3, 18; U.S. Department of Commerce, Bureau of the Census, *Historical Statistics of the United States, Colonial Times to 1970,* part 2; Federal Deposit Insurance Corporation, *Timeline of Banking,* data for 1850–1899; Andrew, *Statistics,* pp. 21–28.
32. Wigmore, *Crash and Its Aftermath*, p. 529.
33. Federal Reserve System, Committee on Branch, Group and Chain Banking, *Dual Banking System,* pp. 181–182.
34. Federal Reserve System, *Changes,* p. 3; U.S. Department of Commerce, Bureau of the Census, *Historical Statistics of the United States, Colonial Times to 1970,* part 2, p. 1038.

Chapter 5. Sunshine Charlie

1. "Damnation of Charles Mitchell"; Wilson, "Sunshine Charley"; Sobel, *Great Bull Market.*
2. "Damnation of Charles Mitchell."
3. Cleveland and Huertas, *Citibank, 1812–1970,* pp. 62–66.
4. Mitchell, *Speculation Economy,* pp. 30–34.

5. Pujo Hearings, *Money Trust Investigation*; "Analysis of 'Money Trust.'"

6. Wilson, "Sunshine Charley."

7. Richardson, *McFadden Act of 1927;* Mote, "Banks and the Securities Markets," part 3; for the McFadden Act itself, see U.S. House of Representatives, Committee on Banking and Currency, *Banking Law, 1913 to 1956.*

8. Mote, "Banks and the Securities Markets."

9. Ibid.; Cleveland and Huertas, *Citibank, 1812–1970,* p. 157; Federal Deposit and Insurance Corporation, *Timeline of Banking,* 1920s; *Federal Reserve Bulletin,* Mar. 1927, p. 181; Kennedy, *Banking Crisis of 1933,* p. 15; Wilmarth, "Prelude to Glass-Steagall," p. 1291, footnote 15 and pp. 1298–1299.

10. "Crash of 1929"; Pecora, *Wall Street under Oath.*

11. Eichengreen, *Hall of Mirrors,* p. 2; Bernanke, *Federal Reserve,* p. 8; Bernanke, *Courage to Act,* p. 47; Federal Deposit Insurance Corporation, *Managing the Crisis.*

12. Bordo, Goldin, and White, *Defining Moment,* pp. 1–20.

Chapter 6. Radio, Rayon, and Retail Credit

1. U.S. Department of Commerce, Bureau of the Census, *Historical Census of Housing Tables,* 1920; Federal Reserve Bank of Boston, *Credit History.*

2. Allen, *Only Yesterday,* p. 136; Ruben, "Radio Activity."

3. Ruben, "Radio Activity."

4. Ibid.

5. Allen, *Only Yesterday.*

6. Ruben, "Radio Activity"; Federal Reserve Bank of Boston, *Credit History,* p. 8; Library of Congress, *Radio.*

7. Library of Congress, *Prosperity and Thrift*; Federal Reserve Bank of Boston, *Credit History;* Thompson, "100-Year March of Technology."

8. Calder, *Financing the American Dream,* p. 37.

9. Ibid. pp. 17, 19, 25, 30, 201, 234.

10. "Crash of 1929," interview with Robert Sobel.

11. Calder, *Financing the American Dream,* p. 21.

12. Ibid., pp. 38, 117.

13. Browne, *Artemus Ward in London,* p. 71.

14. Calder, *Financing the American Dream,* pp. 23, 214.

15. "Henry Ford"; "Frederick Winslow Taylor"; National Park Service, *Ford River Rouge Complex.*

16. Calder, *Financing the American Dream*; Olney, *Buy Now, Pay Later,* introduction, chaps. 1 and 2.

17. Calder, *Financing the American Dream,* p. 191; Olney, *Buy Now, Pay Later,* pp. 127–128.

18. Calder, *Financing the American Dream,* p. 193.

19. Ibid., pp. 283–285.

20. Ibid., p. 193.

21. Ibid., p. 195.

22. Ibid., pp. 194–199.

23. Ibid., p. 111.
24. Ibid., p. 197.
25. Sutch, *Liberty Bonds*; Olney, *Buy Now, Pay Later,* p. 173; "Liberty Bond."
26. Sutch, *Liberty Bonds*.
27. Everts, *How Advertisers Convinced Americans They Smelled Bad.*
28. Calder, *Financing the American Dream,* p. 205.
29. Olney, *Buy Now, Pay Later*, pp. 3–4, 40–47, 86–87, 91, 95, 168–172.
30. Ibid., pp. 86–96; Calder, *Financing the American Dream,* pp. 18–19; Issa, *2017 American Household Credit Card Debt*; Bureau of Labor Statistics, CPI Inflation Calculator.
31. "Review of *Forgotten Depression*"; Wicker, *Banking Panics of the Great Depression,* p. 3; Library of Congress, *Prosperity and Thrift.*
32. "Blue Skies" by Irving Berlin, © Copyright 1926, 1927 by Irving Berlin, © Copyright Renewed, International Copyright Secured, All Rights Reserved, Reprinted by Permission.

Chapter 7. If It Seems Too Good to Be True . . .

1. "Crash of 1929," interview with John Kenneth Galbraith.
2. Darby, "In Ponzi We Trust"; Allen, *Only Yesterday,* pp. 226, 232.
3. Bagehot, *Lombard Street,* chap. 6, p. 40.
4. "Crash of 1929."
5. "Bulls and Bears in a Wild Revel"; Rogers, *Great Activity in Wall Street.*
6. "Crash of 1929."
7. Ibid.; Barton, *Man Nobody Knows*; Raskob, "Everybody Ought to Be Rich."
8. "Crash of 1929."
9. "Floating Brokers."
10. U.S. Senate, *Stock Exchange Practices*; Sobel, *Great Bull Market,* pp. 72–73; "Crash of 1929."
11. "Crash of 1929"; U.S. Senate, *Stock Exchange Practices.*
12. Ibid.
13. Mitchell, "Sound Inflation," pp. 295–296.
14. Sobel, *Great Bull Market,* p. 27; White, "Stock Market Boom and Crash," pp. 67–83.
15. Barton, "Is There Anything Here"; Kennedy, *Banking Crisis of 1933,* p. 114.
16. Pasley, *Al Capone,* p. 64; United Press International, "Stock Market 'Too Crooked' for Al Capone."
17. Hawkins, "Development of Modern Financial Reporting Practices."
18. "Warburg Assails Federal Reserve"; White, "Stock Market Boom and Crash."
19. Fraser, *Every Man a Speculator,* p. 399.
20. Glass, *Adventure in Constructive Finance,* pp. 257–258; Seligman, *Transformation of Wall Street*, p. 7.
21. Ott, *When Wall Street Met Main Street*, p. 2; U.S. Census Bureau, *Households in the U.S.*
22. Galbraith, *Great Crash*, pp. 77–78.
23. Ibid. pp. 21, 77–78.
24. Ibid. pp. 30–31.
25. "Crash of 1929," interview with Galbraith.

26. Galbraith, *Great Crash,* p. 28; Sobel, *Great Bull Market,* p. 57; Bernanke, *Federal Reserve,* p. 19; Eichengreen, *Hall of Mirrors,* pp. 20–21.

27. Myers and Newton, *Hoover Administration,* p. 14.

28. Wigmore, *Crash and Its Aftermath,* p. 529.

29. Bernanke, "On Milton Friedman's Ninetieth Birthday"; Eichengreen, *Hall of Mirrors,* p. 21.

30. Galbraith, *Great Crash,* p. 36.

31. "Unified Banking Put up to Senate."

32. Galbraith, *Great Crash,* p. 25.

33. Bernanke, *Federal Reserve,* pp. 4, 24.

Chapter 8. Crash and Contagion

1. Bernanke, *Federal Reserve,* p. 16.

2. Ibid., pp. 17–19; Calder, *Financing the American Dream,* p. 265; Stock, *Rural Radicals,* p. 79.

3. Green and Wachter, *American Mortgage,* p. 94; Wheelock, "Federal Response," pp. 133–148.

4. Colton, *Housing Finance,* p. 2.

5. Bernanke, *Federal Reserve,* p. 21; Congressional Budget Office, *Fannie Mae, Freddie Mac,* p. 51.

6. U.S. Census Bureau, *Historical Census of Housing Tables*; Federal Deposit Insurance Corporation, *Timeline of Banking,* 1930; Federal Deposit Insurance Corporation, *First Fifty Years,* pp. 35–36; Federal Reserve System, *Changes,* p. 3; U.S. Department of Commerce, Bureau of the Census, *Historical Statistics of the United States: Colonial Times to 1970,* part 2, p. 1038.

7. Silber, "Why Did FDR's Bank Holiday Succeed?," p. 21; Kennedy, *Banking Crisis of 1933,* pp. 96–102.

8. Federal Reserve System, *Changes,* p. 3; U.S. Department of Commerce, Bureau of the Census, *Historical Statistics of the United States; Colonial Times to 1970,* part 2, p. 1038.

9. Lee Davidson, FDIC historian, conversations with the author in 2016.

10. Federal Reserve, *Changes,* p. 1; Federal Deposit Insurance Corporation, *First Fifty Years,* p. 36; Federal Reserve Board, *Banking and Monetary Statistics, 1914–1941,* p. 633; Federal Deposit Insurance Corporation, *Managing the Crisis,* chronological overview, chap. 1; Federal Deposit Insurance Corporation, *Timeline,* 1930s; Bureau of Labor Statistics, CPI Inflation Calculator.

11. Wicker, *Banking Panics of the Great Depression,* p. 154; Bernanke, *Federal Reserve,* pp. 20–24; Hoover, *Memoirs: The Great Depression,* p. 30.

12. Eichengreen and Temin, *Gold Standard,* pp. 7–8.

13. Bernanke, "On Milton Friedman's Ninetieth Birthday."

14. Jones with Angly, *Fifty Billion Dollars,* pp. 4–5.

15. "Bonus Army."

16. Ibid.

17. Stock, *Rural Radicals,* pp. 83–84; Stock, "Violence in the 1930s."

18. "500 Farmers Storm Arkansas Town"; "Arkansas to Urge More Aid"; "Hoover Appeals to Nation"; Quinn, *Furious Improvisation,* p. 61.
19. "500 Farmers Storm Arkansas Town"; Quinn, *Furious Improvisation,* p. 6.
20. Huey Long Project.
21. Kennedy, *Banking Crisis of 1933,* p. 76.
22. Schlesinger, *Crisis of the Old Order,* pp. 267–269; Schlesinger, *Coming of the New Deal,* pp. 3, 22.
23. Blanker, "What a Real Dictator Would Do"; Alpers, *Dictators,* p. 26. Lebovic, *Free Speech,* chap. 2.
24. Blanker, "What a Real Dictator Would Do."
25. Lippmann, "Democracy and Dictatorship."
26. Alpers, *Dictators,* p. 26.
27. Schlesinger, *Crisis of the Old Order,* pp. 267–269.
28. Hoover, *Memoirs: The Great Depression,* vol. 3, p. 36.
29. Kennedy, *Banking Crisis of 1933,* p. 42.
30. Hoover, *Memoirs: The Great Depression,* vol. 3, p. 198.
31. Roosevelt, *Fireside Chats;* "President Franklin Roosevelt's First Fireside Chat."
32. Rogers, "Will Rogers Claps Hands."
33. Silber, "Why Did FDR's Bank Holiday Succeed?"
34. Federal Reserve Bank of Richmond, *Gold and Silver;* U.S. House of Representatives, *Historic Committee Names;* U.S. Capitol Historical Society, *History of the Senate Banking Committee;* "House and Senate Banking Committees Names."
35. Silber, "Why Did FDR's Bank Holiday Succeed?"; Richardson, *Roosevelt's Gold Program;* Greene, *Emergency Banking Act of 1933.*
36. Greene, *Emergency Banking Act of 1933.*
37. Jones with Angly, *Fifty Billion Dollars,* pp. 20, 22; Wigmore, *Crash and Its Aftermath,* pp. 535, 539, 540.
38. Burns, *American Banking Community,* p. 73.
39. Ibid., pp. 10, 16–17; U.S. Secretary of the Treasury, *Annual Report.*
40. Hoover to Shaw, Feb. 17, 1933.
41. Burns, *American Banking Community,* p. 72.
42. Ibid., p. 21; Kennedy, *Banking Crisis of 1933,* pp. 101–128.
43. "La Guardia Charges Pools."
44. U.S. Senate, *Stock Exchange Practices.*
45. Ibid.
46. Ibid.
47. "La Guardia Charges Pools Paid Writers to 'Ballyhoo' Stock."
48. Kennedy, *Banking Crisis of 1933,* p. 111.
49. "Affiliates of Banks Illegal"; Wilmarth, "Prelude to Glass-Steagall," pp. 1292–1294.
50. Hoover to Shaw, Feb. 17, 1933.
51. Ibid.
52. Hoover, *Memoirs: The Great Depression,* p. 461.
53. Roosevelt, *Fireside Chats.*
54. Jones with Angly, *Fifty Billion Dollars,* p. 15.
55. Lamont to FDR, Feb. 27, 1933.

56. Rogers, *Will Rogers' Daily Telegrams*, vol. 4, p. 150. Reprinted with permission from the Will Rogers Memorial Museum & Birthplace Ranch, Claremore, OK.

57. U.S. Senate, *Stock Exchange Practices*, 1st sess., part 2.

58. Chernow, *House of Morgan*, p. 369.

59. Ibid. p. 366.

60. Leuchtenburg, *Franklin D. Roosevelt*, p. 59.

61. "Damnation of Charles Mitchell."

62. Burns, *American Banking Community*, p. 78.

63. Kennedy, *Banking Crisis of 1933*, p. 120.

64. U.S. Senate, *Stock Exchange Practices*, 2nd sess.

65. Ibid.

66. Kennedy, *Banking Crisis of 1933*, pp. 126–127.

67. Wilson, "Sunshine Charley," p. 176; U.S. Senate, *Stock Exchange Practices*, 2nd sess.; Kennedy, *Banking Crisis of 1933*, p. 121.

68. "Affiliates of Banks Illegal."

69. U.S. Senate, *Stock Exchange Practices*, 2nd sess., part 6.

70. "Affiliates of Banks Illegal."

71. Burns, *American Banking Community*, pp. 71–72, 79; Federal Reserve System, Committee on Branch, Group and Chain Banking, *Dual Banking System*.

72. Kennedy, *Banking Crisis of 1933*, p. 126.

73. Burns, *American Banking Community*, pp. 68–72; Bernanke, *Federal Reserve*.

74. Kennedy, *Banking Crisis of 1933*, pp. 127–128.

75. Associated Press, "Rules Mitchell Must Pay Tax Assessment"; "Mitchell Must Pay $364,254 Tax Fine"; "Crash of 1929."

76. Wilmarth, "Prelude to Glass-Steagall," pp. 1289–1300.

Chapter 9. Tickled with Poverty

1. Kennedy, *Banking Crisis of 1933*, p. 159; Burns, *American Banking Community*, p. 40.

2. "Movie Stars"; "Offerings Increase"; "Condemned Men Get Reprieve."

3. Rogers, *Will Rogers' Daily Telegrams*, vol. 4, p. 2. Reprinted with permission from the Will Rogers Memorial Museum & Birthplace Ranch, Claremore, OK.

4. "Trotsky Says We Will Centralize Banks."

5. Green and Wachter, *American Mortgage*.

6. "Industry Control Urged by Chamber."

7. Leuchtenburg, *Franklin D. Roosevelt*, p. 60.

8. Securities and Exchange Commission, "1933 and 1934 Acts."

9. Bernanke, *Federal Reserve*, pp. 3–4; Bernanke, "On Milton Friedman's Ninetieth Birthday."

10. Foster, "Chambers Regalia"; *Federal Reserve Act*.

11. Bernanke, *Federal Reserve*, p. 4.

12. Avraham, Selvaggi, and Vickery, "Structural View."

13. "Unified Banking"; Wyatt, "Constitutionality of Legislation."

14. Gilbert, *Requiem*; Kennedy, *Banking Crisis of 1933*, p. 211.

15. Gilbert, *Requiem*; Bradley, "Historical Perspective," p. 8.

16. Meltzer, *History of the Federal Reserve,* vol. 1, p. 433.

17. Kennedy, *Banking Crisis of 1933,* p. 215.

18. Bodenhorn, "Zombie Banks."

19. Burns, *American Banking Community,* pp. 68–70; Jones with Angly, *Fifty Billion Dollars*, p. 33.

20. Burns, *American Banking Community*, p. 67; U.S. Senate, Banking and Currency Committee, *Hearings S.4115,* p. 160.

21. "Wires Banks."

22. Keeton, "Small and Large Bank Views," p. 31; Burns, *American Banking Community*, p. 68.

23. Keeton, "Small and Large Bank Views," pp. 23–33; Flood, "Great Deposit Insurance Debate," pp. 51–71; Calomiris and White, *Origins of Federal Deposit Insurance*, p. 174; Golembe, "Deposit Insurance Legislation," pp. 181, 189, 197.

24. "Roosevelt 'Won' to Bank Insurance."

25. Roosevelt, *Public Papers and Addresses,* vol. 2, p. 37.

26. Hoover, Annotated memo.

27. Hoover, *Memoirs: The Great Depression,* p. 211; "Farm Groups Urge Deposits Guarantee"; Hoover to James H. Rand Jr., Feb. 28, 1933.

28. Hoover, *Memoirs: The Great Depression*, p. 215.

29. Hoover to FDR, Feb. 18, 1933.

30. Ibid.; Bernanke, "On Milton Friedman's Ninetieth Birthday"; Richardson et al., *Roosevelt's Gold Program.*

31. Wigmore, *Crash and Its Aftermath,* p. 537.

Chapter 10. Moral Hazard

1. U.S. Congress, *Congressional Record,* p. 3728 (May 19, 1933); Flood, "Great Deposit Insurance Debate," pp. 69–70; Golembe, "Deposit Insurance Legislation," pp. 189, 192, 194.

2. U.S. Congress, *Congressional Record,* p. 3908 (May 22, 1933).

3. Ibid., p. 3906.

4. Flood, "Great Deposit Insurance Debate," pp. 70, 71; Calomiris and White, *Origins of Federal Deposit Insurance,* pp. 173, 174.

5. U.S. Senate, *Banking Act of 1935*, p. 20; Flood, "Great Deposit Insurance Debate."

6. Flood, "Great Deposit Insurance Debate," p. 62; Golembe, "Deposit Insurance Legislation," pp. 189, 192, 194.

7. Flood, "Great Deposit Insurance Debate," pp. 51–72; U.S. Senate, *Banking Act of 1935.*

8. U.S. Senate, *Banking Act of 1935.*

9. Ibid.

10. Flood, "Great Deposit Insurance Debate," p. 57.

11. U.S. Senate, *Banking Act of 1935.*

12. Friedman and Schwartz, *Monetary History,* pp. 434–442.

13. Bernanke, *Federal Reserve,* p. 22.

14. Federal Reserve Board, *Banking and Monetary Statistics, 1914–1941*, p. 633.
15. "Roosevelt 'Won' to Bank Insurance."
16. Ibid.
17. "Unified Banking Put up to Senate"; Flood, "Great Deposit Insurance Debate," pp. 51–71.
18. Keeton, "Small and Large Bank Views," pp. 23–33; Flood, "Great Deposit Insurance Debate," pp. 51–71; Calomiris and White, *Origins of Federal Deposit Insurance*, p. 174; Golembe, "Deposit Insurance Legislation," pp. 181, 189, 197; Burns, *American Banking Community*, p. 92.
19. Galbraith, *Money*, p. 209.
20. "Crash of 1929."

Chapter 11. Zombie Banks

1. Day, "Citicorp Inches."
2. Ruebling, *Administration of Regulation Q*.
3. Silber, "How Volcker Launched His Attack"; Day, *S&L Hell*.
4. Silber, "How Volcker Launched His Attack"; Medley, "Volcker's Announcement."
5. Taub, *Other People's Houses*, pp. 61, 69; Day, *S&L Hell*, p. 124.
6. Day, *S&L Hell*, p. 124.
7. Day, "Citicorp Inches."
8. McDowell, "Sifting for Profits."
9. Kapner, "Financier Charles H. Keating Jr."; O'Dell, "Lincoln Savings' Parent Files for Chapter 11"; Day, "Thrift Is the Word"; Corrigan, *Meeting the Challenges*.
10. Federal Deposit Insurance Corporation, "Banking Crises," pp. 1, 4, 8, 10.
11. Federal Deposit Insurance Corporation, *Case Study of Continental Illinois*; Federal Reserve Bank of Richmond, *Failure of Continental Illinois;* Carlson and Rose, *Can a Bank Run Be Stopped?*
12. Federal Reserve Board, "Latin American Debt Crisis."
13. Fromson and Knight, "Saving of Citibank."
14. Day, *S&L Hell*, p. 18.
15. Ibid., p. 20.
16. Ibid., p. 23.
17. Ibid., p. 24. Valentine, "Ex-Fugitive."
18. Ibid., sections on the Ohio and Maryland crises, pp. 15–34.
19. Ibid., p. 25.
20. Ibid., p. 30.
21. Ibid.; Preston, *Report of the Special Counsel*.
22. Day, *S&L Hell*, p. 33.

Chapter 12. The American Home

1. Capra, *It's a Wonderful Life*.
2. Cordery, *British Friendly Societies*, p. 93.

3. Quoted in Day, *S&L Hell,* p. 33.

4. Ibid., p. 40.

5. Cannato, "Home of One's Own."

6. Ibid.

7. Day, *S&L Hell,* p. 41.

8. Post, "Evolution of the U.S. Commercial Paper Market." Federal Reserve Board, *Federal Reserve Issues.*

9. Reagan, "Remarks to State Chairpersons."

10. Quoted in Day, *S&L Hell*, p. 67.

Chapter 13. Financial Cocaine

1. Day, *S&L Hell,* p. 73.

2. Ibid., p. 80.

3. Ibid., p. 88.

4. Jackson, "Bank Board Plan"; ibid., p. 90.

5. Day, *S&L Hell,* p. 98.

6. Ibid., p. 93.

7. Ibid., p. 94.

8. Ibid., p. 96.

9. Ibid., p. 101.

10. Ibid.

11. Mosier, "Convicted I–30 Condo-Fraudster."

12. Federal Deposit Insurance Corporation, press office data provided to the author.

13. Day, *S&L Hell,* p. 192.

14. Ibid., p. 205.

15. Blair, "Future of Banking in America," p. 99; Reagan, "Statement."

16. Day, *S&L Hell,* p. 293.

17. Ibid., p. 114. *Wall Street Journal,* "Paying." Thomas, "At Garn Institute."

Chapter 14. Cover-Up and Bailout

1. Day, *S&L Hell,* p. 282.

2. Ibid., p. 298.

3. Lewis, *Liar's Poker,* pp. 130–131.

4. Nash, "Treasury Now Favors"; Richman, "Who Is Nick Brady?"

5. Day, *S&L Hell,* p. 312.

6. Ibid., pp. 376–378.

7. Ibid., pp. 309–311.

8. Ibid., pp. 311–313.

9. Ibid.

10. Richey, "Newt Gingrich Ethics Investigation"; Yang, "House Reprimands, Penalizes Speaker."

11. Day, *S&L Hell,* pp. 313–314.

12. General Accounting Office, *Financial Audit, Resolution Trust.*

13. Day, *S&L Hell,* p. 350.
14. Ibid.
15. Financial Crisis Inquiry Commission, *Financial Crisis Inquiry Report*, p. 37.
16. Day, *S&L Hell.*

Chapter 15. Russia Defaults

1. Rubin, "Remarks"; Greenspan, "Private-Sector Refinancing"; McDonough, "Statement"; President's Working Group on Financial Markets, *Hedge Funds,* pp. 13–14.
2. Greenspan, "Private-Sector Refinancing"; McDonough, "Statement"; Kirk, "Warning."
3. President's Working Group on Financial Markets, *Hedge Funds,* p. 1; Dodd-Frank Act of 2010, p. 1630.
4. Greenspan, "Private-Sector Refinancing."
5. Scholes, "Derivatives."
6. Roosevelt, *Public Papers and Addresses,* vol. 3, p. 91.
7. Kirk, "Warning."
8. Bank for International Settlements, *Quarterly Review,* Aug. 1999, June 2016; Greenberger, "Overwhelming a Financial Regulatory Black Hole."
9. Ramo, "Three Marketeers."
10. President's Working Group on Financial Markets, *Hedge Funds,* p. 16; General Accounting Office, *Report.*
11. Greenspan, "Private-Sector Refinancing."
12. Ibid.
13. Greenspan to Senator Alphonse D'Amato; Roig-Franzia, "Credit Crisis Cassandra"; Kirk, "Warning"; "Greenspan to the Rescue."
14. McDonough, "Statement."
15. President's Working Group on Financial Markets, *Hedge Funds,* p. 12.
16. Ibid.
17. General Accounting Office, *Report,* p. 11.
18. President's Working Group on Financial Markets, *Hedge Funds,* pp. 21–22, 29.
19. Bianco, "King of Wall Street."
20. Day, "Salomon Suspends 2 Traders."
21. Lewis, *Liar's Poker,* pp. 150–155.
22. Day, "Violations"; Day, "Gutfreund Silent."
23. Day, "Wall Street Giant Shaken."
24. Day, "Violations."
25. Securities and Exchange Commission, "Exchange Act Release No. 34–31554"; Day, "Gutfreund Silent." Day, "A Wall Street Giant Shaken."
26. Mullins, "Statement before the Subcommittee on Telecommunications and Finance," p. 885; Securities and Exchange Commission, "Exchange Act Release No. 34–31554."
27. Siconolfi and Cohen, "Treasury Auction Scandal."
28. Berman, "Deep within Citi."
29. Mullins, "Statement before the Subcommittee on Telecommunications and Finance."
30. Ibid.

31. Mullins, "Statement before the Subcommittee on Oversight."
32. Henriques, "Fischer Black, 57"; Scholes, "Derivatives."
33. President's Working Group on Financial Markets, *Hedge Funds; Brady Report.*
34. Day, "How a Phone Call"; McDonough, "Statement."
35. Greenspan, "Private-Sector Refinancing."
36. Cornwell, "If I Made Myself Clear."
37. Quoted in *New Republic,* Aug. 22, 1988, p. 7.
38. Kirk, "Warning."
39. Parkinson, *Progress Report.*
40. Lowenstein, *When Genius Failed,* p. 179.
41. Berry, "Divided on Derivatives."
42. Lowenstein, *When Genius Failed,* p. 229.
43. Day, "Banks Incur Record Losses"; "Derivatives: Over the Counter, Out of Sight."

Chapter 16. The Committee to Save the World

1. Commodity Futures Trading Commission, "Final Rule," p. 4; Bank for International Settlements, *Quarterly Review* (Nov. 1996).
2. Jereski et al., "Bitter Fruit"; Hansell, "Bankers Trust"; Pollack, "Ending Suit."
3. Financial Crisis Inquiry Commission, *Financial Crisis Inquiry Report,* p. 47.
4. Kirk, "Warning"; Commodity Futures Trading Commission, "Final Rule"; Bank for International Settlements, *Quarterly Review* (Nov. 1996).
5. Healy, "Harvard Ignored Warnings"; Herbst, "Larry Summers' Record"; Salmon, "How Larry Summers Lost Harvard $1.8 Billion"; "Harvard: Inside Story."
6. Ramo, "Three Marketeers."
7. Greenberger, "Overwhelming a Financial Regulatory Black Hole," p. 136.
8. President's Working Group on Financial Markets, *Over-the-Counter Derivatives Markets*, pp. 4–6.
9. Financial Crisis Inquiry Commission, *Financial Crisis Inquiry Report,* p. 48.
10. Alan Greenspan testimony, Oct. 1, 1998, available in Kirk, "Warning."
11. Securities and Exchange Commission, "Dodd-Frank Act Rulemaking: Derivatives"; Greenberger, *Lessons from Enron.*
12. Federal Reserve Board et al., *Joint Report.*
13. Jickling, *Enron Loophole*; Lipton, "Gramm and the Enron Loophole"; Ismail, *Most Favored Corporation;* Presidents Working Group on Financial Markets, *Over-the-Counter Derivatives Markets*, p. 16.
14. Johnson and Day, "Hedge Fund Rule Tossed"; President's Working Group, *Hedge Funds;* President's Working Group, *Over-the-Counter Derivatives Markets.*

Chapter 17. Dysfunctional Oversight

1. Day, "Banking Accord."
2. Day, "Merrill's Fight."
3. Ibid.

4. Numbers obtained by the author from OpenSecrets.org and cited in Friedman, "Did You Hear."

5. Sherman, *Short History,* p. 9; Day, "Ruling."

6. Day, "With Depression-Era Law."

7. Wayne, "Comptroller for the Moment"; Berner and Grow, "They Warned Us"; Carter, "Master of Disaster."

8. O'Hara and Day, "Riggs Bank"; Day, "Chief U.S. Bank Regulator."

9. Hawke, interview with the author, Mar. 2016; Kahn, "Former Treasury Secretary."

10. Sherman, *Short History,* p. 9.

11. Hoenig, "Leverage and Debt."

12. Blair, "Future of Banking in America"; Corrigan, *Federal Reserve Bank of New York.*

13. U.S. House of Representatives, *Banking Law, 1913–1956,* pp. 8–11.

14. Ibid.

15. Corrigan, *Federal Reserve Bank of New York*; Wilmarth, "WalMart," pp. 1539–1622.

16. Day, "With Depression-Era Law."

17. Day, "Thrift Is the Word."

18. Kroszner, *Legacy*; Day, "Piggy Banker?"; Day, "Wal-Mart Defends Its Bid."

19. Financial Crisis Inquiry Commission, *Financial Crisis Inquiry Report,* p. 49.

20. Corrigan, *Federal Reserve Bank of New York.*

21. Ibid.

Chapter 18. Enron

1. McLean, "Why Enron Went Bust."

2. Ibid.; Flanigan, "Enron Is Proving Costly."

3. Partnoy, *Enron and Derivatives*; Greenberger, *Lessons from Enron*; McLean, "Why Enron Went Bust."

4. Oppel and Sorkin, "Enron's Collapse"; McLean, "Why Enron Went Bust"; Howe, "11 Largest Bankruptcies."

5. McLean, interview with C-SPAN.

6. McLean, "Is Enron Overpriced?"

7. McLean, "Why Enron Went Bust"; ibid.

8. McLean and Elkind, *Smartest Guys in the Room,* pp. 325–326.

9. Ibid.

10. McLean, "Why Enron Went Bust"; Oppel and Sorkin, "Enron's Collapse."

11. Oppel and Sorkin, "Enron's Collapse"; McLean, "Is Enron Overpriced?"; "Timeline of Enron's Collapse"; McLean and Elkind, *Smartest Guys in the Room.*

12. Oppel, "Merrill Replaced Research Analyst."

13. Partnoy, *Enron and Derivatives.*

14. Day and Schmidt, "U.S. to Probe Enron"; Greenberger, *Lessons from Enron.*

15. Bajaj and Eichenwald, "Kenneth L. Lay, 64"; Nocera, "Even at the End."

16. Johnson, "Enron's Lay Dies"; Flanigan, "Enron Is Proving Costly."

17. Pellgrini, "Person of the Week."

18. McLean, interview with C-SPAN; Nocera, "Even at the End."

19. Abelson and Glater, "Enron's Collapse."
20. Herbert, "Enron and the Gramms."
21. "Enron Created Fake Trading Room."
22. Morgan and Day, "For Gramms."
23. "History and Timeline"; U.S. Senate, Permanent Subcommittee on Investigations, *Role of the Board*, p. 52; Herbert, "Enron and the Gramms."
24. U.S. Senate, Permanent Subcommittee on Investigations, *Role of the Board*, p. 52; Morgan and Day, "For Gramms"; Arvedlund, "Mr. & Mrs. Enron."
25. Gramm and Thorpe, *Public Comment*; Commodity Futures Trading Commission, "Final Rule," pp. 77961–77993.
26. Gramm and Cochran, *Public Comment*.
27. Fowler, "No Criminal Charges."
28. Lifsher, "10 Enron Ex-Directors."
29. Lipton, "Gramm and the Enron Loophole"; Arvedlund, "Mr. & Mrs. Enron"; Leopold, "McCain Defends."
30. Crawford, "Ex-Tyco CEO."
31. Day and Shin, "Freddie Settles."
32. McKinnon and Hagerty, "How Accounting Issue Crept Up."
33. Day, "Study Finds 'Extensive' Fraud"; Day, "Former Fannie Mae CFO"; Gordon, "Franklin Raines to Pay."
34. U.S. Senate, Permanent Subcommittee on Investigations, *Role of the Financial Institutions*.
35. Day, "Brokerage Settlement"; Alloway, "Banks Seek Changes."
36. B. Masters, "Spitzer"; B. Masters, "Little Guys' Lament"; B. Masters and Day, "Morgan Stanley Settles."
37. Hakim and Rashbaum, "Spitzer"; Harris, "Eliot Spitzer."
38. White and Hilzenrath, "NYSE's Role"; White and Day, "Grasso Critics"; Sloan, "Grasso's Gone."
39. Financial Crisis Inquiry Commission, *Financial Crisis Inquiry Report*, p. 48; U.S. Treasury, *Quarterly Report on Bank Trading*.

Chapter 19. Tent City

1. Seelye, "Sacramento."
2. Financial Crisis Inquiry Commission, *Financial Crisis Inquiry Report*, p. 215; Mian and Sufi, *House of Debt*, pp. 19, 21, 27, 68; Geithner, *Stress Test*, p. 116; Bureau of Labor Statistics, *Recession of 2007–2009;* Rich, "Great Recession."
3. Better Markets, *Cost of the Crisis.*
4. Stockman, "Taxing Wall Street."
5. Galston, *Why the 2005 Social Security Initiative Failed.*
6. Zandi, *Financial Shock,* p. 164.
7. Ibid., pp. 213–215.
8. National Bureau of Economic Research, "NBER's Business Cycle Dating Procedure."
9. Mian and Sufi, *House of Debt*, p. 68; Yagan, *Employment Hysteresis.*
10. Lerner, "After Losing Their Homes"; Hedberg and Krainer, "Credit Access."

11. Bernanke, *Courage to Act*, author's note.
12. Geithner, *Stress Test,* pp. 16–19, 230–241.
13. Paulson, *On the Brink*, pp. 214–215.
14. Geithner, *Stress Test*, pp. 194, 228, 230; Financial Crisis Inquiry Commission, *Financial Crisis Inquiry Report,* pp. 394–365; "Is Dodd-Frank's Failure Resolution Regime Failing?"
15. Financial Crisis Inquiry Commission, *Financial Crisis Inquiry Report,* p. 394.
16. Paulson, *On the Brink,* pp. 160–161.
17. Eichengreen, *Hall of Mirrors,* p. 6.
18. Day, "Villains in the Mortgage Mess?"
19. Day, *S&L Hell*; "Prime Rate History."
20. Zandi, *Financial Shock,* p. 65.
21. U.S. Department of Housing and Urban Development, *Analysis of Mortgage Refinancing*; Financial Crisis Inquiry Commission, *Financial Crisis Inquiry Report,* p. 86.
22. Zandi, *Financial Shock*, pp. 69, 73, 247; Financial Crisis Inquiry Commission, *Financial Crisis Inquiry Report,* p. 85.
23. Day, "Villains in the Mortgage Mess?"; Financial Crisis Inquiry Commission, *Financial Crisis Inquiry Report,* pp. 86, 104; Zandi, *Financial Shock,* pp. 72–75, 247, footnote 7; Bernanke, *Courage to Act,* p. 62.
24. Zandi, *Financial Shock,* p. 13, chart p. 65; Financial Crisis Inquiry Commission, *Financial Crisis Inquiry Report,* p. 86.
25. Kendall and Fishman, *Primer*, p. 38.
26. Davidoff, "Partnership Solution"; Financial Crisis Inquiry Commission, *Financial Crisis Inquiry Report*, p. 61; Cohan, "When Bankers Started Playing with Other People's Money."
27. Financial Crisis Inquiry Commission, *Financial Crisis Inquiry Report,* pp. 61–62.
28. "TimeLine: History of Merrill Lynch"; Wayne, "Going Public"; ibid., pp. 61–64.
29. Financial Crisis Inquiry Commission, *Financial Crisis Inquiry Report*, pp. 63–64; Newman, "How 11 Corporate Titans Profited."
30. Financial Crisis Inquiry Commission, *Financial Crisis Inquiry Report*, xvii.
31. "William McChesney Martin."

Chapter 20. Financial Magic

1. Lewis, *Liar's Poker,* pp. 150–155, 174.
2. Tully, "Lewie Ranieri"; Kendall and Fishman, *Primer,* pp. 32, 42.
3. Kendall and Fishman, *Primer,* p. 31; Eichengreen, *Hall of Mirrors,* pp. 247–250; Congressional Budget Office, *Fannie Mae, Freddie Mac,* p. 50; Goetzmann and Newman, "Securitization in the 1920s."
4. Kendall and Fishman, *Primer,* p. 33; Congressional Budget Office, *Fannie Mae, Freddie Mac*; Lewis, *Liar's Poker.*
5. Rice and Rose, "When Good Investments Go Bad"; Hagerty, *Fateful History,* pp. 38–40, 50, 59; Kendall and Fishman, *Primer*, p. 19; Congressional Budget Office, *Fannie Mae, Freddie Mac*, p. 53; "Blue Sky Law."

6. Hagerty, *Fateful History,* p. 50; Congressional Budget Office, *Fannie Mae, Freddie Mac,* p. 53.

7. Lewis, *Liar's Poker*, p. 116; Kendall and Fishman, *Primer,* p. 40.

8. Congressional Budget Office, *Fannie Mae, Freddie Mac.*

9. Ibid.

10. Kendall and Fishman, *Primer*, p. 33.

11. "Blue Sky Law"; Alger, *Alger Commission Report,* pp. 2–3; ibid., pp. 33–37; Herzog, *History of Mortgage Finance;* Herzog, interview with the author, Aug. 2016; Eichengreen, *Hall of Mirrors,* p. 30.

12. Taub, *Other People's Houses*, p. 10.

13. Securities and Exchange Commission, "Credit Rating Agencies"; Benner, "Fixing the Ratings."

14. Financial Crisis Inquiry Commission, *Financial Crisis Inquiry Report,* p. 119.

15. Kendall and Fishman, *Primer*, pp. 36–38.

16. Congressional Budget Office, *Fannie Mae, Freddie Mac*, pp. 6–7, 54; Financial Crisis Inquiry Commission, *Financial Crisis Inquiry Report,* p. 230.

17. Day, "Villains"; Financial Crisis Inquiry Commission, *Financial Crisis Inquiry Report,* pp. xxvii, 72, 219–221, also John Dugan testimony, app. C., p. 2; Gensler, *Testimony*; Gramlich, *Booms and Busts*; Gramlich, *Subprime Mortgages*; Greenspan, "Economic Development"; Bhutta and Ringo, "Assessing the Community Reinvestment Act's Role."

18. Financial Crisis Inquiry Commission, *Financial Crisis Inquiry Report,* pp. 11, 33–34, 79.

19. Gramlich, *Booms and Busts*; Gensler, *Testimony*; ibid., pp. 70, 104; Zandi, *Financial Shock,* pp. 33, 43.

20. Financial Crisis Inquiry Commission, *Financial Crisis Inquiry Report,* pp. xxvii, 72–74, 220.

21. Natter and Wechsler, "Dodd-Frank Act."

22. Gramlich, *Booms and Busts.*

23. McCoy, *Testimony,* p. 10.

24. Financial Crisis Inquiry Commission, *Financial Crisis Inquiry Report,* p. 79.

25. Brooks and Simon, "Subprime Debacle."

26. U.S. Senate, Special Committee on Aging, *Equity Predators*, p. 80.

27. Bush, "President's Remarks"; Center for Responsible Lending, *Net Drain*; Hedberg and Krainer, "Credit Access."

28. Zuckerman, "Profiting from the Crash."

29. Ibid.

Chapter 21. The Subprime Prisoner's Dilemma

1. Financial Crisis Inquiry Commission, *Financial Crisis Inquiry Report,* p. 85; Federal Housing Finance Agency, *Data,* p. 22.

2. Zandi, *Financial Shock,* pp. 33, 43.

3. Day and Mayer, "Credit Card Penalties, Fees."

4. Congressional Budget Office, *Fannie Mae, Freddie Mac*, p. 6; Zandi, *Financial Shock,* pp. 33–34, 43.

5. Zandi, *Financial Shock*, pp. 33–34, 43; Gramlich, *Booms and Busts*; Financial Crisis Inquiry Commission, *Financial Crisis Inquiry Report,* p. 104.

6. Gramlich, *Subprime Mortgages;* Financial Crisis Inquiry Commission, *Financial Crisis Inquiry Report,* p. 106.

7. Shiller, *Irrational Exuberance*, p. 20.

8. Zandi, *Financial Shock*, pp. 32–36; Financial Crisis Inquiry Commission, *Financial Crisis Inquiry Report*, pp. 85, 104; Gramlich, *Subprime Mortgages*.

9. Financial Crisis Inquiry Commission, *Financial Crisis Inquiry Report,* pp. 80, 86; Center for Responsible Lending, *Net Drain.*

10. Gensler testimony; Saunders and Cohen, "Federal Regulation."

11. Breslow, "S&P to Pay"; Breslow, "Pioneer behind Credit Derivatives"; Kolhatkar, "Legacy."

12. Financial Crisis Inquiry Commission, *Financial Crisis Inquiry Report,* p. 8.

13. Ibid.

14. Ibid., p. 104.

15. Ibid., pp. 31, 103; Investment Company Institute, *Fact Book, 2017,* table 35.

16. Natter, *Home Ownership Equity Act.*

17. U.S. Senate, Special Committee on Aging, *Equity Predators.*

18. Ibid., p. 2.

19. Ibid., p. 93.

20. Ibid., p. 31.

21. U.S. Department of Housing and Urban Development, *Curbing Predatory Home Mortgage Lending*, p. 26.

22. Ibid.

23. Gensler testimony.

24. McCoy testimony; Brooks and Simon, "Subprime Debacle"; Reckard, "Refinance Pitches."

25. U.S. Senate, Committee on Banking, Housing and Urban Affairs, *Predatory Mortgage Lending.*

26. Ibid.

27. Ibid.

28. Ibid.

29. Financial Crisis Inquiry Commission, *Financial Crisis Inquiry Report*, pp. 8, 10.

30. Joint Economic Committee of the House and Senate, U.S. Congress, *Local Look.*

31. Financial Crisis Inquiry Commission, *Financial Crisis Inquiry Report*, pp. 79–80.

32. O'Brien, "Fed Assesses Citigroup Unit."

33. Financial Crisis Inquiry Commission, *Financial Crisis Inquiry Report,* p. 8.

34. Ibid., pp. 188–189.

Chapter 22. Feds Tell States: Shut Up, Sit Down

1. Geiger, "Countrywide's Mozilo"; Geithner, *Stress Test,* p. 122.

2. Bruck, "Angelo's Ashes."

3. Financial Crisis Inquiry Commission, *Financial Crisis Inquiry Report,* pp. 111–113; Saunders and Cohen, "Federal Regulation."

4. Berner and Grow, "They Warned Us."

5. Financial Crisis Inquiry Commission, *Financial Crisis Inquiry Report,* p. 112.

6. Center for Public Integrity, *Subprime 25*; ibid., p. 112; Blair and Kushmeider, *Challenges*; General Accounting Office, *Large Bank Mergers;* Government Accountability Office, *Financial Regulation.*

7. Engel and McCoy, *Subprime Virus*, p. 160.

8. Geithner, *Stress Test,* p. 122.

9. Day, *S&L Hell,* pp. 121–123.

10. Ibid.

11. Ibid.; Shorter, *Resolution Trust*; Financial Crisis Inquiry Commission, *Financial Crisis Inquiry Report,* pp. 68–71.

12. Medley, "Riegle-Neal."

13. Nash, "Treasury Now Favors."

14. Day, *S&L Hell,* p. 123.

15. McCoy testimony; Gramlich, *Subprime Mortgages*; Gramlich, *Booms and Busts*; Financial Crisis Inquiry Commission, *Financial Crisis Inquiry Report,* John Dugan testimony, app. B.

16. Financial Crisis Inquiry Commission, *Financial Crisis Inquiry Report,* p. 142.

17. Ibid., Dugan testimony, app. B, p. 11.

18. Ibid., p. 88.

19. Ibid.

20. Ibid.; Bair, *Bull by the Horns,* p. 57.

21. Federal Deposit Insurance Corporation, press office data provided to the author; Greenfeld, "From IndyMac to OneWest"; Center for Public Integrity, *Subprime 25*.

22. Federal Deposit Insurance Corporation, press office data provided to the author; Greenfeld, "From IndyMac to OneWest."

23. Day, *S&L Hell,* p. 256; Financial Crisis Inquiry Commission, *Financial Crisis Inquiry Report,* pp. 55 and 92.

24. Financial Crisis Inquiry Commission, *Financial Crisis Inquiry Report,* p. 56.

25. Cox, *Testimony.*

26. Propublica, *History of U.S. Government Bailouts,* Apr. 15, 2009 update.

27. Government Accountability Office, *Financial Regulation.* On July 4, 2007, the General Accounting Office changed its name to the Government Accountability Office.

28. Day, *S&L Hell,* p. 256; Day, "Thrift Is the Word"; Day, "With Depression-Era Law"; Financial Crisis Inquiry Commission, *Financial Crisis Inquiry Report,* pp. 55–56, 92; Day, "Wal-Mart Defends Its Bid"; Alvarez, "Industrial Loan Companies"; Barr, "Obama's Banking End Around."

29. Day, *S&L Hell,* p. 256; Financial Crisis Inquiry Commission, *Financial Crisis Inquiry Report,* pp. 55–56, 92; Day, "Wal-Mart Defends Its Bid"; Alvarez, "Industrial Loan Companies"; Barr, "Obama's Banking End Around"; Government Accountability Office, *Bank Holding Company Act*; Day, "Piggy Banker?"; Neely, "Industrial Loan Companies."

30. Geithner, *Stress Test,* p. 96.

31. Avraham, Selvaggi, and Vickery, "Structural View."

32. Cox, *Testimony*; Geithner, *Stress Test*, p. 207.

33. Cox, *Testimony.*

34. Financial Crisis Inquiry Commission, *Financial Crisis Inquiry Report,* p. 350.

35. Kessler, "Ex-AIG Chief."
36. Prial, "SEC"; Financial Crisis Inquiry Commission, *Financial Crisis Inquiry Report*, pp. 55–56.
37. Financial Crisis Inquiry Commission, *Financial Crisis Inquiry Report,* p. 53; Born and Donaldson, "Self-Funding of Regulators."
38. Cox, *Testimony*; Government Accountability Office, *Financial Regulation*; Financial Crisis Inquiry Commission, *Financial Crisis Inquiry Report,* p. 37; "Investment Banks Are Borrowing from the Fed."
39. Wyatt, "SEC Changes Policy."
40. Smith, "Five Things."
41. Center for Public Integrity, *Subprime 25*; "Bailout Tracker," Jan. 13, 2017 update; Paulson, *On the Brink,* pp. 227–228; Geithner, *Stress Test,* p. 98.
42. Day, "Villains."
43. Geiger, "Countrywide's Mozilo."
44. Center for Public Integrity, *Subprime 25.*
45. Alden, "John Mack"; Silver-Greenberg and Craid, "Fined Billions"; Geithner, *Stress Test,* p. 503.
46. Financial Crisis Inquiry Commission, *Financial Crisis Inquiry Report,* p. 36; Day, *S&L Hell.*
47. Eisinger, "Why Haven't Bankers Been Punished?"

Chapter 23. A Number Out of the Air

1. Day, "Villains"; Geithner, *Stress Test,* p. 115.
2. Federal Reserve Bank of St. Louis, *Timeline*; Day, "Villains"; Center for Public Integrity, *Subprime 25*; Kelly, "Bear CEO's Handling of Crisis."
3. Federal Reserve Bank of San Francisco, *Federal Reserve Discount Window Rates.*
4. Federal Reserve Bank of St. Louis, *Timeline*; Federal Reserve Bank of St. Louis, *Effective Federal Funds Rate;* "Financial Crisis Timeline."
5. Day, "Villains."
6. Sorkin, "Paulson's Itchy Finger"; "Bailout Tracker."
7. Smith, "U.S."
8. White and Guerrara, "Investment Banks Split"; Federal Reserve Bank of St. Louis, *Timeline.*
9. Federal Reserve Bank of St. Louis, *Timeline*; Paulson, *On the Brink,* pp. 252–260; Bair, *Bull by the Horns,* pp. 108–115; Geithner, *Stress Test,* pp. 202–235.
10. Ibid.
11. Ibid.; "Adding Up the Government's Total Bailout Tab."
12. Geithner, *Stress Test,* p. 227.
13. Blumenfeld, "$700 Billion Man."
14. Paulson, *On the Brink,* pp. 129, 448.
15. Fox, "Honesty Doesn't Pay."
16. Emergency Economic Stabilization Act of 2008; Securities and Exchange Commission, *2008 Report;* Pozen, "Is It Fair."
17. Shaffer, "Fair Value Accounting."

18. Geithner, *Stress Test,* p. 225.
19. Eichengreen, *Hall of Mirrors*, p. 5; Jones with Angly, *Fifty Billion Dollars*.
20. Kirk et al., "Money, Power and Politics," part 2.
21. Yang, "Fed Aid."
22. Taub, *Other People's Houses,* pp. 2, 5.
23. Mian and Sufi, *House of Debt,* pp. 137–142.
24. Ibid., p. 135.
25. Khanna and Sorg, "Connecting the Dots"; "How Koch Became an Oil Speculation Powerhouse."
26. Benson, "Obama Housing Fix."
27. Mian and Sufi, *House of Debt*, pp. 134–137; Summers, "Lawrence Summers on 'House of Debt.'"
28. Taub, *Other People's Houses,* pp. 138–139.
29. Financial Crisis Inquiry Commission, *Financial Crisis Inquiry Report,* Dugan testimony; Dayen, "Mnuchin Lied"; Orol, "U.S. Breaks Down"; Benson, "Obama Housing Fix."
30. Powell and Morgenson, "MERS?"
31. Dayen, "Mnuchin Lied."
32. Ibid.
33. Xu, "Bye, GMAC."
34. "Bailout Tracker."
35. Atkinson et al. *How Bad Was It?*
36. Financial Crisis Inquiry Commission, *Financial Crisis Inquiry Report,* p. 16.
37. Greenspan, "Remarks via Satellite."
38. Leonhardt, "Fed Missed This Bubble."
39. Zandi, *Financial Shock*, pp. 13, 165.
40. Bernanke, "Subprime Mortgage Market"; Kelly et al. "Two Big Funds."
41. Mufson, "Greenspan Stands His Ground"; Bernanke, *Courage to Act*, pp. 61–63; Mian and Sufi, *House of Debt*, pp. 4–5; Zandi, *Financial Shock*, p. 71; "Greenspan to the Rescue"; General Accounting Office, *Large Bank Mergers*; Financial Crisis Inquiry Commission, *Financial Crisis Inquiry Report*, pp. 55–56, 59, 61, 77, 80, 103.
42. Government Accountability Office, *Financial Regulation*, p. 7.
43. Michael Bradfield, interviews with the author, summer and fall 2016.
44. Federal Reserve Board of Governors, "Federal Reserve to Implement."
45. General Accounting Office, *Large Bank Mergers*; Financial Crisis Inquiry Commission, *Financial Crisis Inquiry Report*, p. 77 and resource library archives, Richard Spillenkothen notes, May 31, 2010.
46. Cox, *Testimony*; Kirk, "Warning"; Rampell, "Lax Oversight."
47. Office of Thrift Supervision, "Housing Conference."
48. Financial Crisis Inquiry Commission, *Financial Crisis Inquiry Report*, pp. 14–15; Frieden, "FBI Warns"; Associated Press, "Mortgage Fraud."
49. Financial Crisis Inquiry Commission, *Financial Crisis Inquiry Report*, pp. xviii, 6, 10, 21, 173; Center for Responsible Lending, *Net Drain*.
50. Home Ownership and Equity Protection Act of 1994.
51. Andrew, "Fed Shrugged."
52. Financial Crisis Inquiry Commission, *Financial Crisis Inquiry Report*, p. 10.

53. Ibid., resource library archives; Financial Crisis Inquiry Commission, "Too Big to Fail," p. 74.

54. National Consumer Law Center, "Simplifying the Home Buying Process."

55. Day, "Villains"; Bush, "President's Remarks."

56. Coalition for Sensible Housing, American Bankers Association, et al., *Updated QRM Proposal*; Zhu, Goodman, and Taz, "Why the GSEs' Support"; Bhutta and Ringo, "Assessing the Community Reinvestment Act's Role."

57. Financial Crisis Inquiry Commission, *Financial Crisis Inquiry Report*, pp. xxvii, 80; U.S. Senate, Special Committee on Aging, *Equity Predators*; U.S. Senate, Committee on Banking, Housing, and Urban Affairs, *Predatory Mortgage Lending*; Center for Responsible Lending, *Net Drain*.

58. U.S. Commission on Civil Rights. *Civil Rights and the Mortgage Crisis*, pp. 47–65, HMDA data on p. 61; Day, "Villains"; Schloemer, *Losing Ground.*

59. Mian and Sufi, *House of Debt*, p. 25; Financial Crisis Inquiry Commission, *Financial Crisis Inquiry Report,* Dugan testimony.

60. Mian and Sufi, *House of Debt*, pp. 19–21, 25–26; Zandi, *Financial Shock*, p. 43.

61. Financial Crisis Inquiry Commission, *Financial Crisis Inquiry Report*, pp. 215–218; Zandi, *Financial Shock*, pp. 34, 44.

62. Leonhardt, "Will the Fed Reserve"; Leonhardt, "Fed Missed This Bubble."

63. Congressional Budget Office, *Housing Wealth*; Mian and Sufi, *House of Debt*, p. 4; Financial Crisis Inquiry Commission, *Financial Crisis Inquiry Report*, p. 7.

64. Leonhardt, "Fed Missed This Bubble."

65. Beim, "It's All about Debt."

66. Mian and Sufi, *House of Debt Blog.*

67. Kindleberger and Aliber, *Manias, Panics, and Crashes*, pp. 41–42; Minsky, "Financial Instability Hypothesis"; Cassidy, "Minsky Moment."

68. Zandi, *Financial Shock,* p. 27, updated ed. p. 42; Financial Crisis Inquiry Commission, *Financial Crisis Inquiry Report,* p. 102; McCoy, *Testimony*; Fishbein, "Going Subprime"; Andrew, "Fed Shrugged."

69. Day, "Villains"; Financial Crisis Inquiry Commission, *Financial Crisis Inquiry Report,* pp. xxvi, 102; Zandi, *Financial Shock,* updated ed. p. 27; Fishbein, "Going Subprime"; Congressional Budget Office, *Fannie Mae, Freddie Mac.*

70. Financial Crisis Inquiry Commission, *Financial Crisis Inquiry Report*, pp. xix, 123–124; Frame et al., *Rescue*, p. 35; Day, "Villains"; Day, "Study Finds 'Extensive' Fraud"; Park, *Fannie, Freddie.*

71. Fishbein, "Going Subprime"; Day, "Study Finds 'Extensive' Fraud."

72. Frame et al., *Rescue*, p. 35; Federal Housing Finance Agency, *Conservatorship*; Zibel, "$2.3 Billion Loss"; Zandi, *Financial Shock,* p. 40.

73. Frame et al., *Rescue, pp.* 11, 39.

74. Ibid., pp. 39, 51; Rice and Rose, "When Good Investments Go Bad"; Congressional Budget Office, *Fannie Mae, Freddie Mac;* Financial Crisis Inquiry Commission, *Financial Crisis Inquiry Report*, pp. 319–321.

75. Day, "Shaky Ground."

76. Rice and Rose, "When Good Investments Go Bad."

77. Financial Crisis Inquiry Commission, *Financial Crisis Inquiry Report*, p. xxvi.

78. Frame et al., *Rescue*; "Bailout Tracker."

79. Day, "Analysis."

80. Financial Crisis Inquiry Commission, *Financial Crisis Inquiry Report*, p. xix.

81. Ibid., pp. xix, xxv, 122.

82. Ibid., p. 118; U.S. Senate, Permanent Subcommittee on Investigations, *Wall Street and the Financial Crisis,* pp. 27, 288.

83. U.S. Senate, Permanent Subcommittee on Investigations, *Wall Street and the Financial Crisis,* p. 288; Financial Crisis Inquiry Commission, *Financial Crisis Inquiry Report,* pp. 118–120; Zandi, *Financial Shock,* p. 141.

84. Protess, "S&P's $1.37 Billion Reckoning."

85. Ibid.

86. Financial Crisis Inquiry Commission, *Financial Crisis Inquiry Report*, p. 18.

87. Delgadillo et al., "Disentangling," p. 313.

88. U.S. Senate, Permanent Subcommittee on Investigations of the Committee on Homeland Security and Governmental Affairs, *Wall Street and the Financial Crisis,* p. 19.

89. Ibid. p. 12.

90. Financial Crisis Inquiry Commission, *Financial Crisis Inquiry Report,* pp. 3–24; Glass, "Inside Job"; U.S. Senate, Permanent Subcommittee on Investigations, *Wall Street and the Financial Crisis,* p. 19.

91. Financial Crisis Inquiry Commission, *Financial Crisis Inquiry Report,* pp. 16–18.

92. Center for Public Integrity, *Subprime 25.*

93. In 2008 an anonymous member of the Wall Street community created a wickedly humorous PowerPoint explaining the mortgage crisis and making clear that Wall Street in fact understood perfectly well how subprime mortgages worked and how ridiculous the system was. It went viral quickly. Anyone offended by foul language should not watch it. For others, it's a hilarious, colorful, and very accurate summation of the crisis, albeit with many four-letter words. In case the anonymous creator comes forward and asserts a copyright claim, I can't reprint it here. But it's easily accessible via an internet search using the phrases "subprime primer" and "stickman presentation." Be sure to watch the version without the narrator. It doesn't need one. And yes, small towns in Norway really did lose money.

94. Mann, "GE Says."

95. Mann and Lublin, "Why General Electric."

96. Gruenberg, "Financial Regulation."

97. Kroszner and Shiller, *Reforming U.S. Financial Markets*, pp. 99, 74–77, 109–110, 114–115; DavisPolk, *Summary.*

98. Day, "Analysis."

99. Financial Crisis Inquiry Commission, *Financial Crisis Inquiry Report,* p. xxvii; U.S. Census Bureau, *Quarterly Residential Vacancies*; Khouri, "Home Ownership Rate"; Zandi, *Financial Shock*, p. 48.

100. "Household Debt Jumps"; El Issa, *2017 American Household Credit Card Debt.*

101. Byrne, "Americans' Household Debt"; Jones-Cooper, "Average U.S. Household Owes"; El Issa, *2017 American Household Credit Card Debt*; Federal Reserve Bank of New York, *Quarterly Report;* Federal Reserve Bank of New York, *Federal Funds Data;* Federal Reserve Bank of New York, Center for Microeconomic Data, *Quarterly Report on Household Debt and Credit.*

Chapter 24. Fake Accounts

1. U.S. Senate, Committee on Banking, Housing and Urban Affairs, "Unauthorized Wells Fargo Accounts."
2. Morrell, "4 Ways"; Lynch, "U.S. Justice."
3. Associated Press, "Wells Fargo Agrees"; Friedman, "Did You Hear."
4. Lynch, "U.S. Justice"; Mount, "Wells Fargo's Fake Accounts"; Arnold, "Reports."
5. Stewart, "Just Deserts."
6. U.S. House of Representatives, Financial Services Committee, *Hearing on Wells Fargo.*
7. Reckard, "Wells Fargo Fires Workers."
8. Freed, "Wells Fargo Uncovers."
9. Stempel, "Lawsuit Says."
10. Freed, "Wells Fargo Uncovers."
11. Day, "Fight"; Dayen, "Donald Trump's Executive Order"; Ritholtz, "It's Too Late"; Hauptman and Roper, *Financial Advisor or Investment Salesperson?*
12. Damato, "Trump Advisor."
13. Powell, "Is Trump a Threat."
14. *Chamber of Commerce et al. v. Secretary of Labor Tomas Perez et al.*
15. Ebling, "Texas Court Ruling."
16. Ibid.
17. Beilfuss, "Fiduciary Rule."
18. Government Accountability Office, *401K Plans.*
19. Day, "Fight."
20. Grimaldi and Overberg, "Many Comments."
21. Peirce, "Five Questions."
22. Stanger, "How Trump Plan Would Ease"; *Do Class Actions Benefit Members?*
23. Consumer Financial Protection Bureau, "We've Issued a New Rule."
24. "Is Dodd-Frank's Failure"; "Financial Regulation."
25. Lynch, "Prudential to Fight"; Bradford, "U.S. Agrees to Delay"; Gray, "AIG Sheds $150M."
26. "Is Dodd-Frank's Failure Resolution Regime Failing"; "Financial Regulation."
27. Levin, "Trump Administration"; Yatter et al., "CFTC Self-Reporting Policy."
28. "Down in the Dumps."
29. Protess and Silver-Greenberg, "Under Trump."
30. Cowley, "With Trump's Signature."
31. Monks and Minow, *Corporate Governance*, pp. 66–69.
32. Financial Crisis Inquiry Commission, *Financial Crisis Inquiry Report*, p. 62.
33. Center for Responsive Politics, Opensecrets.org.
34. Ibid.
35. Confessore et al., "A Wealthy Few"; Yeager, *Differences.*
36. Ibid.; Confessore et al., "Families Funding."
37. Confessore et al., "Families Funding."
38. Ibid.
39. Mider, "Rebekah Mercer"; Bowers, "Hedge Fund House Divided."
40. Mayer, "Reclusive Hedge-Fund Tycoon"; Confessore, "Data Mining Scandal."

41. Confessore et al., "A Wealthy Few."
42. Citigroup, Equity Strategy, "Plutonomy Memos," Oct. 16, 2005, p. 25; Mar. 5, 2006; and Sept. 29, 2006, p. 10.
43. Goldfarb and Boorstein, "Pope Francis Denounces Trickle-Down."
44. Erlanger, "Taking on Adam Smith."
45. Ibid.
46. Saez, "U.S. Top One Percent."
47. Ibid.
48. Piketty, Saez, and Zucman, *Economic Growth.*
49. Ibid.
50. Schwartz, "Velvet Rope Economy."
51. Saez, "U.S. Top One Percent"; Krugman, "'Economics of Inequality,' by Thomas Piketty"; Erlanger, "Taking on Adam Smith"; "*Economist* Explains: Thomas Piketty's 'Capital'"; Bricker et al., "Measuring Income and Wealth."
52. Bricker et al, "Measuring Income and Wealth," p. 269.
53. Pew Research Center, *America's Shrinking Middle Class.*
54. Ibid.
55. Ibid.
56. Federal Reserve Board, "Report on the Economic Well-Being of U.S."
57. Pew Charitable Trusts, *Precarious State.*
58. Ibid.
59. Pew Charitable Trusts, *State of the Union, 2016.*
60. Schwartz, "Can Trump Save Their Jobs?"; Schwartz, "Velvet Rope Economy."
61. Deaton, "It's Not Just Unfair."
62. Freeman and Blasi, "What the Founding Fathers Believed."
63. Washington to Richard Henderson.
64. Freeman and Blasi, "What the Founding Fathers Believed."
65. Ibid.
66. Ibid.
67. Erlanger, "Taking on Adam Smith."
68. Strain, *Want to Fight Economic Inequality?*

Chapter 25. Who Should Own a Bank

1. Nationwide advertisement.
2. Hoenig, "Turning Point."
3. Rosner, "Time Has Come."
4. Allison, "Market Discipline"; Allison, *Financial Crisis.*
5. Bernstein, "Inside the New York Fed."
6. Glass, "Secret Recordings."
7. Bernstein, "Inside the New York Fed"; Bernstein, "High-Level Fed Committee."
8. Ibid.; Eisinger, "Why Haven't Bankers Been Punished?"
9. Ibid.
10. Allison, "Market Discipline"; Perlberg, "Former Fed Governor."
11. Warsh, "Remarks"; Kashkari, *Minneapolis Plan.*

12. Popper and Eavis, "Senate Report"; U.S. Senate, Permanent Subcommittee on Investigations, *Wall Street Bank Involvement*; U.S. Senate, Permanent Subcommittee on Investigations, *Excessive Speculation*.
13. U.S. Senate, Permanent Subcommittee on Investigations, *Wall Street Bank Involvement*.
14. Ibid.
15. Rosner, *Examining Financial Holding Companies*.
16. Cicio, Testimony; U.S. Senate, Permanent Subcommittee on Investigations, *Excessive Speculation*.
17. Lane, "Trump."
18. Foroohar, "Investment Banking."
19. Ibid.; Mann and Lublin, "Why General Electric."
20. Masters, *Accidental Hunt Brothers*.
21. Masters, *Testimony*; Masters, "Masters Sees Correlation"; Masters, "Better Markets," Nov. 20, 2012, and Oct. 18, 2012; Frenk and Turbeville, "Commodity Index Traders."
22. Masters, "Better Markets," Oct. 18, 2012.
23. Masters, "Better Markets," Nov. 20, 2012.
24. Bordelon, "Elizabeth Warren's Wall Street."
25. Volcker, interview with the author, Apr. 2016.
26. Masters, "New York Law Chief."
27. Schmidt, "The CFPB"; Hembree, "Mulvaney Is on the Hot Seat"; Campbell, "Payday Lender."
28. Hembree, "Mulvaney Is on the Hot Seat."
29. Warsh, "Federal Reserve."
30. Appelbaum, "Fed Gets Ready."
31. Kurtzleben, "Donald Trump's Messy Ideas."
32. Gruenberg, "Financial Regulation."
33. Ibid.
34. Pierce, "Queen Asks Why."
35. McLannahan, "Nonprime Has a Nice Ring to It"; Olick, "Subprime Mortgages."
36. Guida, "Fed Slams."
37. U.S. Treasury, Office of the Comptroller of the Currency, "OCC Assesses."
38. Hamilton, "Trump Watchdog."
39. Rappeport and Flitter, "Congress Approves."
40. Westbrook, "Banks Try On."

BIBLIOGRAPHY

Unless otherwise indicated, all websites are current as of April 23, 2018.

Abelson, Reed, and Jonathan D. Glater. "Enron's Collapse: The Auditors; Who's Keeping the Accountants Accountable?" *New York Times,* Jan. 15, 2002, http://www.nytimes.com/2002/01/15/business/enron-s-collapse-the-auditors-who-s-keeping-the-accountants-accountable.html.

Adams, John. Letter to François Adriaan Van der Kemp, Feb. 16, 1809, archived at Founders Online, http://founders.archives.gov/?q=john%20adams%20%22a%20cheat%22&s=1111311111&r=4w.

"Adding Up the Government's Total Bailout Tab." *New York Times,* July 24, 2011, http://www.nytimes.com/interactive/2009/02/04/business/20090205-bailout-totals-graphic.html.

"Affiliates of Banks Illegal, Glass Says." *New York Times,* May 10, 1932.

Alden, William. "John Mack Calls for an End to 'Beating Up' on Wall St. CEOs." *New York Times,* Feb. 11, 2014, https://dealbook.nytimes.com/2014/02/11/john-mack-calls-for-an-end-to-beating-up-on-wall-st-c-e-o-s/.

"Alexander Hamilton Chronology." *American Experience.* PBS, n.d., http://www.pbs.org/wgbh/amex/hamilton/timeline/index.html.

Alger, George W. *The Alger Commission Report.* State of New York, 1934, https://www.aei.org/wp-content/uploads/2012/05/-alger-commission-report_13595669733.pdf.

Allen, Frederick Lewis. *The Lords of Creation.* New York: Harper & Brothers, 1935.

———. *Only Yesterday: An Informal History of the 1920s.* Harper & Row, 1964.

Allison, John A. *The Financial Crisis and the Free Market Cure.* New York: McGraw Hill, 2013.

———. "Market Discipline Beats Regulatory Discipline." *Cato Journal* 34, no. 2 (Spring/Summer 2014), https://object.cato.org/sites/cato.org/files/serials/files/cato-journal/2014/5/cato-journal-v34n2-9.pdf.

Alloway, Tracy, et al. "Banks Seek Changes to Research Settlement." *Financial Times*, Sept. 25, 2012, https://www.ft.com/content/25500cb6-0656-11e2-abdb-00144feabdc0?mhq5j=e1.

Alpers, Benjamin L. *Dictators, Democracy, and American Public Culture: Envisioning the Totalitarian Enemy, 1920–1950.* University of North Carolina Press, 2003.

Alvarez, Scott. "Industrial Loan Companies." Testimony before Subcommittee on Financial Institutions and Consumer Credit, House Financial Services Committee, July 12, 2006, https://www.federalreserve.gov/newsevents/testimony/alvarez20060712a.htm.

American Bar Association. *Annual Issues Chart, 2013.* https://www.americanbar.org/publications/governmental_affairs_periodicals/washingtonletter/2013/january/annualissueschart.html#business.

"Analysis of 'Money Trust': Combination Is Pointed Out and Its Power Pictured." *New York Times,* Mar. 1, 1913.

Andrew, A. Piatt. *Statistics for the United States, 1867–1909.* National Monetary Commission, 61st Cong., 2nd sess., U.S. Government Printing Office, 1910, https://fraser.stlouisfed.org/files/docs/historical/nmc/nmc_570_1910.pdf.

Andrew, Edmund L. "Fed Shrugged as Subprime Crisis Spread." *New York Times,* Dec. 18, 2007, http://www.nytimes.com/2007/12/18/business/18subprime.html.

———. "Small Banks Score a Coup by Lobbying." *New York Times,* Sept. 30, 2008, http://www.nytimes.com/2008/10/01/business/01ideas.html.

Appelbaum, Binyamin. "Debt Concerns, Once a Core Republican Tenet, Take a Back Seat to Tax Cuts." *New York Times,* Nov. 30, 2017.

———. "The Fed Gets Ready for a Reckoning." *New York Times,* Nov. 13, 2016, https://www.nytimes.com/2016/11/13/business/economy/trump-the-fed-yellen-gets-ready-for-reckoning.html.

Aristotle. *Politics,* trans. Ernest Barker. Oxford University Press, 2009.

"Arkansas to Urge More Aid in Drought." *New York Times*, Jan. 5, 1931.

Arnold, Chris. "Reports on Wells Fargo Whistleblowers Spark Inquiry in Congress." National Public Radio, Dec. 30, 2016, http://www.npr.org/2016/12/30/507597691/for-whistleblowers-repercussions-are-felt-beyond-wells-fargo.

Arvedlund, Eric E. "Mr. & Mrs. Enron." *Barron's,* Dec. 10, 2001.

Associated Press. "Mortgage Fraud Becoming an 'Epidemic.'" *USA Today,* Sept. 17, 2004, http://usatoday30.usatoday.com/money/perfi/housing/2004-09-17-mortgage-fraud_x.htm.

———. "Rules Mitchell Must Pay Tax Assessment." *Lewiston Evening Journal,* Mar. 7, 1938, https://news.google.com/newspapers?nid=1913&dat=19380308&id=xbU0AAAAIBAJ&sjid=qmkFAAAAIBAJ&pg=814,5177315&hl=en.

———. "Wells Fargo Agrees to Pay $85 Million over Loans." *New York Times,* July 20, 2011, http://www.nytimes.com/2011/07/21/business/wells-fargo-to-settle-mortgage-charges-for-85-million.html.

Atkinson, Tyler, et al. *How Bad Was It?* Staff Papers, Federal Reserve Bank of Dallas, no. 20, July 2013.

Avery, Robert B., et al. "The 2006 HMDA Data." *Federal Reserve Bulletin* (Dec. 2007): 73–109, http://www.federalreserve.gov/pubs/bulletin/2007/pdf/hmda06final.pdf.

Avraham, Dafna, Patricia Selvaggi, and James Vickery. "A Structural View of U.S. Bank Holding Companies." *FRBNY Economic Policy Review* (July 2012), https://www.newyorkfed.org/medialibrary/media/research/epr/12v18n2/1207avra.pdf.

"Back to the Futures?" *Economist,* Feb. 4, 2013, http://www.economist.com/blogs/freeexchange/2013/02/derivatives-markets-regulation.

Bagehot, Walter. *Lombard Street: A Description of the Money Market.* CreateSpace Independent Publishing, chap. 6, http://www.econlib.org/library/Bagehot/bagLom6.html.

"Bailout Tracker." Propublica. https://projects.propublica.org/bailout/list (updated Jan. 13, 2017).

Bair, Sheila. *Bull by the Horns: Fighting to Save Main Street from Wall Street and Wall Street from Itself.* Simon & Schuster, 2012.

Bajaj, Vikas, and Kurt Eichenwald. "Kenneth L. Lay, 64, Enron Founder and Symbol of Corp. Excess, Dies." *New York Times,* July 6, 2006, http://www.nytimes.com/2006/07/06/business/06lay.html.

Bank for International Settlements. *Quarterly Review: International Banking and Financial Market Developments* (Nov. 1996). http://www.bis.org/publ/r_qt9611.htm.

———. *Quarterly Review: International Banking and Financial Market Developments* (Aug. 1999). http://www.bis.org/publ/r_qt9908.htm.

———. *Quarterly Review: International Banking and Financial Market Developments* (Dec. 2007). http://www.bis.org/publ/qtrpdf/r_qt0712.pdf.

———. *Quarterly Review: International Banking and Financial Market Developments* (Dec. 2008). http://www.bis.org/publ/qtrpdf/r_qt0812.pdf.

———. *Quarterly Review: International Banking and Financial Market Developments* (Dec. 2010). http://www.bis.org/publ/qtrpdf/r_qt1012.pdf.

———. *Quarterly Review: International Banking and Financial Market Developments* (June 2016). http://www.bis.org/publ/qtrpdf/r_qt1606.pdf.

"A Bank Holiday." USHistory.org, n.d. http://www.ushistory.org/us/49a.asp.

Banking Act of 1935. Federal Reserve History, Nov. 22, 2013, https://www.federalreserve history.org/essays/banking_act_of_1935?WT.si_n=Search&WT.si_x=3.

Barr, Colin. "Obama's Banking End Around." *Fortune,* June 22, 2009.

Barth, James, and Moutusi Sau. "The Big Keep Getting Bigger: Too-Big-To-Fail Banks 30 Years Later." Center for Financial Markets, Milken Institute, Sept. 2014.

Barton, Bruce Fairchild. "Is There Anything Here That Other Men Couldn't Do?" *American Magazine,* Feb. 1923.

———. *The Man Nobody Knows: A Discovery of the Real Jesus.* Bobbs-Merrill, 1925.

Beilfuss, Lisa. "Fiduciary Rule Dealt Blow by Circuit Court Ruling." *Wall Street Journal,* Mar. 15, 2018.

Beim, David O. "It's All about Debt." *Forbes,* Mar. 19, 2009, http://www.forbes.com/2009/03/19/household-debt-gdp-markets-beim.html.

Benner, Katie. "Fixing the Ratings Game." *Fortune,* Oct. 4, 2007, http://archive.fortune.com/2007/09/28/news/companies/ratings_agencies.fortune/index.htm.

Benson, Clea. "Obama Housing Fix Faltered as Advisors Chose Carrots, Not Sticks." *Bloomberg,* June 12, 2012, http://www.kcchronicle.com/2012/06/12/obama-housing-fix-faltered-as-advisers-chose-carrots-not-sticks/ag5ew7m/.

Benton, Thomas Hart. *Thirty Years' View: A History of the Working of the American Government for Thirty Years from 1820 to 1850.* D. Appleton and Co., 1883.

Berg, Rebecca. "Koch Group to Take on Wealth-Gap Debate." *RealClear Politics*, July 1, 2015, http://www.realclearpolitics.com/articles/2015/07/01/koch_group_to_take_up_wealth_gap_debate.html.

Berman, Dennis K. "Deep within Citi, the Death of Salomon." *Wall Street Journal,* Sept. 30, 2009.

Bernanke, Benjamin S. *The Courage to Act.* W.W. Norton, 2015.

———. *The Federal Reserve and the Financial Crisis.* Princeton University Press, 2013.

———. "On Milton Friedman's Ninetieth Birthday." Speech, Federal Reserve Board, Nov. 8, 2002, http://www.federalreserve.gov/boarddocs/Speeches/2002/20021108/default.htm.

———. "The Subprime Mortgage Market." Speech at the Federal Reserve Bank of Chicago's 43rd Annual Conference on Bank Structure and Competition, Chicago, May 17, 2007, https://www.federalreserve.gov/newsevents/speech/bernanke20070517a.htm.

Berner, Robert, and Brian Grow. "They Warned Us about the Mortgage Crisis." *Business Week in Depth,* Oct. 9, 2008, https://www.bloomberg.com/news/articles/2008-10-08/they-warned-us-about-the-mortgage-crisis.

Bernstein, Jake. "High-Level Fed Committee Overruled Carmen Segarra's Finding on Goldman." *ProPublica,* Dec. 29, 2014, https://www.propublica.org/article/high-level-fed-committee-overruled-carmen-segarras-finding-on-goldman.

———. "Inside the New York Fed: Secret Recordings and a Culture Clash." *Propublica,* Sept. 26, 2014, partnering with *This American Life,* WBEZ.

Berry, John. "Divided on Derivatives: Greenspan, Buffett at Odds on Risks of the Financial Instruments." *Washington Post,* Mar. 6, 2003.

Berry, John M., and Kathleen Day. "High Stakes as Banks Shed Reins: Taxpayers' Liability, Customers Service at Risk." *Washington Post,* July 26, 1987, http://search.proquest.com/docview/306909898?accountid=11752.

Bhutta, Neil, and Daniel Ringo. "Assessing the Community Reinvestment Act's Role in the Financial Crisis." *Fed Notes,* May 26, 2015, https://www.federalreserve.gov/econresdata/notes/feds-notes/2015/assessing-the-community-reinvestment-acts-role-in-the-financial-crisis–20150526.html.

Bianco, Anthony. "The King of Wall Street." *Business Week,* Dec. 9, 1985.

Blair, Christine E. "The Future of Banking in America: The Mixing of Banking and Commerce: Current Policy Issues." *FDIC Banking Review* 16, no. 4 (2004), https://www.fdic.gov/bank/analytical/banking/2005jan/article3.pdf.

Blair, Christine E., and Rose M. Kushmeider. *Challenges to the Dual Banking System: The Funding of Bank Supervision.* Federal Deposit Insurance Corporation, 2006, https://www.fdic.gov/bank/analytical/banking/2006mar/article1/article1.pdf.

Blanker, Fredericka. "What a Real Dictator Would Do." *North American Review* 234, no. 6 (Dec. 1932): 484–492, http://library.uoregon.edu/ec/e-asia/read/mussolini.pdf.

Blasi, Joseph. "A Founding Father Profit Share Fix for Inequality." *Daily Beast*, July 12, 2014,http://www.thedailybeast.com/articles/2014/07/12/a-founding-father-profit-sharing-fix-for-inequality.html.

Blasi, Joseph, et al. *The Citizen's Share: Putting Ownership Back into Democracy.* Yale University Press, 2013.

Blinder, Alan S. *After the Music Stopped.* Penguin, 2013.

———. "From the New Deal, a Way Out of a Mess." *New York Times,* Feb. 24, 2008, http://www.nytimes.com/2008/02/24/business/24view.html.

Bloomberg Editors. "DeVos Should Stick to the Rules on For-Profit Colleges." Bloomberg.com, June 20, 2017, https://www.bloomberg.com/view/articles/2017-06-20/devos-should-stick-to-the-rules-on-for-profit-colleges.

"Blue Sky Law." Legal Information Institute, Cornell Law School, https://www.law.cornell.edu/wex/blue_sky_law.

Blumenfeld, Laura. "The $700 Billion Man." *Washington Post,* Dec. 6, 2009, http://www.washingtonpost.com/wp-dyn/content/article/2009/12/04/AR2009120402016.html?sid=ST2009120402037.

Bodenhorn, Howard. *State Banking in Early America: A New Economic History.* Oxford University Press, 2003.

———. "Zombie Banks and the Demise of New York's Safety Fund." *Eastern Economic Journal* 22, no. 1 (Winter 1996), http://www.jstor.org/stable/40325677?seq=1#page_scan_tab_contents.

"The Bonus Army: How a Protest Led to the GI Bill." National Public Radio, Nov. 11, 2011, http://www.npr.org/2011/11/11/142224795/the-bonus-army-how-a-protest-led-to-the-gi-bill.

Bookstaber, Richard. Testimony before the Subcommittee on Investigations and Oversight, Committee on Science and Technology, U.S. House of Representatives, 111th Cong., Sept. 10, 2009. https://www.gpo.gov/fdsys/pkg/CHRG–111hhrg51925/html/CHRG–111hhrg51925.htm.

———. Testimony before the U.S. Senate Committee on Agriculture, Nutrition and Forestry. Regulatory Reform and the Derivatives Markets, June 4, 2009, http://rick.bookstaber.com/2009/06/my-senate-testimony-on-derivatives.html.

Bordelon, Brendan. "Elizabeth Warren's Wall Street Double Standard." *National Review,* Oct. 5, 2015, http://www.nationalreview.com/article/425063/elizabeth-warrens-wall-street-double-standard-brendan-bordelon.

Bordo, Michael D., Claudia Goldin, and Eugene N. White, eds. *The Defining Moment: The Great Depression and the American Economy in the Twentieth Century.* University of Chicago Press, 1998.

Bordo, Michael D., and Hugh Rockoff. "Not Just the Great Contraction: Friedman and Schwartz's *A Monetary History of the United States, 1867–1960.*" National Bureau of Economic Research, Feb. 2013, working paper 18828, http://www.nber.org/papers/w18828.pdf.

Born, Brooksley, and William Donaldson. "Self-Funding of Regulators Would Help Fiscal Mess." *Politico,* Mar. 10, 2013, https://www.systemicriskcouncil.org/2013/03/self-funding-of-regulators-would-help-fiscal-mess.

Bowers, John. "A Hedge Fund House Divided: Renaissance Technologies." OpenSecrets.org, June 7, 2016, https://www.opensecrets.org/news/2016/06/a-hedge-fund-house-divided-renaissance-technologies/.

Bradford, Hazel. "U.S. Agrees to Delay MetLife SIFI Designation Appeal." *Pensions & Investments,* May 5, 2017, http://www.pionline.com/article/20170505/ONLINE/170509889/us-agrees-to-delay-metlife-sifi-designation-appeal.

Bradley, Christine M. "A Historical Perspective on Deposit Insurance Coverage." Federal Deposit Insurance Corporation, Dec. 2000, https://www.fdic.gov/bank/analytical/banking/2000dec/brv13n2_1.pdf.

Brady Report: Report of the Presidential Task Force on Market Mechanisms, Submitted to the President of the United States, the Secretary of the Treasury, and the Chairman of the Federal Reserve Board, Jan. 1988. https://archive.org/details/reportofpresiden01unit.

Breslow, Jason. "Goldman Agrees to $5 Billion Deal over Faulty Mortgages." *Frontline,* Jan. 15, 2016, http://www.pbs.org/wgbh/frontline/article/goldman-agrees-to–5-billion-deal-over -faulty-mortgages/.

———. "Pioneer behind Credit Derivatives Is Leaving JPMorgan." *Frontline,* Apr. 3, 2014, http://www.pbs.org/wgbh/frontline/article/pioneer-behind-credit-derivatives-is- leaving-jpmorgan/.

———. "S&P to Pay $1.38 Billion for Once Rave Ravings of Toxic Mortgages." *Frontline,* Feb. 3, 2015, http://www.pbs.org/wgbh/frontline/article/s-p-to-pay-1-38-billion-for-once -rave-ratings-of-toxic-mortgages/.

Bricker, Jesse, et al. "Measuring Income and Wealth at the Top Using Administrative and Survey Data." Brookings Papers on Economic Activity, Spring 2016, https:// www.brookings.edu/wp-content/uploads/2016/03/BrickerEtAl_Measuring IncomeAndWealthAtTheTop_ConferenceDraft.pdf.

Briese, Steve. "Comment on *Barron's* Mr. & Mrs. Enron Story." CommitmentsofTraders.org, Mar. 29, 2008, http://commitmentsoftraders.org/28/what-you-didnt-read-in-the-barrons -cover-story/.

Briscoe v. Bank of the Commonwealth of Kentucky. http://www.oxfordreference.com/ view/10.1093/oi/authority.20110803095527835.

Bromwich, Jonah Engel. "The Wild Inauguration of Andrew Jackson, Trump's Populist Predecessor." *New York Times,* Jan. 20. 2017, https://www.nytimes.com/2017/01/20/us/ politics/donald-trump-andrew-jackson.html?_r=0.

Brooks, Rick, and Ruth Simon. "Subprime Debacle Traps Even Very Credit-Worthy." *Wall Street Journal,* Dec. 3, 2007, http://www.wsj.com/articles/SB119662974358911035.

Browne, Charles Farrar. *Artemus Ward in London, and Other Papers.* New York Printing Co., 1867.

Bruck, Connie. "Angelo's Ashes." *New Yorker,* June 29, 2009, http://www.newyorker.com/ magazine/2009/06/29/angelos-ashes.

Brumbaugh, Dan R., Jr., and Andrew S. Carron. "Thrift Industry Crisis: Causes and Solutions." *Brookings Papers on Economic Activity* 2 (1987), https://www.brookings.edu/ bpea-articles/thrift-industry-crisis-causes-and-solutions/.

Brush, Silla, and Robert Schmidt. "How the Bank Lobby Loosened U.S. Reins on Derivatives." *Bloomberg,* Sept. 4, 2013, http://www.bloomberg.com/news/articles/ 2013-09-04/how-the-bank-lobby-loosened-u-s-reins-on-derivatives.

Bryan, Alfred Cookman. *History of State Banking in Baltimore.* Johns Hopkins University Press, 1899.

Bryn, Michael. *The Great Inflation, 1965–1982.* Federal Reserve Bank of Atlanta, Nov. 22, 2013, https://www.federalreservehistory.org/essays/great_inflation.

"Bulls and Bears in a Wild Revel: Uproarious Fun on the Floor of the Stock Exchange." *New York Times*, Dec. 23, 1900.

Bureau of Economic Analysis. *Percentage Share of Gross Domestic Product.* https://bea. gov/iTable/iTable.cfm?reqid=9&step=3&isuri=1&904=1929&903=14&906=a&905=10 00&910=x&911=0#reqid=9&step=3&isuri=1&904=1929&903=14&906=a&905=1000 &910=x&911=0.

Bureau of Labor Statistics. CPI Inflation Calculator. http://www.bls.gov/data/inflation_ calculator.htm.

————. *The Recession of 2007–2009.* https://www.bls.gov/spotlight/2012/recession/pdf recession_bls_spotlight.pdf.

Burns, Helen M. *The American Banking Community and New Deal Banking Reforms: 1933–1935.* Greenwood Press, 1974.

Bush, George W. "President's Remarks to the National Association of Home Builders." *American Presidency Project,* Oct. 2, 2004, http://www.presidency.ucsb.edu/ws/?pid=64585.

"Bush Signs Stimulus Bill: Rebate Checks Expected in May." CNN, Feb. 13, 2008, http://www.cnn.com/2008/POLITICS/02/13/bush.stimulus/.

Butkiewicz, James L. *Routledge Handbook of Major Events in Economic History,* ed. Randall E. Parker and Robert M. Whaples. Routledge, 2013. Pp. 187–189.

Byrne, John Aidan. "Americans' Household Debt Has Surged by $605B This Year." *New York Post,* Nov. 26, 2017, https://nypost.com/2017/11/26/new-yorkers-household-debt-has-surged-by–605b-this-year/.

Calder, Lendol. *Financing the American Dream.* Princeton University Press, 1999.

Calkins, Laural Brubaker. "Enron's Skilling to Leave Prison in 2017 as Sentence Cut." *Bloomberg,* June 22, 2013, http://www.bloomberg.com/news/articles/2013-06-21/enrons-skilling-sentence-reduced-to–14-years-by-judge.

Calomiris, Charles W. *Banking Approaches the Modern Era.* American Enterprise Institute, July 2002, https://www.aei.org/publication/banking-approaches-the-modern-era/.

Calomiris, Charles, and Joseph R. Mason. *Causes of U.S. Bank Distress during the Depression.* National Bureau of Economic Research, working paper 7919, https://www.aei.org/wp-content/uploads/2011/10/20050817_w7919.pdf.

Calomiris, Charles, and Eugene N. White. *The Origins of Federal Deposit Insurance.* University of Chicago Press, 1994. This was also a chapter in National Bureau of Economic Research, *The Regulated Economy: A Historical Approach to Political Economy*, ed. Claudia Goldin and Gary D. Libecap (conference held May 20–21, 1993), http://www.nber.org/chapters/c6575.pdf. Pp. 145–188.

Campbell, Alexia Fernandez. "A Payday Lender Is Accused of Stealing Millions from Customers. Trump's CFPB Is Now Letting Them off the Hook." Vox.com, Apr. 20, 2018, https://www.vox.com/2018/4/20/17225564/mick-mulvaney-cfpb-payday-loan-cases.

Cannato, Vincent J. "A Home of One's Own." *National Affairs* 35 (Spring 2010), http://www.nationalaffairs.com/publications/detail/a-home-of-ones-own.

Capra, Frank, dir. *It's a Wonderful Life.* Liberty Films, 1946.

Carlson, Mark A., and Jonathan D. Rose. *Can a Bank Run Be Stopped? Government Guarantees and the Run on Continental Illinois.* Finance and Economics Discussion Series, 2016–003, Washington, DC, Board of Governors of the Federal Reserve System, http://dx.doi.org/10.17016/FEDS.2016.003.

Carney, John. "Jimmy Cayne Was Smoking Pot for Years and Years." *Business Insider,* May 12, 2009, http://www.businessinsider.com/jimmy-cayne-was-smoking-pot-for-years-and-years-2009-5.

Carpenter, David H., et al. *The Glass-Steagall Act: A Legal and Policy Analysis.* Congressional Research Service, Jan. 19, 2016.

Carter, Zach. "A Master of Disaster." *The Nation,* Dec. 16, 2009.

————. "Republican Nirvana: Congress Votes on Bill to Aid Wall Street Banks . . . and The Koch Brothers." *Huffington Post,* June 10, 2015.

Cassidy, John. "The Minsky Moment: Subprime Mortgage Crisis and Possible Recession." *New Yorker*, Feb. 4, 2008, https://www.newyorker.com/magazine/2008/02/04/the-minsky-moment.

Center for Public Integrity. *The Subprime 25.* May 6, 2009, https://www.publicintegrity.org/business/finance/whos-behind-financial-meltdown/subprime–25.

Center for Responsible Lending. *Net Drain: A Net Drain on Home Ownership.* CRL Issue Paper 14, Mar. 27, 2007, http://www.responsiblelending.org/mortgage-lending/research-analysis/Net-Drain-in-Home-Ownership.pdf.

Center for Responsive Politics. *Federal Campaign Contributions.* Opensecrets.org, https://www.opensecrets.org/overview/sectors.php?cycle=2016.

———. *Ranked Sectors, Lobbying.* Opensecrets.org, https://www.opensecrets.org/lobby/top.php?indexType=c&showYear=2016.

Chamber of Commerce et al. v. Secretary of Labor Tomas Perez et al. Civil action no. 3:16-cv–1476-M, challenging the Department of Labor's fiduciary rule, http://www.chamberlitigation.com/sites/default/files/cases/files/16161616/DOL%20Fiduciary%20Rule%20Complaint.pdf.

Chase, Samuel. *Report of the Secretary of the Treasury, on the Finances, Containing Estimates of the Public Revenue and Public Expenditures, and Plans for Improving and Increasing the Revenue.* July 1, 1861, https://fraser.stlouisfed.org/scribd/?item_id=5505&filepath=/docs/publications/treasar/AR_TREASURY_1861_2.pdf#scribd-open.

Chernow, Ron. *Alexander Hamilton.* Penguin, 2004.

———. *The House of Morgan.* Touchstone. 1990.

Childress, Sarah. "How Much Did the Financial Crisis Cost?" Frontline, May 31, 2012, http://www.pbs.org/wgbh/frontline/article/how-much-did-the-financial-crisis-cost/.

Cicio, Paul. Testimony, U.S. Senate, Permanent Subcommittee on Investigations of the Committee on Homeland Security and Governmental Affairs. Excessive Speculation in the Natural Gas Market, Hearings, June 25 and July 8 2007, https://www.hsgac.senate.gov/imo/media/doc/REPORTExcessiveSpeculationintheNaturalGasMarket.pdf,   and https://ia801901.us.archive.org/32/items/gov.gpo.fdsys.CHRG–110shrg36616/CHRG–110shrg36616.pdf.

Citigroup, Equity Strategy. "Plutonomy Memos." Oct. 16, 2005, Mar. 5, 2006, Sept. 29, 2006. https://pissedoffwoman.files.wordpress.com/2012/04/citigroup-plutonomy-report-part–1.pdf,   https://pissedoffwoman.files.wordpress.com/2012/04/citigroup-plutonomy-report-part–2.pdf,   https://pissedoffwoman.files.wordpress.com/2012/04/citigroup-plutonomy-report-part–3.pdf.

Cleveland, Harold van B., and Thomas F. Huertas. *Citibank, 1812–1970.* Harvard University Press, 1985.

CNN Enron Timeline. http://www.cnn.com/2013/07/02/us/enron-fast-facts/.

Coalition for Sensible Housing, American Bankers Association, et al. *Updated QRM Proposal Strikes Balance: Preserves Access while Safeguarding Consumers and Market.* Oct. 30, 2013, http://www.sensiblehousingpolicy.org/uploads/QRM_Rule_White_Paper_October_28_2013.pdf.

Cogley, Timothy. *Monetary Policy and the Great Crash of 1929: A Bursting Bubble or Collapsing Fundamentals?* Federal Reserve Bank of San Francisco, Economic Letter, Mar. 26, 1999,

http://www.frbsf.org/economic-research/publications/economic-letter/1999/march/
monetary-policy-and-the-great-crash-of–1929-a-bursting-bubble-or-collapsing-
fundamentals/.

Cohan, William D. "When Bankers Started Playing with Other People's Money." *Atlantic*,
Feb. 28, 2017, https://www.theatlantic.com/business/archive/2017/02/how-wall-street
-went-public/517419/.

Colton, Kent W. *Housing Finance in the United States: The Transformation of the U.S.
Housing System.* Joint Center for Housing Studies, Harvard University, W02–5, July
2002.

Commodity Futures Trading Commission. "Final Rule. A New Regulatory Framework for
Multilateral Transaction Execution Facilities, Intermediaries and Clearing Organizations;
Rules Relating to Intermediaries of Commodity Interest Transactions; A New Regulatory
Framework for Clearing Organizations; Exemption for Bilateral Transactions." *Federal
Register* 65, no. 240 (Dec. 13, 2000): 77961–77993, http://www.cftc.gov/foia/fedreg00/
foi001213b.htm.

"Condemned Men Get Reprieve on Account of Bank Holiday." *New York Times,* Mar. 12,
1933.

Confessore, Nicholas, et al. "The Families Funding the 2016 Presidential Election."
New York Times, Oct. 10, 2015, https://www.nytimes.com/interactive/2015/10/11/us/
politics/2016-presidential-election-super-pac-donors.html?_r=0.

———. "Data Mining Scandal Deals Blow to Clout of Billionaire Donors." *New York Times,*
Apr. 11, 2016.

———. "A Wealthy Few Lead in Giving to Campaigns: Nearly Half of Money from 400
Families." *New York Times,* Aug. 2, 2015, https://www.nytimes.com/2015/08/02/us/
small-pool-of-rich-donors-dominates-election-giving.html.

Congressional Budget Office. *Fannie Mae, Freddie Mac, and the Federal Role in the
Secondary Mortgage Market.* Dec. 2010, https://www.cbo.gov/sites/default/files/111th-
congress–2009-2010/reports/12-23-fanniefreddie.pdf.

———. *Housing Wealth and Consumer Spending.* Jan. 2007, https://www.cbo.gov/sites/
default/files/110th-congress-2007-2008/reports/01-05-housing.pdf.

Congressional Research Service. *Costs of Major U.S. Wars.* 2010, https://www.fas.org/sgp/
crs/natsec/RS22926.pdf.

Connor, John, and Bruce Knecht. "Bankers Trust Facing Action on Derivatives." *Wall Street
Journal,* Dec. 5, 1994.

Consumer Financial Protection Bureau. "CFPB Issues Rule to Ban Companies from Using
Arbitration Clauses to Deny Groups of People Their Day in Court." *CFBP Newsroom,*
July 10, 2017, https://www.consumerfinance.gov/about-us/blog/weve-issued-new-rule-arbitration-
help-groups-people-take-companies-court/.

———. "We've Issued a New Rule on Arbitration to Help Groups of People Take Companies
to Court." Blog entry, July 10, 2017,
https://www.consumerfinance.gov/about-us/newsroom/cfpb-issues-rule-ban-companies-using-
arbitration-clauses-deny-groups-people-their-day-court/.

Copley, Ronald E. "Impact of the Economic Recovery Tax Act of 1981 on Real Estate Tax
Shelters," *Real Estate Issues* (Spring/Summer 1982).

Cordery, S. *British Friendly Societies, 1750–1914.* Palgrave Macmillan, 2003.

Cornwell, Rupert. "If I Made Myself Clear, You Must Have Misunderstood Me." *Independent,* July 13, 1996, http://www.independent.co.uk/news/business/if-ive-made-myself-too-clear-you-must-have-misunderstood-me–1328606.html.

Corrigan, Gerald. *Federal Reserve Bank of New York, 72nd Annual Report, for the Year Ended Dec. 31, 1986.* In author's possession.

———. *Meeting the Challenges of a New Banking Era.* Jan. 1, 1982, https://www.minne apolisfed.org/publications/annual-reports/meeting-the-challenges-of-a-new-banking-era.

The Cost of the Crisis: $20 Trillion and Counting. Better Markets, https://www.bettermar kets.com/costofthecrisis.

Cowen, David Jack. *The Origins and Economic Impact of the First Bank of the United States, 1791–1797.* Garland Publishing, 2000.

Cowley, Stacy. "With Trump's Signature, Dozens of Obama's Rules Could Fall." *New York Times,* Nov. 15, 2016, https://www.nytimes.com/2016/11/16/business/with-trumps-signature-obamas-rules-could-fall.html.

Cox, Christopher. *Testimony Concerning the Role of Federal Regulators: Lessons from the Credit Crisis for the Future of Regulation.* Committee on Oversight and Government Reform, U.S. House of Representatives, Oct. 23, 2008, https://www.sec.gov/news/testi mony/2008/ts102308cc.htm.

"The Crash of 1929." *American Experience.* PBS, 1990, http://www.pbs.org/video/american-experience-the-crash-of–1929.

Crawford, Krysten. "Ex-Tyco CEO Kozlowski Found Guilty." CNN, June 17, 2005, http:// money.cnn.com/2005/06/17/news/newsmakers/tyco_trialoutcome/.

Crouhy, Michel G., et al. *The Subprime Credit Crisis of '07.* Sept. 12, 2007, revised July 4, 2008, https://www.fdic.gov/bank/analytical/cfr/bank-research-conference/annual–8th/turnbull-jarrow.pdf.

Curry, Timothy, and Lynn Shibut. "The Cost of the Savings and Loan Crisis: Truth and Consequences." *FDIC Banking Review* 13, no. 2 (2000), https:// www.fdic.gov/bank/ analytical/banking/2000dec/brv13n2_2.pdf.

Damato, Karen. "Trump Advisor Uses Terrible Food Analogy to Defend Financial Deregulation." *Time,* Feb. 3, 2017, http://time.com/money/4659485/trump-advisor-uses-terrible-food-analogy -to-defend-financial-deregulation/.

Devine, Curt et al. "How Steve Bannon Used Cambridge Analytica to Further his Alt-Right Vision for America." CNN, March 31, 2018. https://www.cnn.com/2018/03/30/politics/ bannon-cambridge-analytica/index.html

"Damnation of Charles Mitchell." *Time.* Mar. 6, 1933, p. 53.

Darby, Mary. "In Ponzi We Trust." *Smithsonian,* Dec. 1998, https://www.smithsonianmag. com/history/in-ponzi-we-trust–64016168/.

Davidoff, Steven M. "A Partnership Solution for Investment Banks?" *New York Times.* Aug. 20, 2008, https://dealbook.nytimes.com/2008/08/20/a-partnership-solution-for-investment -banks/?_r=0.

Davis, Andrew McFarland. *The Origin of the National Banking System.* National Monetary Commission, 2nd sess., 61st Cong. U.S. Government Printing Office, 1910.

DavisPolk. *Summary of the Dodd-Frank Wall Street Reform and Consumer Protection Act,* July 21, 2010.

Day, Kathleen. "Analysis: Credit Agencies Remain Unaccountable." *USA Today,* May 19, 2014,http://www.usatoday.com/story/money/business/2014/05/19/credit-rating-agencies-in-limbo/9290143/.

———. "Banking Accord Likely to Be Law." *Washington Post,* Oct. 23, 1999.

———. "Banks Incur Record Losses on Derivatives." *Washington Post,* Dec. 19, 1998.

———. "Brokerage Settlement Leaves Much Unresolved: SEC Acknowledges Need for New, Specific Rules." *Washington Post,* Apr. 30, 2003.

———. "Chief U.S. Bank Regulator Will Step Down." *Washington Post,* Sept. 10, 2004.

———. "Citicorp Inches toward Nationwide Network." *Washington Post,* June 18, 1986.

———. "The Fight over Protecting Retirement Savings." Ozy.com, Oct. 27, 2014 (updated in 2015), http://www.ozy.com/fast-forward/the-fight-over-protecting-retirement-savings/36788.

———. "Former Fannie Mae CFO Joins Debate on Its Future." *USA Today,* Jan. 27, 2014, http://www.usatoday.com/story/money/business/2014/01/27/former-fannie-mae-cfo-mortgage-wars/4773547/.

———. "Gutfreund Silent at July Meeting." *Washington Post,* Aug. 29, 1991.

———. "How a Phone Call Set the Rescue Effort into Motion." *Washington Post,* Oct. 2, 1998.

———. "Merrill's Fight for Bank Reform: Industry Insiders Say Firm Was Worried about Its Survival." *Washington Post,* Oct. 16, 1998.

———. "Piggy Banker?" *Washington Post,* Feb. 12, 2006, http://www.washingtonpost.com/wp-dyn/content/article/2006/02/11/AR2006021100252.html.

———. "Probe Examining Fannie's Promises." *Washington Post,* Sept. 4, 2004, http://www.washingtonpost.com/wp-dyn/articles/A43161-2004Sep22.html.

———. "Ruling Grants Commercial Banks Some Investment Banking Powers." *Washington Post,* July 8, 1987.

———. *S&L Hell: The People and the Politics behind the $1 Trillion Savings and Loan Scandal.* W.W. Norton & Co., 1993.

———. "Salomon Suspends Two Traders in Bond Market Probe." *Washington Post,* Aug. 10, 1991.

———. "Sarbanes Delays Banking Nomination." *Washington Post,* Oct. 28, 1998.

———. "'Shaky Ground' Exposes Zombie Side of Freddie, Fannie." *USA Today,* Oct. 20, 2015, http://www.usatoday.com/story/money/2015/10/20/book-review-shaky-ground-exposes-zombie-side-freddie-fannie/74237976/.

———. "Study Finds 'Extensive' Fraud at Fannie Mae: Bonuses Allegedly Drove the Scheme." *Washington Post,* May 24, 2006.

———. "Thrift Is the Word: Thrifts Rush for Charters to Sell Banking Services, Avoid Bank Regulations." *Washington Post,* Dec. 13, 1998.

———."Top Salomon Executives to Resign; Major Investor Warren Buffett Is to Take Charge Temporarily." *Washington Post,* Aug. 17, 1991.

———. "Villains in the Mortgage Mess? Start at Wall Street. Keep Going." *Washington Post,* June 1, 2008. http://www.washingtonpost.com/wp-dyn/content/article/2008/05/30/AR2008053002568_pf.html.

———. "Violations Detailed by Salomon." *Washington Post,* Aug. 15, 1991.

———. "A Wall Street Giant Shaken." *Washington Post,* Aug. 16, 1991.

———. "Wal-Mart Defends Its Bid to Enter Banking." *Washington Post,* Apr. 11, 2006, http://www.washingtonpost.com/wp-dyn/content/article/2006/04/10/AR2006041001594. html.

———. "White House to Urge New Rules for Hedge Funds." *Washington Post,* Apr. 29, 1991.

———. "With Depression-Era Law about to Be Rewritten, the Future Remains Unclear." *Washington Post,* Oct. 31, 1999.

Day, Kathleen, and Caroline Mayer. "Credit Card Penalties, Fees Bury Debtors." *Washington Post,* Mar. 6, 2005, http://www.washingtonpost.com/wp-dyn/content/article/2005/03/25/ AR2005032502675.html.

Day, Kathleen, and Annys Shin. "Fannie to Settle Charges, Pay Fine." *Washington Post,* May 23, 2006.

———. "Freddie Settles Investor Lawsuits." *Washington Post,* Apr. 21, 2006.

Day, Kathleen, and Susan Schmidt. "U.S. to Probe Enron Tie to Energy Prices; Senators from West Voice Concern about Alleged Manipulation." *Washington Post,* Jan. 30, 2002.

Dayen, David. "Donald Trump's Executive Order Will Let Private Equity Funds Drain Your 401K." *Intercept,* Feb. 6, 2017, https://theintercept.com/2017/02/06/donald-trumps -executive-order-will-let-private-equity-funds-drain-your-401k/.

———. "Mnuchin Lied about His Bank's History of Robosigning." *Intercept,* Jan. 25, 2017, https://theintercept.com/2017/01/25/mnuchin-lied-about-his-banks-history-of-robo- signing-foreclosure-documents/AP.

Deaton, Angus. "It's Not Just Unfair: Inequality Is a Threat to Our Governance." *New York Times,* Mar. 20, 2017, https://www.nytimes.com/2017/03/20/books/review/crisis-of-the- middle-class-constitution-ganesh-sitaraman-.html.

Delgadillo, Lucy M., et al. "Disentangling the Difference between Abusive and Predatory Lending: Professionals' Perspectives." *Journal of Consumer Affairs* 42, no. 3 (Fall 2008): 313, http://www05.usu.edu/today/pdf/2008/october/itn1002085.pdf.

"Derivatives: Over the Counter, Out of Sight." *Economist,* Nov. 12, 2009.

DeSilver, Drew. *U.S. Income Inequality, on Rise for Decades, Is Now Highest since 1928.* Pew Research, Dec. 5, 2013.

De Tocqueville, Alexis. *Democracy in America,* vol. 2, ed. Eduardo Nolla. Liberty Fund, Inc. 2010, http://classiques.uqac.ca/classiques/De_tocqueville_alexis/democracy_in_america_ historical_critical_ed/democracy_in_america_vol_2.pdf.

Dewey, Davis Rich, and Martin Joseph Shugrue. *Banking and Credit: A Textbook for Colleges and Schools of Business Administration.* Ronald Press Co., 1922.

Dillistin, William H. *Bank Note Reporters and Counterfeit Detectors, 1826–1866.* Numismatic Notes and Monographs, no. 114. New York: American Numismatic Society, 1949.

Dimitri, Carolyn, Anne Effland, and Conklin Neilson. *The 20th Century Transformation of U.S. Agriculture and Farm Policy.* U.S. Department of Agriculture, Economic Research Service, *Economic Information Bulletin,* no. 3 (2005), http://www.ers.usda.gov/ media/259572/eib3_1_.pdf.

"The Dinner Table Bargain, June 1790." *American Experience.* PBS, n.d., http://www.pbs. org/wgbh/amex/hamilton/peopleevents/e_dinner.html dinner deal on potomac and debt assumption.

Do Class Actions Benefit Members? An Empirical Analysis of Class Actions. Chamber of
    Commerce, Institute for Legal Reform, 2013, http://www.instituteforlegalreform.com/
    uploads/sites/1/Class_Action_Study.pdf.

Dodd, Randall. *Industrial Loan Banks: Regulatory Loopholes as Big as a Wal-Mart*
    Financial Policy Center, Special Policy Report 13 (Mar. 2006), http://www.financial
    policy.org/fpfspr13.pdf.

Dodd-Frank Act of 2010. 111th Cong., 1st sess., U.S. Government Printing Office, 2010,
    https://www.congress.gov/bill/111th-congress/house-bill/4173.

"Down in the Dumps." *Economist,* Feb. 26, 2009, http://www.economist.com/node/
    13135413.

Dugan, John. *Statement before the Financial Crisis Inquiry Commission.* Apr. 8, 2010,
    https://www.gpo.gov/fdsys/pkg/GPO-FCIC/pdf/GPO-FCIC.pdf.

Ebling, Ashlea. "Texas Court Ruling Backs DOL Fiduciary Rule Despite Trump and DOJ
    Appeal for Delay." *Forbes,* Feb. 9, 2017, http://www.forbes.com/sites/ashleaebeling/
    2017/02/09/texas-court-ruling-backs-dol-fiduciary-rule-despite-trump-and-doj-appeal-
    for-delay/#7cf38bc06a8.

"The East India Company." *Economist,* Dec. 11, 2011, http://www.economist.com/
    node/21541753.

"*The Economist* Explains: Thomas Piketty's 'Capital,' Summarized in Four Paragraphs."
    Economist, May 4, 2014.

Eichengreen, Barry. *Hall of Mirrors: The Great Depression, the Great Recession, and the
    Uses—and Misuses—of History.* Oxford University Press, 2015.

Eichengreen, Barry, and Peter Temin. *The Gold Standard and the Great Depression.* National
    Bureau of Economic Research, Working Paper no. 6060, June 1997, http://www.nber.org/
    papers/w6060.pdf.

Eisinger, Jesse. "Why Haven't Bankers Been Punished? Just Read These Insider SEC Emails."
    ProPublica, Apr. 21, 2016, https://www.propublica.org/article/why-havent-bankers
    -been-punished-just-read-these-insider-sec-emails.

El Issa, Erin., *2017 American Household Credit Card Debt Study.* Nerd Wallet, Dec. 2017,
    https://www.nerdwallet.com/blog/average-credit-card-debt-household/.

Ellis, Joseph J. *The Quartet: Orchestrating the Second American Revolution, 1783–1789.*
    First Vintage Books, 2016.

Ely, Bert. "The Savings and Loan Crisis." In *The Concise Encyclopedia of Economics,* 2nd
    ed., ed. David R. Henderson, http://www.econlib.org/library/Enc/SavingsandLoanCrisis.
    html.

"Embarrassed Giant: How Bank of America Took $37 Million Bath in a Mortgage Scheme—
    It Was Escrow Agent in Deal Arranged by Two Felons; Some Directors in Dark—the
    Demise of Oxford Court—A *Wall Street Journal* News Roundup." *Wall Street Journal,*
    Feb. 4, 1985.

Emergency Economic Stabilization Act of 2008. https://www.congress.gov/110/plaws/
    publ343/PLAW-110publ343.pdf.

Engel, Katherine, and Patricia McCoy. *The Subprime Virus: Reckless Credit, Regulatory
    Failure and Next Steps.* Oxford University Press, 2016.

"Enron Created Fake Trading Room." *BBC News,* Feb. 21, 2002, http://news.bbc.co.uk/2/hi/
    business/1833221.stm.

Erlanger, Steven. "Taking on Adam Smith (and Karl Marx)." *New York Times,* Apr. 19, 2014, https://www.nytimes.com/2014/04/20/business/international/taking-on-adam-smith-and-karl-marx.html.

"Establishing a National Bank." *American Experience,* PBS, http://www.pbs.org/wgbh/amex/hamilton/peopleevents/e_bank.html.

Everts, Sarah. *How Advertisers Convinced Americans They Smelled Bad.* Smithsonian.com, Aug. 2, 2012, http://www.smithsonianmag.com/history/how-advertisers-convinced-americans-they-smelled-bad–12552404/?no-ist.

Fang, Lee. "Emails Reveal Coziness between Lobbyists and Regulators." *Intercept*, June 12, 2015.

———. *Report: How Koch Industries Makes Billions by Demanding Bailouts and Taxpayer Subsidies.* ThinkProgress, Mar. 1, 2011, https://thinkprogress.org/report-how-koch-industries-makes-billions-by-demanding-bailouts-and-taxpayer-subsidies-part-1-6c9653356142.

"Fannie Mae and Freddie Mac." Legal Information Institute, Cornell Law School, https://www.law.cornell.edu/uscode/text/12/24.

"Farm Groups Urge Deposits Guarantee." *New York Times,* Mar. 10, 1933.

Faux, Zeke, and Laura Keller. "Wells Fargo CEO Stumpf Quits in Fallout from Fake Accounts." *Bloomberg,* Oct. 12, 2016, https://www.bloomberg.com/news/articles/2016-10-12/wells-fargo-ceo-stumpf-steps-down-in-fallout-from-fake-accounts.

"FDR Message to Congress, 1934, on Introduction of the Commodity Exchange Act." *Time*, June 29, 1936, http://content.time.com/time/magazine/article/0,9171,770228,00.html.

Federal Deposit Insurance Corporation. "Banking Crises of the 1980s and Early 1990s." *FDIC Banking Review* 11, no. 1 (1998), https://www.fdic.gov/bank/analytical/banking/brspecial.pdf.

———. *A Brief History of Deposit Insurance in the United States.* https://www.fdic.gov/bank/historical/brief/brhist.pdf.

———. *Case Study of Continental Illinois.* https://www.fdic.gov/bank/historical/managing/history2-04.pdf.

———. *The First Fifty Years, 1933–1983.* https://www.fdic.gov/bank/analytical/firstfifty/chapter3.pdf.

———. *Improvement Act of 1991.* https://www.fdic.gov/regulations/laws/rules/8000-2400.html.

———. *Managing the Crisis: The FDIC and RTC Experience.* Aug. 1998. Vols. 1 and 2 and overview: https://www.fdic.gov/bank/historical/managing/; full text: https://babel.hathitrust.org/cgi/pt?id=mdp.39015043145542;page=root;seq=1;view=plaintext;size=100;orient=0; table of contents: https://www.fdic.gov/bank/historical/managing/contents.pdf; chronological overview: https://www.fdic.gov/bank/historical/managing/Chron/pre-fdic/.

———. *Managing the Crisis: The FDIC and RTC Experience.* Vol. 1: History; Part II Chapter 3, "Penn Square Bank," pp. 527–542, https://www.fdic.gov/bank/historical/managing/documents/history-consolidated.pdf.

———. *The Savings and Loan Crisis and Its Relationship to Banking.* https://www.fdic.gov/bank/historical/history/167_188.pdf.

———. *Study on History of the 1980s.* https://www.fdic.gov/bank/historical/history/vol1.html.

———. *Timeline of Banking.* https://www.fdic.gov/about/history/timeline/.

Federal Housing Finance Agency. *Annual Report to Congress, 2009.* http://ccc.sites.unc.edu/ files/2013/02/FannieFreddieForeclosure.pdf.

———. *Conforming Loan Limits.* https://www.fhfa.gov/Media/PublicAffairs/Pages/FHFA -Announces-Increase-in-Maximum-Conforming-Loan-Limits-for-Fannie-Mae-and-Fred die-Mac-in–2017.aspx.

———. *Conservatorship of Fannie Mae and Freddie Mac.* Nov. 7, 2008, https://www.fhfa. gov/Media/PublicAffairs/Pages/Conservatorship-of-Fannie-Mae-and-Freddie-Mac.aspx.

———. *Data on the Risk Characteristics and Performance of Single-Family Mortgages Originated from 2001 through 2008 and Financed in the Secondary Market.* Sept. 13, 2010, https://www.fhfa.gov/PolicyProgramsResearch/Research/PaperDocuments/20100913_ RP_DataRiskPerformance_2001-2008_508.pdf.

Federal Housing Finance Agency, Office of the Inspector General. *A Brief History of the Housing Government-Sponsored Enterprises.* http://fhfaoig.gov/Content/Files/History% 20of%20the%20Government%20Sponsored%20Enterprises.pdf.

Federal National Mortgage Association. *Record.* National Archives, http://www.archives. gov/research/guide-fed-records/groups/294.html.

Federal Reserve Act: Public Law 63-43, 63d Cong., H.R. 7837. An Act to Provide for the Establishment of Federal Reserve Banks, to Furnish an Elastic Currency, to Afford Means of Rediscounting Commercial Paper, to Establish a More Effective Supervision of Banking in the United States, and for Other Purposes. https://fraser.stlouisfed.org/scribd/?title_ id=966&filepath=/docs/historical/fr_act/nara-dc_rg011_e005b_pl63-43.pdf.

Federal Reserve Bank of Boston. *Credit History: The Evolution of Consumer Credit in America.* https://www.bostonfed.org/education/ledger/ledger04/sprsum/credhistory.pdf.

———. Depository Institutions Deregulation and Monetary Control Act of 1980.

Federal Reserve Bank of Kansas. *Balance of Power: The Political Fight for an Independent Central Bank.* https://www.kansascityfed.org/publicat/balanceofpower/balanceofpower. pdf.

———. *Economic Policy Symposium Proceedings.* https://www.kansascityfed.org/publica tions/research/escp.

Federal Reserve Bank of Minneapolis. *The Bank that Hamilton Built.* https://www.minne apolisfed.org/publications/the-region/the-bank-that-hamilton-built.

Federal Reserve Bank of New York. *Federal Funds Data.* https://apps.newyorkfed.org/ markets/autorates/fed%20funds.

———. *Primary Dealers.* https://www.newyorkfed.org/markets/primarydealers.

Federal Reserve Bank of New York, Center for Microeconomic Data. *Household Debt and Credit.* https://www.newyorkfed.org/microeconomics/hhdc/background.html (see fourth quarter 2017).

———. *Quarterly Report on Household Debt and Credit.* Feb. 2018, https://www. newyorkfed.org/medialibrary/interactives/householdcredit/data/pdf/HHDC_2017Q4. pdf.

Federal Reserve Bank of Philadelphia. *The First Bank of the United States.* https://www. philadelphiafed.org/-/media/publications/economic-education/first-bank.pdf.

———. *The Second Bank of the United States.* https://www.philadelphiafed.org/results?sort =rel&start=0&text=The+state+and national+bank+eras.

————. *The State and National Banking Eras.* https://www.philadelphiafed.org/-/media/publications/economic-education/state-and-national-banking-eras.pdf.

Federal Reserve Bank of Richmond. *Failure of Continental Illinois.* May 1984, http://www.federalreservehistory.org/Events/DetailView/47.

————. *Gold and Silver.* https://www.richmondfed.org/faqs/gold_silver.

Federal Reserve Bank of San Francisco. *Federal Reserve Discount Window Rates.* http://www.frbsf.org/banking/discount-window/discount-rate.

————. *Is the Federal Reserve a Privately Owned Corporation?* http://www.frbsf.org/education/publications/doctor-econ/2003/september/private-public-corporation/.

Federal Reserve Bank of St. Louis. *Effective Federal Funds Rate.* https://fred.stlouisfed.org/series/FEDFUNDS.

————. *Timeline of the Financial Crisis.* https://www.stlouisfed.org/financial-crisis/full-timeline.

Federal Reserve Board. *Banking and Monetary Statistics, 1914–1941.* https://fraser.stlouisfed.org/docs/publications/bms/1914-1941/BMS14-41_complete.pdf.

————. *Federal Reserve Bulletin.* Mar. 1927, https://fraser.stlouisfed.org/scribd/?item_id=20663&filepath=/files/docs/publications/FRB/1920s/frb_031927.pdf.

————. *Federal Reserve Bulletin.* Sept. 1937, https://fraser.stlouisfed.org/files/docs/publications/FRB/1930s/frb_091937.pdf.

————. "Final Rule Mandating Assessing Ability to Repay." July 14, 2008, https://www.federalreserve.gov/newsevents/press/bcreg/20080714a.htm.

————. "Latin American Debt Crisis of the 1980s." http://www.federalreservehistory.org/Events/DetailView/46.

————. "Outstanding Household Debt in Aggregate, 1981–2015." http://www.federalreserve.gov/releases/z1/current/z1r–2.pdf.

————. "The Panic of 1907." Dec. 2015, http://www.federalreservehistory.org/Events/PrintView/97.

————. "Report on the Economic Well-Being of U.S. Households in 2015." May 2016, https://www.federalreserve.gov/2015-report-economic-well-being-us-households–201605.pdf.

————. "The Stock Market Crash of 1929." http://www.federalreservehistory.org/Events/DetailView/74.

————. "Who Owns the Federal Reserve?" https://www.federalreserve.gov/faqs/about_14986.htm.

Federal Reserve Board et al. *Joint Report on Retail Swaps.* Dec. 2001, https://www.treasury.gov/resource-center/fin-mkts/Documents/rss-final.pdf.

Federal Reserve Board of Governors. "Federal Reserve to Implement Consumer Compliance Supervision Program of Nonbank Subsidiaries of Bank Holding Companies and Foreign. Banking Organizations." Press release, Sept. 15, 2009, https://www.federalreserve.gov/newsevents/pressreleases/bcreg20090915a.htm.

Federal Reserve Board of Governors. "Federal Reserve Issues Final Rule to Repeal Regulation Q." Press release, July 14, 2011.

Federal Reserve Board of Governors. "Consumer Credit Outstanding." https://www.federalreserve.gov/releases/g19/hist/cc_hist_sa_levels.html.

————. *Report to the Congress on Practices of the Consumer Credit Industry in Soliciting and Extending Credit and Their Effects on Consumer Debt and Insolvency.* June 2006, https://www.federalreserve.gov/boarddocs/rptcongress/bankruptcy/bankruptcybill study200606.pdf.

———. "Survey of Consumer Finances." https://www.federalreserve.gov/econres/scfindex.htm.

Federal Reserve Board of Governors, Division of Consumer and Community Affairs. "Policy of Not Routinely Conducting Consumer Compliance Examinations." Jan. 20, 1998, https://www.federalreserve.gov/boarddocs/caletters/1998/9801/caltr9801.htm.

Federal Reserve System. *Changes in the Number and Size of Banks in the United States, 1834–1931*. Material prepared for the information of the Federal Reserve System by the Federal Reserve Committee on Branch, Group, and Chain Banking, https://fraser.stlou isfed.org/scribd/?title_id=804&filepath=/docs/historical/federal%20reserve%20history/ frcom_br_gp_ch_banking/changes_in_banks.pdf#scribd-open.

Federal Reserve System, Committee on Branch, Group and Chain Banking. *The Dual Banking System in the United States: 1935.* https://fraser.stlouisfed.org/files/docs/historical/federal% 20reserve%20history/frcom_br_gp_ch_banking/dual_banking_system_us.pdf.

Felsenfeld, Carl, and David L. Glass. *Banking Regulation in the United States,* 3rd ed. Juris Publishing, 2011.

Financial Crisis Inquiry Commission. *The Financial Crisis Inquiry Report.* Jan. 2011, https://www.gpo.gov/fdsys/pkg/GPO-FCIC/pdf/GPO-FCIC.pdf.

———. "Too Big to Fail." Sept. 2, 2010, hearing, https://fcic-static.law.stanford.edu/cdn_ media/fcic-testimony/2010-0902-Transcript.pdf.

"Financial Crisis Timeline: What the Fed Did." Bankrate.com, Sept. 17, 2015. https://www. bankrate.com/finance/federal-reserve/financial-crisis-timeline.aspx.

"Financial Reform: Trust Us." *Economist,* Apr. 15, 2010, http://www.economist.com/blogs/ freeexchange/2010/04/financial_reform.

"Financial Regulation—A Post-Crisis Perspective." Brookings Institution Forum, Nov. 14, 2017, https://www.brookings.edu/events/financial-regulation-a-post-crisis-perspective/.

Fishback, Price. "The Real Facts about the Original Home Owners' Loan Corporation (and What They Mean for a Modern Incarnation)." *Freakonomics*, Oct. 17, 2008, http://freako nomics.com/2008/10/17/economist-price-fishback-the-real-facts-about-the- original-home-owners-loan-corporation-and-what-they-mean-for-a-modern-incarnation/.

Fishbein, Alan. "Going Subprime: Will Low-Income Homebuyers Gain or Lose When Fannie Mae and Freddie Mac Move into the Subprime Lending Market?" *Shelterforce* (National Housing Institute) 125 (Sept./Oct. 2002), http://www.nhi.org/online/issues/125/ goingsubprime.html.

Fisher, Irving. "The Debt-Deflation Theory of Great Depressions." *Econometrica* 1, no. 4 (Oct. 1933): 337–357, http://www.jstor.org/stable/1907327.

"500 Farmers Storm Arkansas Town Demanding Food for Their Children." *New York Times,* Jan. 4, 1931.

Flanigan, James. "Enron Is Proving Costly to Economy." *Los Angeles Times,* Jan. 20, 2002, http://webcache.googleusercontent.com/search?q=cache:3zGgEnq3COwJ: articles.latimes.com/2002/jan/20/news/mn–23790+&cd=3&hl=en&ct=clnk&gl=usE nron%20Is.

Flint Hill Resources. *Lobbying for Koch Industries.* OpenSecrets.org., 2008, 2009, https:// www.opensecrets.org/lobby/firmbills.php?id=D000021216.

"Floating Brokers." *Time*, Aug. 12, 1929.

Flood, Mark D. "The Great Deposit Insurance Debate." *Federal Reserve Bank of St. Louis* (July–Aug. 1992), https://research.stlouisfed.org/publications/review/92/07/Deposit_Jul_Aug1992.pdf.

Foroohar, Rana. "Investment Banking: Too Many Businesses Want a Piece of the Financial Action." *Financial Times,* May 15, 2016, https://www.ft.com/content/ed421ea4-1925-11e6-b197-a4af20d5575e.

Foster, J. D. "Chambers Regalia Puts Microscope on Federal Reserve's Regulatory Approach." https://www.uschamber.com/above-the-fold/chambers-regalia-puts-microscope-federal-reserve-s-regulatory-approach.

Fowler, Thomas. "No Criminal Charges against Enron's Board Members." *Houston Chronicle,* July 8, 2004, http://www.seattlepi.com/business/article/No-criminal-charges-are-expected-against-Enron-s-1148994.php.

Fox, Justin. "Honesty Doesn't Pay but It Sure Has Its Uses." *Harvard Business Review,* May 19, 2010.

Frame, Scott W., et al. *The Rescue of Fannie Mae and Freddie Mac.* Federal Reserve Bank of New York, staff report 719, Mar. 2015.

Fraser, Steve. *Every Man a Speculator: A History of Wall Street in American Life.* Harper Perennial, 2005.

Freed, Dan. "Wells Fargo Uncovers More Fake Accounts in Drawn-Out Scandal." Reuters, Aug. 31, 2017, https://www.reuters.com/article/us-wells-fargo-accounts/wells-fargo-uncovers-more-fake-accounts-in-drawn-out-scandal-idUSKCN1BB1QF.

Freeman, Richard B., and Joseph Blasi. "What the Founding Fathers Believed: Stock Ownership for All." *PBS News Hour,* Nov. 15, 2013, http://www.pbs.org/newshour/making-sense/what-the-founding-fathers-beli/.

Foner, Eric, and John A. Garraty, eds. *The Reader's Companion to American History.* Houghton Mifflin Harcourt, 1991.

"Frederick Winslow Taylor." *Who Made America?* PBS, http://www.pbs.org/wgbh/theymadeamerica/whomade/taylor_hi.html.

Frenk, David, and Wallace Turbeville. "Commodity Index Traders and Boom/Bust in Commodities Prices." Better Markets, Oct. 14, 2011, https://bettermarkets.com/sites/default/files/Better%20Markets-%20Commodity%20Index%20Traders%20and%20Boom-Bust%20in%20Commodities%20Prices.pdf.

Frieden, Terry. "FBI Warns of Mortgage Fraud 'Epidemic,' Seeks to Head Off 'Next S&L Crisis.'" CNN, Sept. 17, 2004, http://www.cnn.com/2004/LAW/09/17/mortgage.fraud/.

Friedman, Milton, and Anna Jacobson Schwartz. *A Monetary History of the United States, 1867–1960.* Princeton University Press, 1963.

Friedman, Thomas. "Did You Hear the One about the Banker?" *New York Times,* Oct. 30, 2011, http://www.nytimes.com/2011/10/30/opinion/sunday/friedman-did-you-hear-the-one-about-the-bankers.html.

Fromson, Brett D., and Jerry Knight. "The Saving of Citibank." *Washington Post,* May 16, 1993, https://www.washingtonpost.com/archive/politics/1993/05/16/the-saving-of-citibank/64323ac1-db21-43e4-b89e-a3171324c202/.

Galbraith, John Kenneth. *The Great Crash: 1929.* Houghton Mifflin Harcourt, 2009.

———. *Money: Whence It Came, Where It Went.* Penguin, 1976.

———. *A Short History of Financial Euphoria.* Penguin, 1993.

Gallatin, Albert. *The Writings of Albert Gallatin*, ed. Henry Adams. J.B. Lippincott, 1879.

Galston, William A. *Why the 2005 Social Security Initiative Failed, and What It Means for the Future.* Brookings, Sept. 21, 2007, https://www.brookings.edu/research/why-the-2005-social-security-initiative-failed-and-what-it-means-for-the-future/.

Gandel, Stephen. "Wells Fargo Exec Who Headed Phony Accounts Unit Collected $125 Million." *Fortune*, Sept. 12, 2016, http://fortune.com/2016/09/12/wells-fargo-cfpb-carrie-tolstedt/.

Geiger, Keri, et al. "Countrywide's Mozilo Off Hook as U.S. Said to Abandon Suit." *Bloomberg,* June 17, 2006, https://www.bloomberg.com/news/articles/2016-06-17/countrywide-s-mozilo-off-the-hook-as-a-u-s-said-to-abandon-suit.

Geisst, Charles. *Wall Street: A History.* Oxford University Press, 2012.

Geithner, Timothy. *Stress Test.* Broadway Books, 2014.

General Accounting Office. *The Commodity Exchange Act.* May 1999, https://www.gao.gov/assets/230/227199.pdf.

———. *Financial Audit, Resolution Trust Corporation's 1995 and 1994 Financial Statements.* July 1996, GAO/AIMD-96-123.

———. *Financial Crisis Management: Four Financial Crises in the 1980s.* GAO/GGD-97-96 (May 1997).

———. *Large Bank Mergers: Fair Lending Review Could Be Enhanced with Better Coordination.* GAO/GGD-00-16 (Nov. 1999).

———. *Report to Senators Byron L. Dorgan, Tom Harkin and Harry Reid and Rep. Edward J. Markey on Long-Term Capital.* GAO/GGD-00-3 (Oct. 29, 1999), B-281371, Long-Term Capital Management.

General Motors Acceptance Corporation. "History." https://history.gmheritagecenter.com/wiki/index.php/General_Motors_Acceptance_Corporation_(GMAC).

Gensler, Gary. Testimony before the House Financial Services Committee. May 24, 2000, https://archives-financialservices.house.gov/banking/52400gen.shtml.

Gilbert, Alton R. *Requiem for Regulation Q: What It Did and Why It Went Away.* Feb. 1986, https://research.stlouisfed.org/publications/review/86/02/Requiem_Feb1986.pdf.

Gilder Lehrman Institute of American History. *George Washington and the Newburgh Conspiracy, 1783.* https://www.gilderlehrman.org/history-by-era/war-for-independence/resources/george-washington-and-newburgh-conspiracy-1783.

Glass, Carter. *An Adventure in Constructive Finance.* Doubleday, 1927; also in *Review of Reviews,* Sept. 1928, pp. 257–258.

Glass, Ira. "Inside Job." *This American Life.* Apr. 9, 2010, https://www.thisamericanlife.org/radio-archives/episode/405/transcript.

———. "The Secret Recordings of Carmen Seggara." *This American Life.* Sept. 26, 2014, https://www.thisamericanlife.org/radio-archives/episode/536/transcript.

"The Global Settlement: An Overview." *Frontline,* May 8, 2003, http://www.pbs.org/wgbh/pages/frontline/shows/wallstreet/fixing/settlement.html.

Goetzmann, William, and Frank Newman. "Securitization in the 1920s." National Bureau of Economic Research, working paper 155650, Jan. 2010, http://nber.org/papers/w15650, http://www.nber.org/digest/may10/w15650.html.

Goldfarb, Zachary A., and Michelle Boorstein. "Pope Francis Denounces Trickle-Down Economic Theories in Sharp Criticism of Inequality." *Washington Post,* Nov. 13, 2013, https://www.washingtonpost.com/business/economy/pope-francis-denounces-trickle-down-economic-theories-in-critique-of-inequality/2013/11/26/e17ffe4e–56b6–11e3–8304-caf30787c0a9_story.html?utm_term=.f1f29f877d98.

Goldstein, Deborah, and Stacy Strohauer Son. *Why Prepayment Penalties Are Abusive in Subprime Home Loans.* Center for Responsible Lending, policy paper 4, Apr. 2, 2003, http://www.responsiblelending.org/mortgage-lending/research-analysis/PPP_Policy_Paper2.pdf.

Golembe, Carter H. "The Deposit Insurance Legislation of 1933: An Examination of Its Antecedents and Its Purposes." *Political Science Quarterly* 75, no. 2 (June 1960).

Gordon, Marcy. "Franklin Raines to Pay $24.7 Million to Settle Fannie Mae Lawsuit." Associated Press, Apr. 18, 2008, http://old.seattletimes.com/html/businesstechnology/2004358433_webraines18.html.

Government Accountability Office. *Bank Holding Company Act.* Jan. 2012, GAO-12-160, http://www.gao.gov/assets/590/587830.pdf.

———. *Fannie Mae and Freddie Mac: Analysis of Options for Revising the Housing Enterprises' Long-Term Structures.* (Sept. 2009), http://www.gao.gov/new.items/d09782.pdf.

———. *Financial Regulation: Review of Regulators' Oversight of Risk Management Systems at a Limited Number of Large, Complex Financial Institutions.* GAO-09-449T, Mar. 18, 2009.

———. *401K Plans: Improved Regulation Could Better Protect Participants from Conflicts of Interest.* January 2011, https://www.gao.gov/assets/320/315363.pdf.

Gramlich, Edward M. *Booms and Busts: The Case of Subprime Mortgages.* Federal Reserve Bank of Kansas City symposium, "Housing, Housing Finance, and Monetary Policy," Jackson Hole, WY, Aug. 30–Sept. 1, 2007. www.KansasCityFed.org.

———. *Subprime Mortgages: America's Latest Boom and Bust.* Urban Institute Press, 2007.

Gramm, Wendy, and Jay Cochran. *Public Comment: Security Holder Director Nominations; Proposed Rule. 2003, 2004,* https://www.sec.gov/rules/proposed/s71903/mercatus122203.htm.

Gramm, Wendy, and Jane K. Thorpe. *Public Comment: The Commodity Futures Trading Commission's Proposed Rules Relating to a New Regulatory Framework for Multilateral Transaction Execution Facilities, Intermediaries and Clearing Organizations, and Exemption for Bilateral Transactions.* Mercatus Center, June 22, 2000, https://www.mercatus.org/system/files/MC_RSP_PIC2000-17CFTC_NewRegFramework_000821.pdf.

Grant, Michael. "RESPA: The Inside Story." *Mortgage Banking* (Nov. 1999), https://www.questia.com/magazine/1G1-63800718/respa-the-inside-story.

Gray, Allistair. "AIG Sheds $150M in Costs along with Sifi Label." *Financial Times,* Oct. 1, 2017, https://www.ft.com/content/31b36b9a-a662-11e7-93c5-648314d2c72c.

Green, Harlan. "So Freddie and Fannie Weren't the Problem." PopularEconomics.com, May 21, 2014, http://www.huffingtonpost.com/harlan-green/so-fannie-and-freddie-wer_b_5009851.html.

Green, Richard K., and Susan M. Wachter. *The American Mortgage in Historical and International Context.* Penn Institute for Urban Research, Sep. 21, 2005, http://repository.upenn.edu/cgi/viewcontent.cgi?article=1000&context=penniur_papers.

Greenberger, Michael. *Lessons from Enron: An Oversight Hearing on Gas Prices and Energy Trading.* Senate Democratic Policy Committee Hearing, May 8, 2006, http://

digitalcommons.law.umaryland.edu/cgi/viewcontent.cgi?article=1017&context =cong_test.

———. "Overwhelming a Financial Regulatory Black Hole with Legislative Sunlight." *Journal of Business and Technology Law* 6, no. 1 (2011), http://digitalcommons.law. umaryland.edu/jbtl/vol6/iss1/6.

Greene, Stephen. *Emergency Banking Act of 1933.* Federal Reserve Bank of St. Louis, Nov. 22, 2013, http://www.federalreservehistory.org/Events/DetailView/23.

Greenfeld, Karl Taro. "From IndyMac to OneWest: Steven Mnuchin's Big Score." *Bloomberg,* Mar. 22, 2012.

Greenspan, Alan. "Economic Development in Low-and Moderate-Income Communities." Remarks at a Community Forum on Community Reinvestment and Access to Credit: California's Challenge, Los Angeles, Jan. 12, 1998, https://www.federalreserve.gov/ boarddocs/speeches/1998/19980112.htm.

———. Letter to Sen. Alfonse D'Amato, Chair, Committee on Banking, Housing and Urban Affairs. Oct. 20, 1998.

———. "Private-Sector Refinancing of the Large Hedge Fund, Long-Term Capital Management." Testimony before the Committee on Banking and Financial Services, U.S. House of Representatives. Oct. 1, 1998, https://www.federalreserve.gov/boarddocs/testi mony/1998/19981001.htm.

———. "Remarks via Satellite to the Annual Convention of the Independent Community Bankers of America," Mar. 4, 2003, https://fraser.stlouisfed.org/scribd/?item_id =8783&filepath=/files/docs/historical/greenspan/Greenspan_20030304.pdf.

———. *Statements and Speeches of Alan Greenspan,* https://fraser.stlouisfed.org/title/452.

———. *Waxman Testimony, Oct. 23, 2008.* https://www.c-span.org/video/?c3342718/ waxman-greenspan-testimony, and https://www.youtube.com/watch?v=R5lZPWNFizQ.

"Greenspan to the Rescue." *Economist,* Apr. 19, 2001, http://www.economist.com/node/581508.

Grimaldi, James V., and Paul Overberg. "Many Comments of 'Fiduciary' Rule Are Fake." *Wall Street Journal,* Dec. 27, 2017, https://www.wsj.com/articles/many-comments-critical-of-fiduciary-rule-are-fake–1514370601.

Gross, Daniel. "The Gang of Five, and How They Nearly Ruined Us." *Slate*, Jan. 29, 2010, http://www.slate.com/articles/business/moneybox/2010/01/the_gang_of_five_and _how_they_nearly_ruined_us.html.

Gruenberg, Martin. "Financial Regulation: A Post-Crisis Perspective." Speech at the Brookings Institution, Nov. 14, 2017, https://www.brookings.edu/events/financial-regulation-a -post-crisis-perspective/.

Guida, Victoria. "Fed Slams Wells Fargo with Penalty, as Four Board Members Ousted." *Politico,* Feb. 2, 2018, https://www.politico.com/story/2018/02/02/federal-reserve-wells -fargo-penalty–389073.

Hagerty, James R. *The Fateful History of Fannie Mae: New Deal Birth to Mortgage Crisis Fall.* History Press, 2012.

Hakim, Danny, and William K. Rashbaum. "Spitzer Is Linked to Prostitution Ring." *New York Times,* Mar. 20, 2008, http://www.nytimes.com/2008/03/10/nyregion/10cnd-spitzer. html.

Hakkio, Craig S. *The Great Moderation, 1982–2007.* Federal Reserve Bank of Kansas City, Nov. 22, 2013, https://www.federalreservehistory.org/essays/great_moderation.

Hamilton, Alexander. *Alexander Hamilton's Papers on Public Credit, Commerce, and Finance,* ed. Samuel McKee, Jr. Liberal Arts Press, 1957.

———. *The Working Papers of Alexander Hamilton,* ed. Harold C. Syrett, vol. 8: *Feb. 1791–July 1791.* Columbia University Press, 1965. (See p. 122 for the definition of a bank and p. 101 for the discussion of incorporation; on p. 102, in a footnote, Jefferson makes a case for having multiple banks because the competition will benefit all.)

———. *The Working Papers of Alexander Hamilton,* ed. Harold C. Syrett, vol. 12: *July 1792–Oct. 1792.* Columbia University Press, 1965.

———. *The Working Papers of Alexander Hamilton,* ed. Harold C. Syrett, vol. 15: *June 1793–Jan. 1794.* Columbia University Press, 1965.

———. *The Works of Alexander Hamilton: Comprising His Correspondence and His Political and Official Writings,* vol. 4, ed. John C. Hamilton. Charles S. Francis & Co., 1850.

Hamilton, Jesse. "Trump Watchdog Tells Banks He Really, Really Likes Them." Bloomberg. com, Apr. 9, 2018, https://www.bloomberg.com/news/articles/2018-04-09/trump-picked -watchdog-tells-banks-he-really-really-likes-them.

Hammond, Bray. *Banks and Politics in America: From the Revolution to the Civil War.* Princeton University Press, 1991.

Hammond, John Scott, et al. *Campaigning for President in America, 1788–2016.* ABC-CLIO, 2016.

Hansell, Saul. "Bankers Trust Settles Suit with P&G." *New York Times,* May 10, 1996, http:// www.nytimes.com/1996/05/10/business/bankers-trust-settles-suit-with-p-g.html.

Harris, Paul. "Eliot Spitzer: Wall Street's Fallen Angel." *Guardian,* Feb. 26, 2011, https:// www.theguardian.com/world/2011/feb/27/eliot-spitzer-wall-street-fallen-angel.

"Harvard: The Inside Story of Its Financial Meltdown." *Forbes,* Feb. 26, 2009, https://www. forbes.com/forbes/2009/0316/080_harvard_finance_meltdown.html#4a1eb0e251dd.

Harvard Management Company. *Annual Endowment Report, 2014.* http://www.hmc. harvard.edu/docs/Final_Annual_Report_2014.pdf.

———. *Annual Endowment Report, 2016.* http://www.hmc.harvard.edu/docs/Final_ Annual_Report_2016.pdf.

Hattem, Michael. *Newburgh Conspiracy.* http://www.mountvernon.org/digital-encyclopedia/ article/newburgh-conspiracy/.

Hauptman, Micah, and Barbara Roper. *Financial Advisor or Investment Salesperson? Brokers and Insurers Want to Have It Both Ways.* Consumer Federation of America, Jan. 18, 2017, http://consumerfed.org/wp-content/uploads/2017/01/1-18-17-Advisor-or-Salesperson_Report.pdf.

Hawkins, David F. "The Development of Modern Financial Reporting Practices among American Manufacturing Corporations." *Business History Review* 37, no. 3 (Fall 1963): 135–168.

Healy, Beth. "Harvard Ignored Warnings about Investments." *Boston Globe,* Nov. 29, 2009.

Hedberg, William, and John Krainer. "Credit Access Following a Mortgage Default." *Federal Reserve Bank of San Francisco Economic Letter,* Oct. 29, 2012, http://www.frbsf.org/ economic-research/publications/economic-letter/2012/october/credit-access-following -a-mortgage-default/.

Helderman, Leonard C. *National and State Banks: A Study of Their Origins.* Houghton Mifflin, 1931, https://catalog.hathitrust.org/Record/005923277.

Hembree, Diana. "Mulvaney Is on the Hot Seat for His Stunning 'Pay to Play' Remarks." *Forbes,* Apr. 6, 2018, https://www.forbes.com/sites/dianahembree/2018/04/26/cfpbs-mulvaney-is-on-the-hot-seat-for-his-pay-to-play-remark/#70c8858d4417.

Henriques, Diana B. "Fault Lines of Risk Appear as Market Hero Stumbles." *New York Times,* Sept. 27, 1998.

———. "Fischer Black, 57, Wall Street Theorist, Dies." *New York Times,* Aug. 31, 1995.

"Henry Ford." *Who Made America?* PBS, http://www.pbs.org/wgbh/theymadeamerica/whomade/ford_hi.html.

Herbert, Bob. "Enron and the Gramms." *New York Times,* Jan. 17, 2002, http://www.nytimes.com/2002/01/17/opinion/enron-and-the-gramms.html.

Herbst, Moira. "Larry Summers' Record Should Rule Him out of the Fed Chairmanship." *Guardian,* Aug. 12, 2013.

Herzog, Thomas N. *History of Mortgage Finance with an Emphasis on Mortgage Insurance.* Society of Actuaries, 2009, http://citeseerx.ist.psu.edu/viewdoc/summary?doi=10.1.1.514.857.

Hessen, Robert. *In Defense of the Corporation.* Hoover Press, 1979, https://books.google.com/books?id=P8mMyuYtwpIC&source=gbs_slider_cls_metadata_7_mylibrary.

Hirschman, Charles, and Elizabeth Mogford. "Immigration and the American Industrial Revolution from 1880 to 1920." *Social Science Research* 38, no. 4 (Dec. 2009): 897–920, http://www.ncbi.nlm.nih.gov/pmc/articles/PMC2760060/.

"History and Timeline." Mercatus.org, https://www.mercatus.org/content/history-and-timeline.

Hoenig, Thomas. "Leverage and Debt: The Impact of Today's Choices on Tomorrow." Speech, Kansas Bankers Association Meeting, Aug. 6, 2009, https://www.kansascityfed.org/~/media/files/publicat/speechbio/hoenigpdf/hoenigkba080609.pdf.

———. "A Turning Point: Defining the Financial Structure." Speech, 22nd Annual Hyman P. Minsky Conference at the Levey Economics Institute of Bard College, Apr. 17, 2013, https://www.fdic.gov/news/news/speeches/spapr1713.pdf.

Home Ownership and Equity Protection Act of 1994. Summary: https://www.congress.gov/bill/103rd-congress/house-bill/3474; full text: https://www.congress.gov/bill/103rd-congress/house-bill/3474/text.

Home Owners' Loan Act of 1933. https://fraser.stlouisfed.org/scribd/?title_id=850&filepath=/docs/historical/congressional/hola1933_congress.pdf.

Homer, Sidney, and Richard Sylla. *A History of Interest Rates,* 4th ed. John Wiley & Sons, 2005.

Hoover, Herbert. Letter to Arch Shaw, Feb. 17, 1933. Herbert Hoover Presidential Library and Museum.

———. Annotated memo, "The Plan for Government Guarantee of Bank Deposits." Herbert Hoover Presidential Library and Museum.

———. Letter to FDR, Feb. 18, 1933, in George McJimsey, ed., *Documentary History of the Franklin D. Roosevelt Presidency,* vol. 3: *The Bank Holiday and the Emergency Banking Act, March 1933.* University Publications of America, 2001.

———. Letter to James H. Rand Jr., Feb. 28, 1933. Presidential papers, Herbert Hoover Presidential Library and Museum.

———. *The Memoirs of Herbert Hoover: The Cabinet and the Presidency, 1920–1933.* Macmillan, 1952, https://hoover.archives.gov/research/ebooks/B1V2_Full.pdf.

———. *Memoirs of Herbert Hoover: The Great Depression: 1929–1941.* Macmillan, 1952, https://hoover.archives.gov/sites/default/files/research/ebooks/b1v3_full.pdf,

"Hoover Appeals to Nation on Radio to Aid Red Cross; Coolidge, Smith Add Pleas." *New York Times,* Jan. 23, 1931.

"Hoover Orders Eviction." *New York Times.* July 29, 1932.

"House and Senate Banking Committees Names." http://uschs.org/explore/historical-articles/senate-banking-committee-history/, http://history.house.gov/Records-and-Research/FAQS/Committee-Names/.

"Household Debt Jumps as 2017 Marks the Fifth Consecutive Year of Positive Annual Growth since Post-Recession Deleveraging." Federal Reserve Bank of New York, Feb. 13, 2018, https://www.newyorkfed.org/newsevents/news/research/2018/rp180213.

Howe, Alex. "The 11 Largest Bankruptcies in American History." *Business Insider,* Nov. 29, 2011, http://www.businessinsider.com/largest-bankruptcies-in-american-history-2011-11?op=1/#cific-gas-and-electric-co-1.

"How Koch Became an Oil Speculation Powerhouse." ThinkProgress, June 6, 2011, https://thinkprogress.org/how-koch-became-an-oil-speculation-powerhouse–706d135e412f.

Huey Long Project. http://www.hueylong.com/programs/share-our-wealth-speech.php.

"Incorporating the Republic: The Corporation in Antebellum Political Culture." *Harvard Law Review* 102, no. 8 (1989): 1883–1903, http://www.jstor.org/stable/1341360.

Industrial Energy Consumers of America. "Position Statement before the Federal Energy Regulatory Commission." Docket no. AD06-11-000, Oct. 13, 2006.

"Industry Control Urged by Chamber." *New York Times*, May 6, 1933.

International Swaps and Derivatives Association, Inc. *ISDA Market Surveys,* http://www.isda.org/statistics/pdf/ISDA-Market-Survey-historical-data.pdf, and http://www.isda.org/statistics/pdf/ISDA-Market-Survey-annual-data.pdf.

"Is Dodd-Frank's Failure Resolution Regime Failing?" Transcript of the Brookings Institution forum in Washington, D.C., June 6, 2017, https://www.brookings.edu/events/is-dodd-franks-failure-resolution-regime-failing/.

"Investment Banks Are Borrowing from the Fed." Reuters, Mar. 19, 2008, https://www.reuters.com/article/us-usbanks-fed/investment-banks-are-borrowing-from-fed-idUSN1954536520080319.

Investment Company Institute, *Fact Book, 2007.* https://www.ici.org/pdf/2017_factbook.pdf.

Ismail, Asif F. *A Most Favored Corporation: Enron Prevailed in Federal, State Lobbying Efforts 49 Times.* Center for Public Integrity, May 19, 2014, https://www.publicintegrity.org/2003/01/06/3160/most-favored-corporation-enron-prevailed-federal-state-lobbying-efforts–49-times.

Issa, Erin El. *2017 American Household Credit Card Debt Study.* Nerdwallet, https://www.nerdwallet.com/blog/average-credit-card-debt-household/.

Jackson, Brooks. "Bank Board Plan to Fund Failing S&Ls Seems Unswayed by Reagan Opposition." *Wall Street Journal,* June 4, 1981.

Jalil, Andrew J. *A New History of Banking Panics in the United States, 1825–1929: Construction and Implications.* Aug. 2014, https://www.oxy.edu/sites/default/files/assets/Economics/Jalil_ANewHistoryofBankingPanicsAug2014.pdf.

Jaremski, Matthew. *State Banks and the National Banking Acts: A Tale of Creative Destruction.* Vanderbilt University, Nov. 2010, http://econ.as.nyu.edu/docs/IO/18865/Jaremski_20110218.pdf.

Jefferson, Thomas. *The Complete Anas of Thomas Jefferson,* ed. Franklin B. Sawvel. Roundtable Press, 1903, https://archive.org/details/completeanastho00sawvgoog.

———. *Jefferson's Account of the Bargain on the Assumption and Residence Bills,* https://founders.archives.gov/documents/Jefferson/01-17-02-0018-0012.

———. Letter to Charles Pinckney, Sept. 30, 1820, http://founders.archives.gov/documents/Jefferson/98-01-02-1544.

———. Letter to Edmund Pendleton, July 24, 1791, http://founders.archives.gov/documents/Jefferson/01-20-02-0318.

———. Letter to John Adams, Aug. 22, 1813, https://archive.org/stream/writingsofthomas-09jeffiala/writingsofthomas09jeffiala_djvu.txt.

———. Letter to John Wayles Eppes, Sept. 11, 1813, http://founders.archives.gov/documents/Jefferson/03-06-02-0388.

———. Letter to Madison, Oct. 1, 1792, arguing that any person in Virginia who recognized the national bank was guilty of treason and should be executed, http://founders.archives.gov/documents/Jefferson/01-24-02-0392.

Jefferson, Thomas. *Papers of Thomas Jefferson,* vol. 22: *6 August 1791–31 December 1791,* ed. Charles T. Cullen. Princeton University Press, 1986.

———. *The Writings of Thomas Jefferson,* comp. and ed. Paul Leicester Ford. G.P. Putnam's Sons, 1892–1899, https://catalog.hathitrust.org/Record/000366341.

Jereski, Laura, et al. "Bitter Fruit: Orange County, Mired in Investment Mess, Files for Bankruptcy." *Wall Street Journal,* Dec. 7, 1994, http://search.proquest.com/docview/398545040?accountid=11752.

Jickling, Mark. *The Enron Loophole.* Congressional Research Service. July 7, 2008, RS22912.

Johnson, Carrie. "Enron's Lay Dies of Heart Attack." *Washington Post,* July 6, 2006, http://www.washingtonpost.com/wp-dyn/content/article/2006/07/05/AR2006070500523.html.

Johnson, Carrie, and Kathleen Day. "Hedge Fund Rule Tossed: Appeals Court Says SEC Went Too Far in Oversight Effort." *Washington Post,* June 24, 2006.

Joint Economic Committee of the House and Senate, U.S. Congress. *A Local Look at the National Foreclosure Crisis: Cleveland Families, Neighborhoods, Economy under Siege from the Subprime Mortgage Fallout.* U.S. Government Printing Office, July 25, 2007, https://www.gpo.gov/fdsys/pkg/CHRG–110shrg38266/html/CHRG–110shrg38266.htm.

Jones, Jesse H., with Edward Angly. *Fifty Billion Dollars: My Thirteen Years with the RFC.* MacMillan, 1951.

Jones-Cooper, Brittany. "Average U.S. Household Owes $15,654 in Credit Card Debt." *Yahoo Finance,* Dec. 11, 2017, https://finance.yahoo.com/news/average-us-household-owes–15654-credit-card-debt–171830579.html.

JPMorganChase. *Historical Prime Rate.* https://www.jpmorganchase.com/corporate/About-JPMC/historical-prime-rate.htm.

Kahn, Joseph A. "Former Treasury Secretary Joins Leadership Triangle at Citigroup." *New York Times,* Oct. 27, 1999, http://www.nytimes.com/1999/10/27/business/former-treasury-secretary-joins-leadership-triangle-at-citigroup.html.

Kane, Muriel. "California Town to Pay Off All City Employees, Disband Police." *Raw Story,* June 23, 2010, http://www.rawstory.com/2010/06/california-town-law-city-employees-disband-police/.

Kapner, Suzanne. "Financier Charles H. Keating Jr. Symbolized the Savings and Loan Crisis Era." *Wall Street Journal,* Apr. 1, 2014, https://www.wsj.com/articles/SB1000142405270 2304432604579476340331548028.

Kashkari, Neel. *Minneapolis Plan to End Too Big to Fail.* Federal Reserve Bank of Minneapolis, https://www.minneapolisfed.org/publications/special-studies/endingtbtf.

Kaufman, George G. and Robert A. Eisenbeis. "Deposit Insurance Issues in the Post 2008 Crisis World." *The Oxford Handbook of Banking,* 2nd ed., ed. Allen N. Berger, Philip Molyneux, and John O. S. Wilson. Oxford University Press, 2015.

Keeton, William R. "Small and Large Bank Views of Deposit Insurance: Today vs. the 1930s." *Federal Reserve Bank of Kansas City, Economic Review* (Sept./Oct. 1990): 23–35.

Kelly, Kate. "Bear CEO's Handling of Crisis Raises Questions." *Wall Street Journal,* Nov. 1, 2007, http://www.wsj.com/articles/SB119387369474078336.

Kelly, Kate, et al. "Two Big Funds at Bear Stearns Face Shutdown." *Wall Street Journal,* June 20, 2007, http://www.wsj.com/articles/SB118230204193441422.

Kendall, Leon T., and Michael J. Fishman, eds. *A Primer on Securitization.* Paperback ed. MIT Press, 2000.

Kennedy, Susan Estabrook. *The Banking Crisis of 1933.* University Press of Kentucky, 1973.

Kessler, Aaron. "Ex-AIG Chief Wins Bailout Suit, But Gets No Damages." *New York Times,* June 15, 2015, https://www.nytimes.com/2015/06/16/business/dealbook/judge-sides-with-ex-aig-chief-greenberg-against-us-but-awards-no-money.html?_r=0.

Keyfetz, Lisa. "The Home Ownership and Equity Protection Act of 1994: Extending Liability for Predatory Subprime Loans to Secondary Mortgage Market Participants." *Loyola Consumer Law Review* 18, no. 2 (2005): article 3, https://pdfs.semanticscholar.org/54f2/ff526c9ad93c01ebec82e63c69c70bce40b0.pdf.

Khanna, Samiha, and Lisa Sorg. "Connecting the Dots on Americans for Prosperity." Indyweek.com,https://www.indyweek.com/indyweek/connecting-the-dots-on-americans-for-prosperity/Content?oid=1396475.

Kher, Unmesh. "The End of Arthur Andersen?" *Time,* Mar. 11, 2002, http://content.time.com/time/business/article/0,8599,216386,00.html.

Khouri, Andrew. "Home Ownership Rate Falls to 20-Year Low." *Los Angeles Times,* Jan. 29, 2015, http://www.latimes.com/business/la-fi-home-ownership-20150129-story.html.

Kiel, Paul. "The Bailout by the Actual Numbers." Propublica, Sept. 6, 2012, https://www.propublica.org/article/the-bailout-by-the-actual-numbers.

Kilborn, Peter T. "Reagan Advisors Blame U.S. Policy for Savings Crisis." *New York Times,* Jan. 11, 1989.

Kindleberger, Charles P., and Ribert Z. Aliber. *Manias, Panics and Crashes: A History of Financial Crises,* 7th ed. Palgrave Macmillan, 2015.

King, Gilbert. "The Man Who Busted the 'Banksters.'" *Smithsonian,* Nov. 29, 2011.

Kirk, Michael. "The Warning: How Greenspan, Summers and Rubin Conspired to Silence Derivatives Whistleblower Brooksley Born." *Frontline,* 2009, http://www.pbs.org/wgbh/pages/frontline/warning/etc/script.html.

Kirk, Michael, et al. "Money, Power and Politics: Inside the Meltdown." *Frontline,* Apr. 24, 2012, http://pages.suddenlink.net/dfrentrup/MoneyPowerAndWallStFrontline.htm#g2.

Klein, Matthew C. "Larry Summers's Billion-Dollar Bad Bet at Harvard." *Bloomberg,* July 18, 2013, https://www.bloomberg.com/view/articles/2013-07-18/larry-summers-s-billion-dollar-bad-bet-at-harvard.

Klingaman, William. *1929: The Year of the Great Crash.* Harper & Row, 1989.

Knox, John J. *A History of Banking in the United States.* Bradford Rhodes & Co. 1903.

Kocieniewski, David. "A Shuffle of Aluminum, But to Banks, Pure Gold." *New York Times,* July 30, 2013, http://www.nytimes.com/2013/07/21/business/a-shuffle-of-aluminum-but-to-banks-pure-gold.html.

Kolhatkar, Sheelah. "The Legacy of JPMorgan's Blythe Masters." *Bloomberg,* Apr. 3, 2014, https://www.bloomberg.com/news/articles/2014-04-03/the-legacy-of-jpmorgans-blythe-masters.

Krantz, Matt. "Well Fargo CEO Stumpt Retires with $134 Million." *USA Today,* Oct. 12, 2016,http://www.usatoday.com/story/money/markets/2016/10/12/wells-fargo-ceo-retires-under-fire/91964778/.

Kroszner, Randall S. *The Legacy of the Separation of Banking and Commerce Continues in Gramm-Leach-Bliley,* June 1, 2000, https://www.minneapolisfed.org/publications/the-region/the-legacy-of-the-separation-of-banking-and-commerce-continues-in-grammleachbliley?sc_device=Default.

Kroszner, Randall S., and Robert J. Shiller. *Reforming U.S. Financial Markets: Reflections before and beyond Dodd-Frank.* MIT Press, 2011.

Krugman, Paul. "'The Economics of Inequality, by Thomas Piketty." *New York Times,* Aug. 2,2015,https://www.nytimes.com/2015/08/03/books/review-the-economics-of-inequality-by-thomas-piketty.html?_r=0.

———. "Paul Krugman Reviews 'The Rise and Fall of American Growth.'" *New York Times,* Jan. 25, 2016.

Kumpa, Peter. "The Bank of Maryland Fiasco: Anarchy in the Streets of Baltimore." *Baltimore Sun,* Oct. 8, 1990, http://articles.baltimoresun.com/1990–10–08/news/1990281121_1_bank-of-maryland-reverdy-johnson-lynching.

Kurtzleben, Danielle. "Donald Trump's Messy Ideas for Handling the National Debt, Explained." National Public Radio, May 9, 2016, http://www.npr.org/2016/05/09/477350889/donald-trumps-messy-ideas-for-handling-the-national-debt-explained.

Labaton, Stephen. "Agency's '04 Rule Let Banks Pile Up New Debt, and Risk." *New York Times,* Oct. 3, 2008.

"La Guardia Charges Pools Paid Writers to 'Ballyhoo' Stock." *New York Times,* Apr. 27, 1932.

Lamont, Thomas. Letter to FDR, Feb. 27, 1933. In George McJimsey, ed., *Documentary History of the Franklin D. Roosevelt Presidency,* vol. 3: *The Bank Holiday and the Emergency Banking Act, March 1933.* University Publications of America, 2001.

Lander, Mark. "Obama Signs Bill to Promote Start-up Investments." *New York Times,* Apr. 5, 2012, http://www.nytimes.com/2012/04/06/us/politics/obama-signs-bill-to-ease-investing-in-start-ups.html.

Lane, Sylvan. "Trump: Dodd-Frank Rollback 'Should Be Done Fairly Quickly.'" *The Hill,* Apr. 5, 2018, http://thehill.com/policy/finance/381851-trump-dodd-frank-rollback-should-be-done-fairly-quickly.

Lapowsky, Issie. "A Lot of People Are Saying Trump's New Data Team Is Shady." *Wired,* Aug. 15, 2016, https://www.wired.com/2016/08/trump-cambridge-analytica/.

Lattman, Peter. "The Law Blog History Lesson: The Enron-Insull Connection." *Wall Street Journal,* Mar. 26, 2006, http://blogs.wsj.com/law/2006/05/26/law-blog-history-lesson-the-enron-insull-connection/.

Lebovic, Sam. *Free Speech and Unfree News: The Paradox of Press Freedom in America.* Harvard University Press, 2016.

Lee, Mike, and Jeb Henserling. "National Review: A Stronger Congress, A Healthier Republic." *National Review,* Feb. 2, 2016, http://www.nationalreview.com/article/430703/step-congress-reclaim-constitutional-authority.

Lehrman Institute. "Abraham Lincoln." http://www.abrahamlincolnsclassroom.org/abraham-lincoln-in-depth/abraham-lincoln-and-civil-war-finance/#nscuf.

———. "Alexander Hamilton." http://lehrmaninstitute.org/history/foundingeconomists.html.

———. "Andrew Jackson." http://lehrmaninstitute.org/history/Andrew-Jackson–1837.html.

Leonhardt, David. "Fed Missed This Bubble. Will It See a New One?" *New York Times,* Jan. 5, 2010, http://www.nytimes.com/2010/01/06/business/economy/06leonhardt.html.

———. "Will the Fed Reserve the Housing Slump?" *New York Times,* Sept. 19, 2007, http://www.nytimes.com/2007/09/19/business/19leonhardt.html.

Leopold, Jason. "McCain Defends 'Enron Loophole.'" *Public Record,* May 20, 2008.

Lerner, Michele. "After Losing Their Homes in the Foreclosure Crisis, Boomerang Buyers Are Back." *Washington Post,* Aug. 21, 2008, https://www.washingtonpost.com/realestate/after-losing-their-homes-in-the-foreclosure-crisis-boomerang-buyers-are-back/2014/08/21/1a6f7092–18ca–11e4–9e3b–7f2f110c6265_story.html?utm_term=.c7f8cd3add23.

Leuchtenburg, William. *Franklin D. Roosevelt and the New Deal, 1932–1940.* Harper & Row, 1963.

Levin, Bess. "Trump Administration Wants Wall Street to 'Self Report' Its Crimes." *Vanity Fair,* Sept. 25, 2017, https://www.vanityfair.com/news/2017/09/trump-administration-wants-wall-street-to-self-report-its-crimes.

Levin, Carl. Interview with *PBS News Hour.* July 30, 2002.

Levine, Jonathan. "Credit Where It Is Due: A Social History of Consumer Credit in America." Ph.D. diss., American Studies, New York University, Sept. 2008, http://gradworks.umi.com/33/30/3330146.html.

Lewis, Michael. "How the Eggheads Cracked: Inside Long-Term Capital." *New York Times,* Jan. 24, 1999.

———. *Liar's Poker: Rising through the Wreckage on Wall Street.* W.W. Norton. 1989.

"Liberty Bond." Museum of American Finance, image from exhibit *Checks & Balances,* http://www.moaf.org/exhibits/checks_balances/woodrow-wilson/liberty-bond.

Library of Congress. *Bonus Army.* https://www.loc.gov/exhibits/treasures/trm203.html.

———. *Prosperity and Thrift: The Coolidge Era and the Consumer Economy.* https://memory.loc.gov/ammem/coolhtml/coolhome.html.

———. *Radio: A Consumer Product and a Producer of Consumption.* Coolidge-Consumerism Collection, http://lcweb2.loc.gov:8081/ammem/amrlhtml/inradio.html, and http://lcweb2.loc.gov:8081/ammem/amrlhtml/inmenu.html.

Lifsher, Marc. "10 Enron Ex-Directors to Pay $13 million to Settle Suit by UC and Other Investors." *Los Angeles Times*, Jan. 8, 2005.

Lippmann, Walter. "Democracy and Dictatorship." *Milwaukee Journal,* Feb. 25, 1933, https://news.google.com/newspapers?nid=1368&dat=19330225&id=JHxhAAAAIBAJ &sjid=_gwEAAAAIBAJ&pg=6474,3330435&hl=en.

Lipton, Eric. "Gramm and the Enron Loophole." *New York Times,* Nov. 14, 2008, http://www.nytimes.com/2008/11/17/business/17grammside.html.

Logan, Lorie K. "Implementing Monetary Policy: Perspective from the Open Market Trading Desk." Federal Reserve Bank of New York, May 18, 2017, https://www.newyorkfed.org/newsevents/speeches/2017/log170518.

Long, Huey. Radio address proposing his "Share Our Wealth" program. Feb. 23, 1934, http://www.hueylong.com/programs/share-our-wealth-speech.php.

Loomis, Carol. "A House Built on Sand: John Meriwether's Once-Mighty Long-Term Capital Has All but Crumbled." *Fortune,* Oct. 26, 1998.

Lowenstein, Roger. *America's Bank: The Epic Struggle to Create the Federal Reserve.* Penguin Press, 2015.

———. "Before There Was Enron, There Was Insull." *New York Times,* Mar. 19, 2006.

———. *When Genius Failed: The Rise and Fall of Long-Term Capital Management.* Random House, 2000.

Ludwig, Eugene. "We Are the Neiman Marcus and Tiffany of Bank Charters." *Washington Post,* Jan. 30, 1997, https://www.washingtonpost.com/archive/business/1997/01/30/comptroller-of-the-controversy/88daabe4-400d-4cc5-acca-efd3d62de530/.

Lutrell, David, et al. "Assessing the Costs and Consequences of the 2007–2009 Financial Crisis and Its Aftermath." Federal Reserve Bank of Dallas, *Economic Letter* 8, no. 7 (Sept. 2013), https://www.dallasfed.org/research/eclett/2013/el1307.cfm.

Lutz, Bryon, et al. *The Housing Crisis and State and Local Government Tax Revenue: Five Channels.* Finance and Economics Discussion Series, Divisions of Research & Statistics and Monetary Affairs, Federal Reserve Board, Washington, D.C., Aug. 2010.

Lynch, Sarah. "Prudential to Fight U.S. Proposal to Label it 'Systemic.' " Reuters, July 2, 2013, https://www.reuters.com/article/us-gecapital-fsoc/prudential-to-fight-u-s-proposal-to-label-it-systemic-idUSBRE96115Z20130702.

———. "U.S. Justice Dept. Orders Whistleblower to Testify in Wells Fargo Probe." Reuters, Dec. 23, 2017, https://www.reuters.com/article/us-wells-fargo-accounts-whistleblower/u-s-justice-dept-orders-whistleblower-to-testify-in-wells-fargo-probe-idUSKBN14C234.

Macey, Jonathan R., and Geoffrey P. Miller. *Double Liability of Bank Shareholders: History and Implications.* Yale Law School, Faculty Scholarship Series, paper 1642, 1992, http://digitalcommons.law.yale.edu/fss_papers/1642.

Madison, James. *Debates on the Adoption of the Constitution,* vol. 5, ed. Jonathon Elliot. J.B. Lippincott Co., 1901, https://babel.hathitrust.org/cgi/pt?id=njp.32101075729101;view=1up;seq=7.

———. Letter to Thomas Jefferson, Oct. 17, 1788, http://press-pubs.uchicago.edu/founders/documents/v1ch14s47.html.

———. *The Papers of James Madison,* vols. 1–10, ed. William T. Hutchinson et al. University of Chicago Press, 1962–1977.

Mahon, Joe. *Financial Services Modernization Act of 1999, Commonly Called Gramm-Leach-Bliley.* Federal Reserve Bank of Minneapolis, Nov. 12, 1999, http://www.federalreservehistory.org/Events/DetailView/53.

Malkin, Lawrence. "Procter & Gamble's Tale of Derivatives Woe." *New York Times,* Apr. 14, 1994.

Mann, Ted. "GE Says Justice Department Sent to GE Capital, WMC in Subprime Probe." *Wall Street Journal,* Feb. 26, 2016.

Mann, Ted, and Joann Lublin. "Why General Electric Is Unwinding Its Finance Arm." *Wall Street Journal*, Oct. 13, 2015.

Masters, Brooke A. "Little Guys' Lament; Abuses Shake Investors' Confidence in Mutual Fund Industry." *Washington Post,* Sept. 14, 2003.

———. "New York Law Chief Turns Spotlight on Dark Pools." *Financial Times*, June 27, 2014, https://www.ft.com/content/0f4daecc-fd2c-11e3-8ca9-00144feab7de.

———. "Spitzer Alleges Improprieties." *Washington Post,* Sept. 4, 2003.

Masters, Brooke A., and Kathleen Day. "Morgan Stanley Settles with SEC, NASD; Firm Accused of Failing to Disclose Funds' Payments." *Washington Post,* Nov. 18, 2003.

Masters, Michael W. *The Accidental Hunt Brothers.* Special Report, July 31, 2008, https://www.loe.org/images/content/080919/Act1.pdf.

———. "Better Markets and Masters Capital Management." YouTube, Oct. 18, 2012, https://www.youtube.com/watch?v=bxkZIOlYVyE.

———. "Better Markets and Masters Capital Management." YouTube, Nov. 20, 2012, https://www.youtube.com/watch?v=LsAJTxWN3h4.

———. "Masters Sees Correlation between Oil Prices, Speculation." *Bloomberg,* June 8, 2011, https://www.youtube.com/watch?v=q5MXWJkdsow.

———. *Testimony before the U.S. Senate Committee on Homeland Security and Government Affairs.* June 24, 2008, http://www.hsgac.senate.gov//imo/media/doc/062408Masters.pdf?attempt=2.

"The Match King." *Economist,* Dec. 19, 2007.

Mayer, Jane. "The Reclusive Hedge-Fund Tycoon behind the Trump Presidency." *New Yorker,* Mar. 27, 2017, https://www.newyorker.com/magazine/2017/03/27/the-reclusive-hedge-fund-tycoon-behind-the-trump-presidency.

McBride, James. *Council on Foreign Relations Backgrounder: Understanding the LIBOR Scandal,* Oct. 12, 2016, http://www.cfr.org/united-kingdom/understanding-libor-scandal/p28729.

McCombs, Phil. "Keating, Failed King of Thrifts." *Washington Post,* Mar. 5, 1990, https://www.washingtonpost.com/archive/lifestyle/1990/03/05/keating-failed-king-of-thrifts/d19b16ed-2e10-4b4f-bdf6-912f4e8bae83/.

McCoy, Patricia A. Testimony before the U.S. Senate Committee on Banking, Housing and Urban Affairs. Mar. 3, 2009, https://papers.ssrn.com/sol3/papers.cfm?abstract_id=1367977.

McCulloch v. Maryland. PBS, *Thirteen: Media with Impact,* http://www.pbs.org/wnet/supremecourt/antebellum/landmark_mcculloch.html.

McDonough, William J. *Statement before the Committee on Banking and Financial Services, U.S. House of Representatives*, Oct. 1, 1998, https://www.newyorkfed.org/newsevents/speeches/1998/mcd981001.html.

McDowell, Edwin. "Sifting for Profits in Keating's Desert Monument." *New York Times,* Aug. 26, 1992.

McKinnon, John D., and James R. Hagerty. "How Accounting Issue Crept up on Fannie's Pugnacious Chief." *Wall Street Journal,* Dec. 17, 2004, http://www.wsj.com/articles/SB110323877001802691.

McLannahan, Ben. "Nonprime Has a Nice Ring to It: The Return of the High-Risk Mortgage." *Financial Times,* Aug. 31, 2017, https://www.ft.com/content/3c245dee–8d0f–11e7-a352-e46f43c5825d.

McLean, Bethany. Interview with C-SPAN, May 19, 2005, https://www.c-span.org/video/?186818–1/qa-bethany-mclean.

———. "Is Enron Overpriced?" *Fortune,* Mar. 5, 2001, http://money.cnn.com/2006/01/13/news/companies/enronoriginal_fortune/.

———. *Shaky Ground: The Strange Saga of the Mortgage Giants.* Columbia Global Reports, 2015.

———. "Why Enron Went Bust: Start with Arrogance." *Fortune,* Dec. 24, 2001, http://archive.fortune.com/magazines/fortune/fortune_archive/2001/12/24/315319/index.htm.

McLean, Bethany, and Peter Elkind. *The Smartest Guys in the Room: The Amazing Rise and Scandalous Fall of Enron.* Penguin Group, 2003.

McLean, Bethany, and Joe Nocera. *All the Devils Are Here.* Portfolio/Penguin, 2010.

McMahan, John. "Impact of New Tax Reform Legislation on Real Estate." *Real Estate* (Fall/Winter 1986).

McNamara, Robert. *Loco-Foco.* http://history1800s.about.com/od/1800sglossary/g/Loco-Foco-definition.htm.

McNeill, Allison, et al. "Causes of the Great Depression." Pp. 1–20 in Allison McNeill et al., eds., *Great Depression and the New Deal Reference Library,* vol. 1: *Almanac.* UXL, 2003.

MeasuringWorth.com. "What Was the U.S. GDP Then?" http://www.measuringworth.org/usgdp/.

Medley, Bill. "Riegle-Neal Interstate Banking and Branching Act of 1994." Federal Reserve Bank of Kansas, Sept. 1994, https://www.federalreservehistory.org/essays/riegle_neal_act_of_1994.

———. "Volcker's Announcement of Anti-Inflation Measures." Federal Reserve Bank of Kansas City, Nov. 22, 2013, http://www.federalreservehistory.org/Events/PrintView/41.

Meltzer, Allan H. *A History of the Federal Reserve,* vol. 1: *1913–1951.* University of Chicago Press, 2003.

Mian, Atif, and Amir Sufi. *House of Debt.* University of Chicago Press, 2015, http://houseofdebt.org/2014/03/15/household-debt-and-the-great-depression.html.

———. *House of Debt Blog: Household Debt and the Great Depression,* Mar. 15, 2014, http://houseofdebt.org/2014/03/15/household-debt-and-the-great-depression.html.

Mider, Zachary. "Rebekah Mercer, Daughter of Major Donor, Named to Trump Role." *Bloomberg,* Nov. 11, 2016, https://www.bloomberg.com/politics/articles/2016-11-11/rebekah-mercer-daughter-of-major-donor-named-to-trump-role.

"Midget Placed in Lap of Morgan: He Is Flabbergasted at Press Agent Stunt but Chats with Tiny Woman." *New York Times,* June 2, 1933.

Miller, Peter. "Why Is GE Leaving the Mortgage Business?" *RealtyTrac,* May 1, 2015, http://www.realtytrac.com/news/real-estate-investing/why-is-ge-capital-leaving-the-mortgage-business/.

Minsky, Hyman P. "The Financial Instability Hypothesis." Levy Economics Institute of Bard College, working paper 74, May 1992, http://www.levy.org/pubs/wp74.pdf.

"Minsky's Moment." *Economist,* July 30, 2016, https://www.economist.com/news/economics-brief/21702740-second-article-our-series-seminal-economic-ideas-looks-hyman-minskys.

Mitchell, Charles. "Sound Inflation." *Magazine of Wall Street* (June 9, 1917): 295–296, https://babel.hathitrust.org/shcgi/pt?id=pst.000068191016;view=1up;seq=329.

Mitchell, Lawrence E. *The Speculation Economy: How Finance Triumphed over Industry.* Berrett-Koehler, 2007.

"Mitchell Must Pay $364,254 Tax Fine." *New York Times,* May 8, 1938.

Moen, Jon R., and Ellis W. Tallman. "The Panic of 1907." *Federal Reserve History,* Dec. 4, 2015, https://www.federalreservehistory.org/essays/panic_of_1907.

"Money and the Constitution." *American History: From Revolution to Reconstruction and Beyond,* http://www.let.rug.nl/usa/essays/general/a-brief-history-of-central-banking/money-and-the-constitution.php.

Monks, Robert A. G., and Nell Minow. *Corporate Governance,* 5th ed. John Wiley & Sons, 2011.

Morgan, Dan, and Kathleen Day. "For Gramms, Enron Is Hard to Escape." *Washington Post,* Jan. 25, 2007.

Morrell, Alex. "The 4 Ways Wells Fargo Employees Were Ripping Off Customers, Earning the Bank a $185 Million Fine." *Business Insider,* Sept. 9, 2016, http://www.businessinsider.com/the-four-ways-wells-fargo-bank-employees-were-ripping-off-customers-2016-9.

Mosier, Jeff. "Convicted I–30 Condo-Fraudster D. L. 'Danny' Faulkner Dies." *Dallas Morning News,* May 31, 2012, https://www.dallasnews.com/obituaries/obituaries/2012/05/31/convicted-i-30-condo-fraudster-d.l.-danny-faulkner-dies.

Mote, Larry R. "Banks and the Securities Markets: The Controversy." *Economic Perspectives,* Federal Reserve Board of Chicago, Mar.–Apr. 1979, part 3.

Mount, Ian. "Wells Fargo's Fake Accounts May Go Back More Than 10 Years." *Fortune,* Oct. 12, 2016, http://fortune.com/2016/10/12/wells-fargo-fake-accounts-scandal/.

"Movie Stars Lack for Ready Cash." *New York Times,* Mar. 4, 1933.

Mufson, Steven. "Greenspan Stands His Ground." *Washington Post,* Mar. 21, 2008, http://www.washingtonpost.com/wp-dyn/content/article/2008/03/20/AR2008032003708.html.

Mullins, David W., Jr. "Statement before the Subcommittee on Oversight of the Committee on Ways and Means." U.S. House of Representatives, Feb. 3, 1992, in *Federal Reserve Bulletin* 78, no. 4 (1992): 251.

———. "Statement before the Subcommittee on Telecommunications and Finance of the Committee on Energy and Commerce." U.S. House of Representatives, Sept. 4, 1991, in *Federal Reserve Bulletin* 77, no. 11 (Nov. 1991): 885.

Murray, John C. "Enforceability of Mortgage Due-On-Sale Clauses—An Update." American Bar Association, 2015, http://www.americanbar.org/content/dam/aba/publishing/rpte_ereport/2015/2-March/enforceability_of_mortgage.authcheckdam.pdf.

Myers, William Starr, and Walter H. Newton. *The Hoover Administration: A Documented Narrative.* C. Scribner's Sons, 1936.

Nakamoto, Michiyo. "Citigroup Chief Bullish on Buy-Outs." *Financial Times,* July 9, 2007.

Nash, Nathaniel C. "Task Force Ties Market Collapse to Big Investors' Program Trades," *New York Times,* Jan. 9, 1998.

———. "Treasury Now Favors Creation of Huge Banks." *New York Times,* June 7, 1987, http://www.nytimes.com/1987/06/07/us/treasury-now-favors-creation-of-huge-banks. html?pagewanted=all.

"National Banking Acts of 1863 and 1864." *American History: From Revolution to Reconstruction and Beyond,* http://www.let.rug.nl/usa/essays/general/a-brief-history-of-central-banking/national-banking-acts-of–1863-and–1864.php.

National Bureau of Economic Research. "The NBER's Business Cycle Dating Procedure." http://www.nber.org/cycles/recessions.html.

National Consumer Law Center. "Simplifying the Home Buying Process: HUD's Proposal to Reform RESPA." Testimony before the House Financial Services Committee, 2001, https://www.nclc.org/images/pdf/foreclosure_mortgage/archive/respa_revised.pdf.

National Park Service. *Ford River Rouge Complex.* https://www.nps.gov/nr/travel/detroit/ d38.htm.

Nationwide advertisement. https://www.youtube.com/watch?v=jpHcFzJ6glI.

Natter, Raymond. *Home Ownership Equity Protection Act of 1994.* http://apps.americanbar. org/buslaw/committees/CL130000pub/newsletter/200708/natter.pdf.

Natter, Raymond, and Katie Wechsler. "Dodd-Frank Act and National Bank Preemption: Much Ado about Nothing." *Virginia Law & Business Review* 7, no. 2 (Fall 2012), http:// ssrn.com/abstract=2046173.

Neal, Michael. "Written Submission of GE Capital to the Financial Crisis Inquiry Commission by Michael A. Neal, Chairman and CEO of GE Capital and Vice Chairman of GE." May 6, 2010, http://fcic-static.law.stanford.edu/cdn_media/fcic-testimony/2010-0506-Neal.pdf.

Neely, Michelle Clark. *Industrial Loan Companies Come out of the Shadows.* Federal Reserve Bank of St. Louis, July 2007, https://www.stlouisfed.org/publications/regional-economist/july–2007/industrial-loan-companies-come-out-of-the-shadows.

Newman, Rick. "How 11 Corporate Titans Profited after Failure." *U.S. News,* June 29, 2011, http://money.usnews.com/money/blogs/flowchart/2011/06/29/how–11-corporate -titans-profited-after-failure.

Nocera, Joe. "Corporate Welfare for the Kochs." *New York Times*, Oct. 10, 2015, https:// www.nytimes.com/2015/10/11/opinion/sunday/corporate-welfare-for-the-kochs.html.

———. "Even at the End, Ken Lay Didn't Get It." *New York Times,* July 6, 2006, http:// www.nytimes.com/2006/07/06/business/06nocera.html.

Norris, Floyd. "Orange County's Bankruptcy." *New York Times,* Dec. 8, 1994.

Noyes, Alexander D. *History of the National Bank Currency.* National Monetary Commission, 61st Cong., 2d. sess., U.S. Government Printing Office, 1910, https://fraser.stlouisfed.org/ scribd/?title_id=635&filepath=/files/docs/historical/nmc/nmc_572_1910.pdf

Obeidat, Sara. "Justice Department Signals a Shift in Policing of Wall Street." *Frontline,* Sept. 10, 2015, http://www.pbs.org/wgbh/frontline/article/justice-department-signals-a-shift-in-its-policing-of-wall-street/ (part of *The Untouchables* series).

O'Brien, Timothy L. "Fed Assesses Citigroup Unit $70 Million in Loan Abuse." *New York Times,* May 28, 2004.

O'Dell, John. "Lincoln Savings' Parent Files for Chapter 11." *Los Angeles Times,* Apr. 14, 1989, http://articles.latimes.com/1989-04-14/business/fi–1760_1_lincoln-savings-parent-files-john-h-rousselot-s-l-regulators.

"Offerings Increase in Chicago Churches." *New York Times,* Mar. 13, 1933.

Office of the Special Inspector General for the Troubled Asset Relief Program (SIGTARP). *Quarterly Report to Congress.* July 21, 2009, https://www.sigtarp.gov/Quarterly%20 Reports/July2009_Quarterly_Report_to_Congress.pdf.

Office of Thrift Supervision. "Housing Conference, Dec. 3, 2007." https://www.c-span.org/ video/?202638–1/housing-market-outlook-panel–1.

O'Hara, Terence, and Kathleen Day. "Riggs Bank Hid Assets of Pinochet Senate Report Says." *Washington Post,* July 15, 2004, http://www.washingtonpost.com/wp-dyn/articles/ A50222-2004Jul14.html.

Olick, Diana. "Subprime Mortgages Make a Comeback—With a New Name and Soaring Demand."CNBC,April12,2018,https://www.cnbc.com/2018/04/12/sub-prime-mortgages-morph-into-non-prime-loans-and-demand-soars.html

Olney, Martha L. *Buy Now, Pay Later: Advertising, Credit and Consumer Durables in the 1920s.* University of North Carolina Press, 1991.

Oppel, Richard A. "Merrill Replaced Research Analyst Who Upset Enron." *New York Times,* July 30, 2002, http://mobile.nytimes.com/2002/07/30/business/merrill-replaced-research-analyst-who-upset-enron.html.

Oppel, Richard A., and Andrew Ross Sorkin. "Enron's Collapse: The Overview." *New York Times,* Dec. 3, 2001, http://www.nytimes.com/2001/12/03/business/enron-s-collapse-the-overview-enron-corp-files-largest-us-claim-for-bankruptcy.html.

Orol, Ronald. "U.S. Breaks Down $9.3 Billion Robo-Signing Settlement." *MarketWatch,* Feb. 28, 2013, http://www.marketwatch.com/story/us-breaks-down–93-bln-robo-signing-settlement-2013-02-28.

Ott, Julia C. "The Free and Open People's Market: Political Ideology and Retail Brokerage at the New York Stock Exchange, 1913–1933." *Journal of American History* (June 2009).

———. *When Wall Street Met Main Street: The Quest for an Investors' Democracy.* Harvard University Press, 2011.

"Overnight Reverse Repurchase Agreement Facility." Board of Governors of the Federal Reserve System, Jan. 3, 2018, https://www.federalreserve.gov/monetarypolicy/overnight-reverse-repurchase-agreements.htm.

Pace University Law School. *Financial Crisis and Recovery: Financial Crisis Timeline.* http://libraryguides.law.pace.edu/financialcrisis.

Park, Kevin. *Fannie, Freddie, and the Foreclosure Crisis.* Center for Community Capital, University of North Carolina, Sept. 2010, http://ccc.sites.unc.edu/files/2013/02/ FannieFreddieForeclosure.pdf.

Parkinson, Patrick M. *Progress Report by the President's Working Group on Financial Markets.* Testimony before the Committee on Agriculture, Nutrition and Forestry, U.S. Senate, Dec. 16, 1998, https://www.federalreserve.gov/boarddocs/testimony/1998/19981216.htm.

Partnoy, Frank. *Enron and Derivatives.* Testimony before the U.S. Senate Committee on Governmental Affairs, Jan. 24, 2002.

———. "Enron Trading Risks," *PBS NewsHour,* Mar. 19, 2002.

————. *The Match King: The Financial Genius behind a Century of Wall Street Scandals.* Public Affairs, 2009.

Pasley, Fred. D. *Al Capone: The Biography of a Self-Made Man.* University of Illinois, 1930, https://archive.org/stream/alcaponebiograp0pasl/alcaponebiograp0pasl_djvu.txt.

Paulson, Henry M., Jr. *On the Brink.* Updated trade ed. Hachette Book Group, 2013.

Pecora, Ferdinand. *Wall Street under Oath: The Story of Our Modern Money Changers.* 1939; Graymalkin Media, 2014.

Peirce, Charles. *A Meteorological Account of the Weather in Philadelphia: From January 1, 1790 to January 1, 1847.* Lindsay and Blakiston, 1847.

Peirce, Hester. "Five Questions about the DoL Fiduciary Rules." Brown Brothers Harriman website, May 15, 2017, https://ontheregs.com/2017/05/15/five-questions-about-the-dol-fiduciary-rule/.

Pellgrini, Frank. "Person of the Week: 'Enron Whistleblower' Sherron Watkins." *Time,* Jan. 18, 2002, http://content.time.com/time/nation/article/0,8599,194927,00.html.

Perino, Michael. *The Hellhound of Wall Street.* Penguin, 2011.

Perlberg, Steven. "Former Fed Governor." *Business Insider,* Jan. 14, 2014, http://www.businessinsider.com/kevin-warsh-too-big-to-fail-2014-1.

Pew Charitable Trusts. *Home Foreclosures Could Decrease Municipal Tax Base by $356 Billion.* Government Finance Officers Association, June 2008.

————. *The Precarious State of Family Balance Sheets.* Jan. 2015, http://www.pewtrusts.org/en/research-and-analysis/reports/2015/01/the-precarious-state-of-family-balance-sheets.

————. *State of the Union, 2016.* http://www.pewtrusts.org/en/research-and-analysis/analysis/2016/01/13/state-of-the-union–2016-securing-the-american-dream.

————. *America's Shrinking Middle Class: A Close Look at Changes within Metropolitan Areas.* May 11, 2016, http://www.pewsocialtrends.org/2016/05/11/americas-shrinking-middle-class-a-close-look-at-changes-within-metropolitan-areas/.

Peyton, Rupert. "Amazing Stunts and Escapades Featured Career of 'Kingfish.'" *Berkeley Daily Gazette*, Sept. 10, 1935.

Phillips, Matt. "The Long Story of U.S. Debt." *Atlantic,* Nov. 13, 2012, http://www.theatlantic.com/business/archive/2012/11/the-long-story-of-us-debt-from-1790-to-2011-in-1-little-chart/265185/.

Pierce, Andrew. "The Queen Asks Why No One Saw the Crunch Coming." *Telegraph,* Nov. 5, 2008, http://www.telegraph.co.uk/news/uknews/theroyalfamily/3386353/The-Queen-asks-why-no-one-saw-the-credit-crunch-coming.html.

Piketty, Thomas. *Capital in the 21st Century.* Harvard University Press, 2014.

Piketty, Thomas, and Emmanuel Saez. "Income Inequality in the United States, 1913–1998." *Quarterly Journal of Economics* 118, no. 1 (Feb. 2003), https://eml.berkeley.edu/~saez/pikettyqje.pdf.

Piketty, Thomas, Emmanuel Saez, and Gabriel Zucman. *Economic Growth in the United States: A Tale of Two Countries.* Washington Center for Economic Growth, Dec. 6, 2016, http://equitablegrowth.org/research-analysis/economic-growth-in-the-united-states-a-tale-of-two-countries/.

Pollack, Andrew. "Ending Suit, Merrill Lynch to Pay California County $400 Million." *New York Times,* June 3, 1998, http://www.nytimes.com/1998/06/03/business/ending-suit-merrill-lynch-to-pay-california-county-400-million.html.

Ponczek, Sarah. "Greenspan Says He Would Like to See Dodd-Frank Bank Law Repealed." *Bloomberg,* Sept. 22, 2016, https://www.bloomberg.com/news/articles/2016-09-22/greenspan-says-he-would-like-to-see-dodd-frank-bank-law-repealed.

Popper, Nathaniel. "Senate Spars with Goldman Sachs over Commodities." *New York Times,* Nov. 20, 2014, https://dealbook.nytimes.com/2014/11/20/goldman-in-testy-exchange-at-senate-panel-over-its-role-in-commodities-market/?_r=0.

Popper, Nathaniel, and Peter Eavis. "Senate Report Finds Goldman and JPMorgan Can Influence Commodities." *New York Times,* Nov. 19, 2014, https://dealbook.nytimes.com/2014/11/19/senate-report-criticizes-goldman-and-jpmorgan-over-their-roles-in-commodities-market/?ref=dealbook.

Post, Mitchell A. "The Evolution of the U.S. Commercial Paper Market since 1980." Federal Reserve Board, Dec. 1992, https://fraser.stlouisfed.org/files/docs/publications/FRB/pages/1990–1994/32988_1990–1994.pdf.

Powell, Michael, and Gretchen Morgenson. "MERS? It May Have Swallowed Your Loan." *New York Times,* Mar. 5, 2011.

Powell, Robert. "Is Trump a Threat to the Fiduciary Rule?" *MarketWatch,* Jan. 28, 2017, http://www.marketwatch.com/story/what-if-trump-kills-the-fiduciary-rule-2017-01-23?mod=MW_video_latest_news.

Pozen, Robert C. "Is It Fair to Blame Fair Value Accounting for the Financial Crisis?" *Harvard Business Review* (Nov. 2009).

President's Working Group on Financial Markets. *Hedge Funds, Leverage and the Lessons of Long-Term Capital Management.* Apr. 1999, https://www.treasury.gov/resource-center/fin-mkts/Documents/hedgfund.pdf.

———. *Over-the-Counter Derivatives Markets and the Commodity Exchange Act.* Nov. 1999, https://www.treasury.gov/resource-center/fin-mkts/Documents/otcact.pdf.

Preston, Howard Hall. *History of Banking in Iowa.* Iowa City, State Historical Society of Iowa, 1922, https://archive.org/stream/historyofbanking00presrich#page/8/mode/2up.

Preston, Wilbur D., Jr., *Report of the Special Counsel of the Savings and Loan Crisis.* Jan. 8, 1986, http://msa.maryland.gov/megafile/msa/speccol/sc5300/sc5339/000113/016000/016697/unrestricted/20130665e.pdf.

Prial, Dustan. "SEC: Self-Funding vs. Congressional Appropriations," *Fox Business,* May 17, 2013, http://www.foxbusiness.com/politics/2013/05/16/sec-self-funding-vs-congressional-appropriations.html.

"Prime Rate History." *Wall Street Journal,* http://www.fedprimerate.com/wall_street_journal_prime_rate_history.htm.

Propublica. *History of U.S. Government Bailouts.* Updated Apr. 15, 2009, https://projects.propublica.org/bailout/.

Protess, Ben. "S&P's $1.37 Billion Reckoning over Crisis-Era Misdeeds." *New York Times,* Feb. 3, 2015, http://dealbook.nytimes.com/2015/02/03/s-p-announces-1-37-billion-settlement-with-prosecutors/.

Protess, Ben, and Jessica Silver-Greenberg. "Under Trump, Banking Watchdog Trades Its Bite for a Tamer Stance," *New York Times,* Nov. 15, 2017, https://www.nytimes.com/2017/11/15/business/bank-regulation.html.

Pujo Hearings. *Money Trust Investigation: Investigation of Financial and Monetary Conditions in the United States under House Resolutions Nos. 429 and 504, before a Subcommittee of the Committee on Banking and Currency, 1912–1913.* https://fraser.stlouisfed.org/title/80.

———. *Report of the Committee Appointed Pursuant to House Resolutions 429 and 504 to Investigate the Concentration of Control of Money and Credit.* https://www.scribd.com/doc/34121180/Pujo-Committee-Report-Report-of-the-Committee-Appointed-Pursuant-to-House-Resolutions-429-and-504-1912-1913-Pujo-Committee-Report.

"Queen Told How Economists Missed Financial Crisis." *Telegraph,* July 26, 2009, http://www.telegraph.co.uk/news/uknews/theroyalfamily/5912697/Queen-told-how-economists-missed-financial-crisis.html.

Quinn, Susan. *Furious Improvisation: How the WPA and a Cast of Thousands Made High Art Out of Desperate Times.* Walker & Co., 2008.

Quint, Michael. "Citibank Rethinks Its Lending." *New York Times,* Jan. 6, 1993, https://www.washingtonpost.com/archive/politics/1993/05/16/the-saving-of-citibank/64323ac1-db21-43e4-b89e-a3171324c202/.

Ramo, Joshua Cooper. "The Three Marketeers." *Time*, Feb. 15, 1999.

Rampell, Catherine. "Lax Oversight Caused Crisis, Bernanke Says." *New York Times,* Jan. 3, 2010, http://www.nytimes.com/2010/01/04/business/economy/04fed.html.

Rappeport, Alan, and Amy Flitter. "Congress Approves First Big Dodd-Frank Rollback." *New York Times,* May 22, 2018.

Raskob, John J. "Everybody Ought to Be Rich." *Ladies' Home Journal,* Aug. 1929, https://www.joshuakennon.com/wp-content/uploads/2013/01/Everybody-Ought-to-Be-Rich.pdf.

"Raskob Radio Pool Realized $5,000,000." *New York Times*, May 20, 1932.

Reagan, Ronald. "Statement on the Competitive Equality Banking Act of 1987." http://www.presidency.ucsb.edu/ws/?pid=34677.

Reagan, Ronald. "Remarks to State Chairpersons of the National White House Conference on Small Business." Aug. 15, 1986, https://www.reaganlibrary.gov/sites/default/files/archives/speeches/1986/081586e.htm.

Reckard, Scott E. "Refinance Pitches in Sub-Prime Tone." *Los Angeles Times,* Apr. 22, 2007, http://articles.latimes.com/2007/oct/29/business/fi-loanpitch29.

———. "Wells Fargo Fires Workers Accused of Cheating on Sales Goals." *Los Angeles Times,* Oct. 3, 2013, http://articles.latimes.com/2013/oct/03/business/la-fi-mo-wells-fargo-workers-fired-20131003.

———. "Wells Fargo's Pressure-Cooker Sales Culture Comes at a Cost." *Los Angeles Times,* Dec. 21, 2013, http://www.latimes.com/business/la-fi-wells-fargo-sale-pressure-20131222-story.html.

Rennison, Joe. "New Treasuries 'Rep' Rate to Replace Libor." *Financial Times,* June 22, 2017.

Renzulli, Kerri Anne. "This Is How Much Debt the Average American Has Now." *Time*, Apr. 13, 2018, http://time.com/money/5233033/average-debt-every-age/.

"Reports on Wells Fargo Whistleblowers Spark Inquiry in Congress." National Public Radio, Dec. 30, 2016, http://www.npr.org/2016/12/30/507597691/for-whistleblowers-repercussions-are-felt-beyond-wells-fargo.

Republican Platform, 2016. https://prod-cdn-static.gop.com/media/documents/DRAFT_12_FINAL[1]-ben_1468872234.pdf.

"Review of *The Forgotten Depression: 1921: The Crash That Cured Itself*, by James Grant." *Economist,* Nov. 8, 2014.

Rice, Laura. *Maryland History in Prints.* Maryland Historical Society, 2001.

Rice, Tata, and Jonathan Rose. "When Good Investments Go Bad: The Contraction in Community Bank Lending after the 2008 GSE Takeover." Board of Governors of the Federal Reserve System, International Finance Discussion Papers 1045, Mar. 2012, https://www.federalreserve.gov/pubs/ifdp/2012/1045/default.htm.

Rich, Richard. "The Great Recession." *Federal Reserve History,* Nov. 22, 2013, https://www.federalreservehistory.org/essays/great_recession_of_200709.

"Richard Whitney, 1888–1974." *Harvard Crimson,* Dec. 13, 1974, http://www.thecrimson.com/article/1974/12/13/richard-whitney-1888-1974-pbbby-the-time/.

Richardson, Gary, et al. *McFadden Act of 1927.* http://www.federalreservehistory.org/Events/DetailView/11.

———. *Roosevelt's Gold Program, Spring 1933.* http://www.federalreservehistory.org/Events/DetailView/24.

Richey, Warren. "Newt Gingrich Ethics Investigation: 4 Facts You Haven't Heard from Him." *Christian Science Monitor,* Feb. 6, 2012, http://www.csmonitor.com/USA/Elections/President/2012/0206/Newt-Gingrich-ethics-investigation–4-facts-you-haven-t-heard-from-him/Gingrich-not-exonerated-of-ethics-violations.

Richman, Louis S. "Who Is Nick Brady? Why It Matters." *Fortune*, May 22, 1989.

Ritholtz, Barry. "It's Too Late for Trump to Stop This Financial Rule." *Washington Post,* Feb. 6, 2017, https://www.washingtonpost.com/news/wonk/wp/2017/02/06/its-too-late-for-trump-to-stop-this-financial-rule/?utm_term=.bc7d55bc752a.

Rivlin, Alice M., and John B. Soroushian. "Credit Rating Agency Reform Is Incomplete." *Brookings,* Mar. 6, 2017, https://www.brookings.edu/research/credit-rating-agency-reform-is-incomplete/.

Rogers, W. A. *Great Activity in Wall Street.* Editorial cartoon, 1908. Library of Congress, Prints & Photographs Division, http://www.loc.gov/pictures/item/2010717683/.

———. Series of Editorial Cartoons at the turn of the century showing sheep being taken advantage of by the bulls and bears of Wall Street. http://www.loc.gov/pictures/search/?q=lambs%2C%20bears%20and%20bulls.

———. "Will Rogers Claps Hands for the President's Speech." *New York Times,* Mar. 14, 1933.

———. *Will Rogers' Daily Telegrams,* vol. 4: *The Roosevelt Years.* Oklahoma State University Press, 1979. Revised and reprinted online by Will Rogers Memorial Museums, Claremore, OK, 2008, https://drive.google.com/file/d/0Bz3yw4a2bM_Wd0xBajY5cEFkczA/view.

Roig-Franzia, Manuel. "Credit Crisis Cassandra." *Washington Post,* May 26, 2009, http://www.washingtonpost.com/wp-dyn/content/article/2009/05/25/AR2009052502108_pf.html.

Roosevelt, Franklin D. *Fireside Chats.* http://www.presidency.ucsb.edu/fireside.php.

———. *On Our Way.* John Day Co., 1934.

———. "President Franklin Roosevelt's First Fireside Chat." C-SPAN video archive, Mar. 12, 1933, https://www.c-span.org/video/?298210–1/president-franklin-roosevelts-fireside-chat.

———. *The Public Papers and Addresses of Franklin D. Roosevelt,* vols. 2 and 3. Random House, 1938, http://quod.lib.umich.edu/p/ppotpus/4925381.1933.001?rgn=works;view=toc;rgn1=author;q1=roosevelt%2C+franklin.

"Roosevelt 'Won' to Bank Insurance." *New York Times*, Oct. 27, 1936.

Rosner, Joshua. *Examining Financial Holding Companies: Should Banks Control Power Plants, Warehouses and Oil Refineries?* July 23, 2013, U.S. House Committee on Financial Services, https://www.gpo.gov/fdsys/pkg/CHRG–113shrg82568/pdf/CHRG–113shrg82568.pdf.

———. *Fannie Mae and Freddie Mac: How Government Housing Policy Failed Homeowners and Taxpayers and Led to the Financial Crisis.* Testimony before the U.S. House Financial Services Committee, Subcommittee on Capital Markets and Government Sponsored Enterprises, Mar. 6, 2012, http://financialservices.house.gov/uploadedfiles/hhrg–113-ba16-wstate-jrosner–20130306.pdf.

———. "Housing in the New Millennium: A Home without Equity Is Just a Rental with Debt." Graham Fisher & Co., June 29, 2001, http://ssrn.com/abstract=1162456.

———. "The Time Has Come to Turn the GSEs into Utilities." *American Banker,* Aug. 4, 2016.

Rothbard, Murray N. *An Austrian Perspective on the History of Economic Thought,* vol. 2. Ludwig von Mises Institute, 2010. Pp. 212–213.

Rowe, James L. Jr., "Penn Square: A Painful Lesson." *Washington Post,* Aug. 1, 1982.

Ruben, Marina Koestler. "Radio Activity: The 100th Anniversary of Public Broadcasting." Smithsonian.com, Jan. 26, 2010, http://www.smithsonianmag.com/history/radio-activity-the–100th-anniversary-of-public-broadcasting–6555594/.

Rubin, Robert E. "Remarks to Woodrow Wilson International Center for Scholars." Oct. 20, 1998, https://www.treasury.gov/press-center/press-releases/Pages/rr2766.aspx.

Ruebling, Charlotte E. *The Administration of Regulation Q.* Federal Reserve Bank of St. Louis, Feb. 1970.

Saez, Emmanuel. "Striking It Richer, The Evolution of Top Incomes in the United States." University of California, Berkeley, Sept. 3, 2013, http://eml.berkeley.edu//~saez/saez-UStopincomes–2012.pdf.

———. "U.S. Top One Percent of Income Earners Hit New High in 2015 amid Strong Economic Growth." Equitablegrowth.org, July 1, 2016.

Salmon, Felix. "How Larry Summers Lost Harvard $1.8 Billion." Reuters, Nov. 29, 2009, http://blogs.reuters.com/felix-salmon/2009/11/29/how-larry-summers-lost-harvard–18-billion/.

Saunders, Lauren K. *Preemption and Regulatory Reform: Restore the States' Traditional Role as "First Responder."* National Consumer Law Center, Sept. 2009.

Saunders, Margot, and Alys Cohen. "Federal Regulation of Consumer Credit: The Cause or the Cure for Predatory Lending?" Harvard University, Joint Center for Housing Studies Working Paper Series, BABC 02–21, Mar. 2004.

Scharf, John Thomas. *History of Baltimore City and County.* https://babel.hathitrust.org/cgi/pt?id=loc.ark:/13960/t5n87w204;view=1up;seq=9.

Schlesinger, Arthur M., Jr. *The Coming of the New Deal.* Houghton Mifflin, 1959.

———. *The Crisis of the Old Order, 1919–1933.* Houghton Mifflin, 1957.

Schloemer, Ellen, et al. *Losing Ground.* Center for Responsible Lending, 2006, http://www.peri.umass.edu/fileadmin/pdf/conference_papers/SAFER/Schloemer_etal_Losing_Ground.pdf.

Schmidt, Robert. "The CFPB: Center for Partisan Bickering." *Bloomberg,* Nov. 30, 2017, https://www.bloomberg.com/news/articles/2017-11-30/the-cfpb-center-for-partisan-bickering.

Scholes, Myron S. "Derivatives in a Dynamic Environment." Nobel Lecture, Dec. 8, 1997, http://www.nobelprize.org/nobel_prizes/economic-sciences/laureates/1997/scholes-lecture.pdf.

Schwartz, John. "Enron's Collapse: The Analyst; Man Who Doubted Enron Enjoys New Recognition." *New York Times,* Jan. 21, 2002, http://mobile.nytimes.com/2002/01/21/business/enron-s-collapse-the-analyst-man-who-doubted-enron-enjoys-new-recognition.html.

Schwartz, Nelson. "Can Trump Save Their Jobs?" *New York Times*, Nov. 13, 2016.

———. "Velvet Rope Economy." *New York Times,* Apr. 24, 2016, http://www.nytimes.com/2016/04/24/business/economy/velvet-rope-economy.html?_r=0 WEALTH GAP.

Securities and Exchange Commission. "Credit Rating Agencies and Nationally Recognized Statistical Rating Organizations (NRSROs)." https://www.sec.gov/answers/nrsro.htm.

———. Description of mutual funds and hedge funds. https://www.sec.gov/investor/pubs/inwsmf.htm.

———. "Dodd-Frank Act Rulemaking: Derivatives." May 4, 2015, https://www.sec.gov/spotlight/dodd-frank/derivatives.shtml.

———. "Exchange Act Release No. 34-31554." Securities Exchange Act of 1934 in the Matter of John H. Gutfreund et. al., Administrative Proceeding File 3-7930, Dec. 3, 1992, http://ocw.mit.edu/courses/sloan-school-of-management/15-649-the-law-of-mergers-and-acquisitions-spring-2003/study-materials/class13gutfreund.pdf.

———. Governing laws. https://www.sec.gov/about/laws.shtml.

———. "1933 and 1934 Acts." https://www.sec.gov/about/laws.shtml, and https://www.sec.gov/answers/about-lawsshtml.html.

———. *2008 Report from the Office of the Chief Accountant. Report and Recommendations Pursuant to Section 133 of the Emergency Economic Stabilization Act of 2008: Study on Mark-To-Market Accounting.* https://www.sec.gov/files/marktomarket123008.pdf.

Securities and Exchange Commission v. Syron et al. at Freddie Mac. https://www.sec.gov/litigation/complaints/2011/comp-pr2011-267-freddiemac.pdf.

Seelye, Katherine. "Sacramento and Its Riverside Tent City." *New York Times,* Mar. 11, 2009, http://thelede.blogs.nytimes.com/2009/03/11/tent-city-report/?_r=0.

Seligman, Joel. *The Transformation of Wall Street.* Aspen Publishers, 2003.

Servon, Lisa J. "The High Cost, for the Poor, of Using a Bank." *New Yorker*, Oct. 9, 2013, http://www.newyorker.com/business/currency/the-high-cost-for-the-poor-of-using-a-bank.

Shaffer, Sanders. "Fair Value Accounting: Villain or Innocent Victim?" Federal Reserve Bank of Boston, Jan. 31, 2010.

Shalhope, Robert E. *The Baltimore Bank Riot: Political Upheaval in Antebellum Maryland.* University of Illinois Press, 2009.

Sherman, Matthew. *A Short History of Financial Deregulation in the United States.* Center for Economic and Policy Research, July 2009.

Shiller, Robert J. *Finance and the Good Society.* Princeton University Press, 2012.

———. *Irrational Exuberance,* 2nd ed. Doubleday, 2005.

Shorter, Gary. *The Resolution Trust Corp.: Historical Analysis.* Congressional Research Service. Sept. 26, 2008, https://www.everycrsreport.com/files/20080926_RS22959_ea6bff6b53cc5935a48babae0cd85400cda96cf8.pdf.

Siconolfi, Michael, and Laurie P. Cohen. "The Treasury Auction Scandal at Salomon—Sullied Solly." *Wall Street Journal,* Aug. 19, 1991.

Silber, William L. "How Volcker Launched His Attack on Inflation." *Bloomberg,* Aug. 20, 2012, https://www.bloomberg.com/view/articles/2012-08-20/how-volcker-launched-his-attack-on-inflation.

———. "Why Did FDR's Bank Holiday Succeed?" Federal Reserve Bank of New York, *Economic Policy Review,* July 2009, https://www.newyorkfed.org/medialibrary/media/research/epr/09v15n1/0907silb.pdf.

Silver-Greenberg, Jessica, and Susanne Craid. "Fined Billions, JPMorgan Will Give Dimon a Raise." *New York Times,* Jan. 23, 2014, https://dealbook.nytimes.com/2014/01/23/fined-billions-bank-approves-raise-for-chief/.

Simon, Ruth. "The Prepayment Trap: Lenders Put Penalties on Popular Mortgages." *Wall Street Journal,* Mar. 10, 2005, http://www.wsj.com/articles/SB111041540322375313.

Sirota, David. "Charles Koch Blasts Subsidies and Tax Credits, but Has Taken $195 Million Worth of Them." *International Business Times,* Aug. 2, 2015, http://www.ibtimes.com/charles-koch-blasts-subsidies-tax-credits-his-firm-has-taken–195-million-worth-them–2034949.

Sloan, Allen. "Grasso's Gone but Plenty of Corporate and Political Excesses Remain." *Washington Post,* Sept. 23, 2003.

Smith, Aaron. "Five Things You Don't Know about Bernie Madoff's Epic Scam." CNN, Dec. 11, 2013, http://money.cnn.com/2013/12/10/news/companies/bernard-madoff-ponzi/.

Smith, Yves. "U.S.: The Most Deceitful Form of Socialism?" *Naked Capitalism,* July 12, 2008, https://www.nakedcapitalism.com/2008/07/us-most-deceitful-form-of-socialism.html.

Sobel, Robert. *The Great Bull Market: Wall Street in the 1920s.* W.W. Norton, 1968.

Sorkin, Andrew Ross. "Paulson's Itchy Finger, on the Trigger of a Bazooka." *New York Times,* Sept. 8, 2008, http://www.nytimes.com/2008/09/09/business/09sorkin.html.

Sprague, O. M. W. *History of Crises under the National Banking System.* https://fraser.stlouisfed.org/scribd/?title_id=633&filepath=/files/docs/historical/nmc/nmc_538_1910.pdf.

Stanger, Tobie. "How Trump Plan Would Ease Mortgage-Lending Rules." *Consumer Reports,* June 14, 2017, https://www.consumerreports.org/mortgages/how-trump-plan-would-ease-mortgage-lending-rules/.

Stashenko, Joel. "AG, State Regulators Vow to Defend 'Blue Sky' Laws from Trump." Law.com, Nov. 17, 2016, http://www.law.com/sites/almstaff/2016/11/17/ag-state-regulators-vow-to-defend-blue-sky-laws-from-trump/?slreturn=20170001194343.

Steelman, Aaron. *The Federal Reserve's "Dual Mandate": The Evolution of an Idea.* Federal Reserve Bank of Richmond, Economic Brief, Dec. 2011, https://www.richmondfed.org/~/media/richmondfedorg/publications/research/economic_brief/2011/pdf/eb_11-12.pdf.

Stempel, Jonathon. "Lawsuit Says Wells Fargo Auto Insurance Charges Were a Fraud." Reuters, July 31, 2017, https://www.reuters.com/article/us-wells-fargo-insurance/lawsuit-says-wells-fargo-auto-insurance-charges-were-a-fraud-idUSKBN1AG20Q.

Stewart, James. "Just Deserts, or Just Cruel?" *New York Times,* Apr. 20, 2018.

Stock, Catherine McNicol. *Rural Radicals: Righteous Rage in the American Grain.* Cornell University Press, 1996.

———. "Violence in the 1930s." *New York Times,* Jan. 10, 2011.

Stockman, David. "Taxing Wall Street down to Size." *New York Times,* Jan. 19, 2010, http://www.nytimes.com/2010/01/20/opinion/20stockman.html.

Stojanovic, Dusan, and Mark D. Vaughan. "Is Federal Home Loan Bank Funding a Risky Business for the FDIC?" Federal Reserve Bank of St. Louis, https://www.stlouisfed.org/publications/regional-economist/october–2000/is-federal-home-loan-bank-funding-a-risky-business-for-the-fdic.

Stone, Peter. "Data Firm in Talks for Role in White House Messaging—and Trump Business." *Guardian,* Nov. 23, 2016, https://www.theguardian.com/us-news/2016/nov/23/donald-trump-cambridge-analytica-steve-bannon.

Strain, Michael. *Want to Fight Economic Inequality? Focus on Growing the Economy Faster.* American Enterprise Institute, Oct. 21, 2015, https://www.aei.org/publication/why-we-need-economic-growth-more-than-we-need-democratic-socialism/.

Summers, Larry. "Lawrence Summers on 'House of Debt.'" *Financial Times*, June 6, 2014, https://www.ft.com/content/3ec604c0-ec96-11e3-8963-00144feabdc0#axzz34AYqP5mO.

"Supreme Court History: The First 100 Years." PBS, *Thirteen: Media with Impact,* Dec. 2006, https://www.thirteen.org/wnet/supremecourt/antebellum/landmark.html.

Sutch, Richard. *Liberty Bonds.* http://www.federalreservehistory.org/Events/DetailView/100.

Sylla, Richard. "Early American Banking: The Significance of the Corporate Form." *Business and Economic History,* 2nd ser., vol. 14, 1985, Library of Congress Catalog no. 85-072859.

———. "Federal Policy, Banking Market Structure, and Capital Mobilization in the United States, 1863–1913." *Journal of Economic History* 29 (1969): 657–686.

———. "Forgotten Men of Money: Private Bankers in Early U.S. History." *Journal of Economic History* 36, no. 1 (Mar. 1976): 173–188.

———. "The U.S. Banking System: Origin, Development and Regulation." *Journal of the Gilder Lehrman Institute,* https://www.gilderlehrman.org/history-by-era/hamiltoneconomics/essays/us-banking-system-origin-development-and-regulation (accessed Dec. 22, 2017).

Sylla, Richard, John B. Legler, and John J. Wallis. "Banks and State Public Finance in the New Republic: The United States, 1790–1860." *Journal of Economic History* 47, no. 2 (June 1987): 391–403.

Taub, Jennifer. *Other People's Houses.* Yale University Press, 2014.

Terrell, Ellen. *History of the U.S. Income Tax.* Library of Congress, https://www.loc.gov/rr/business/hottopic/irs_history.html.

Thomas, Paulette. "Seidman Raises Estimate of Size of FDIC Deficit." *Wall Street Journal,* June 28, 1991.

———. "At Garn Institute, S&L Executives Get to Rub Shoulders with U.S. Regulators." *Wall Street Journal,* Nov. 16, 1989.

Thompson, Derek. "The 100-Year March of Technology." *Atlantic,* Apr. 7, 2012, https://www.theatlantic.com/technology/archive/2012/04/the–100-year-march-of-technology-in–1-graph/255573/.

Thompson, Robert B. "Piercing the Corporate Veil: An Empirical Study." *Cornell Law Review* 76, 1036 (1991), http://scholarship.law.cornell.edu/clr/vol76/iss5/2.

"TimeLine: History of Merrill Lynch." Reuters, Sept. 15, 2008, http://www.nytimes.com/1986/01/27/business/going-public-on-wall-street.html?pagewanted=all.

"Timeline of Enron's Collapse." The *Washington Post*'s Series on the Enron Scandal, 2002, http://www.washingtonpost.com/wp-srv/business/enron/front.html.

"Timeline of Wall Street." PBS, *American Experience*, http://www.pbs.org/wgbh/americanexperience/features/timeline/crash/.

"Top 10 Bankruptcies." *Time*, n.d., http://content.time.com/time/specials/packages/article/0,28804,1841334_1841431_1841358,00.html.

"Trotsky Says We Will Centralize Banks and Be Financially Stronger Than Ever." *New York Times,* Mar. 18, 1933.

Tully, Shawn. "Lewie Ranieri Wants to Fix the Mortgage Mess." *Fortune*, Dec. 9, 2009, http://archive.fortune.com/2009/12/08/real_estate/lewie_ranieri_mortgages.fortune/index.htm.

Twain, Mark, and Charles Dudley Warner. *The Writings of Mark Twain: The Gilded Age.* American Publishing, 1899.

Unger, Irwin. *The Greenback Era: A Social and Political History of American Finance, 1865–1879.* Princeton University Press, 1964.

"Unified Banking Put up to Senate." *New York Times*, Mar. 30, 1933.

United Press International. "Stock Market 'Too Crooked' for Al Capone." *Salt Lake Telegram,* Nov. 3, 1929, https://newspapers.lib.utah.edu/details?id=15615975#t_15615975.

U.S. Capitol Historical Society. *A History of the Senate Banking Committee.* http://uschs.org/explore/historical-articles/senate-banking-committee-history/.

U.S. Chamber of Congress. "U.S. Chamber Outlines Reforms to Make Federal Reserve Regulation More Accountable, Transparent." July 12, 2016, https://www.uschamber.com/press-release/us-chamber-outlines-reforms-make-federal-reserve-regulation-more-accountable.

U.S. Commission on Civil Rights. *Civil Rights and the Mortgage Crisis.* Sept. 2009, http://www.usccr.gov/pubs/CRMORTGAGE092509.pdf.

U.S. Congress. *The Competitive Equality Banking Act of 1987,* https://www.gpo.gov/fdsys/pkg/STATUTE–101/pdf/STATUTE–101-Pg552.pdf.

———. "A Concurrent Resolution Reaffirming that Deposits, up to the Statutorily Prescribed Amount, in Federally Insured Depository Institutions, Are Backed by the Full Faith and Credit of the United States." Mar. 16, 1982, https://www.govtrack.us/congress/bills/97/hconres290.

———. *Congressional Record,* vol. 77, pt. 2, 73rd Cong., 1st sess. (Apr. 1933).

————. *Congressional Record,* vol. 77, pt. 4, 73rd Cong., 1st sess. (May 1933).

————. Documents and Statements Pertaining to the Banking Emergency, Presidential Proclamations, Federal Legislation, Executive Orders, Regulations, and Other Documents and Official Statements, part 1, Feb. 25 to Mar. 31, 1933. https://fraser.stlouisfed.org/scribd/?item_id=23564&filepath=/files/docs/historical/federal%20reserve%20history/bank_holiday/bank_emerg_pt1_19330225.pdf.

U.S. Department of Commerce, Bureau of the Census. *Historical Census of Housing Tables.* https://www.census.gov/hhes/www/housing/census/historic/owner.html.

————. *Historical Statistics of the United States, Colonial Times to 1957,* p. 633, on banking, https://fraser.stlouisfed.org/docs/publications/histstatus/hstat_1957_cen_1957.pdf.

————. *Historical Statistics of the United States, Colonial Times to 1970,* part 2, on bank suspensions by state and nationally, https://www.census.gov/history/pdf/1933-46suspensions.pdf.

————. *Households in the U.S.* http://www.census.gov/hhes/families/data/households.html.

————. *Quarterly Residential Vacancies and Homeownership, First Quarter, 2016.* http://www.census.gov/housing/hvs/files/currenthvspress.pdf.

————. *Quarterly Residential Vacancies and Homeownership, Third Quarter, 2016.* http://www.census.gov/housing/hvs/files/currenthvspress.pdf.

U.S. Department of Commerce, Bureau of Economic Analysis. *National Data.* Number on consumer expenditures as a percentage of GNP, https://www.bea.gov/iTable/iTable.cfm?reqid=19&step=2#reqid=19&step=2&isuri=1&1921=survey.

U.S. Department of Health and Human Services. "The Great Pandemic." http://www.flu.gov/pandemic/history/1918/the_pandemic/influenza/index.html.

U.S. Department of Housing and Urban Development. *An Analysis of Mortgage Refinancing, 2001–2003.* Nov. 2004, https://www.huduser.gov/Publications/pdf/MortgageRefinance03.pdf.

————. *Curbing Predatory Home Mortgage Lending.* June 2000, https://www.huduser.gov/portal/publications/hsgfin/curbing.html.

U.S. Department of Justice. "Federal Government and State Attorneys General Reach $25 Billion Agreement with Five Largest Mortgage Servicers to Address Mortgage Loan Servicing and Foreclosure Abuses." Press release, Feb. 9, 2012, https://www.justice.gov/opa/pr/federal-government-and-state-attorneys-general-reach–25-billion-agreement-five-largest.

————. "Former Enron CEO Jeffrey Skilling Resentenced to 168 Months for Fraud, Conspiracy Charges." Press release, June 21, 2013, https://www.justice.gov/opa/pr/former-enron-ceo-jeffrey-skilling-resentenced–168-months-fraud-conspiracy-charges.

U.S. Department of Justice, Federal Bureau of Investigation. "Former Enron Chief Financial Officers Andrew Fastow Pleads Guilty to Conspiracy to Commit Securities and Wire Fraud." Jan. 14, 2004, https://archives.fbi.gov/archives/news/pressrel/press-releases/former-enron-chief-financial-officer-andrew-fastow-pleads-guilty-to-conspiracy-to-commit-securities-and-wire-fraud.

U.S. House of Representatives. *Guide to House Records: Chapter 5, Records of the Banking and Currency Committees,* https://www.archives.gov/legislative/guide/house/chapter–05.html.

————. *Historic Committee Names.* http://history.house.gov/Records-and-Research/FAQs/Committee-Names/.

———. *Report 112–196, Asset-Backed Market Stabilization Act of 2011*. https://www. congress.gov/congressional-report/112th-congress/house-report/196/1?resultIndex =121.

U.S. House of Representatives, Committee on Banking and Currency. *Banking Law, 1913 to 1956*. https://fraser.stlouisfed.org/files/docs/historical/congressional/bankinglaw1913–1956_ complete.pdf.

U.S. House of Representatives, Committee on Oversight and Government Reform. *The Financial Crisis and the Role of Federal Regulators*. Oct. 23, 2008, https://www.gpo.gov/ fdsys/pkg/CHRG–110hhrg55764/html/CHRG–110hhrg55764.htm.

U.S. House of Representatives, Financial Services Committee. *Hearing on Wells Fargo: Holding Wall Street Accountable*. C-SPAN, Sept. 29, 2016, https://www.c-span.org/ video/?415981-1/ceo-john-stumpf-testifies-unauthorized-wells-fargo-accounts.

U.S. Secretary of the Treasury. *Annual Report: FY June 30, 1932*. https://archive.org/stream/ annualreportofse1932unit/annualreportofse1932unit_djvu.txt.

U.S. Senate. *Banking Act of 1935: Hearings before a Subcommittee of the Committee on Banking and Currency, U.S. Senate, 74th Cong., 1st sess., on S. 1715 and H.R. 7617, Bills to Provide for the Sound, Effective, and Uninterrupted Operation of the Banking System, and for Other Purposes. Consolidated, April 19 to June 3, 1935*. http://www.archive.org/ stream/bankingactheari00jrgoog/bankingactheari00jrgoog_djvu.txt.

———. *History of the Committee's Laws*. https://www.banking.senate.gov/public/index. cfm/milestones.

———. *Stock Exchange Practices: Hearings before the Committee on Baking and Currency, 72nd Congress, 1932–1934*. 1st sess. on S. Res. 84, pts. 1 & 2, and sess. 2, https://fraser. stlouisfed.org/title/87.

U.S. Senate, Banking and Currency Committee. *Hearings S.4115, Part I, March 23 to 25, 1933. A Bill to Provide for the Safer and More Effective Use of the Assets of Federal Reserve Banks and of National Banking Associations, to Regulate Interbank Control, to Prevent the Undue Diversion of Funds into Speculative Operations and for Other Purposes*. https://babel.hathitrust.org/cgi/pt?id=mdp.39015037397562;view=1up;seq=5.

U.S. Senate, Committee on Banking, Housing and Urban Affairs. *Financial Services Modernization Act, Gramm-Leach-Bliley. Summary of Provisions*. 1999. http://www. banking.senate.gov/conf/grmleach.htm.

———. *Predatory Mortgage Lending: The Problem, Impact and Responses*. Hearing before the Committee on Banking, Housing and Urban Affairs, July 26 and 27, 2001, https:// www.gpo.gov/fdsys/pkg/CHRG–107shrg82969/pdf/CHRG–107shrg82969.pdf.

———. *Milestones*. https://www.banking.senate.gov/public/index.cfm/milestones.

———. "Unauthorized Wells Fargo Accounts." C-SPAN, Sept. 20, 2016, https://www.c-span.org/video/?415547-1/ceo-john-stumpf-testifies-unauthorized-wells-fargo-accounts.

U.S. Senate, Permanent Subcommittee on Investigations. *Excessive Speculation in the Natural Gas Market*. Hearings, June 25 and July 8, 2007, https://www.hsgac.senate.gov/ imo/media/doc/REPORTExcessiveSpeculationintheNaturalGasMarket.pdf, and https:// ia801901.us.archive.org/32/items/gov.gpo.fdsys.CHRG–110shrg36616/CHRG– 110shrg36616.pdf.

———. *The Role of the Board of Directors in Enron's Collapse*. July 8, 2002, https://www. gpo.gov/fdsys/pkg/CPRT–107SPRT80393/pdf/CPRT–107SPRT80393.pdf.

———. *The Role of the Financial Institutions in Enron's Collapse,* July 23 and 30, 2002, https://www.gpo.gov/fdsys/pkg/CHRG-107shrg81313/html/CHRG-107shrg81313.htm.

———. *Wall Street and the Financial Crisis: Anatomy of a Financial Collapse.* Apr. 13, 2001, https://www.gpo.gov/fdsys/pkg/CHRG–112shrg57323/pdf/CHRG–112shrg57323. pdf.

———. *Wall Street Bank Involvement with Physical Commodities.* Nov. 20 and 21, 2014, https://www.hsgac.senate.gov/imo/media/doc/REPORT-Wall%20Street%20Bank%20 Involvement%20With%20Physical%20Commodities%20(12–5–14).pdf.

U.S. Senate, Special Committee on Aging. *Equity Predators: Stripping, Flipping and Packing Their Way to Profits.* Mar. 16, 1998, http://www.aging.senate.gov/imo/media/ doc/publications/3161998.pdf (chaired by Sen. Charles E. Grassley).

"U.S. Senator Seeks to Strip 'Loophole.'" Reuters, Apr. 14, 2016, http://www.reuters.com/ article/usa-congress-cftc-idUSL2N17H0NN.

U.S. State Department. *Debt of the U.S.* https://history.state.gov/milestones/1784-1800/loans.

U.S. Treasury. *Quarterly Report on Bank Trading and Derivatives Activities: First Quarter 2016 and 2008.* https://www.occ.gov/topics/capital-markets/financial-markets/deriva-tives/dq116.pdf and https://occ.gov/topics/capital-markets/financial-markets/derivatives/ derivatives-quarterly-report.html.

U.S. Treasury, Office of the Comptroller of the Currency. Final Rule from Federal Bank Regulators on Real Estate Lending. Federal Reserve Board 12 CFR Part 208, in *Federal Register* 57 FR 62890, Dec. 31, 1992, https://fcic-static.law.stanford.edu/cdn_media /fcic-docs/1992–12–31%20Final%20Rule%20Real%20Estate%20Lending%20 Standards.pdf.

———. "OCC Assesses $500 Million Penalty against Wells Fargo, Orders Restitution for Unsafe or Unsound Practices." Apr. 20, 2018, https://www.occ.gov/news-issuances/news-releases/2018/nr-occ–2018–41.html.

Valentine, Paul. "Ex-Fugitive S&L Chief Convicted." *Washington Post,* April 2, 1994.

Wall Street Journal. "Paying for Ethics." Nov. 17, 1989.

Walsh, Mary Williams. "S&P Seeks Dismissal of U.S. Suit over Rating of Mortgage Debt." *New York Times,* Apr. 22, 2013, http://dealbook.nytimes.com/2013/04/22/s-p-responds-to-mortgage-ratings-case/.

"Warburg Assails Federal Reserve." *New York Times,* Mar. 8, 1929.

Warsh, Kevin. "The Federal Reserve Needs New Thinking." *Wall Street Journal,* Aug. 25, 2016, http://www.hoover.org/research/federal-reserve-needs-new-thinking.

———. "Regulatory Reform: A Practitioner's Perspective." Speech, Stanford Law School, Apr. 25, 2012.

———. "Remarks: The Volcker Alliance and the Institute for New Economic Thinking Forum." Dec. 5, 2016, https://www.ineteconomics.org/events/financial-crises.

Washington, George. Letter to Richard Henderson, June 19, 1788. https://founders.archives. gov/documents/Washington/04-06-02-0304.

Washington Center for Equitable Growth. http://www.equitablegrowth.org.

Wayne, Leslie. "The Comptroller for the Moment: Banking Lawyer May Have Trod on Some Senatorial Toes." *New York Times,* Dec. 8, 1998, http://www.nytimes.com/ 1998/12/08/business/comptroller-for-moment-banking-lawyer-may-have-trod-some-senatorial-toes.html.

———. "Going Public on Wall Street." *New York Times,* Jan. 27, 1986, http://www.nytimes. com/1986/01/27/business/going-public-on-wall-street.html?pagewanted=all.

Webel, Baird. "Insurance Regulation: Background, Overview, and Legislation in the 114th Congress." Congressional Research Service, Sept. 16, 2015, https://www.everycrsreport. com/files/20150527_R44046_e2d6a0fd05b2d1dcd592275e5255335db2500cec.pdf.

Weber, Warren. *Balance Sheets for U.S. Antebellum State Banks.* Research Department, Federal Reserve Bank of Minneapolis, 2008, http://research.mpls.frb.fed.us/research/ economists/wewproj.html.

———. *Listing of All State Banks with Beginning and Ending Dates.* Research Department, Federal Reserve Bank of Minneapolis, 2005, https://www.minneapolisfed.org/research/ wp/wp634.pdf.

Weisberger, Bernard. *The Dream Maker: William C. Durant, Founder of General Motors.* Little, Brown, 1979.

Wells Fargo. "Proxy Statement 2015." https://www08.wellsfargomedia.com/assets/pdf/ about/investor-relations/annual-reports/2015-proxy-statement.pdf.

Westbrook, Jesse, and Benjamin Bain. "Banks Try on New Volcker Rule, Like Its Wiggle Room." Bloomberg, June 6, 2018.

"What You Need to Know about SIFIs." *Wall Street Journal,* Mar. 30, 2016, https://blogs. wsj.com/briefly/2016/03/30/what-you-need-to-know-about-sifis-the-short-answer/.

Wheelock, David C. "The Federal Response to Home Mortgage Distress: Lessons from the Great Depression." *Federal Reserve Bank of Saint Louis Review* 90, no. 3, pt. 1 (May/June 2008): 133–148, https://research.stlouisfed.org/publications/review/08/05/Wheelock.pdf.

White, Ben. "Banks Celebrate Dawn of Trump Era." *Politico,* Nov. 17, 2016, http://www. politico.com/story/2016/11/donald-trump-wall-street-bankers–231524.

White, Ben, and Kathleen Day. "Grasso Critics Extend to NYSE Board: Wall Street Executives Seeking Changes." *Washington Post,* Sept. 16, 2003.

White, Ben, and Francesco Guerrara. "Investment Banks Split over Fed Loan Facility." *Financial Times,* May 27, 2008, https://www.ft.com/content/0ccfc5ec–2c2a–11dd–9861– 000077b07658.

White, Ben, and David S. Hilzenrath. "NYSE's Role as Regulator Questioned: Industry Group's Protection of Investors Seen as Secondary." *Washington Post,* Sept. 14, 2003.

White, Eugene N. "The Comptroller and the Transformation of American Banking, 1960– 1990." Comptroller of the Currency, 1962, https://books.google.com/books/about/The_ Comptroller_and_the_Transformation_o.html?id=sII_dLAeZBgC&printsec=frontcover &source=kp_read_button&hl=en&output=reader&pg=GBS.PA11.

———. "The Stock Market Boom and Crash of 1929 Revisited." *Journal of Economic Perspectives* 4, no. 2 (Spring 1990): 67–83.

"Why Is the Federal Reserve Paying Banks Interest?" Board of Governors of the Federal Reserve System, Dec. 16, 2015, https://www.federalreserve.gov/faqs/why-is-the-federal- reserve-paying-banks-interest.htm.

Wicker, Elmus. *The Banking Panics of the Great Depression.* Cambridge University Press, 1996.

Wigmore, Barrie A. *The Crash and Its Aftermath: A History of Securities Markets in the United States, 1929–1933.* Greenwood Press, 1985, https://books.google.com/books?id=I_Bs3s3rd HwC&printsec=frontcover&source=gbs_ge_summary_r&cad=0#v=onepage&q&f=false.

"William McChesney Martin, the Fed's Happy Puritan, Died on July 27th, Aged 91." *Economist,* Aug. 6, 1998, http://www.economist.com/node/171026.

Wilmarth, Arthur E., Jr. *Citigroup: A Case Study in Managerial and Regulatory Failures.* GW Law Faculty Publications and Other Works, 2013, http://scholarship.law.gwu.edu/cgi/viewcontent.cgi?article=2234&context=faculty_publications.

———. "Did Universal Banks Play a Significant Role in the U.S. Economy's Boom-and-Bust Cycles of 1921–1933? A Preliminary Assessment." GWU Legal Studies Research Paper 171, in *Current Developments in Monetary and Financial Law* 4 (2005): 559–645, http://ssrn.com/abstract=838267.

———. "Prelude to Glass-Steagall: Abusive Securities Practices by National City Bank and Chase National Bank during the 'Roaring Twenties.'" GW Law School Public Law and Legal Theory Paper 2016–35, in *Tulane Law Review* (2016).

———. "Wal-Mart and the Separation of Banking and Commerce." *Connecticut Law Review* 39, no. 4 (May 2007): 1539–1622.

Wilson, Edmund. "Sunshine Charley." *New Republic,* June 28, 1933, pp. 176–178.

Wilson, Janet. "The Bank of North America and Pennsylvania Politics: 1781–1787." *Pennsylvania Magazine of History and Biography* 66, no. 1 (Jan. 1942): 3–28, http://www.jstor.org/stable/20087443.

Winski, Sarah. "The Dinner-Party Compromise That Resolved a Debt Crisis (and Gave Us Washington, DC)." National Constitution Center Blog, June 13, 2011, http://blog.constitutioncenter.org/2011/06/the-dinner-party-compromise-that-resolved-a-debt-crisis-and-gave-us-washington-d-c/.

"Wires Banks to Urge Veto of Glass Bill: Bankers Association Attacks Deposits Guarantee in Message to Its Members." *New York Times,* June 16, 1933.

Woodruff, Nan Elizabeth. *As Rare as Rain: Federal Relief in the Great Southern Drought of 1930–1931.* University of Illinois Press, 1985.

Wright, Robert, and David J. Cowen. *Financial Founding Fathers: The Men Who Made America Rich.* University of Chicago Press, 2006, http://www.press.uchicago.edu/Misc/Chicago/910687.html (see excerpt of chapter on Hamilton).

Wyatt, Edward. "SEC Changes Policy on Firms' Admissions of Guilt." *New York Times,* Jan. 6, 2012, https://mobile.nytimes.com/2012/01/07/business/sec-to-change-policy-on-companies-admission-of-guilt.html.

Wyatt, Walter. "The Constitutionality of Legislation Providing a Unified Commercial Banking System for the United States." *Federal Reserve Bulletin,* Mar. 1933, https://fraser.stlouisfed.org/files/docs/historical/meyer/mss52019_121_010.pdf.

Xu, Jodi. "Bye Bye, GMAC: Will 'Ally Bank" Work or Not?" *Wall Street Journal,* May 15, 2009, http://blogs.wsj.com/deals/2009/05/15/bye-bye-gmac-will-ally-bank-work-or-not/.

Yagan, Danny. *Employment Hysteresis from the Great Recession.* National Bureau of Economic Research, Sept. 2017, http://papers.nber.org/tmp/29035-w23844.pdf.

Yang, Jie Lynn, et al. "Fed Aid in Financial Crisis Went beyond U.S. Banks to Industry, Foreign Firms." *Washington Post,* Dec. 2, 2010, http://www.washingtonpost.com/wp-dyn/content/article/2010/12/01/AR2010120106870.html.

Yang, John. "House Reprimands, Penalizes Speaker." *Washington Post,* Jan. 22, 1997.

Yatter, Douglas, et al. "CFTC Self-Reporting Policy Leaves Open Several Questions." *Law 360,* Oct. 5, 2017, https://www.lw.com/thoughtLeadership/cftc-self-reporting-policy-several-questions.

Yeager, Melissa. *The Differences between Super PACs and Dark Money Groups.* Sunlight Foundation, Oct. 30, 2015, https://sunlightfoundation.com/2015/10/30/the-difference-between-super-pacs-and-dark-money-groups/.

Yglesias, Matthew. "Lies and Libor." *Slate,* July 9, 2012, http://www.slate.com/articles/business/moneybox/2012/07/what_is_the_libor_scandal_how_the_interest_rate_rigging_should_destroy_the_credibility_of_banks_once_and_for_all.html.

Zandi, Mark. *Financial Shock.* Pearson Education, 2009. Updated edition where noted.

Zarroli, Jim. "Trump Favors Returning to the Gold Standard, Few Economists Agree." National Public Radio, June 16, 2016, http://www.npr.org/2016/06/16/482279689/trump-favors-returning-to-the-gold-standard-few-economists-agree.

Zhu, Jun, Laurie Goodman, and George Taz. "Why the GSEs' Support of Low-Downpayment Loans Again Is No Big Deal." *Urban Wire*, Nov. 4, 2014, http://www.urban.org/urban-wire/why-government-sponsored-enterprises-support-low-down-payment-loans-again-no-big-deal.

Zibel, Alan. "Liar Loans Threaten to Prolong Mortgage Crisis." Associated Press, Aug. 18, 2008.

———. "$2.3 Billion Loss Forces Drastic Cuts at Fannie Mae." Associated Press, Aug. 9, 2008, updated May 26, 2013, http://www.tbo.com/business/business/2008/aug/09/bz–23-billion-loss-forces-drastic-cuts-at-fannie-m-ar–140867/.

Zuckerman, Gregory. "Profiting from the Crash." *Wall Street Journal,* Mar. 31, 2009, http://www.wsj.com/articles/SB10001424052748703574604574499740849179448.

Zuil, Lilla. "AIG's Title as World's Largest Insurer Gone Forever." *Insurance Journal,* Apr. 9, 2009, http://www.insurancejournal.com/news/national/2009/04/29/100066.htm.

INDEX

Page numbers in *italics* refer to illustrations.